WAR, CHRISTIANITY, AND THE STATE

ESSAYS ON THE FOLLIES OF CHRISTIAN MILITARISM

Books by Laurence M. Vance

The Other Side of Calvinism
A Brief History of English Bible Translations
The Angel of the Lord
Archaic Words and the Authorized Version
A Practical Grammar of Basic Biblical Hebrew
Double Jeopardy: The NASB Update
Christianity and War and Other Essays Against the Warfare State
King James, His Bible, and Its Translators
Greek Verbs in the New Testament and Their Principal Parts
War, Foreign Policy, and the Church
Guide to Prepositions in the Greek New Testament
The Myth of the Just Price and the Biblical Case for Laissez Faire
Guide to Nouns in the Greek New Testament
Guide to Adjectives in the Greek New Testament
Guide to Pronouns in the Greek New Testament
The Revolution that Wasn't
Rethinking the Good War
Galatians 1 & 2: Exposition, Commentary, Application
The Quatercentenary of the King James Bible
The War on Drugs Is a War on Freedom
War, Christianity, and the State: Essays on the Follies of
Christian Militarism

WAR, CHRISTIANITY, AND THE STATE

ESSAYS ON THE FOLLIES OF CHRISTIAN MILITARISM

by

Laurence M. Vance

Vance Publications
www.vancepublications.com

War, Christianity, and the State:
Essays on the Follies of Christian Militarism

ISBN 978-0-9823697-6-0

Published and Distributed by: Vance Publications
P.O. Box 780671, Orlando, FL 32878
E-mail: vancepub@vancepublications.com
Website: www.vancepublications.com

Printed in the United States of America

TABLE OF CONTENTS

CHAPTER ONE

CHRISTIANITY AND WAR

CHAPTER TWO

CHRISTIANITY AND THE MILITARY

CHAPTER THREE

CHRISTIANITY AND THE WARFARE STATE

CHAPTER FOUR

CHRISTIANITY AND TORTURE

INTRODUCTION

These essays, although organized under four headings, have one underlying theme: the relation of Christianity to war, the military, and the warfare state. If there is any group of people that should be opposed to war, torture, militarism, and the warfare state with its suppression of civil liberties, imperial presidency, government propaganda, and interventionist foreign policy it is Christians, and especially conservative, evangelical, and fundamentalist Christians who claim to strictly follow the dictates of Scripture and worship the Prince of Peace.

These seventy-six essays also have one thing in common—they were all published on the premier anti-state, anti-war, pro-market website, LewRockwell.com, during the period from October 29, 2003, to March 28, 2013. The vast majority of them first appeared on and were written exclusively for that website. LewRockwell.com is the brainchild of Lew Rockwell, the founder and chairman of the Ludwig von Mises Institute in Auburn, Ala., and a leading opponent of the central state, its wars, and its socialism.

Thirty-five of the essays contained in this work originally appeared in the second edition of the author's book *Christianity and War and Other Essays Against the Warfare State*, published in 2008. Four of them appeared there and in that book's first edition, published in 2005. In addition to essays relating to Christianity and war and Christianity and the military, that book also included essays on war and peace, the military, the war in Iraq, other wars, and the U.S. global empire. Although a third edition was planned, two things served to redirect my intentions.

Because the second edition had already grown in size to seventy-nine essays in 432 pages and I had written so much on these subjects since its publication early in 2008, a third edition would just be too large of a book if I tried to include everything I had written on these subjects since the publication of the second edition. Additionally, since one part of the book and much additional material consisted of essays with a decidedly Christian theme, while the other part of the book and much additional material was more secular in nature, it seemed best to organize the existing and new material along these themes. So, instead of issuing an unwieldy one volume third edition, I opted to collect all of the former material into *War, Christianity, and the State: Essays on the Follies of*

Christian Militarism, and issue the latter material in a companion volume titled *War, Empire, and the Military: Essays on the Follies of War and U.S. Foreign Policy.*

Each essay is reprinted verbatim, with the exception of the correction of a few minor errors. It should be noted, however, that the original spelling, capitalization, and punctuation are followed in all quotations. Because they were published on the Internet, most of the essays originally contained numerous links to documentation and further information on the Web that the reader could click on if he desired. Because this feature is not possible in a printed format, the reader is encouraged to consult the online versions of each essay at LewRockwell.com where they are archived. Many of the essays also originally included pictures, which, for space considerations, are not included here.

Although many of these essays reference contemporary events, the principles discussed in all of them are timeless: war, militarism, the warfare state, and especially the proper Christian attitude toward these things. The essays in each chapter are listed in their order of publication. Each chapter as well as its individual essays can be read in any order.

In chapter 1, "Christianity and War," Christian enthusiasm for war and the military is shown to be an affront to the Saviour, contrary to Scripture, and a demonstration of the profound ignorance many Christians have of history. In chapter 2, "Christianity and the Military," the idea that Christians should have anything to do with the military is asserted to be illogical, immoral, and unscriptural. In chapter 3, "Christianity and the Warfare State," I argue that Christians who condone the warfare state, its senseless wars, its war on a tactic (terrorism), its nebulous crusades against "evil," its aggressive militarism, its interventions into the affairs of other countries, and its expanding empire have been duped. In chapter 4, "Christianity and Torture," I contend that it is reprehensible for Christians to support torture for any reason.

The books listed at the close under "For Further Reading" include not only some of the more important books referenced in the essays, but other recommended works that relate in some way to Christianity and war, the the military, and the warfare state. Most of them are available from Amazon.com. The inclusion of any book should not be taken as a blanket endorsement of everything contained in the book or anything else written by the author.

It is my desire in all of these essays to show that war and militarism are incompatible with biblical Christianity.

CHAPTER 1
CHRISTIANITY AND WAR

CHRISTIANITY AND WAR

"We will export death and violence to the four corners of the earth in defense of our great nation." ~ The Bush Administration

"From whence come wars and fightings among you? Come they not hence, even of your lusts that war in your members?" ~ James 4:1

"War is the health of the state." ~ Randolph Bourne

"War is a racket. It always has been. It is possibly the oldest, easily the most profitable, surely the most vicious. It is the only one international in scope. It is the only one in which the profits are reckoned in dollars and the losses in lives." ~ U.S. Marine Corps Major General Smedley Butler

"War prosperity is like the prosperity that an earthquake or a plague brings. The earthquake means good business for construction workers, and cholera improves the business of physicians, pharmacists, and undertakers; but no one has for that reason yet sought to celebrate earthquakes and cholera as stimulators of the productive forces in the general interest." ~ Ludwig von Mises

"War is God's judgment on sin here; hell is God's judgment on sin hereafter." ~ Bob Jones Sr.

"I saw in the whole Christian world a license of fighting at which even barbarous nations might blush. Wars were begun on trifling pretexts or none at all, and carried on without any reference of law, Divine or human." ~ Hugo Grotius

"Our wars, for the most part, proceed either from ambition, from anger and malice, from the mere wantonness of unbridled power, or from some other mental distemper." ~ Desiderius Erasmus

That the ongoing undeclared "war" in Iraq is supported by

apologists for what World War II general, and later president, Dwight Eisenhower, called the "military-industrial complex" is no surprise. What is surprising, however, is the present degree of Christian enthusiasm for war.

Our Christian forefathers thought differently, as will presently be seen.

"Just war theory," although it has been misused by political leaders to encourage soldiers to needlessly fight, kill, bleed, and die, with the full support of the civilian populace, including many of its Christians, is nevertheless still relevant in this age of tanks, bombs, land mines, and "weapons of mass destruction."

In his 1625 treatise *De Jure Belli Ac Pacis (On the Law of War and Peace)*, the famed Dutch Christian, Hugo Grotius (1538–1645), universally recognized as the "Father of International Law," set forth six *jus ad bellum* (just recourse to war) conditions that limit a nation's legitimate recourse to war: just cause (correct intention [self-defense] with an objective), proportionality (grave enough situation to warrant war), reasonable chance for success (obtainable objectives), public declaration (fair warning, opportunity for avoidance), declaration only by legitimate authority, and last resort (all other options eliminated).

Or, as the historian and economist, Murray Rothbard (1926–1995), said, in making his case that America has only had two just wars (1776 & 1861), "A just war exists when a people tries to ward off the threat of coercive domination by another people, or to overthrow an already-existing domination. A war is unjust, on the other hand, when a people try to impose domination on another people, or try to retain an already existing coercive rule over them."

Grotius also articulated three *jus in bello* (justice in the course of war) conditions that govern just and fair conduct in war: legitimate targets (only combatants, not civilians), proportionality (means may not exceed what is warranted by the cause), and treatment of prisoners (combatants are through capture rendered noncombatants).

Grotius' fellow Dutchman, Desiderius Erasmus (1466–1536), was certainly no pacifist, yet he lamented: "War would be understandable among the beasts, for they lack natural reason; it is an aberration among men because the evil of war can be easily understood through the use of reason alone. War, however, is inconceivable among Christians because it is not only rationally objectionable but, even more important, ethically inadmissible."

The fact that a government claims a war is just is irrelevant, for American history is replete with examples of American presidents who have exaggerated, misinformed, misrepresented, and lied to deceive the American people into supporting wars that they would not have supported if they had known the facts.

In 1846 President James Polk, after Texas' accession to the union, deliberately put U.S. troops into an area still complicated by the existence of a boundary dispute with Mexico so as to be able to go to Congress with an incident and get a declaration of war.

In 1861 President Abraham Lincoln waged war on his own people after declaring in his First Inaugural Address: "I have no purpose, directly or indirectly, to interfere with the institution of slavery in the States where it exists. I believe I have no lawful right to do so, and I have no inclination to do so."

In 1898 President William McKinley began a "splendid little war" with Spain over Cuba. Its sequel to secure U.S. colonial power in the Philippines left dead 4,000 U.S. troops, more than 20,000 Filipino fighters, and more than 220,000 Filipino civilians, all based on the news-media slogan "Remember the *Maine*!"

In 1916 President Woodrow Wilson sought reelection on the slogan "he kept us out of war," but then proceeded, soon after his second inauguration, to ask Congress for a declaration of war: "a war to end all wars" to "make the world safe for democracy."

In 1940 President Franklin Roosevelt campaigned for his third term, saying, "I have said this before, but I shall say it again and again: Your boys are not going to be sent into any foreign wars." It was not long, however, before our "boys" were back once again on European soil.

In 1964 President Lyndon Johnson announced to a crowd at Akron University: "We are not about to send American boys 9 or 10,000 miles away from home to do what Asian boys ought to be doing for themselves." This was followed by the 1964 Gulf of Tonkin Resolution that saw over 500,000 "American boys" fight an "Asian boys" war. Over 50,000 of them came home in body bags.

In 1991 President George Bush I used faked satellite photos to gain Saudi participation in the first Gulf War, and to convince the American people that Hussein must be stopped from conquering the whole region.

In 2003 President George Bush II insisted on the need to "end a brutal regime, whose aggression and weapons of mass destruction make it a unique threat to the world." The holes in this statement have been unfolding before our eyes.

Yet, the gullible Christian theologian Loraine Boettner (1901–1990), in his book *The Christian Attitude Toward War*, claims that the United States has "never had a militarist president." He even advocates that the government "should be given the benefit of the doubt" when it comes to waging war.

But contrary to Boettner, and as mentioned previously, our Christian forefathers, being much better read and having a much better grasp of history than the modern Christian who spends all his time in front of the Internet and the television, had no enthusiasm for war at all.

Back before the Civil War, when the Christians published theological journals worth reading, two Baptist ministers writing in the *Christian Review* demonstrated that Christian war fever was contrary to the New Testament.

Veritatis Amans, in his 1847 article "Can War, Under Any Circumstances, Be Justified on the Principles of the Christian Religion?" approached the subject from the standpoint of war being justified only in cases of self-defense. Another Baptist preacher, in an unsigned article from 1838 titled "Wickedness of War," approached the subject from the standpoint of the nature of war in general. Both articles look to the New Testament as their authority.

Amans begins: "War has ever been the scourge of the human race. The history of the past is little else than a chronicle of deadly feuds, irreconcilable hate, and exterminating warfare. The extension of empire, the love of glory, and thirst for fame, have been more fatal to men than famine or pestilence, or the fiercest elements of nature."

"And what is more sad and painful, many of the wars whose desolating surges have deluged the earth, have been carried on in the name and under the sanction of those who profess the name of Christ."

"It has not been till recently, that the disciples of Christ have been conscious of the enormous wickedness of war as it usually exists. And even now there are many who do not frown upon it with that disapprobation and abhorrence, which an evil of such magnitude as an unjust war deserves."

"Wars of every kind may be included under two classes—offensive and defensive. Concerning the former we shall say nothing. We need not delay a moment to discuss a question so directly at variance with the dictates of conscience, and the principles of revealed religion."

"But under what circumstances is war truly defensive? We reply, when its object is to repel an invasion; when there is no alternative but to submit to bondage and death, or to resist."

The anonymous Baptist preacher writing in a 1838 issue of the *Christian Review* continues: "The war spirit is so wrought into the texture of governments, and the habits of national thinking, and even into our very festivals and pomps, that its occasional recurrence is deemed a matter of unavoidable necessity."

War "contradicts the genius and intention of Christianity," "sets at nought the example of Jesus," and "is inconsistent not only with the general structure and nature of Christianity and the example of Jesus, but it violates all the express precepts of the New Testament."

"Christianity requires us to seek to amend the condition of man. But war cannot do this. The world is no better for all the wars of five thousand years. Christianity, if it prevailed, would make the earth a paradise. War, where it prevails, makes it a slaughter-house, a den of thieves, a brothel, a hell. Christianity cancels the laws of retaliation. War is based upon that very principle. Christianity is the remedy for all human woes. War produces every woe known to man."

"The causes of war, as well as war itself, are contrary to the gospel. It originates in the worst passions and the worst aims. We may always trace it to the thirst of revenge, the acquisition of territory, the monopoly of commerce, the quarrels of kings, the intrigues of ministers, the coercion of religious opinion, the acquisition of disputed crowns, or some other source, equally culpable; but never has any war, devised by man, been founded on holy tempers and Christian principles."

"It should be remembered, that in no case, even under the Old Testament, was war appointed to decide doubtful questions, or to settle quarrels, but to inflict national punishment. They were intended, as are pestilence and famine, to chastise nations guilty of provoking God. Such is never the pretext of modern war; and if it were, it would require divine authority, which, as has just been said, would induce even members of the Peace Society to fight."

The "criminality of war," as Howard Malcom, president of Georgetown College, wrote in 1845, is not "that tyrants should lead men into wars of pride and conquest," but that "the people, in governments comparatively free, should so readily lend themselves to a business in which they bear all the sufferings, can gain nothing, and may lose all." That people would act this way, Malcom says, is an "astonishment indeed." "But," he continues, "the chief wonder is that Christians, followers of the Prince of Peace, should have concurred in this mad idolatry of strife, and thus been inconsistent not only with themselves, but with the very genius of their system."

The Founding Fathers of this country, many of whom were deists, had more sense than many twenty-first-century Christians when it came to espousing a policy of peace through nonintervention; in other words, not being "a busybody in other men's matters" (1 Peter 4:15). George Washington: "The great rule of conduct for us in regard to foreign nations is, in extending our commercial relations to have with them as little political connection as possible." Thomas Jefferson: "Peace, commerce, and honest friendship with all nations—entangling alliances with none." John Quincy Adams: "America . . . goes not abroad seeking monsters to destroy."

So the War on Terrorism, like the War on Poverty and the War on Drugs, is in so many ways just a tragic joke. But why Christians support any of these bogus "wars" is an even greater tragedy.

* * * * *

FALWELL'S FOLLY

Jerry Falwell has done it again. Just like Jacob's sons Simeon and Levi made him "stink among the inhabitants of the land" (Genesis 34:30), so Falwell has made Christians stink. Case in point—Falwell's recent *WorldNetDaily* article in which he made an attempt, and a very feeble one, to justify, with Scripture, President Bush's invasion of Iraq—an invasion which has resulted, and continues to result, in the senseless deaths of American servicemen. And if the article itself wasn't bad enough, he had the audacity to entitle it: "God is pro-war." As a Christian of the Independent Baptist persuasion (like Falwell), I am almost ashamed to identify myself as such. Although Falwell has been an embarrassment to Independent Baptists for years, his recent article is just too much to stomach.

Falwell is certainly correct when he says about war that "the Bible is not silent on the subject." Yes, it is true that "just as there are numerous references to peace in the Bible, there are frequent references to God-ordained war." And yes, it is true that Jesus is depicted in Revelation 19 as "bearing a 'sharp sword' and smiting nations, ruling them with 'a rod of iron.'" And yes again, it is true that "the Song of Victory in Exodus 15 hails God as a God of war." Furthermore, no one can deny that "God actually strengthened individuals for war, including Moses, Joshua, and many of the Old Testament judges who demonstrated great faith in battle." And finally, it is true that "the Bible tells us war will be a reality until Christ returns. And when the time is right, Jesus will indeed come again, ending all wars."

Falwell is also correct when he says about society that "we continue to live in violent times." And yes, "America continues to face the horrible realities of our fallen world. Suicide bombings and terrorist actions are beamed live into our homes daily."

The problem with Falwell's article is not with these observations that anyone who read the Bible and watched the nightly news already knew. The problem with the article is the numerous distortions of Scripture and the truth that occur in it.

Falwell's first distortion is the inappropriate use of that portion of Scripture that prefaces his article: "To every thing there is a season, and a time to every purpose under the heaven: A time to be born . . . , *a time of war*." This implies that the present war in Iraq is just because, after all, there is "a time of war." If the United States was invaded then it would certainly be "a time of war." But it would be a morally justifiable defensive war against an aggressor. The war in Iraq is neither defensive nor against an aggressor.

Falwell's second distortion is the title of his article itself: "God is pro-war." To say that because God permitted wars to take place, and even commanded the nation of Israel in the Old Testament to conduct them, that he is "pro-war" is ludicrous. We know from the Bible that God is pro-holiness and pro-righteousness, but to say that God is "pro-war" doesn't sound like any description of God's attributes that I ever read in a systematic theology book. Was God pro-Crimean War? Was God pro-War of the Austrian Succession? Was God pro-War of the Roses? Whose side was he on in these conflicts? What Falwell really means is that God is pro-American wars. Falwell's shameless pseudo-patriotism is a violation of the third commandment in the Bible he professes to believe: "Thou shalt not take the name of the LORD thy God in vain" (Exodus 20:7).

Falwell's third distortion: "God even gives counsel to be wise in war. Proverbs 20:18: 'Every purpose is established by counsel: and with good advice make war.'" How this verse is supposed to mean that "God even gives counsel to be wise in war" is beyond me. Nothing in the verse or the context suggests that God is giving the counsel or the advice. Did God give Hitler and Stalin counsel to be wise in war? Did God give Pol Pot and Ho Chi Min advice to make war? Oh, I guess it just means that God only gives U.S. presidents counsel and advise to be wise in war? But could that even be the case? Did God give Lincoln counsel to invade the South after Lincoln said: "I have no purpose, directly or indirectly, to interfere with the institution of slavery in the States where it exists. I believe I have no lawful right to do so, and I have no inclination to do so."? Did God give advice to Wilson to make the world safe for democracy after Wilson sought reelection on the slogan "he kept us out of war"?

Falwell's fourth distortion: "It is apparent that our God-authored freedoms must be defended. Throughout the book of Judges, God calls the Israelites to go to war against the Midianites and Philistines. Why?

Because these nations were trying to conquer Israel, and God's people were called to defend themselves." But what does invading Iraq have to do with defending our God-authored freedoms? For this analogy to be credible, several things must of necessity be true. First, Iraq would had to have been trying to conquer the United States—which it wasn't, and couldn't possibly have done so if it tried. Second, the citizens of the United States would have to be God's people—quite strange in view of the fact that God and his Bible are unwelcome in most of the country's schools. Christians can quote 2 Chronicles 7:14 all they want, but it still won't change the fact that America is not made up of God's people like Israel of the Old Testament. Third, invading another country would have to be a means of defending our God-authored freedoms. That is, we owe our freedoms to offensive wars by the United States military away from American soil in places that most Americans couldn't locate on a map. And fourth, the state would have to be the defender of our God-given freedoms. But who has always been the greatest opponent of anyone's God-authored freedoms? Why, the state, of course.

Falwell's fifth distortion: "President Bush declared war in Iraq to defend innocent people. This is a worthy pursuit. In fact, Proverbs 21:15 tells us: 'It is joy to the just to do judgment: but destruction shall be to the workers of iniquity.'" Well, first of all, according to that archaic, neglected document in Washington known as the Constitution, the power to declare war belongs exclusively to Congress (Art. I, Sec. 8, Par. 11). The fact that Congress hasn't officially issued a declaration of war since World War II doesn't change anything. It only demonstrates that the Iraq fiasco is not any more constitutional than the Korea or Vietnam fiascos were. Secondly, I thought the war was all about finding weapons of mass destruction, destroying chemical weapons labs, or uncovering Iraq's nascent nuclear capability? If the United States is so interested in defending innocent people in Iraq then why was not Saddam Hussein removed during the First Gulf War? Why let them suffer all these years? And why stop at Iraq? Why not defend the innocent people in North Korea who have suffered under oppressive regimes for decades? And if it is such a worthy pursuit to defend innocent people in Iraq, then why not defend innocent people in America? How many millions of unborn children have been slaughtered in the United States since the 1973 *Roe v. Wade* decision? How many thousands of people are languishing in U.S. prisons for victimless crimes? There are also two problems with Falwell's equating the destruction of Iraq by the U.S. Military with the destruction of the workers of iniquity. First off, I don't recall reading in Proverbs that it is the job of the United States to destroy the workers of iniquity. And second, if "destruction shall be to the workers of iniquity," then the United States is in trouble, for we have worked iniquity all over the globe for the past fifty years.

Falwell's sixth distortion: "One of the primary purposes of the church is to stop the spread of evil, even at the cost of human lives. If we do not stop the spread of evil, many innocent lives will be lost and the kingdom of God suffers." I thought one of the primary purposes of the church was to preach the gospel? I thought one of the primary purposes of the church was to teach converts? There is no mention anywhere in the New Testament of the church being commanded to stop the spread of evil. Only God himself can stop the spread of evil. The Apostle Paul preached the gospel and taught converts (Acts 14:21), he didn't waste five minutes trying to stop the spread of something as nebulous as evil. And then there is the "cost of human lives." Should the church practice evil to stop evil? Does the end justify the means? Falwell apparently thinks it does, even though the Apostle Paul said it was slanderously reported that he was saying: "Let us do evil, that good may come?" (Romans 3:8). Falwell's attitude is like the then U.S. ambassador to the United Nations, Madeleine Albright, in 1996, saying that the deaths of 500,000 Iraqi children because of U.S. sanctions was "worth it" in order to punish Saddam Hussein.

Falwell's seventh distortion: "Some reading this column will surely ask, 'Doesn't the sixth commandment say, "Thou shalt not kill?"' Actually, no; it says: 'Thou shalt not commit murder.' There is a difference between killing and murdering. In fact, many times God commanded capital punishment for those who break the law." Falwell is exactly right, there is a difference between killing and murdering. The question then is this: Is dropping bombs on countries thousands of miles away for dubious reasons killing or murdering? I think the answer is quite obvious.

In addition to mentioning war, the writer of Ecclesiastes also says that there is "a time to keep silence" (Ecclesiastes 3:7). Mr. Falwell, are you listening?

* * * * *

GOTT MIT UNS

> "Religion is the sigh of the oppressed creature, the heart of a heartless world and the soul of soulless conditions. It is the opium of the people" (Karl Marx—*Critique of Hegel's Philosophy of Right*).

Marx was right.

This admission may sound strange coming from someone who is both a conservative Christian and an unabashed advocate of laissez faire, but what Marx said about religion being a drug is nevertheless correct. He may never have said anything else in his entire life that was true or worth reading, and probably didn't, but even a broken clock is right twice a day.

It goes without saying that people high on drugs do not act normal. They may think, say, and do strange things that they would not normally do. They may even do some wild and crazy things that they would never dream of doing when they were not high.

Many supporters of the senseless war in Iraq are high on religion. Add a religious element to a war and the faithful will come out in droves in support of it. In the case of the current war in Iraq this is easy to do. Because the United States is supposedly a "Christian nation," the war can be turned into a modern-day crusade since Iraq is a "Muslim nation."

The use of religion in war is as old as history itself. If there is one thing that men are willing to fight and die for it is their religious beliefs. But unfortunately, it is also historically true that many are willing to kill or justify killing under the guise of religion.

This is especially disheartening of those who would defend aggression in the name of Christianity. As the Baptist minister who called himself Veritatis Amans lamented in the pages of the *Christian Review* back in 1847:

> War has ever been the scourge of the human race. The history of the past is little else than a chronicle of deadly feuds, irreconcilable hate, and exterminating warfare. The extension of empire, the love of glory, and thirst for fame, have been more fatal to men than famine or pestilence, or the fiercest elements of nature. The trappings and tinsel of war, martial prowess, and military heroism, have, in all ages, been venerated and lauded to the skies. And what is more sad and painful, many of the wars whose desolating surges have deluged the earth, have been carried on in the name and under the sanction of those who profess the name of Christ.

The last time the United States experienced such religious intensity during a war was back during the misnamed conflict commonly called the Civil War. The blasphemous "Battle Hymn of the Republic" is still sung today in many northern churches around the fourth of July and Veterans Day.

American preachers were used during World War I to keep war fever high. Here is a typical example: "It is God who has summoned us to this war. It is his war we are fighting.... This crusade is indeed a crusade.

The greatest in history—the holiest ... a Holy War. Yes, it is Christ, the King of Righteousness, who calls us to grapple in deadly strife with this unholy and blasphemous power" (Randolph McKim, *For God and Country or the Christian Pulpit in War Time*, 1918). For more on religion during World War I and the Progressive Era see Richard Gamble's *The War for Righteousness: Progressive Christianity, the Great War, and the Rise of the Messianic Nation.*

President Bush has mastered the art of using religious rhetoric to capture the support of gullible evangelical Christians. Even while the federal debt and deficit skyrocket, the body count in Iraq continues to rise, and he makes war on the Bill of Rights, Bush has continued to maintain that he is a man of faith who is doing the will of the Lord. And so have others: see Stephen Mansfield's *The Faith of George Bush* and David Aikman's *A Man Of Faith: The Spiritual Journey of George W. Bush.* Christian "leaders" like Pat Robertson, Ralph Reed, James Dobson, Donald Wildmon, Tim LaHaye, D. James Kennedy, John Hagee, and Jerry Falwell are some of the most vocal apologists for Bush and the Republican Party. Even that great paragon of virtue, Rudolph Giuliani, has gotten on the religious bandwagon, recently saying that "there was some divine guidance in the President being elected."

It is no overstatement to say that many of these so-called Christian leaders consider George Bush to be God's gift to the human race. Jerry Falwell, who, in the wake of the elections, has resurrected his Moral Majority organization, said his group would capitalize on the momentum of the elections "to maintain an evangelical revolution of voters who will continue to go the polls to 'vote Christian.'" Said Falwell: "On election night, I actually shed tears of joy as I saw the fruit of a quarter century of hard work. Nearly 116 million Americans voted. More than 30 million were evangelical Christians who, according to the pollsters, voted their moral convictions. I proudly say . . . they voted Christian!!" Although Bush fails on all three counts, Falwell has actually called him a "socially, fiscally, and politically conservative president." When it comes to the subject of politics, Christian leaders and their followers are a perfect example of the blind leading the blind (Matthew 15:14).

There is another regime in recent history that used religious rhetoric in wartime. Soldiers in the German Wehrmacht wore belt buckles inscribed with *Gott Mit Uns* (God is with us). Now, I am not in any way comparing the United States to Nazi Germany or George Bush to Adolph Hitler. However, there are an abundance of Bush/Hitler comparisons out there, most perhaps written by "any Democrat-but-Bush" leftists, but some that are at least worth reading—like the one that was linked to on

LRC, and a recent one that raises some good points. Anyway, there really is no comparison between the two "leaders," for as has been pointed out, Bush is not the orator that Hitler was, and he doesn't promote the production of small, cheap cars.

But in all seriousness, there are two passages in Hitler's *Mein Kampf*, which was published in two volumes in 1925–1926, and which can be read today in print or online, that are uncanny.

In volume I, at the end of chapter 2, the Führer said: "Hence today I believe that I am acting in accordance with the will of the Almighty Creator: by defending myself against the Jew, I am fighting for the work of the Lord." Substitute "Muslim" or "terrorists" for "Jew" and this sounds like George Bush. According to Bob Woodward's book *Plan of Attack*, Bush prayed as he walked outside the Oval Office after giving the order to begin the attack on Iraq: "Going into this period, I was praying for strength to do the Lord's will. . . . I'm surely not going to justify war based upon God. Understand that. Nevertheless, in my case I pray that I be as good a messenger of His will as possible."

In chapter 13 of volume 2, Hitler mentions the German people asking God to bless their troops:

> Each point of that Treaty [of Versailles] could have been engraved on the minds and hearts of the German people and burned into them until sixty million men and women would find their souls aflame with a feeling of rage and shame; and a torrent of fire would burst forth as from a furnace, and one common will would be forged from it, like a sword of steel. Then the people would join in the common cry: "To arms again!"
>
> Then, from the child's story-book to the last newspaper in the country, and every theatre and cinema, every pillar where placards are posted and every free space on the hoardings should be utilized in the service of this one great mission, until the faint-hearted cry, "Lord, deliver us," which our patriotic associations send up to Heaven today would be transformed into an ardent prayer: "Almighty God, bless our arms when the hour comes. Be just, as Thou hast always been just. Judge now if we deserve our freedom. Lord, bless our struggle."

For an unpretentious war prayer that no Christian "leader" would dare to pray—see Mark Twain's "The War Prayer."

In fairness to Bush, the "Gott Mit Uns" belt buckle was not just used by Germany in World War II—it was also worn by German soldiers in World War I. But contrast this with the supposedly "Christian" United

States, where, as defense consultant Josh Pollack, in his "Saudi Arabia and the United States, 1931–2002," has documented, Air Force chaplains were forbidden to wear Christian insignia or hold formal services during the early decades of the American troop presence in Saudi Arabia. It is also true that during the first war in Iraq, the importation of Bibles for Christian troops was discouraged, and no alcohol was permitted to U.S. troops in accordance with Islamic Law.

The lesson here is clear: The state uses religion for its own sinister purposes, and especially for that most destructive purpose of all—what Jefferson called "the greatest scourge of mankind" and Washington called "the plague of mankind"—war. But if war is so destructive then why does the state engage in it? As Randolph Bourne (1886–1918) so succinctly stated: "War is the health of the State."

* * * * *

CHARLES SPURGEON ON CHRISTIAN WAR FEVER

We know all too well about Christian war fever—that sickening blind worship of the state that elevates George W. Bush to Messiah status and seeks to justify his immoral, unscriptural, unconstitutional war in Iraq by incessantly repeating the mantras "obey the powers that be" and "God is a God of war." But who is Charles Spurgeon and why should we care what he said about war?

Charles Haddon Spurgeon (1834–1892) was an English Baptist minister who served as pastor of the Metropolitan Tabernacle in London from 1861 until his death. But Spurgeon was no ordinary minister. He was a pastor, a preacher, a teacher, an author, an editor, and the overseer of a pastor's college, a Christian literature society, and an orphanage. He is still widely revered today among Baptists (and others as well) as one of the greatest Baptist ministers in history.

Spurgeon preached his first sermon as a teenager and, in 1854, was called to the pastorate of the historic New Park Street Church, Southwark, London. During his thirty-eight-year tenure, the church increased from 232 to over 5,000. During the remodeling of the Park Street chapel to house the growing congregation, Spurgeon preached at the 5,000-seat Exeter Hall, a public auditorium. But because the remodeled chapel was still too small to accommodate the crowds, the church began construction of the Metropolitan Tabernacle, which sat 5,500 and had standing room for 500 more. In the interim, Spurgeon preached to thousands at the Surrey Gardens Music Hall. He was truly one of the most popular preachers in history. When he died in 1892, 60,000 people filed past his casket in the Tabernacle.

Spurgeon lives today through his sermons. From 1855 until his death, his Sunday morning sermons were published weekly. By 1865, Spurgeon's sermons were selling 25,000 copies every week. They would eventually be translated into more than twenty languages. The sermons were then collected in one volume and reissued at the end of each year in book form. After Spurgeon's death, the series continued until 1917 using his Sunday evening sermons. The six volumes of the *New Park Street Pulpit* (1855–1860) and the fifty-seven volumes of the *Metropolitan Tabernacle Pulpit* (1861–1917) contain 3,561 sermons, 25 million words, and fill 41,500 pages. Many of these volumes are available online, and most are in print.

Unlike some Baptist preachers today who shamelessly serve as spokesmen or apologists for Bush and his "splendid little war" in Iraq, Spurgeon was not the least bit excited about war and war fever.

Spurgeon on War

Spurgeon's comments on war can be found in his sermons on a variety of topics. He rarely preached a sermon that was specifically about war. His observations about war are overwhelmingly negative:

> Long have I held that war is an enormous crime; long have I regarded all battles as but murder on a large scale ("India's Ills and England's Sorrows," September 6, 1857, Music Hall, Royal Surrey Gardens).

> So combustible are the materials of which this great world is made, that I am ever apprehensive of war. I do not account it wonderful that one nation should strive against another, I account if far more wonderful that they are not all at arms. Whence come wars and fightings? Come they not from your lusts? Considering how much lust there is in the world, we might well conceive that there would be more war than we see. Sin is the mother of wars; and remembering how plentiful sin is, we need not marvel if it brings forth multitudes of them. We may look for them. If the coming of Christ be indeed drawing nigh, then we must expect wars and rumors of wars through all the nations of the earth ("The God of Peace," November 4, 1855, New Park Street Chapel).

> There is yet one more point which I must mention here in which the gospel is the best help to man. We must remember to-day, that

there are districts of the earth where the ground is yet red with blood. There are sad portions of our globe that as yet must have the name of Aceldama, the field of gore, there are spots where the horse-hoof is splashed with blood; where the very carcasses of men are the food of ravens and of jackalls, the mounds of Balaclava are as yet scarcely green, and the spots where rest the relics of our own murdered sisters and brothers are not covered with the memorial stone. War has ravaged whole districts; even in these late times the dogs of war are not yet muzzled. Oh! what shall we do to put an end to war? Mars, where is the chain that shall bind thee like Prometheus, to the rock? How shall we imprison thee for ever, thou cruel Moloch; how shall we for ever chain thee? Behold here is the great chain, that which one day is to bind the great serpent; it has the blood-red links of love. The gospel of Jesus Christ the crucified one, shall yet hush the clarion of war, and break the battle-bow in sunder ("The Cry of the Heathen," April 25, 1858, Music Hall, Royal Surrey Gardens).

It is astonishing how distance blunts the keen edge of anything that is disagreeable. War is at all times a most fearful scourge. The thought of slain bodies and of murdered men must always harrow up the soul; but because we hear of these things in the distance, there are few Englishmen who can truly enter into their horrors. If we should hear the booming of cannon on the deep which girdles this island; if we should see at our doors the marks of carnage and bloodshed; then should we more thoroughly appreciate what war means. But distance takes away the horror, and we therefore speak of war with too much levity, and even read of it with an interest not sufficiently linked with pain ("A Present Religion," May 30, 1858, Music Hall, Royal Surrey Gardens).

Better far for us to have famine than war. From all civil war and all the desperate wickedness which it involves, good Lord deliver us; and if thou smitest us as thou hast done, it is better to fall into the hand of God than into the hand of man ("Christian Sympathy," November 9, 1862, Metropolitan Tabernacle).

Oh! that God would put an end in the world to all wars between nations, as well as all strifes between individuals ("The Fruits of Grace," January 21, 1872, Metropolitan Tabernacle).

Spurgeon on Peace

Like Thomas Jefferson, Spurgeon did not just speak about the evils of war without also relating the blessings of peace:

> He is the God of peace, for he is the restorer of it; though wars have broken out through sin. He is the preserver of peace. Whenever I see peace in the world, I ascribe it to God, and if it is continued, I shall always believe it is because God interferes to prevent war ("The God of Peace," November 4, 1855, New Park Street Chapel).

> Have you not noticed how magnificently peace winneth its reprisals at the hand of war? Look through this country. Methinks if the angel of peace should go with us, as we journey through it, and stop at the various ancient towns where there are dismantled castles, and high mounds from which every vestige of a building has long been swept, the angel would look us in the face, and say, "I have done all this: war scattered my peaceful subjects, burned down my cottages, ravaged my temples, and laid my mansions with the dust. But I have attacked war in his own strongholds and I have routed him. Walk through his halls. Can you hear now the tramp of the warrior? Where now the sound of the clarion and the drum?" The sheep is feeding from the cannon's mouth, and the bird builds his nest where once the warrior did hang his helmet. As rare curiosities we dig up the swords and spears of our forefathers, and little do we reck that in this we are doing tribute to peace. For peace is the conqueror. It hath been a long duel, and much blood hath been shed, but peace hath been the victor. War, after all, has but spasmodic triumphs; and again it sinks—it dies, but peace ever reigneth. If she be driven from one part of the earth, yet she dwelleth in another; and while war, with busy hand, is piling up here a wall, and there a rampart, and there a tower, peace with her gentle finger, is covering over the castle with the mees and the ivy, and eating the stone from the top, and letting it lie level with the earth. . . . I think this is a fine thought for the lover of peace; and who among us is not? Who among us ought not to be? Is not the gospel all peace? ("The Desolations of the Lord, the Consolation of His Saints," April 28, 1858, Music Hall, Royal Surrey Gardens, on behalf of the Baptist Missionary Society).

Spurgeon on Imperialism in the Name of Christianity

Imperialism is bad enough, but it is even worse when it is done in the name of Christianity. Unlike Christian pragmatists today who think that U.S. wars and interventions will be a boon to Christianity, Spurgeon was not deceived:

The church, we affirm, can neither be preserved nor can its interests be promoted by human armies. We have all thought otherwise in our time, and have foolishly said when a fresh territory was annexed to our empire, "Ah! what a providence that England has annexed Oude,"—or taken to itself some other territory—"Now a door is opened for the Gospel. A Christian power will necessarily encourage Christianity, and seeing that a Christian power is at the head of the Government, it will be likely that the natives will be induced to search into the authenticity of our revelation, and so great results will follow. Who can tell but that, at the point of the British bayonet, the Gospel will be carried, and that, by the edge of the true sword of valiant men, Christ's Gospel will be proclaimed?" I have said so myself; and now I know I am a fool for my pains, and that Christ's church hath been also miserably befooled; for this I will assert, and prove too, that the progress of the arms of a Christian nation is not the progress of Christianity, and that the spread of our empire, so far from being advantageous to the Gospel, I will hold, and this day proclaim, hath been hostile to it.

But I have another string to my bow, I believe that the help of Government would have been far worse than its opposition, I do regret that the [East India] Company sometimes discourages missionary enterprise; but I believe that, had they encouraged it, it would have been far worse still, for their encouragement would have been the greatest hindrance we could receive. If I had to-morrow to go to India to preach the Gospel, I should pray to God, if such a thing could be, that he would give me a black face and make me like a Hindoo; for otherwise I should feel that when I preached I should be regarded as one of the lords—one of the oppressors it may sometime be added—and I should not expect my congregation to listen to me as a man speaking to men, a brother to brother, a Christian full of love, but they would hear me, and only cavil at me, because even my white face would give me some appearance of superiority. Why in England, our missionaries and our clergymen have assumed a kind of superiority and dignity over the people; they have called themselves clergy, and the people laity; and the result has been that they have weakened their influence. I have thought it right to come amongst my fellow men, and be a man amongst men, just one of themselves, their equal and their friend; and they have rallied around me, and not refused to love me. And I should not expect to be successful in preaching the gospel, unless I might stand and feel that I am a brother, bone of their bone, and flesh of their flesh. If I cannot stand before them thus, I cannot get at their hearts. Send me, then, to India as one of the dominant ruling race, and you give me a work I cannot accomplish when you tell me to evangelise its inhabitants. In that day when John Williams fell in Erromanga, ye wept, but it was a more hopeful day for Erromanga than the day when our missionaries in India first landed there. I had rather go to preach to the greatest savages that live, than I would go to preach in the place that is under British rule. Not for the fault of Britain, but simply because I, as a Briton, would be looked upon as one of the superiors, one of the lords, and that would take away much of my power to do good. Now, will you just cast your eye upon the wide world? Did you ever hear of a nation under British rule being converted to God? Mr. Moffat and our great friend Dr. Livingstone have been laboring in Africa with great success, and many have been converted. Did you ever hear of Kaffir tribes protected by England, ever being converted? It is only a people that have been left to themselves, and preached to by men as men, that have been brought to God. For my part, I conceive, that when an enterprise begins in martyrdom, it is none the less likely to succeed, but when conquerors begin to preach the gospel to those they have conquered, it will not succeed, God will teach us that it is not by might All swords that have ever flashed from scabbards have not aided Christ a single grain. Mahommedans' religion might be sustained by scimitars, but Christians' religion must be sustained by love. The great crime of war can never promote the religion of peace. The battle, and the garment rolled in blood, are not a fitting prelude to "peace on earth, goodwill to men." And I do firmly hold, that the slaughter of men, that bayonets, and swords, and guns, have never yet been, and never can be, promoters of the gospel. The gospel will proceed without them, but never through them. "Not by might." Now don't be fooled again, if you hear of the English conquering in China, don't go down on your knees and thank God for it, and say it's such a heavenly thing for the spread of the gospel—it just is not. Experience teaches you that, and if you look upon the map you will find I have stated only the truth, that where our arms have been victorious, the gospel has been hindered rather than not; so that where South Sea Islanders have bowed their knees and cast their idols to the bats, British Hindoos have kept their idols, and where Bechuanas and Bushmen have turned unto the Lord, British Affairs have not been converted, not perhaps because they were British, but because the very fact of the missionary being a Briton, put him above them, and weakened their influence. Hush thy trump, O war; put away thy gaudy trappings and thy bloodstained drapery, if thou thinkest that the cannon with the cross upon it is really sanctified, and if thou imaginest that thy banner hath become holy, thou dreamest

> of a lie. God wanteth not thee to help his cause. "It is not by armies, nor by power, but by my Spirit, saith the Lord" ("Independence of Christianity," August 31, 1857, Music Hall, Royal Surrey Gardens).
>
> While, however, we shall anxiously watch the contest, it will be quite as well if we mingle in it ourselves. Not that this nation of England should touch it; God forbid. If tyrants fight, let them fight; let free men stand aloof. Why should England have aught to do with all the coming battles? As God has cut us off from Europe by a boisterous sea, so let us be kept apart from all the broils and turmoils into which tyrants and their slaves may fall ("War! War! War!" May 1, 1859, Music Hall, Royal Surrey Gardens).

Spurgeon on Christianity and War

If there is anyone who should be opposed to strife and bloodshed it is the man that names the name of Christ. Spurgeon considered the spirit of war to be absolutely foreign to the spirit of Christianity:

> The Church of Christ is continually represented under the figure of an army; yet its Captain is the Prince of Peace; its object is the establishment of peace, and its soldiers are men of a peaceful disposition. The spirit of war is at the extremely opposite point to the spirit of the gospel ("The Vanguard and Rereward of the Church," December 26, 1858, Music Hall, Royal Surrey Gardens).
>
> Far be it from us to lay the blood of men at God's door. Let us not for one moment be guilty of any thought that the sin and the iniquity which have brought war into the world is of God ("The Desolations of the Lord, the Consolation of His Saints," April 28, 1858, Music Hall, Royal Surrey Gardens, on behalf of the Baptist Missionary Society).
>
> What saves us from war at this moment? What influence is it that is always contrary to war, and always cries for peace? Why, it is the Christian element among us which counts anything better than bloodshed! ("Jesus—'All Blessing and All Blest'," February 1, 1891, Metropolitan Tabernacle).
>
> The Lord's battles, what are they? Not the garment rolled in blood, not the noise, and smoke, and din of human slaughter. These may be the devil's battles, if you please, but not the Lord's. They may be days of God's vengeance but in their strife the servant of Jesus

> may not mingle. We stand aloof. Our kingdom is not of this world; else would God's servants fight with sword and spear. Ours is a spiritual kingdom, and the weapons of our warfare are not carnal, but spiritual, and mighty through God, to the pulling down of strongholds ("War! War! War!" May 1, 1859, Music Hall, Royal Surrey Gardens).
>
> War is to our minds the most difficult thing to sanctify to God. The genius of the Christian religion is altogether contrary to everything like strife of any kind, much more to the deadly clash of arms. . . . Now I say again, I am no apologist for war, from my soul I loathe it, and I do not understand the position of a Christian man as a warrior, but still I greatly rejoice that there are to be found at this present day in the ranks many of those who fear God and adorn the doctrine of God their Saviour ("A Peal of Bells," July 7, 1861, Metropolitan Tabernacle).
>
> If men receive Christ, there will be no more oppression: the true Christian does to others as he would that they should do to him, and there is no more contention of classes, nor grinding of the faces of the poor. Slavery must go down where Christianity rules, and mark you, if Romanism be once destroyed, and pure Christianity shall govern all nations, war itself must come to an end; for if there be anything which this book denounces and counts the hugest of all crimes, it is the crime of war. Put up thy sword into thy sheath, for hath not he said, "Thou shalt not kill," and he meant not that it was a sin to kill one but a glory to kill a million, but he meant that bloodshed on the smallest or largest scale was sinful. Let Christ govern, and men shall break the bow and cut the spear in sunder, and burn the chariot in the fire. It is joy to all nations that Christ is born, the Prince of Peace, the King who rules in righteousness. ("Joy Born at Bethlehem," December 24, 1871, Metropolitan Tabernacle).

Spurgeon on True Christian Warfare

As I have previously pointed out, there is no denying the fact that the Bible likens a Christian to a soldier. But as Spurgeon points out, the Christian's true warfare is a spiritual one:

> First of all, note that this crusade, this sacred, holy war of which I speak, is *not with men*, but with Satan and with error. "We wrestle not with flesh and blood." Christian men are not at war with any man that walks the earth. We are at war with infidelity,

but the persons of infidels we love and pray for; we are at warfare with any heresy, but we have no enmity against heretics; we are opposed to, and cry war to the knife with everything that opposes God and his truth: but towards every man we would still endeavour to carry out the holy maxim, "Love your enemies, do good to them that hate you." The Christian soldier hath no gun and no sword, for he fighteth not with men. It is with "spiritual wickedness in high places" that he fights, and with other principalities and powers than with those that sit on thrones and hold sceptres in their hands. I have marked, however, that some Christian men—and it is a feeling to which all of us are prone—are very apt to make Christ's war a war of flesh and blood, instead of a war with wrong and spiritual wickedness. Have you never noticed in religious controversies how men will fall foul of each other, and make personal remarks and abuse each other? What is that but forgetting what Christ's war is? We are not fighting against men; we are fighting for men rather than against them. We are fighting for God and his truth against error and against sin; but not against men. Woe, woe, to the Christian who forgets this sacred canon of warfare. Touch not the persons of men, but smite their sin with a stout heart and with strong arm. Slay both the little ones and the great; let nothing be spared that is against God and his truth; but we have no war with the persons of poor mistaken men ("The War of Truth," January 11, 1857, Music Hall, Royal Surrey Gardens).

But now let us observe that the warfare which the Christian carries on, may be said for his encouragement, to be a most *righteous* warfare. In every other conflict in which men have engaged, there have been two opinions, some have said the war was right, and some have said it was wrong; but in regard to the sacred war in which all believers have been engaged, there has been only one opinion among right-minded men. When the ancient priest stirred up the Crusaders to the fight, he made them shout *Deus vult—God wills it.* And we may far more truly say the same. A war against falsehood, a war against sin, is God's war; it is a war which commends itself to every Christian man, seeing he is quite certain that he has the seal of God's approval when he goes to wage war against God's enemies. Beloved, we have no doubt whatever, when we lift up our voices like a trumpet against sin, that our warfare is justified by the eternal laws of justice. Would to God that every war had so just and true an excuse as the war which God wages with Amalek—with sin in the world! ("The War of Truth," January 11, 1857, Music Hall, Royal Surrey Gardens).

Spurgeon on Christian War Fever

Spurgeon's remarks about war can be found not only in his sermons, but also in the monthly magazine he edited, *The Sword and the Trowel*. In an article from April of 1878, "Periodical War Madness," Spurgeon issued his most scathing denunciation of Christian war fever:

> A friend who was some long time ago prostrated by African fever assures us that he still feels it once a year. The enemy was repulsed in its first assault, but it annually resumes the attack, and will probably do so as long as our friend survives. This curious phenomenon has its parallel in the moral world, for certain evils may be subdued and apparently driven out of a man, and yet they return with great fury and resume their former sway. The like is true of races and nations. At intervals the world goes mad, and mad in the very same direction in which it had confessed its former insanity, and resolved never to rave again. England, at set seasons, runs wild with the war lunacy, foams at the mouth, bellows out "Rule Britannia," shows her teeth, and in general behaves herself like a mad creature: then her doctors bleed her, and put her through a course of depletion until she comes to her senses, settles down to her cotton-spinning and shop-keeping, and wonders what could have ailed her. A very few months ago it would have been difficult to discover an apologist for the Crimean war, and yet in this year of grace 1878 we find ourselves surrounded by a furious crowd whose intemperate language renders it almost a miracle that peace yet continues. If they do not desire war, they are mere bullies; but if they do desire it, they certainly go the right way to bring it about.
>
> One stands amazed at the singular change which has come over the populace, who, if they are faithfully represented by their journals, have learned nothing by experience, but long to throat their burned hand again into the fire. The mistakes of former days should minister to the wisdom of the present generation, for history is a nation's education; it is, therefore, to the last degree, unfortunate when the people relapse into their acknowledged errors, and repeat the blunders of their sires. If our country has been fairly depicted by the advocates for war, its condition is disappointing to the believer in progress, and alarming to the patriot who gazes into the future. We are still pugnacious, still believers in brute force, still ready to shed blood, still able to contemplate ravaged lands and murdered thousands without horror, still eager to test our ability to kill our fellow men. We are

persuaded that a large portion of our fellow citizens are clear of this charge, but the noisier, if not the more numerous party, clamour for a warlike policy as loudly as if it involved no slaughter, and were rather a boon to mankind than an unmitigated curse. A mysterious argument, founded upon the protection of certain mythical "British interests" is set up as an excuse, but the fact is that the national bull-dog wants to fix his teeth into somebody's leg, and growls because he does not quite see how to do it. The fighting instinct is asking to be gratified, and waxes violent because it is denied indulgence.

It is cause for gratitude that the cool heads among us are now sufficiently numerous to act as a check upon the more passionate. We are not now *all* mad at the same time, nor are quite so many bitten by the ban-dog. When last our people barked at the Russian bear, Messrs. Cobden and Bright and a small band of sensible men entered a protest which only enraged the fighting party; but now, thank God, the advocates of peace are heard, and even though abused, their power is felt. They may be unpopular, but they are certainly influential; their opponents have to stand upon the defensive, and exhibit some show of apologetic argument, whereas aforetime they laughed the peace-man to scorn as un-English, fanatical, and idiotic. Though our people have not advanced as we could desire, yet there has been progress, and that of a solid kind. Statesmen are now found who forego considerations of party to obey the higher dictates of humanity; ministers of the gospel now more frequently denounce the crime of carnage and pray for peace and among the masses there are juster ideas of the lamentable results of war. We are bound to be thankful even for small mercies, and on that ground we rejoice in the faintest sign of advance towards truthful estimates of bloodshed; but we are sorry to temper our rejoicing with a large measure of regret that our fellow countrymen, ay, and fellow Christians are still so far from being educated upon this most important subject. Many who did run well apparently, and were theoretical lovers of peace, lost their heads in the general excitement and went over to the enemy; some of them, fearful lest English prestige, alias British swagger, should suffer; others afraid that Russia, by capturing Constantinople, would block our road to India; and a third class, carried away by unreasoning sympathy with the dominant feeling around them. Times of feverish excitement test our attachment to great principles, and are probably intended by providence to act as a gauge as to their real growth; viewing the past few months in that light, there has been cause for congratulation, but greater reason for regret.

What is the cause of these periodical outbreaks of passion? Why does a peaceful nation bluster and threaten for a few months, and even commence fighting, when in a short time it sighs for peace, and illuminates its streets as soon as peace is proclaimed? The immediate causes differ, but the abiding reason is the same—man is fallen, and belongs to a race of which infallible revelation declares "their feet are swift to shed blood; destruction and misery are in their ways, and the way of peace they have not known." Wars and fightings arise from the inward lusts of the corrupt heart, and so long as human nature is unrenewed, battles and sieges, wars and rumours of wars will make up the history of nations. Civilized man is the same creature as the savage; he is washed and clothed, but intrinsically he is the same being. As beneath the Russian's skin you find the Tartar, so the Englishman is the savage Briton, or plundering Saxon, wearing broadcloth made from the wool of the sheep, but with a wild fierce heart within his breast. A prizefight a few years ago excited universal interest, and would do so again if it exhibited gameness and pluck, endurance and mettle. As a race we have these qualities and admire them, and it is idle to deny that if we were unrestrained by education and unrenewed by grace, there is not a man among us but would delight to see, or at least to read of, a fair stand-up fight, whether between fighting men or fighting cocks. We are not cruel, and therefore the brutal contests of Roman gladiators, or the disgusting scenes of Spanish bull-fights, would never be tolerated among us; but we are a fighting nation, and are never better pleased than when we see an exhibition of spirit and courage. Doubtless some good runs side by side with this characteristic of our countrymen, and we are far from wishing to depreciate bravery and valour, but at the same time this is one of the difficulties which the peace advocate must not fail to recognize. A tamer people might more readily adopt our tenets, not from conviction, but from force of circumstances; we find a warrior race slow to learn the doctrine of "peace on earth, good will toward men"; nor may this discourage us, for such a race is worth instructing, and when thoroughly indoctrinated will be mighty to spread abroad the glorious truth. Rome covets England because she knows it to be the centre and pivot of the world, and we covet it also for the self-same reason: let Great Britain once declare from her heart that her empire is peace, and the whole earth shall be in a fair way to sit still and be at rest. We are far from this consummation at present, nor need we wonder when we remember the hearts of men and the passions which rage therein, and especially when we note the peculiarly warlike constituents of which our nation is composed. Observe the bold dash of the Irish, the stern valour of the Scotch, the fierce fire of the Welsh, and the dogged resolution of the English, and you see before you stormy elements ready at any time to brew a tempest.

What, then, is to be done? Shall we unite with the clamorous patriots of the hour and sacrifice peace to political selfishness? Or shall we in silence maintain our own views, and despair of their ever being received by our own countrymen? There is no need to take either course: let us believe in our principles, and wait till the present mania comes to an end. We would persuade all lovers of peace to labour perseveringly to spread the spirit of love and gentleness, which is indeed the spirit of Christ, and to give a practical bearing to what else may become mere theory. The fight-spirit must be battled with in all its forms, and the genius of gentleness must be cultivated. Cruelty to animals, the lust for destroying living things, the desire for revenge, the indulgence of anger—all these we must war against by manifesting and inculcating pity, compassion, forgiveness, kindness, and goodness in the fear of the Lord. Children must be trained with meekness and not with passion, and our dealings with our fellow-men must manifest our readiness to suffer wrong rather than to inflict it upon others. Nor is this all: the truth as to war must be more and more insisted on: the loss of time, labour, treasure, and life must be shown, and the satanic crimes to which it leads must be laid bare. It is the sum of all villainies, and ought to be stripped of its flaunting colours, and to have its bloody horrors revealed; its music should be hushed, that men may hear the moans and groans, the cries and shrieks of dying men and ravished women. War brings out the devil in man, wakes up the hellish legion within his fallen nature, and binds his better faculties hand and foot. Its natural tendency is to hurl nations back into barbarism, and retard the growth of everything good and holy. When undertaken from a dire necessity, as the last resource of an oppressed people, it may become heroic, and its after results may compensate for its immediate evils; but war wantonly undertaken, for self-interest, ambition, or wounded pride is evil, only evil, and that continually. It ought not to be smiled upon as a brilliant spectacle, nor talked of with a light heart; it is a fitter theme for tears and intercessions. To see a soldier a Christian is a joy; to see a Christian a soldier is another matter. We may not judge another man, but we may discourage thoughtless inclinations in the young and ignorant. A sweeping condemnation would arouse antagonism, and possibly provoke the very spirit we world allay; while quiet and holy influence may sober and ultimately overcome misdirected tendencies. Many of our bravest soldiers are on the side of peace, and in the present crisis have spoken out more boldly on the right side than we might reasonably have expected of them. This must be duly acknowledged and taken into account, and we must speak accordingly. Rash advocates mar the cause they love, and this also is not to be wondered at, since a portion of the same fighting nature is in them also, and leads them to be furious for peace, and warlike on behalf of love. The temptation to fight Christ's battles with the devil's weapons comes upon us all at times, and it is not marvellous that men speak of "fighting Quakers," and "bigots for liberality." We must guard our own spirits, and not lend ourselves to the service of strife by bitter contentions for peace; this, we fear, has not always been remembered, and the consequences have been more lamentable than would at first sight appear: opponents have been needlessly created, and prejudices have been foolishly confirmed. Let us profit by all the mistakes of zealots, and at the same lime let us not become so extremely prudent as to lose all earnestness. The cause is a good one, let us urge it onward with blended vigour and discretion.

Seeing that the war-spirit is not slain, and only at the best wounded, we must in quiet times industriously inculcate the doctrines of peace. The work begun must be deepened and made more real, and where nothing has been taught we must begin in real earnest. It is wise to keep the evil spirit down when it is down. We had better shear its locks while it sleeps, for if once the giant awakes it snaps all arguments as Samson broke the new ropes. As a drunkard should be reasoned with in his sober intervals, and not when he is in liquor, so must our nation be instructed in peace when it's fit of passion is over, and not when it is enraged. Have we well and wisely used the period since the last great war? Perhaps not; and it may be that the late ebullition has come to warn us, lest we beguile ourselves into the false notion that a millennium has commenced, and dream that men are about to beat their spears into pruning-hooks. Peace teaching, which is but another name for practical gospel teaching, must be incessant, line upon line, precept upon precept, here a little and there a little. "Thou shalt love thy neighbour as thyself" must resound from our pulpits, and be practised in our homes. "Let us love one another, for love is of God," must be more in our hearts and lives. Above all we must evangelize the masses, carry the truth of the loving God to their homes, preach Jesus and his dying love in their streets, and gather men to his fold. All soul-saving work is a blow at the war-spirit. Make a man a Christian, and he becomes a lover of his race; instruct him, and he becomes ashamed of blows and battles; sanctify him, and he sweetens into an embodiment of love. May the Holy Ghost do such work on all sides among our

> countrymen, and we shall see their outbursts of rage become less frequent and less violent, for there will be a strong counteracting influence to keep down the evil, and to restrain it when in a measure it breaks loose.

Charles Spurgeon was not alone, for as I have pointed out elsewhere, Baptist ministers in America during the nineteenth century held the same opinions about Christianity and war. Christian agitation or apology for war is an aberration from the principles of Christianity, the folly of which is exceeded only by its appalling misuse of Scripture.

Modern conservative, fundamentalist, and evangelical Christians, all of whom might claim him as one of their own, have much to learn from Spurgeon, not only for his example of an uncompromising and successful Christian minister, but also for his consistent opposition to war and Christian war fever.

* * * * *

ARE YOU A CHRISTIAN WARMONGER?

It is appalling that many defenders of the war in Iraq are Christians; it is even worse when they appeal to Scripture to excuse or justify a senseless war that has now resulted in the deaths of over 1,500 Americans and the wounding of countless thousands more.

When the president of the Ayn Rand Institute, Yaron Brook, appeared last December on The O'Reilly Factor and called for "harsher military measures in Iraq," it was disheartening to hear him advocate that the U.S. military should "be a lot more brutal," "bring this war to the civilians," and "turn Fallujah into dust." As reprehensible as these statements are, they come as no surprise since Brook is guided by Objectivism and not Christianity.

But the sad fact is that some Christian warmongers are just as militant. They consider this war to be a Christian crusade against Islam and view the thousands of dead Iraqi civilians as collateral damage. Congressman Sam Johnson (R–TX), when speaking on February 19 at Suncreek United Methodist Church in Allen, Texas, related to the congregation how he told President Bush: "Syria is the problem. Syria is where those weapons of mass destruction are, in my view. You know, I can fly an F-15, put two nukes on 'em and I'll make one pass. We won't have to worry about Syria anymore." Although Johnson later claimed to be joking, it is strange that "the crowd roared with applause" instead of with laughter.

Other Christians are passive Christian warmongers. Although they don't actively participate in the war in Iraq, cherish the thought of dead Iraqis, or "joke" about nuking Muslims, they excuse, dismiss, make apologies for, and defend the war (and sometimes even the torture of prisoners and the killing of civilians) with such profound scriptural and logical assertions as "we should always obey the government," "Bush is a Christian so we should follow his leadership," or "doesn't the Bible say there is 'a time of war'?"

The following test is designed for Christians of any stripe to determine to what degree, if any, that they are a Christian warmonger. These statements are based on things I have read or been told by Christians seeking to excuse or justify the war in Iraq in order to defend President Bush. The statements are not in any particular order. Each statement is designed to be answered with either "true" or "false." A "true" answer receives 1 point and a "false" answer receives no points. Add up your points and consult the scale at the bottom to obtain the results.

1. The commandment "Thou shalt not kill" (Exodus 20:13) never applies to killing in war.
2. We should follow President Bush's leadership because he is a Christian.
3. Torturing Iraqi prisoners to obtain information is okay if it saves the life of one American.
4. The command to "submit yourselves to every ordinance of man for the Lord's sake" (1 Peter 2:13) means that we should kill foreigners in their country if the government says to do so.
5. U.S. intervention in the Middle East is necessary to protect Israel from the Arabs.
6. Muslim civilians killed by the U.S. military in Iraq and Afghanistan are just collateral damage.
7. A preemptive war against Iraq is nothing to be concerned about because the Bible says there is "a time of war" (Ecclesiastes 3:8).
8. It is okay to kill Muslims in Iraq because the terrorists who kill Jews are Muslims.
9. Since the Bible says that "the powers that be are ordained of God" (Romans 13:1), we should always obey the government when it comes to war.
10. U.S. wars and interventions abroad are ultimately a good thing because they pave the way for the spread of the gospel.
11. The command to "obey magistrates" (Titus 3:1) means that it is not immoral to drop bombs on foreign countries if the government says it should be done.

12. The U.S. should take vengeance on Muslims because of the September 11th attacks.
13. A perpetual war against the Muslim world in order to fight terrorism is just because "The LORD is a man of war" (Exodus 15:3).
14. Christians can wholeheartedly participate in their government's wars since God commanded the Jews in the Old Testament to go to war.
15. Christians can proudly serve in the military in any capacity.
16. Christians can proudly serve in the CIA in any capacity.
17. The command to "obey God rather than men" (Acts 5:29) does not apply to refusing to kill for the state in a war.
18. God approves of the war in Iraq because Islam is a false religion.
19. Muslims in the Middle East hate Americans because of their Christianity, their freedoms, and their democratic values.
20. Christians in Iraq are better off now than they were under Saddam Hussein.

1 _____ 2 _____ 3 _____ 4 _____ 5 _____

6 _____ 7 _____ 8 _____ 9 _____ 10 _____

11 _____ 12 _____ 13 _____ 14 _____ 15 _____

16 _____ 17 _____ 18 _____ 19 _____ 20 _____

Total _____

If you scored:

0 You are truly a man of peace.

1–4 You are not a Christian warmonger, but you may want to reevaluate some of your beliefs.

5–8 You are on your way to becoming a Christian warmonger, but there is still hope for you; repent.

9–12 You are a Christian warmonger; turn from the error of your ways.

13–16 You are a militant Christian warmonger; get right with God.

17–20 You may be a Christian but you are a crazed warmonger whose idea of Christianity is seriously defective.

* * * * *

THE WARMONGER'S BEATITUDES

The tragic waste of American lives in Iraq (the death count is now up to 1,601) has caused support for Bush's war to decline. Evangelical Christian support for the war also appears to be waning. Unfortunately, however, it is generally not out of principle, but only because the war is going so badly. Thus, many Christians who now oppose the war in Iraq are still warmongers at heart.

The Beatitudes found at the opening of the Sermon on the Mount in Matthew 5:3–12 have been a source of inspiration to Christians for centuries:

> Blessed are the poor in spirit: for theirs is the kingdom of heaven.
> Blessed are they that mourn: for they shall be comforted.
> Blessed are the meek: for they shall inherit the earth.
> Blessed are they which do hunger and thirst after righteousness: for they shall be filled.
> Blessed are the merciful: for they shall obtain mercy.
> Blessed are the pure in heart: for they shall see God.
> Blessed are the peacemakers: for they shall be called the children of God.
> Blessed are they which are persecuted for righteousness' sake: for theirs is the kingdom of heaven.
> Blessed are ye, when men shall revile you, and persecute you, and shall say all manner of evil against you falsely, for my sake.
> Rejoice, and be exceeding glad: for great is your reward in heaven: for so persecuted they the prophets which were before you.

It is a shame that some of the same Christians who have found comfort and direction in the Beatitudes can also be found making apologies for the state and its wars. Rather than be a hypocrite, they should rewrite the Beatitudes so as to make them more in line with their theology.

Since no one has done so yet, I have taken the liberty to revise the Beatitudes as the Warmonger's Beatitudes:

> Blessed are the defense contractors: for theirs is the taxpayers' money.
> Blessed are they that kill: for they shall not comfort.
> Blessed are the soldiers: for they shall bomb the earth.
> Blessed are they which do hunger and thirst after blood: for they shall shed it.

Blessed are the vengeful: for they shall not show mercy.
Blessed are the war lovers in heart: for they shall see combat.
Blessed are the warmongers, for they shall be called the children of Mars.
Blessed are they which persecute for the state's sake: for theirs is a government contract.
Blessed are ye when ye shall revile foreigners, and persecute them, and say all manner of evil against them falsely, for the state's sake. Rejoice, and be exceeding glad: for great is your reward in the military: for so persecuted the military foreigners which were before you.

That many evangelical Christians have started questioning the necessity and morality of Bush's war, just as some in the military have repudiated their service in Iraq for the state, is a welcome sight. The real test will be when the United States bombs the next country.

* * * * *

VICESIMUS KNOX: MINISTER OF PEACE

Christian, is your preacher a minister of war or a minister of peace?

It is a horrible blight on Christianity that many of the preachers in America today who claim to be conservative Christians waste their time defending the president and upholding the Republican Party instead of defending the Bible and upholding Christianity. Instead of indoctrinating their congregations in the Christian faith, they propagandize them in government falsehood. Instead of exalting the name of Jesus Christ, they exalt the name of George Bush. Instead of diligently studying and giving their church members the truth, they indolently watch Fox News and give their church members government lies. Instead of helping their parishioners grow in their Christian life, they help them grow in their admiration for the state.

What an embarrassment that some preachers parrot Fox News instead of preach the gospel! What a shame to hear a sermon that glorifies the sacrifices of U.S. troops in Iraq instead of the sacrifice of Christ on Calvary! What a disgrace that some preachers are ministers of war instead of ministers of peace!

A Minister of Peace

Warmongering and making apologies for the state were not always the forte of preachers. The British preacher Vicesimus Knox (1752–1821) was a minister of peace.

Knox was educated at home by his father of the same name until he was fourteen. After graduating from St. John's College, Oxford, he became a fellow of the college and was ordained a priest in the Church of England. He served as the headmaster of Tonbridge School from 1778 to 1812. He was preceded by his father, who was headmaster from 1772 to 1778, and succeeded by his son, Thomas, who was headmaster from 1812 to 1843. Knox was said to be "a good scholar, an impressive preacher, and a popular and voluminous writer." He was both an advocate of civil liberties and an adversary of offensive war. Knox's collected works of letters, sermons, educational writings, and political pamphlets take up seven volumes.

The Prospect of Perpetual and Universal Peace

In 1793, Knox preached a sermon in the parish church at Brighton on the unlawfulness of offensive war. This sermon, "The Prospect of Perpetual and Universal Peace to Be Established on the Principles of Christian Philanthropy," which is available online and in print, was attended by some officers from the local army garrison. Several days later, these same officers compelled Knox and his family to leave a play at the Brighton theatre when they spotted him in one of the boxes. The text of Knox's sermon was "Glory to God in the highest, and on earth peace, good will toward men" (Luke 2:14). He begins by imploring his hearers to

> consider whether among those who bear rule, by power or by example, GLORY IS DULY GIVEN TO GOD; whether they do really promote to the utmost of their power, PEACE ON EARTH; and whether they seem to entertain GOOD WILL TOWARDS MEN, in that extent and degree which the Gospel of Jesus Christ requires of all who profess to believe it, and who expect the rewards of the pious and the peaceful.

He concludes that such is not the case:

> The picture is sadly shaded with misery. Peace on earth! Alas where is it? amid all our refinement in the modes of cultivated life, all our elegant pleasures, all our boasted humanity, WAR, that giant fiend, is stalking over empires in garments dropping with the blood of men, shed by men, personally unoffended and unoffend-

ing; of men, professing to love as brethren, yet cutting off each other from the land of the living, long before the little time allotted them by nature is elapsed; and increasing beyond measure, all the evils to which man is naturally and morally doomed, at the command of a narrow shortsighted human policy, and an ambition which, considering the calamities causes, I must call accursed.

By all but the vulgar and the creatures of despotism, offensive war, with all its pompous exterior, must be deprecated as the disgrace and calamity of human nature. Poor outside pageantry! What avails the childish or womanish finery of gaudy feathers on the heads of warriors? Though tinged with the gayest colours by the dyer's art, they appear to the eye of humanity, weeping over the fields of battle, dipt in gore. What avails the tinsel, the trappings, the gold and the scarlet? Ornaments fitter for the pavilions of pleasure than the field of carnage. Can they assuage the anguish of a wound, or call back the departed breath of the pale victims of war; poor victims, unnoticed and unpitied, far from their respective countries, on the plains of neighhouring provinces, the wretched seat of actual war; not of parade, the mere play of soldiers, the pastime of the idle spectator, a summer day's sight for the gazing saunterer; but on the scene of carnage, the Aceldama, the field of blood, where, in the fury of the conflict, man appears to forget his nature and exhibits feats at which angels weep, while nations shout in barbarous triumph.

The elegant decorations of a sword, wantonly drawn in offensive war, what are they, but a mockery of the misery it was intended to create? An instrument of death to a fellow-creature who has never injured me, a holiday ornament! Colours of the darkest hue might form the appropriate habiliments of those who art: causelessly sent as the messengers of death; of death, not to animals of another species, fierce and venomous; but to those who like themselves, were born of woman, who sucked the breast of a woman, and who, if spared by the ruthless sword, must like themselves in a few short years die by the necessity of nature; die, and moulder into dust, under the turf once verdant and flowery, but now crimsoned with human gore. Alike born the victors and the vanquished, alike they die if spared in the battle; and alike must stand at the latter day, all stript of the distinctions of finer dress and superior rank, in the presence of those whom they cut off in this world before their time, in youth and health, like rose-buds cropt in the bud of existence.

Oh war! thy blood-stained visage cannot be disguised by the

politician's artifice. Thy brilliant vestments are to him who sympathizes with human woe in all climes and conditions, no better than sable mourning; thy melody, doleful discord, the voice of misery unutterable. Decked, like the harlot, in finery not thine own, thou art even the pest of man nature; and in countries where arbitrary power prevails, the last sad refuge of selfish cruel despotism, building its gorgeous palaces on the ruins of those who support its grandeur by their personal labour; and whom it ought to protect and to nourish under the olive shade of peace.

What feeling man can cast his eyes (as he proceeds in contemplating the picture) over the tented plains, on the theatre, glittering in the sunbeams with polished arms and gay with silken banners, without a sigh, if he views it undazzled by the "pride, pomp and circumstance," which the wisdom of this world has, from the earliest times, devised to facilitate its own purposes; purposes, it is to be feared, that have little reference to him who said, *that his kingdom was not of this world*; and whose religion was announced by a proclamation of peace on earth. What a picture is the tablet we are viewing of the heart of man, and of the misery of man! that he should thus find it necessary to defend himself with so much effort, at such expense of blood and treasure, not, as I said before, against the beast of the forest, not against the tiger and the wolf, for then it were well; but against his fellow man, his Christian brother, subject to the same wants, agonized with the same natural sufferings, doomed to the same natural death, and as a Christian, hoping for the same salvation; and perhaps separated from him only by a few leagues of intervening ocean.

Lo! in countries where war actually rages, thousands and tens of thousands of our fellow-creatures, all perhaps Christians in profession, many in the flower of their youth, torn from the peaceful vale, the innocent occupations of agriculture, or the useful employments of mechanic arts, to learn with indefatigable pains (separated at the same time from all the sweet endearments and duties of domestic life) to learn the art of spreading devastation and most expeditiously and effectually destroying those of their fellow-creatures, whom politicians have bade them consider as enemies, and therefore to cut off in their prime; but whom Christ taught, even if they were personal enemies, to love, to pity, and to save. Do they not, thoughtless as they are, require to be reminded of the gracious proclamation from Heaven, "On earth peace, Good-will towards men."

I wish not to dwell on the gloomy picture exhibited by various nations of Europe, professing Christianity as part of their respective constitutions; but acting towards each other with the ferocity of such savages as never heard that invitation of Christ; *Come unto me, all ye that labour and are heavy laden and I will give you rest.*

Alas! is it not enough that age, disease, death, and misery, in a hundred forms, are hourly waging war with all mankind; but they must add to the sting of death new venom; new anguish to every pang by waging war with each other? Men who as individuals are kind and humane, appear as nations, still in a state of barbarism and savage nature.

Yet we must believe and maintain the political necessity of war, though the greatest evil which can be endured by a civilized, flourishing and free people; we must believe its political necessity, because they, who in the various nations of the world, seem to claim an hereditary right to wisdom, as well as power, have, in all ages and in the most enlightened and Christian countries, so determined; yet, with all due submission to that wisdom and to that power, let every man who justly glories in the name and feelings of a man, mourn and lament the existence of that political necessity; and if it be such, pray to the father of us all, of every clime and colour, that under the benign influence of that Christianity which we profess, war may be no more on the face of the whole earth, and the sword every where converted into the pruning hook and the plough share.

O! that the still small voice of religion and philosophy could be heard amidst the cannon's roar, the shouts of victory, and the clamours of discordant politicians! It would say to all nations and to all people "Come unto me, all ye that labour in the field of battle, heavy laden with the weapons of war, worn out with its hardships, arid in jeopardy every hour; come unto me and I will give you rest; I will be unto you as a helmet, and a shield from the fiery darts of the common enemy of all mankind; and will lead you, after having rendered you happy and safe in this world, to the realms of everlasting peace."

As much as he hated war, Knox was not a pacifist: "Defensive war, in the present disordered state of human affairs, is sometimes as necessary as it is honourable; necessary to maintain peace, and the beautiful gradations of a well regulated society." But he believed that faithful ministers of the Gospel, are on our part bound by our duty, to pray for peace; to promote peace as much as in us lies; to preach peace, to cry aloud for peace and spare not, even though the instigators to war should frown upon us; and in defiance of the God of peace, prepare for the battle, It is our indispensable duty.

As a minister, Knox's answer to the problems of the world was, of course, Christianity:

> If the Christian religion, apparently laid aside, when to lay it aside suits the convenience of politicians, were indeed allowed to influence above every thing else the conduct of princes, and the councils of all cabinets, how different would be the picture of Europe.
>
> If the Christian religion in all its purity, and in its full force, were suffered to prevail universally, the sword of offensive war must be sheathed for ever, and the din of arms would at last he silenced in perpetual peace.

He finishes his sermon with a prayer that is rather unlike the war prayer recorded by Mark Twain:

> O thou God of mercy, grant that the sword may return to its scabbard for ever; that the religion of Jesus Christ may be duly understood, and its benign influence powerfully felt by all kings, princes, rulers, nobles, counsellors, and legislators, on the whole earth; that they may all combine in a league of philanthropy, to enforce by reason and mild persuasion, the law of love, or Christian charity, among all mankind, in all climes, and in all sects; consulting, like superior beings, the good of those beneath them; not endeavouring to promote their own power and aggrandizement by force and arms; but building their thrones, and establishing their dominion on the hearts of their respective people, preserved from the horrors of war by their prudence and clemency: and enjoying, exempt from all unnecessary burthens, the fruits of their own industry; every nation thus blest, permitting all others under the canopy of heaven to enjoy the same blessings uninterrupted, in equal peace and security.

The Spirit of Despotism

But it was not just in his sermons that Knox spoke out against war. His main work, *The Spirit of Despotism*, written in 1795, is an analysis of how political despotism at home can arise under the cover of fighting a foreign war. The complete text is available online and the complete chapters from which the following abstracts are taken are available in print.

Knox begins in his preface:

> I attribute war, and most of the artificial evils of life, to the Spirit of Despotism, a rank poisonous weed, which grows and flourishes even in the soil of liberty, when over-run with corruption.
>
> I have frequently lifted up my voice—a feeble one indeed—against war, that great promoter of despotism; and while I have liberty to write, I will write for liberty.

In section X, "When Human Life is held cheap, it is a Symptom of a prevailing Spirit of Despotism," he says of war:

> Despotism delights in war. It is its element. As the bull knows, by instinct, that his strength is in his horns, and the eagle trusts in his talons; so the despot feels his puissance most, when surrounded by his soldiery arrayed for battle. With the sword in his hand, and his artillery around him, he rejoices in his might, and glories in his greatness. Blood must mark his path; and his triumph is incomplete, till death and destruction stalk over the land, the harbingers of his triumphant cavalcade.
>
> We hear much of necessary wars; but it is certainly true, that a real, absolute, unavoidable necessity for war, such as alone can render it just, has seldom occurred in the history of man. The pride, the wanton cruelty of absolute princes, caring nothing for human life, have in all ages, without the least necessity, involved the world in war; and therefore it is the common cause of all mankind to abolish absolute power; and to discourage, by every lawful means, the spirit that leads to any degree of it. No individual, however good, is fit to be trusted with so dangerous a deposit. His goodness may be corrupted by the magnitude of the trust; and it is the nature of power, uncontrolled by fear or law, to vitiate the best dispositions. He who would have shuddered to spill a drop of blood, in a hostile contest, as a private man, shall deluge whole provinces, as an absolute prince, and laugh over the subjugated plains which he has fertilized with human gore.
>
> What are the chief considerations with such men, previously to their going to war, and at its conclusion? Evidently the expense of money. Little is said or thought of the lives lost, or devoted to be lost, except as matters of pecuniary value. Humanity, indeed,

> weeps in silence and solitude, in the sequestered shade of private life; but is a single tear shed in courts, and camps, and cabinets? When men high in command, men of fortune and family, fall, their deeds are blazoned, and they figure in history; but who, save the poor widow and the orphan, inquire after the very names of the rank and file? There they lie, a mass of human flesh, not so much regretted by the despots as the horses they rode, or the arms they bore. While ships often go down to the bottom, struck by the iron thunderbolts of war, and not a life is saved; the national loss is estimated by the despot, according to the weight of metal wasted, and the magnitude and expense of the wooden castle.
>
> Great numbers of men, trained to the trade of human butchery, have been constantly ready to be let to hire, to carry on the work of despotism, and to support, by the money they earned in this hellish employment, the luxurious vices of the wretch who called them his property.

In section XVII, "On debauching the Minds of the rising Generation and a whole People, by giving them Military Notions in a free and commercial Country," he says of war:

> The abettors of high prerogative, of absolute monarchy, and aristocratical pride, always delight in war. Not satisfied with attacking foreign nations, and keeping up a standing army even in time of peace, they wish, after they have once corrupted the mass of the people by universal influence, to render a whole nation military. The aggregate of military force, however great, being under their entire direction, they feel their power infinitely augmented, and bid defiance to the unarmed philosopher and politician, who brings into the field truth without a spear, and argument unbacked with artillery.
>
> The diffusion of a military taste among all ranks, even the lowest of the people, tends to a general corruption of morals, by teaching habits of idleness, or trifling activity, and the vanity of gaudy dress and empty parade.
>
> The strict discipline which is found necessary to render an army a machine in the hands of its directors, requiring, under the severest penalties, the most implicit submission to absolute command, has a direct tendency to familiarize the mind to civil despotism. Men, rational, thinking animals, equal to their commanders by nature, and often superior, are bound to obey the

impulse of a constituted authority, and to perform their functions as mechanically as the trigger which they pull to discharge their muskets. They cannot indeed help having a will of their own; but they must suppress it, or die. They must consider their official superiors as superiors in wisdom and in virtue, even though they know them to be weak and vicious. They must see, if they see at all, with the eyes of others: their duty is not to have an opinion of their own, but to follow blindly the behest of him who has had interest enough to obtain the appointment of a leader. They become living automatons, and self-acting tools of despotism.

While a few only are in this condition, the danger may not be great to constitutional liberty; but when a majority of the people are made soldiers, it is evident that the same obsequiousness will become habitual to the majority of the people. Their minds will be broken down to the yoke, the energy of independence weakened, the manly spirit tamed; like animals, that once ranged in the forest, delighting in their liberty, and fearless of man, caught in snares, confined in cages, and taught to stand upon their hind legs, and play tricks for the entertainment of the idle. They obey the word of command given by the keeper of the menagerie, because they have been taught obedience by hunger, by the lash of the whip, by every mode of discipline consistent with their lives, which are saleable property. But they are degenerate, contemptible animals.

The whole of the military system is much indebted for its support to that prevailing passion of human nature, pride. Politicians know it, and flatter pride even in the lowest of the people. Hence recruiting-officers invite gentlemen only, who are above servile labour. "The vanity of the poor men" (says a sagacious author) "is to be worked upon at the cheapest rate possible. Things we are accustomed to we do not mind, or else what mortal, that never had seen a soldier, could look, without laughing, upon a man accoutred with so much paltry gaudiness and affected finery? The coarsest manufacture that can be made of wool, dyed of a brick-dust colour, goes down with him, because it is in imitation of scarlet or crimson cloth; and to make him think himself as like his officer as it is possible, with little or no cost, instead of silver or gold lace, his hat is trimmed with white or yellow worsted, which in others would deserve bedlam; yet these fine allurements, and the noise made upon a calf-skin, have drawn in and been the destruction of more men in reality, than all the killing eyes and bewitching voices of women ever slew in jest."

The spirit of pride is in fact the spirit of despotism; especially

> when it is that sort of pride which plumes itself on command, on external decoration, and the idle vanity of military parade.
>
> When this pride takes place universally in a nation, there will remain little industry, and less independence. The grand object will be to rise above our neighbours in show and authority. All will bow to the man in power, in the hope of distinction. Men will no longer rely on their own laborious exertions; but the poor man will court, by the most obsequious submission, the favour of the esquire; the esquire cringe to the next lord, especially if he be a lord-lieutenant of the county; and the lord-lieutenant of the county, will fall prostrate before the first lord of the treasury; and the first lord of the treasury will idolize prerogative. Thus the military rage will trample on liberty; and despotism triumphant march through the land, with drums beating and colours flying.

In section XXX, "The Spirit of Despotism delights in War or systematic Murder," he says of war:

> Fear is the principle of all despotic government, and therefore despots make war their first study and delight. No arts and sciences, nothing that contributes to the comfort or the embellishment of human society, is half so much attended to, in countries where the spirit of despotism is established, as the means of destroying human life. Tigers, wolves, earthquakes, inundations, are all innocuous to man, when compared with the fiercest of monsters, the gory despots. Fiends, furies, demons of destruction! may the day be near, when, as wolves have been utterly exterminated from England, despots may be cut off from the face of the whole earth; and the bloody memory of them loaded with the execration of every human being, to whom God has given a heart to feel, and a tongue to utter!
>
> Wherever a particle of their accursed spirit is found, there also will be found a propensity to war. In times of peace, the grandees find themselves shrunk to the size of common mortals. A finer house, a finer coach, a finer coat, a finer livery than others can afford, is all that they can display to the eye of the multitude, in proof of their assumed superiority. Their power is inconsiderable. But no sooner do you blow the blast of war, and put armies under their command, than they feel themselves indeed great and powerful. A hundred thousand men, in battle array, with all the instruments of destruction, under the command of a few grandees, inferior, perhaps, in bodily strength, to every one of the subject train, and

but little superior in intellect or courage, yet holding all, on pain of death, in absolute subjection; how must it elevate the little despots in their own opinion! "This it is to live," (they exclaim, shaking hands with each other) "this is to be great indeed. Now we feel our power. Glory be to us on high; especially as all our fame and greatness is perfectly compatible with our personal safety; for we will not risk our precious persons in the scene of danger, but be content with our extended patronage, with the delight of commanding the movements of this human machine, and with reading of the blood, slaughter, and burnt villages, in the Gazette, at our fire-side."

All the expense of war is paid by the people, and most of the personal danger incurred by those, who, according to some, have no political existence; I mean the multitude, told by the head, like sheep in Smithfield. Many of these troublesome beings in human form, are happily got rid of in the field of battle, and more by sickness and hardship previous or subsequent to the glorious day of butchery. Thus all makes for the spirit of despotism. There are, in consequence of a great carnage, fewer wretches left to provide for, or to oppose its will; and all the honour, all the profit, all the amusement, falls to the share of the grandees, thus raised from the insignificance and inglorious indolence of peace, to have their names blown over the world by the trumpet of Fame, and recorded in the page of history.

But a state of war not only gives a degree of personal importance to some among the great, which they could never obtain by the arts of peace, but greatly helps the cause of despotism. In times of peace the people are apt to be impertinently clamorous for reform. But in war, they must say no more on the subject, because of the public danger. It would be ill-timed. Freedom of speech also must be checked. A thousand little restraints on liberty are admitted, without a murmur, in a time of war, that would not be borne one moment during the halcyon days of peace. Peace, in short, is productive of plenty, and plenty makes the people saucy. Peace, therefore, must not continue long after a nation has arrived at a certain degree of prosperity. This is a maxim of Despotism.

And finally, in section XL, "The Pride which produces the Spirit of Despotism conspicuous even on the Tombstone. It might be treated with total Neglect, if it did not tend to the Oppression of the Poor, and to Bloodshed and Plunder," Knox warns of the dangers of standing armies:

> Standing armies are therefore the glory and delight of all who are actuated by the spirit of despotism. They would have no great objection to military government and martial law, while power is in their own hands, or in the hands of their patrons. The implicit submission of an army, the doctrine, which the military system favours, that men in subaltern stations are to act as they are bidden, and never to deliberate on the propriety of the command, is perfectly congenial with the spirit of despotism. The glitter, the pomp, the parade and ostentation of war are also highly pleasing to minds that prefer splendour and pageantry to solid and substantial comfort. The happiness, which must ever depend on the tranquillity of the people, is little regarded, when set in competition with the gratification of personal vanity. Plumes, lace, shining arms, and other habiliments of war, set off the person to great advantage; and as to the wretches who are slain or wounded, plunged into captivity and disease, in order to support this finery, are they not paid for it? Besides, they are, for the most part, in the lowest class, and those whom nobody knows.
>
> Such is the love of standing armies, in some countries, that attempts are made to render even the national militia little different from a standing army. This circumstance alone is a symptom of the spirit of despotism. A militia of mercenary substitutes, under officers entirely devoted to a minister, must add greatly to a standing army, from which, in fact, it would differ only in name. Should the people be entirely disarmed, and scarcely a musket and bayonet in the country but under the management of a minister, through the agency of servile lords lieutenant and venal magistrates, what defence would remain, in extremities, either for the king or the people?

Included in the works of Knox is also his translation of a work of Erasmus, "Antipolemus, or the Plea of Reason, Religion, and Humanity against War," that examines why Christian nations are constantly at war. This is also available online and in print. Knox added a lengthy preface in which he said of war:

> There will never be wanting pamphleteers and journalists to defend war, in countries where prime ministers possess unlimited patronage in the church, in the law, in the army, in the navy, in all public offices, and where they can bestow honours, as well as emoluments, on the obsequious instruments of their own ambition.
>
> Near three hundred years have elapsed since the composition of

this Treatise. In so long a period, the most enlightened which the history of the world can display, it might be supposed that the diffusion, of Christianity, and the improvements in arts, sciences, and civilisation, would either have abolished war, or have softened its rigour. It is however a melancholy truth, that war still rages in the world, polished as it is, and refined by the beautiful arts, by the *belles lettres*, and by a most liberal philosophy.

To eradicate from the bosom of man principles which argue not only obduracy, but malignity, is certainly the main scope of the Christian religion; and the clergy are never better employed in their grand work, the melioration of human nature, the improvement of general happiness, than when they are reprobating all propensities whatever, which tend, in any degree, to produce, to continue, or to aggravate the calamities of war; those calamities which, as his majesty graciously expressed it, in one of his speeches from the throne, are inseparable from a state of war.

There is nothing so heterodox, I speak under the correction of the reverend prelacy, as war, and the passions that lead to it, such as pride, avarice, and ambition. The greatest heresy I know, is to shed the blood of an innocent man, to rob by authority of a Christian government, to lay waste by law, to destroy by privilege, that which constitutes the health, the wealth, the comfort, the happiness, the sustenance of a fellow-creature, and a fellow Christian. This is heresy and schism with a vengeance!

I hope the world has profited too much by experience, to encourage any offensive war, under the name and pretext of a holy war.

Let Mahomet mark the progress of the faith by blood. Such modes of erecting the Cross are an abomination to Jesus Christ. Is it, after all, certain, that the slaughter of the unbelievers will convert the survivors to the religion of the slaughterers? Is the burning of a town, the sinking of a ship, the wounding and killing hundreds of thousands in the field, a proof of the lovely and beneficent spirit of that Christianity to which the enemy is to be converted, by the philanthropic warriors?

They who defend war, must defend the dispositions which lead to war; and these dispositions are absolutely forbidden by the gospel. The very reverse of them is inculcated in almost every page. Those dispositions being extinguished, war must cease; as the rivulet ceases to flow when the fountain is destitute of water; or as the tree no longer buds and blossoms, when the fibres, which extract the moisture from the earth, are rescinded or withered. It is not necessary that there should be in the gospel an absolute prohibition of war in so many express words; it is enough that malice and revenge are prohibited. The cause ceasing, the effect can be no more. Therefore I cannot think it consistent with the duty of a bishop, or any other clergyman, either to preach or pray in such a manner as to countenance, directly or indirectly, any war, but a war literally, truly, and not jesuitically, a defensive war *pro aris et focis*; and even then, it would be more characteristic of Christian divines to pray for universal peace, for a peaceable conversion of the hearts of our enemies, rather than for bloody victory.

Wars of ambition, for the extension of empire or for the gratification of pride, envy, and malice, can never be justified; and therefore it is, that all belligerent powers agree to call their several wars defensive in the first instance, and then, just and necessary. This is a tacit, but a very striking acknowledgment, on all sides, that offensive war is unjustifiable. But the misfortune is, that power is never without the aid of ingenious sophistry to give the name of right to wrong; and, with the eloquence which Milton attributes to the devil, to make the worse appear the better cause.

But as war is confessedly PUBLICA MUNDI CALAMITAS, the common misfortune of all the world, it is time that good sense should interpose, even if religion were silent, to controul the mad impetuosity of its cause, ambition.

War has certainly been used by the great of all ages and countries except our own, as a means of supporting an exclusive claim to the privileges of enormous opulence, stately grandeur, and arbitrary power. It employs the mind of the multitude, it kindles their passions against foreign, distant, and unknown persons, and thus prevents them from adverting to their own oppressed condition, and to domestic abuses. There is something fascinating in its glory, in its ornaments, in its music, in its very noise and tumult, in its surprising events, and in victory. It assumes a splendour, like the harlot, the more brilliant, gaudy, and affected, in proportion as it is conscious to itself of internal deformity. Paint and perfume are used by the wretched prostitute in profusion, to conceal the foul ulcerous sores, the rottenness and putrescence of disease. The vulgar and the thoughtless, of which there are many in the highest ranks, as well as in the lowest, are dazzled by outward glitter. But improvement of mind is become almost universal, since the invention of printing; and reason, strengthened by reading, begins to discover, at first sight and with accuracy, the difference between paste and diamonds, tinsel and bullion. It begins to see that there can be no glory in mutual destruction; that real glory can be derived only from beneficial exertions, from contributions to the conveniencies and accommodations of life; from arts, sciences, commerce, and agriculture; to all which war is the bane.

The total abolition of war, and the establishment of perpetual and universal peace, appear to me to be of more consequence than any thing ever achieved, or even attempted, by mere mortal man, since the creation.

I detest and abhor atheism and anarchy as warmly and truly as the most sanguine abettors of war can do; but I am one who thinks, in the sincerity of his soul, that reasonable creatures ought always to be coerced, when they err, by the force of reason, the motives of religion, the operation of law; and not by engines of destruction. In a word, I utterly disapprove all war, but that which is strictly defensive.

The Need of the Hour

We need preachers who will serve as ministers of peace instead of ministers of war. We need preachers who will preach the Bible instead of Bush's "compassionate conservatism." We need preachers who will refuse to defend the president with the words: "But he's a Christian." We need preachers who will refuse to make excuses for Bush's warped and unorthodox view of Christianity. We need preachers with some backbone who will not blindly follow the state as they incessantly repeat the mantra: "Obey the powers that be." We need preachers who are willing to apply the commandment, "Thou shalt not kill" (Exodus 20:13), to killing in an unjust, immoral war. We need preachers who are as concerned about killing on the battlefield as they are about killing in the womb.

We need more preachers like Vicesimus Knox and fewer preachers like Jerry Falwell.

* * * * *

THE EARLY CHRISTIAN ATTITUDE TO WAR

Were the early Christians warmongers like too many Christians are today? Did they idolize the Caesars like some Christians idolize President Bush? Did they make signs that said "the emperor" similar to the ones we see on cars today that refer to Bush as "the president"? Did they make apologies for the Roman Empire like some Christian apologists make for the U.S. Empire? Did they venerate the institution of the military like many Christians do today?

C. John Cadoux would say no.

Some books are instant classics. Once published, they are the final word on a subject. Such is the case with Cadoux's 1919 book, *The Early Christian Attitude to War: A Contribution to the History of Christian Ethics* (London: Headley Bros. Publishers, xxxii+272 pages). Although I have published a small collection of essays called *Christianity and War*, and have since written many more essays on this topic, Cadoux's book is truly the definitive work on the subject of the Christian attitude toward war and military service. I am pleased to report that *The Early Christian Attitude to War* is now available online, both in PDF and HTML, and in a printed, hardbound reprint edition.

Although Cadoux's book was written just after World War I, nothing written since then on this important subject is comparable in any way to it. Given the violent history of the twentieth century, and the continued participation by Christians in the state's wars, this book is just as relevant today as when it was written. In fact, many statements Cadoux makes sound like they could have been written yesterday:

> Among the many problems of Christian ethics, the most urgent and challenging at the present day is undoubtedly that of the Christian attitude to war. Christian thought in the past has frequently occupied itself with this problem; but there has never been a time when the weight of it pressed more heavily upon the minds of Christian people than it does to-day. The events of the past few years have forced upon every thoughtful person throughout practically the whole civilized world the necessity of arriving at some sort of a decision on this complicated and critical question—in countless cases a decision in which health, wealth, security, reputation, and even life itself have been involved.

The book is divided into four parts:

- The Teaching of Jesus
- Forms of the Early Christian Disapproval of War
- Forms of the Early Christian Acceptance of War
- Summary and Conclusion

These are preceded by a foreword, a very detailed table of contents, a chronological table, and an introduction. The book also includes an index.

Cadoux explains his purpose in his introduction:

> The purpose of the following pages is not to force or pervert the history of the past in the interests of a present-day controversy, but plainly and impartially to present the facts as to the early Christian attitude to war—with just so much discussion as will suffice to make this attitude in its various manifestations clear and intelligible—and to do this by way of a contribution towards the settlement of the whole complicated problem as it challenges the Christian mind to-day. Having recently had occasion for another purpose to work through virtually the whole of pre-Constantinian Christian literature, the present writer has taken the opportunity to collect practically all the available material in the original authorities. His work will thus consist largely of quotations from Christian authors, translated into English for the convenience of the reader, and arranged on a systematic plan.

And although he cautions that "the example of our Christian forefathers indeed can never be of itself a sufficient basis for the settlement of our own conduct to-day," Cadoux believes that "at the same time the solution of our own ethical problems will involve a study of the mind of Christendom on the same or similar questions during bygone generations: and, for this purpose, perhaps no period of Christian history is so important as that of the first three centuries."

The Teaching of Jesus

In part one, Cadoux readily acknowledges that the Lord Jesus "gave his disciples no explicit teaching on the subject of war." But, since "the proportion of soldiers and policemen to civilians must have been infinitesimal," and "no Jew could be compelled to serve in the Roman legion," and "there was scarcely the remotest likelihood that any disciple of Jesus would be pressed into the army," there was no occasion that "presented itself to him for any explicit pronouncement on the question as to whether or not his disciples might serve as soldiers." Therefore, "the silence of Jesus" does not mean that "no definite conclusion on the point is to be derived from the Gospels."

After discussing, among other things, the non-resistance teaching in the Sermon on the Mount and pointing out Jesus' refusal to advance his ideals by political or coercive means, Cadoux concludes that his arguments constitute a strong body of evidence for the belief that Jesus both abjured for himself and forbade to his disciples all use of physical violence as a means of checking or deterring wrongdoers, not excluding even that use of violence which is characteristic of the public acts of society at large as distinct from the individual. On this showing, participation in warfare is ruled out as inconsistent with Christian principles of conduct.

Forms of the Early Christian Disapproval of War

In part two will be found the bulk of the material that substantiates Cadoux's thesis. He divides it into five sections:

- The Condemnation of War in the Abstract
- The Essential Peacefulness of Christianity
- The Christian Treatment of Enemies and Wrongdoers
- The Christians' Experience of Evil in the Character of Soldiers
- The Christian Refusal to Participate in War

Cadoux properly opens the first part of this chapter with the statement: "The conditions under which the books of the New Testament were written were not such as to give occasion for Christian utterances on the wrongfulness of war." The early Christians, however, did write on the subject, and were especially critical of the Roman Empire. Cadoux points out how Arnobius contrasted Christ with the Roman emperors: "Did he, claiming royal power for himself, occupy the whole world with fierce legions, and, (of) nations at peace from the beginning, destroy and remove some, and compel others to put their necks beneath his yoke and obey him?" Lactantius says of the Romans:

> They despise indeed the excellence of the athlete, because there is no harm in it; but royal excellence, because it is wont to do harm extensively, they so admire that they think that brave and warlike generals are placed in the assembly of the gods, and that there is no other way to immortality than by leading armies, devastating foreign (countries), destroying cities, overthrowing towns, (and) either slaughtering or enslaving free peoples. Truly, the more men they have afflicted, despoiled, (and) slain, the more noble and renowned do they think themselves; and, captured by the appearance of empty glory, they give the name of excellence to their crimes. Now I would rather that they should make gods for themselves from the slaughter of wild beasts than that they should approve of an immortality so bloody. If any one has slain a single

> man, he is regarded as contaminated and wicked, nor do they think it right that he should be admitted to this earthly dwelling of the gods. But he who has slaughtered endless thousands of men, deluged the fields with blood, (and) infected rivers (with it), is admitted not only to a temple, but even to heaven.

Writing before Lactantius, Cyprian speaks of the idea that "homicide is a crime when individuals commit it, (but) it is called a virtue, when it is carried on publicly." This idea that mass killing in war is acceptable but only the killing of one's neighbor violates the Sixth Commandment is unfortunately a very prevalent idea among some Christians. Cadoux concludes:

> This collection of passages will suffice to show how strong and deep was the early Christian revulsion from and disapproval of war, both on account of the dissension it represented and of the infliction of bloodshed and suffering which it involved. The quotations show further how closely warfare and murder were connected in Christian thought by their possession of a common element—homicide; and the connection gives a fresh significance for the subject before us to the extreme Christian sensitiveness in regard to the sin of murder—a sensitiveness attested by the frequency with which warnings, prohibitions, and condemnations in regard to this particular sin were uttered and the severity with which the Church dealt with the commission of it by any of her own members. The strong disapprobation felt by Christians for war was due to its close relationship with the deadly sin that sufficed to keep the man guilty of it permanently outside the Christian community.

Cadoux then takes up the very nature of Christianity. If there was anything at all advocated by the early Christians it was peace. After all, they had some New Testament admonitions to go by:

- Blessed are the peacemakers (Matthew 5:9)
- Live peaceably with all men (Romans 12:18)
- Follow peace with all men (Hebrews 12:14)

So, as Cadoux says: "The natural counterpart of the Christian disapproval of war was the conception of peace as being of the very stuff and substance of the Christian life." Although this was ultimately based on first having peace with God ("Therefore being justified by faith, we have peace with God through our Lord Jesus Christ" [Romans 5:1]), this private concept of peace was made into a public one. Cadoux quotes Justin Martyr, from his *Apology* and from his *Dialogue with Truphon the Jew*:

> For from Jerusalem twelve men went out into the world, and these (were) unlearned, unable to speak; but by (the) power of God they told every race of men that they had been sent by Christ to teach all (men) the word of God. And we, who were formerly slayers of one another, not only do not make war upon our enemies, but, for the sake of neither lying nor deceiving those who examine us, gladly die confessing Christ.

> And we who had been filled with war and mutual slaughter and every wickedness, have each one—all the world over—changed the instruments of war, the swords into ploughs and the spears into farming instruments, and we cultivate piety, righteousness, love for men, faith, (and) the hope which is from the Father Himself through the Crucified One.

Cadoux also refers to the words of Tertullian:

> The old law vindicated itself by the vengeance of the sword, and plucked out eye for eye, and requited injury with punishment; but the new law pointed to clemency, and changed the former savagery of swords and lances into tranquillity, and refashioned the former infliction of war upon rivals and foes of the law into the peaceful acts of ploughing and cultivating the earth.

In his third section, Cadoux then explains how the attitude of the early Christians toward their enemies and wrongdoers also demonstrates the early Christian disapproval of war. First, since it is recurrent theme of the New Testament, Cadoux quotes, among others, these passages:

- Dearly beloved, avenge not yourselves, but rather give place unto wrath (Romans 12:19)
- As we have therefore opportunity, let us do good unto all men (Galatians 6:10)
- See that none render evil for evil unto any man; but ever follow that which is good (1 Thessalonians 5:15)

And second, he again refers to the Church Fathers. Cadoux wonders what Justin Martyr would have thought about Christians serving in the military when he said in his *Apology*:

> We who hated and slew one another, and because of (differences in) customs would not share a common hearth with those who were not of our tribe, now, after the appearance of Christ, have become sociable, and pray for our enemies, and try to persuade those who hate (us) unjustly, in order that they, living according to the good suggestions of Christ, may share our hope of obtaining the same (reward) from the God who is Master of all.

Lactantius describes Christians as "those who are ignorant of wars, who preserve concord with all, who are friends even to their enemies, who love all men as brothers, who know how to curb anger and soften with quiet moderation every madness of the mind." The just man, according to Lactantius, "inflicts injury on none, nor desires the property of others, nor defends his own if it is violently carried off, since he knows also (how) to bear with moderation an injury inflicted on him, because he is endowed with virtue, it is necessary that the just man should be subject to the unjust, and the wise man treated with insults by the fool."

Unlike many Christians today who have a superstitious reverence for the military, the early Christians did not think too highly of the Roman legions, as Cadoux shows in section four. Ignatius referred to soldiers as "beasts." Cadoux recounts case after case of Roman soldiers abusing, persecuting, and killing Christians. He refers to the account of Eusebius of the suffering of Christians in which "soldiers appear at every turn of the story, as the perpetrators either of the diabolical and indescribable torments inflicted on both sexes or of the numerous other afflictions and annoyances incidental to the persecution." He also mentions the *Didascalia*, which forbids the acceptance of money for the church "from soldiers who behave unrighteously or from those who kill men or from executioners or from any (of the) magistrate(s) of the Roman Empire who are stained in wars and have shed innocent blood without judgment."

If part two contains the bulk of the material that substantiates Cadoux's thesis, then the fifth section, "The Christian Refusal to Participate in War," is the quintessence of that material. Cadoux begins by quoting the church historian Adolf von Harnack (1851–1930) on the features of military life that would have presented great difficulty to Christians:

> The shedding of blood on the battlefield, the use of torture in the law-courts, the passing of death-sentences by officers and the execution of them by common soldiers, the unconditional military oath, the all-pervading worship of the Emperor, the sacrifices in which all were expected in some way to participate, the average

> behaviour of soldiers in peace-time, and other idolatrous and offensive customs—all these would constitute in combination an exceedingly powerful deterrent against any Christian joining the army on his own initiative.

Cadoux's extended quotations from Tertullian and Origen offer definitive proof that the early Christians were averse to war and military service.

Writing in defense of a Christian soldier who had refused to wear a garland on the emperor's birthday, Tertullian addresses the question of whether a Christian ought to be in the military in the first place:

> And in fact, in order that I may approach the real issue of the military garland, I think it has first to be investigated whether military service is suitable for Christians at all. Besides, what sort (of proceeding) is it, to deal with incidentals, when the (real) fault lies with what has preceded them? Do we believe that the human 'sacramentum' may lawfully be added to the divine, and that (a Christian) may (give a promise in) answer to another master after Christ, and abjure father and mother and every kinsman, whom even the Law commanded to be honoured and loved next to God, (and) whom the Gospel also thus honoured, putting them above all save Christ only? Will it be lawful (for him) to occupy himself with the sword, when the Lord declares that he who uses the sword will perish by the sword? And shall the son of peace, for whom it will be unfitting even to go to law, be engaged in a battle? And shall he, who is not the avenger even of his own wrongs, administer chains and (im)prison(ment) and tortures and executions? Shall he now go on guard for another more than for Christ, or (shall he do it) on the Lord's Day, when (he does) not (do it even) for Christ? And shall he keep watch before temples, which he has renounced? and take a meal there where the Apostle has forbidden it? And those whom he has put to flight by exorcisms in the daytime, shall he defend (them) at night, leaning and resting upon the pilum with which Christ's side was pierced? And shall he carry a flag, too, that is a rival to Christ? And shall he ask for a watchword from his chief, when he has already received one from God? And (when he is) dead, shall he be disturbed by the bugler's trumpet—he who expects to be roused by the trumpet of the angel? And shall the Christian, who is not allowed to burn (incense), to whom Christ has remitted the punishment of fire, be burned according to the discipline of the camp? (And) how many other sins can be seen (to belong) to the functions of camp (life)—(sins) which must be explained as a transgression (of

God's law). The very transference of (one's) name from the camp of light to the camp of darkness, is a transgression. Of course, the case is different, if the faith comes subsequent(ly) to any (who are) already occupied in military service, as (was, for instance, the case) with those whom John admitted to baptism, and with the most believing centurions whom Christ approves and whom Peter instructs: all the same, when faith has been accepted and signed, either the service must be left at once, as has been done by many, or else recourse must be had to all sorts of cavilling, lest anything be committed against God—(any, that is, of the things) which are not allowed (to Christians) outside the army, or lastly that which the faith of (Christian) civilians has fairly determined upon must be endured for God. For military service will not promise impunity for sins or immunity from martyrdom. The Christian is nowhere anything else (than a Christian).... With him (i.e. Christ) the civilian believer is as much a soldier as the believing soldier is a civilian. The state of faith does not admit necessities. No necessity of sinning have they, whose one necessity is that of not sinning.... For (otherwise) even inclination can be pleaded (as a) necessity, having of course an element of compulsion in it. I have stopped up that very (appeal to necessity) in regard to other cases of (wearing) garlands of office, for which (the plea of) necessity is a most familiar defence; since either (we) must flee from (public) offices for this reason, lest we fall into sins, or else we must endure martyrdoms, that we may break (off our tenure of public) offices. On (this) first aspect of the question, (namely) the illegitimacy of the military life itself, I will not add more, in order that the second (part of the question) may be restored to its place—lest, if I banish military service with all my force, I shall have issued a challenge to no purpose in regard to the military garland.

Those who think the military is tame now compared to the military in days gone by have never read the testimony of veterans on the subject.

Turning next to Origen, Cadoux remarks that "his defence of the early Christian refusal to participate in war is the only one that faces at all thoroughly or completely the ultimate problems involved." In his *Against Celsus*, Origen remarks:

To those who ask us whence we have come or whom we have (for) a leader, we say that we have come in accordance with the counsels of Jesus to cut down our warlike and arrogant swords of argument into ploughshares, and we convert into sickles the spears we formerly used in fighting. For we no longer take "sword against a nation," nor do we learn "any more to make war," having

> become sons of peace for the sake of Jesus, who is our leader, instead of (following) the ancestral (customs) in which we were strangers to the covenants.

In response to the appeal of Celsus that Christians should serve as soldiers for the emperor, Origen says:

> Celsus next urges us to help the Emperor with all (our) strength, and to labour with him (in maintaining) justice, and to fight for him and serve as soldiers with him, if he require (it), and to share military command (with him). To this it has to be said that we do help the Emperors as occasion (requires) with a help that is, so to say, divine, and putting on "the whole armour of God." And this we do in obedience to the apostolic voice which says: "I therefore exhort you firstly that supplications, prayers, intercessions, thanksgivings, be made for all men, for Emperors and all who are in high station"; and the more pious one is, so much the more effectual is he in helping the Emperors than (are) the soldiers who go forth in battle-array and kill as many as they can of the enemy. And then we should say this to those who are strangers to the faith and who ask us to serve as soldiers on behalf of the community and to kill men: that among you the priests of certain statues and the temple-wardens of those whom ye regard as gods keep their right-hand(s) unstained for the sake of the sacrifices, in order that they may offer the appointed sacrifices to those whom ye call gods, with hands unstained by (human) blood and pure from acts of slaughter; and whenever war comes, ye do not make the priests also serve. If then it is reasonable to do this, how much more (reasonable is it, that), when others are serving in the army, these (Christians) should do their military service as priests and servants of God, keeping their right-hands pure and striving by prayers to God on behalf of those who are righteously serving as soldiers and of him who is reigning righteously, in order that all things opposed and hostile to those that act righteously may be put down?

Forms of the Early Christian Acceptance of War

In part three, Cadoux turns from "the various ways in which the Christian abhorrence and disapproval of war expressed itself" to "the various conditions and connections in which war was thought of by Christian people without that association of reproach which so frequently attached to it."

Cadoux begins by correctly noting the biblical use of military terms to illustrate the Christian life:

- Put on the whole armour of God (Ephesians 6:11)
- Thou therefore endure hardness, as a good soldier of Jesus Christ (2 Timothy 2:3)
- War a good warfare (1 Timothy 1:18)

He then further points out that the Church Fathers likewise used "military metaphors and similes" in their writings. But as Cadoux explains: "For the purpose of pointing an argument or decorating a lesson, a writer will sometimes use rhetorical analogies which seem likely to carry weight, but which do not represent his own considered opinions on that from which the analogy is drawn." Thus, when the Bible says: "Then the LORD awaked as one out of sleep, and like a mighty man that shouteth by reason of wine" (Psalm 78:65), it doesn't mean that God condones drunkenness.

What, then, caused some of the early Christians to "accept" war? In addition to the aforementioned biblical use of military terms, Cadoux gives six factors:

> *The wars of the Old Testament*: some early Christians "accepted" war because they could not separate the divine sanction of war against the enemies of God in the Old Testament from the New Testament ethic that taught otherwise.
>
> *Apocalyptic wars*: some early Christians "accepted" war because of references in the Old Testament and the Apocalypse that told of a victorious war to be waged by the Messiah against the enemies of God.
>
> *The destruction of Jerusalem*: some early Christians "accepted" war because they believed that the destruction of Jerusalem "was a divinely ordained punishment inflicted on the Jewish nation for its sin in rejecting and crucifying Christ."
>
> *War as an instrument of divine justice*: some early Christians "accepted" war because of the generally accepted belief that war was a form of divine chastisement.
>
> *The Christian view of the state*: some early Christians "accepted" war because they believed war to be included in their belief that "the State was a useful and necessary institution, ordained by God for the security of life and property, the preservation of peace, and the prevention and punishment of the grosser forms of human sin."

> *The good character of some soldiers*: some early Christians "accepted" war because they saw kindness exhibited by some pagan soldiers.

The fact that some early Christians were influenced by one or more of these factors is irrelevant. None of these influences necessitated Christian participation in war or military service. There is nothing in the New Testament from which to draw the conclusion that killing is somehow sanctified if it is done in the name of the state.

Regarding war as an instrument of divine chastisement, Cadoux explains that

> a belief in the use of war for the divine chastisement of the Jews and of others who have been guilty of great offences, whatever theological problems it may raise, certainly does not involve the believer in the view that it is right or permissible for him to take a part in inflicting such penalties. While Christians agreed that the fall of Jerusalem and its accompanying calamities were a divine chastisement, no one thought of inferring from that that the Roman army was blameless or virtuous in the bloodthirsty and savage cruelty it displayed in the siege. And in regard to the more general view of war as a divine chastisement, if it could be inferred from the fact of its being so that a Christian might lawfully help to inflict it, it would follow that he might also under certain conditions help to cause and spread a plague or to inflict persecution on his fellow-Christians—for both plagues and persecutions were regarded as divine chastisements just as war was. The obvious absurdity of this conclusion ought to be enough to convince us that the Christian idea of war being used by God to punish sin certainly does not mean that the Christian may take part in it with an easy conscience: on the contrary, the analogy of pestilence, famine, persecution, etc., which are often coupled with war, strongly suggests that participation in it could not possibly be a Christian duty. And there can be no doubt that the vast majority of early Christians acted in conformity with that view, whether or not they theorized philosophically about it.

And regarding the state in particular, Cadoux adds:

> There was nothing in the relative justification which Christians accorded to the ordinary functions of government, including even its punitive and coercive activities, which logically involved them in departing from the ethics of the Sermon on the Mount and personally participating in those activities.

Cadoux's conclusion: "None therefore of the various forms in which Christians may be said to have 'accepted' war necessarily committed them to participation in it." This does not mean that there were no Christian soldiers in the Roman army. Cadoux freely acknowledges this fact, although he does point out that "there is no trace of the existence of any Christian soldiers" until about the year 170.

Summary and Conclusion

Cadoux very nicely summarizes his research into the early Christian attitude to war. He concludes that

> The early Christians took Jesus at his word, and understood his inculcations of gentleness and non-resistance in their literal sense. They closely identified their religion with peace; they strongly condemned war for the bloodshed which it involved; they appropriated to themselves the Old Testament prophecy which foretold the transformation of the weapons of war into the implements of agriculture; they declared that it was their policy to return good for evil and to conquer evil with good.

Because of their new outlook on life, refusal to serve in the military was the normal policy of the early Christians. Soldiers left the army upon their conversion to Christianity. And while "a general distrust of ambition and a horror of contamination by idolatry entered largely into the Christian aversion to military service," it was "the sense of the utter contradiction between the work of imprisoning, torturing, wounding, and killing, on the one hand, and the Master's teaching on the other" that "constituted an equally fatal and conclusive objection."

W.E. Orchard, who wrote the foreword to Cadoux's book almost ninety years ago, explains why Christians in the twenty-first century will reject Cadoux's thesis:

> The only real objection which can be urged against the revival of the early Christian attitude is that Christianity has accepted the State, and that this carries with it the necessity for coercive discipline within and the waging of war without; in which disagreeable duties Christians must as citizens take their part. To refuse this will expose civilization to disaster. It may perhaps serve to provoke reflection to notice in passing that this was the argument of Celsus and is the general attitude which determines German thought on this subject. The truth is that the way of war, if persisted in, is going to destroy civilization anyhow, and the

> continual demand for war service will, sooner or later, bring the modern State to anarchy.

Christians, of all people, should stop making excuses for the necessity of war. Cadoux's work proves, at least on this point, that the early Christians had better sense.

* * * * *

HUMPTY DUMPTY RELIGION

> "When I use a word," Humpty Dumpty said, in rather a scornful tone, "it means just what I choose it to mean—neither more nor less."
>
> "The question is," said Alice, "whether you can make words mean so many different things."
>
> "The question is," said Humpty Dumpty, "which is to be master—that's all."
>
> ~ *Through the Looking Glass*

Lewis Carroll (1832–1898), the author of *Through the Looking Glass* (the sequel to *Alice in Wonderland*) had nothing on the twenty-first-century Christian warmonger.

Some Christian warmongers seek to get around the plain truth of the commandment, "Thou shalt not kill" (Exodus 20:13), by taking the Humpty Dumpty approach.

But first, a word about the term "Christian warmonger." Yes, it is spoken in derision. And yes, it is a pejorative term that is meant to agitate and incite Christians who continue to support, what is becoming more and more evident everyday, an unnecessary, unscriptural, immoral, and unjust war that is needlessly killing and injuring American soldiers, creating terrorists faster than we can kill them, increasing the hatred many foreigners around the world have for the United States, and dividing churches and families across the country. In light of what Christian peace advocates are called by Christian war supporters (liberal, communist, anti-war weenie, traitor, coward, America-hater), I think the term "Christian warmonger" is justified. The term does not mean, as one of my critics recently said, that a Christian warmonger "cherishes the thought of any war." It is merely a short way of saying:

> defender of Bush's war in Iraq because Republicans and conservatives support the war, Bush is a Christian, "The LORD is a man of war," Iraq was responsible for September 11th, Islam is a false religion, U.S. intervention in the Middle East is necessary to protect Israel, dead Muslims are just collateral damage, U.S. soldiers are fighting for our freedoms, the military is a great institution, and we should "obey the powers that be."

But the term is also meant to provoke Christians to reexamine their support for Bush, his war in Iraq, the interventionist foreign policy of the United States, and war in general.

Here are two examples of the Humpty Dumpty mentality.

In the opening chapter of George Orwell's novel *Nineteen Eighty-Four*, we read of three slogans of the Party emblazoned "in elegant lettering" on the "glittering white concrete" of The Ministry of Truth building:

WAR IS PEACE

FREEDOM IS SLAVERY

IGNORANCE IS STRENGTH

In the movie *Saving Private Ryan*, Captain Miller (played by Tom Hanks) says to Sergeant Horvath (played by Tom Sizemore):

> You see, when you end up killing one of your men you tell yourself it happened so you could save the lives of two or three or ten others. Maybe a hundred others. You know how many men I've lost under my command? Ninety-four. But that means I've saved the lives of ten times that many, doesn't it? Maybe even twenty, right, twenty times as many? And that's how simple it is. That's how you rationalize making the choice between the mission and the men.

This Humpty Dumpty attitude cannot be dismissed because it is just found in a novel or a movie and is therefore not representative of the real world. An "Intelligence Analyst," in his one-sentence response to an article of mine that he did not name, made this statement:

> It didn't change my belief in the thought that when I pull the trigger it is to save a life, not take a life.

Killing is saving? This is Humpty Dumpty religion. Evil is good; malevolence is benevolence; torture is hazing; destruction is nation building; invasion is deliverance.

Christianity has always been plagued by advocates of Humpty Dumpty religion:

- The Bible is not really the word of God.
- The creation account in Genesis is just an allegory.
- Hell is just separation from God.
- The Second Coming was the destruction of Jerusalem in the first century.

The difference between these things and the subject of war is that it is conservative Christians who are manifesting Humpty Dumpty religion, not those viewed as unorthodox, liberals, modernists, or heretics

A variation of this attitude is that the commandment, "Thou shalt not kill," does not apply to killing in war. Thus, killing someone you don't know, and have never seen, in his own territory, who was no threat to anyone until the United States invaded his country, is not murder if the U.S. government says that he should be killed. Therefore, Christians can in good conscience join the military, not only knowing that they might have to go to Iraq and bomb, maim, "interrogate," and kill for the state, but can actually do these things without any fear of negative consequences by God at the judgment because they "obeyed orders" and "obeyed the powers that be." This attitude I have written about elsewhere.

Still another variety of Humpty Dumpty religion is the approach that reasons: Since the commandment "Thou shalt not kill" obviously doesn't mean "the taking of any life," one cannot apply it to killing in war. Every Christian I have ever talked to or read who took that position was trying to justify Christians killing for the state in Iraq.

This was the approach taken by a critic of my quiz: "Are You a Christian Warmonger." This is a twenty-question, true/false test designed for Christians of any stripe to determine to what degree, if any, that they are a Christian warmonger. I was informed by my critic that "the questions are rife with logical fallacies." He specifically mentioned the following: non sequiturs, red herrings, straw man arguments, sweeping generalizations, appeals to pity, complex questions, and false dichotomies. My quiz "is a logically fallacious quiz which appears to be deliberately designed to mislead those taking it into agreeing with your position—not out of genuine moral concern and logical reasoning, but rather out of trickery."

I was impressed with my critic's knowledge of logical fallacies and Latin; however, I was not impressed with my critic's ability to read simple English.

First, he defined a Christian warmonger as a Christian who "cherishes the thought of any war"—something that I never said or implied in that article or any article I have ever written. See above on what I mean by Christian warmonger.

Second, I was told that I should "repair the flaws" in my argument if I wish my quiz "to be a part of a genuine scholarly debate on the subject." But I never intended the quiz "to be part of a genuine scholarly debate on the subject." It was deliberately meant to be pithy, humorous, and thought provoking. It was definitely not intended to be a serious quiz along the lines of the "Are You an Austrian?" quiz offered by the Ludwig von Mises Institute.

Third, as to my quiz questions being or containing logical fallacies, I clearly stated in the introduction to the quiz: "These statements are based on things I have read or been told by Christians seeking to excuse or justify the war in Iraq in order to defend President Bush." If any of my statements contain logical fallacies then it is those Christians who seek to defend Bush and his war that are responsible.

My first question was: "The commandment 'Thou shalt not kill' (Exodus 20:13) never applies to killing in war." My critic first terms this a "complex question." Incredibly, he equates it with the question: "Have you stopped beating your wife?" He maintains that the question "presupposes that the Scripture, 'Thou shalt not kill,' refers to the taking of any life—a fact which has not yet been established."

But not only does the question presuppose nothing of the kind, this is not a fact that anyone with any sense would attempt to establish. When my critic informs me that "for generations, Hebrews have interpreted that passage as non-contradictory to God's required destruction of evil cultures in battle," he is preaching to the choir. Before God gave this commandment in Exodus chapter twenty, he allowed for the killing of animals for clothing (Genesis 3:21), food (Genesis 9:3), and sacrifices (Genesis 8:20), as well as the killing of men via capital punishment (Genesis 9:6). And after God gave this commandment, he instructed the Jews to destroy the Canaanites, Perizzites, Hivites, and Jebusites (Deuteronomy 20:17). Why would anyone ever presuppose that the commandment, "Thou shalt not kill," referred to the absolute "taking of any life."

My critic continues: "In fact, the literal Hebrew translation of the word for 'kill' (ratsach) is 'to murder,' and is otherwise used in the Bible only in phrases which refer to taking lives without just cause." Is that so?

Well, I taught basic biblical Hebrew for a number of years and even wrote a basic Hebrew grammar, so let's see if this is true. The word *ratsach* occurs fifty times in the Hebrew Old Testament. It is often used to refer to murder (e.g., Job 24:14, Psalm 94:6, Jeremiah 7:9); however, not always. As for instance:

> Whoso killeth any person, the murderer shall be put to death by the mouth of witnesses: but one witness shall not testify against any person to cause him to die (Numbers 35:30).

The word "murderer" in this verse is from the word *ratsach*, but so is the phrase "shall be put to death." The ones carrying out capital punishment are obviously not committing murder. So, the word *ratsach* is not "otherwise used in the Bible only in phrases which refer to taking lives without just cause."

My critic next terms my first question a "false dichotomy." Here is the question again: "The commandment 'Thou shalt not kill' (Exodus 20:13) never applies to killing in war." He reasons: "By asking if the commandment 'never' applies, you are stating that there are only two positions regarding this verse: if you answer 'True' then you must claim that there are never unjustified killings in war; if answering 'False' then you are claiming that there are never justified killings in war."

I stand by my first question; it is exactly what Christian defenders of Christians killing for the state in Iraq have told me. These Christians would answer "True" because they actually believe that the state can sanctify killing—even in an unjust war. I have even heard Christians defend the My Lai Massacre. And furthermore, it is simply not true that you believe that "there are never justified killings in war" if you answer "False." It depends on the war and the circumstances.

Since I do not intend to issue a separate reply answering every charge against my "Christian warmonger" quiz raised by my critic, I would like to address the criticism of another question from my "Christian Warmonger" quiz even though it is not related to the commandment, "Thou shalt not kill." My seventh true/false question was: "A preemptive war against Iraq is nothing to be concerned about because the Bible says there is 'a time of war' (Ecclesiastes 3:8)."

My critic comments:

> This is a straw man fallacy, whereby you set up an unfairly simplistic opponent simply to provide easy attack. Few Christians who support the war in Iraq do so for the sole purpose that

> Ecclesiastes says there is a "time of war." To do so would be a logical flaw on their fault—Ecclesiastes never mentions Iraq or 2005 or Hussein or the War on Terror, so one cannot assume that the verse indicates that the "time of war" is now and against Iraq. And, for that reason, I have never heard a Christian claim this as their argument. Some may use it as proof that God is not opposed to war at certain times if the need is great, but no one argues in defense of the war solely based on this verse. Thus, it is an unfairly simplistic opponent which you have set up here to attack.

My critic is suffering from something far worse than committing a logical fallacy: he can't read. I never said that any Christian supported the war in Iraq "for the sole purpose that Ecclesiastes says there is a 'time of war.'" And yes, Christians, such as Jerry Falwell, have used this verse to justify the war in Iraq. The fact that my critic "never heard a Christian claim this as their argument" means absolutely nothing. I have, and that's why I included it in my quiz.

With all the Bush administration lies that have been exposed, the only way a Christian can continue to justify the invasion, destruction, and occupation of Iraq, as well as Christians participating in the bombing, maiming, torturing, and killing of Iraqis at the behest of the state, is by adopting the "killing is saving" Humpty Dumpty approach.

God deliver us from Humpty Dumpty religion!

* * * * *

THE WICKED BIBLE AND THE WICKED WAR

> "Thou shalt not commit adultery." ~ The Holy Bible
> "Thou shalt commit adultery." ~ The Wicked Bible

Does the Bible condone adultery? At one time that depended on which Bible you read.

The introduction of the computer has certainly made it easier for printers to set type. Although occasionally a typesetting error still gets by the proofreaders, it is rare to see a blatant typo in a book produced since the advent of computers. Since printers in the seventeenth century didn't have that luxury, it is a wonder that books published back then don't contain more errors than they do.

Misprints in the Bible have always been of particular concern. An edition in 1631, nicknamed the "Wicked Bible," omitted the word not from Exodus 20:14, changing the prohibition against adultery into the command: "Thou shalt commit adultery." A contemporary historian recorded that

> His Majesties Printers, at or about this time, had committed a scandalous mistake in our *English* Bibles, by leaving out the word *Not* in the Seventh Commandment. His Majesty being made acquainted with it by the Bishop of *London*, Order was given for calling the Printers into the *High-Commission*, where upon Evidence of the Fact, the whole Impression was called in, and the Printers deeply fined, as they justly merited. With some part of this Fine *Laud* [Archbishop William Laud] caused a fair Greek Character to be provided, for publishing such Manuscripts as Time and Industry should make ready for the Publick view.

Okay, the misprint was fixed, and most people are against adultery, so what is my point?

My point is simply this: Bush apologists, Republican loyalists, Christian warmongers, and other assorted defenders of the war in Iraq are doing just what the king's printer did back in 1631, but only worse since they are doing it deliberately. By justifying U.S. troops killing for the state in Iraq they are effectively removing the word not from another commandment: "Thou shalt not kill" (Exodus 20:13).

This is done in a number of ways: the commandment never applies to killing in war, the commandment obviously doesn't mean "the taking of any life," so it cannot be applied to killing in war, the commandment doesn't apply if you are just following orders, the commandment doesn't mean what it says, the commandment is different now because of September 11th, the commandment doesn't apply to Muslim infidels, the commandment is not being violated if you kill for the state, the commandment doesn't apply if you're in the military.

Because the U.S. military does very little to actually defend this country, but instead is used to invade, occupy, bomb, or defend other countries, military recruiters, pastors, and parents who encourage young men and women to join the military are in effect saying "Thou shalt kill." They may call it defending our freedoms, regime change, fighting the war on terror, liberating Iraq, or spreading democracy, but it is still a wicked endeavor in a wicked war.

Friends, family, and supporters of U.S. soldiers: We have a holy Bible not a wicked Bible. What part of "Thou shalt not kill" is so hard to understand?

* * * * *

IS IT OR ISN'T IT?

"Thou shalt not kill" (Exodus 20:13)

There seems to be an inordinate number of Hebrew scholars who support the war in Iraq. It was not until recently, however, that I realized just how many of them are readers of this website. True, I always hear from one or two whenever I write about Christianity and war and happen to reference the above commandment, but the last time I wrote about this subject, the Hebrew scholars came out in droves.

I was told that a more [appropriate, proper, precise, preferred] translation of the sixth commandment, according to the original Hebrew, would be: "Thou shalt not commit murder" or "Thou shalt do no murder." My rendering of the sixth commandment (actually, it is the rendering found in the Holy Bible) is unjustified and simplistic.

I was then informed of the following four facts to show me that some killing is justifiable:

- Men have God's permission to kill animals for food.
- Men have the right of self-defense, including the use of deadly force if necessary.
- There were many crimes in the Old Testament punishable by death.
- God commanded the Jews in the Old Testament to war against their enemies.

Since I discuss the truth of all of these things in several of my previous articles on Christianity and war, and especially the articles "Christian Killers?" and "Humpty Dumpty Religion," next time perhaps these wannabe Hebrew scholars will tell me something I don't know.

What, then, is the point of all this quibbling about the translation of a Hebrew word? Why are some people so adamant about limiting the sixth commandment to murder? Simply this: They are ideologically driven by a desire to legitimatize killing in war, and especially the current war in Iraq. The line of reasoning is as follows: If the commandment in question only prohibits murder, then killing someone in war is okay, and will not subject one to negative consequences by God at the judgment, since it is not murder to kill a man on the battlefield.

Is it or isn't it?

The wannabe Hebrew scholars who conclude that the word "kill" in the sixth commandment should be translated as "murder" are not off the hook. Even if we grant that it is merely murder which is prohibited by the sixth commandment (which I have shown in previous articles and will show again in future articles that such is not the case), they are still responsible for explaining how U.S. soldiers killing for the state in Iraq is anything but murder.

Is it murder to travel thousands of miles away from your home and drop a bomb, scatter cluster bomblets, throw a grenade, launch a missile, or fire a gun at someone in his home that you have never met who was no threat to you until the United States invaded his country? If it is not murder then what are you going to call it? Justifiable homicide? Manslaughter? Self-defense? Perhaps it can be masked as collateral damage, peacekeeping, or spreading democracy?

Any sane man would say that if you travel thousands of miles from your home in Florida to California and blow up a building so as to kill the people inside then you are a murderer. What is it that separates murder from mere killing? What makes the difference? Does killing someone in a foreign country instead of on U.S. soil make the difference? Does the religion of the people you kill make the difference? Does wearing a uniform make the difference? Does getting a paycheck from the government make the difference? Does using a government-issued weapon make the difference? Does following a government order make the difference?

Apologists for U.S. soldiers killing in Iraq would have us to believe that the killings are justified because they are done in self-defense. The terrible truth is that most killing in war is simply murder under the guise of self-defense. Those darn Iraqis were trying to kill me so I just had to kill them. All I wanted them to do was to welcome me as a liberator, write a constitution, and hold an election (and perhaps give me a little cheap oil), and look how they are treating me.

Let's see if I understand the self-defense argument. A U.S. solider participates in the invasion of a country thousands of miles away that has never attacked his country. He has his weapon loaded, his finger on the trigger, and the weapon pointed straight ahead. Someone who objects to his country being invaded then loads his weapon, puts his finger on the trigger, and points it at the invading U.S. soldier. The soldier shoots and kills the foreigner. It's not murder; it's self-defense. The "enemy combatant" should have surrendered peacefully. So likewise, I suppose that if an armed robber stands on someone's driveway and aims his weapon at the owner of the house standing in the garage and puts his finger on the trigger, but then the owner of the house points a shotgun at him, that the robber could shoot and kill the homeowner and say that he was simply defending himself. "But the robber was trespassing," you say. And U.S.

troops are not? What else are you going to call it? Importing democracy? Regime change? Nation building? It is all of these things and more, but at the point of a gun.

U.S. soldiers killing for the state in Iraq cannot claim to be acting in self-defense because the war itself was not for self-defense. It was an act of aggression that was supposed to be a cakewalk, but it backfired with disastrous results for the United States. We have sown the wind, but shall reap the whirlwind (Hosea 8:7). There is no saving face. Withdraw now. If you want to do it in a safe, reasonable, timely, and just manner, follow the seven steps I have previously outlined. Just withdraw the troops, now.

Is it murder or isn't it?

In the end it doesn't matter what you call it. Thousands of Iraqis don't care about the semantic word games played by wannabe Hebrew scholars, Bush apologists, Republican loyalists, Christian warmongers, and other supporters or defenders of this senseless war in Iraq—they're dead. It is of no concern to them if they were killed via murder, accident, manslaughter, self-defense, collateral damage, justifiable homicide, assassination, or execution—they're just as dead as the 2,327 American soldiers who have died "defending our freedoms."

Is it murder or isn't it? I would not want to face God at the judgment with blood on my hands.

* * * * *

THE PRESIDENT'S PRAYER

Just after the war in Iraq began three years ago, I saw this message on the sign of a conservative Baptist church in the town where I live (Pensacola, Fla.). It was gone after a few weeks, never to reappear. I don't know why. Perhaps the church or the pastor had a change of heart. Or perhaps whoever maintains the sign never uses the same message twice. I have noticed recently that some churches still have similar signs. It is unfortunate that many Christians initially supported the president's endeavor; it is tragic that some of them still do.

Evangelical Christian support for the president and his war is waning. Perhaps it is not out of principle, but at least support for *this* war has diminished somewhat (although gullible Christians can be counted on to support the *next* intervention or war if a Republican president undertakes it). But it is a blight on Christianity that many of those who continue to support Bush and his war are evangelical Christians. To their everlasting shame, I suspect that it is evangelical Christians who will support

Bush until the bitter end—no matter how many more U.S. soldiers are killed, no matter long the war continues, no matter how many more billions of dollars are wasted, and no matter what outrages the president commits against the Constitution, the rule of law, and Christianity itself.

There is a king mentioned in the Old Testament named Darius who was so full of himself that he signed a decree drawn up by "all the presidents of the kingdom, the governors, and the princes, the counselors, and the captains" which stated that "whosoever shall ask a petition of any God or man for thirty days, save of thee, O King, he shall be cast into the den of lions" (Daniel 6:7). This was done to trap Daniel the prophet, who prayed three times a day toward Jerusalem to the true God. The king later regretted his decision to sign the decree; but nevertheless, since "no decree nor statute which the king established" (Daniel 6:15) could be changed, Daniel was cast into the den of lions. As it turned out, God delivered Daniel, and the king had the men thrown into the den of lions who had accused him.

I haven't heard of any Christians asking petitions of Bush as a form of prayer as yet, but should they decide to do so, I will make it easy for them.

All Christians are familiar with the Lord's Prayer—the model prayer that Jesus taught his disciples found in the sixth chapter of Matthew's gospel:

> Our Father which art in heaven, Hallowed be thy name.
> Thy kingdom come. Thy will be done in earth, as it is in heaven.
> Give us this day our daily bread.
> And forgive us our debts, as we forgive our debtors.
> And lead us not into temptation, but deliver us from evil: For thine is the kingdom, and the power, and the glory, for ever. Amen.

Just as Christian warmongers who are honest should recite the Warmonger's Psalm and assent to the Warmonger's Beatitudes, so they should pray the President's Prayer:

> Our President which art in Washington, May the U.S. empire be called after thy name.
> Thy military come. Thy war be done in Iran, as it is in Iraq and Afghanistan.
> Give us this day our daily battle.
> And forgive us our pacifism, as we ridicule the critics of your wars.
> And lead us into combat, but deliver us from Muslims: For thine

> is the army, and the navy, and the air force, until your term is up. Amen.

Am I really serious? Perhaps a better question would be: "Are Christians who defend, promote, and support Bush's unjust, immoral, and unscriptural war really serious?" Or perhaps this: "Are Christians who consider Bush to be a great Christian president, God's anointed, or the fourth member of the Trinity really serious?" The way some Christians hagiographically describe the president or blindly support his war—it is only natural to think that the next step would be to offer prayer to him.

Christian, which prayer is it going to be? Is Christ the Lord or is Bush the Lord? If you would never think of praying the President's Prayer then why do you still so highly regard the president after you have had five years to observe his anti-Christian actions? Your standard of Christianity has been lowered to the ground.

And to those Christians who don't care much for the president (and perhaps even loathe him), but are still making excuses for his war of death and destruction in Iraq—because "9/11 changed everything," "we are protecting Israel," "Islam is a false religion," "we must support our troops," "the Lord is a man of war," "the military is defending our freedoms," "we must obey the government," or some other substitute for sound doctrine—I would say this: how many more dead American soldiers and billions of dollars will it take before you finally say enough is enough? Some of you would probably still support the war in Vietnam if it was still going on. I know you don't care about dead Iraqi soldiers and civilians—they are on their way to hell anyway is your attitude. I know you don't care about Iraqis in U.S. custody being abused and tortured—they tried to kill Americans you would say. But what about American soldiers? When more U.S. soldiers are killed in Iraq than people were killed in the September 11th attacks—will you then begin to question the war? What about the dollars of American taxpayers? When the cost of the war reaches a trillion dollars—will you then call for a cost-benefit analysis?

Christian soldiers who would never think of praying the President's Prayer are not off the hook, for they cannot pray Lord's Prayer either. In his immortal work, *The Complaint of Peace*, Erasmus asks us to

> imagine we hear a soldier, among these fighting christians, saying the Lord's prayer. "Our Father," says he; O hardened wretch! can you call him father, when you are just going to cut your brother's throat? "Hallowed be thy name:" how can the name of God be more impiously unhallowed, than by mutual bloody murder among

> you, his sons? "Thy kingdom come": do you pray for the coming of his kingdom, while you are endeavouring to establish an earthly despotism, by spilling the blood of God's sons and subjects? "Thy will be done on earth as it is in heaven": his will in heaven, is for peace, but you are now meditating war. Dare you to say to your Father in heaven "Give us this day our daily bread"; when you are going, the next minute perhaps, to burn up your brother's corn-fields; and had rather lose the benefit of them yourself, than suffer him to enjoy them unmolested? With what face can you say, "Forgive us our trespasses as we forgive them that trespass against us," when, so far from forgiving your own brother, you are going, with all the haste you can, to murder him in cold blood, for an alleged trespass that, after all, is but imaginary. Do you presume to deprecate the danger of temptation, who, not without great danger to yourself, are doing all you can to force your brother into danger? Do you deserve to be delivered from evil, that is, from the evil being, to whose impulse you submit yourself, and by whose spirit you are now guided, in contriving the greatest possible evil to your brother?

Erasmus, who did not know George WMD Bush, nevertheless remarked in his *The Education of a Christian Prince* that "it happens sometimes that princes enter into mutual agreements and carry on a war on trumped-up grounds so as to reduce still more the power of the people and secure their own positions through disaster to their subjects." His admonition to the president to consider all the catastrophes that would come to the world if he launches a war, which obviously went unheeded, was to think over in his own mind:

> Shall I, one person, be the cause of so many calamities? Shall I alone be charged with such an outpouring of human blood; with causing so many widows; with filling so many homes with lamentation and mourning; with robbing so many old men of their sons; with impoverishing so many who do not deserve such a fate; and with such utter destruction of morals, laws, and practical religion? Must I account for all these things before Christ?

Did the president even remotely consider the potential damage to not only the United States, but civilization itself, that his war might cause? I would not want to be in Bush's shoes at the judgment. Or in the shoes of a Christian who in any way defended, supported, promoted, apologized for, or made excuses for the president and his war. I have enough of my own sins to be concerned about without adding to them the blood of thousands of American soldiers and tens of thousands of Iraqi civilians. Don't we all?

* * * * *

BEAM CHRISTIANS

> "And why beholdest thou the mote that is in thy brother's eye, but considerest not the beam that is in thine own eye?
> Or how wilt thou say to thy brother, Let me pull out the mote out of thine eye; and, behold, a beam is in thine own eye?
> Thou hypocrite, first cast out the beam out of thy own eye; and then shalt thou see clearly to cast out the mote out of thy brother's eye" (Matthew 7:3–5).

Opponents of Bush and his war in Iraq are a diverse lot. Christian apologists for the state, its president, its military, and its wars have tried to capitalize on this diversity by using the old "guilt by association" argument. Cindy Sheehan appeared with Jesse Jackson at an anti-war protest; most of the congressmen who speak out against the war are Democrats; the Hollywood actors who oppose the war are political leftists; therefore, if you oppose Bush and his war then you are a liberal, a peacenik, or an anti-war weenie.

They are beam Christians.

The fact that Jesse Jackson, Democratic congressmen, and Hollywood actors are right for once in their life (and in some cases perhaps the only time in their life) is immaterial. Many of us have opposed this unnecessary, senseless, and immoral war from the beginning because we saw it not only as a grave injustice and a monstrous evil, but as benefiting only the state in its quest for more power and its defense contractors in their lust for more of the taxpayers' money. If all the liberal activists in the country suddenly announced that they too were opposed to the war then what difference would it make? Those of us who have opposed this war from the beginning (and will oppose the next one with Iran) do so because we are standing for what is right—life, liberty, peace, nonintervention, limited government, and allowing the taxpayers to better spend the $7.4 million per hour that the war is costing—and are not concerned with whoever else happens to be standing with us. We are standing with or without their support. We don't wet our finger and hold it up to check how the political winds are blowing before we take a position.

Christian warmongers are beam Christians. They would rather be associated with Bush and the war than with people whom they and others have deemed undesirable. In actuality, however, they are choosing to be associated with a war criminal and murder than with the truth just because some people who are usually wrong happen to be right on this particular issue.

Beam Christians are generally savvy e-mail users. Some have even convinced themselves (and others gullible enough to believe them) that they are champion e-mail debaters when in reality they are guilty of sowing "discord among brethren" (Proverbs 6:19). Here are a couple of e-mails that, even though they may not have been created by Christians, have nevertheless made the rounds in Christian circles.

Exhibit A is a multiple-choice history test that has not only circulated via e-mail, but also appears in an interactive version online. These are the questions:

> In 1968 Bobby Kennedy was shot and killed by:
> In 1972 at the Munich Olympics, athletes were kidnapped and massacred by:
> In 1979, the US embassy in Iran was taken over by:
> During the 1980's a number of Americans were kidnapped in Lebanon by:
> In 1983, the US Marine barracks in Beirut was blown up by:
> In 1985 the cruise ship Achille Lauro was hijacked and a 70 year old American passenger was murdered and thrown overboard in his wheelchair by:
> In 1985 TWA flight 847 was hijacked at Athens, and a US Navy diver trying to rescue passengers was murdered by:
> In 1988, Pan Am Flight 103 was bombed by:
> In 1993 the World Trade Center was bombed the first time by:
> In 1998, the US embassies in Kenya and Tanzania were bombed by:
> On 9/11/01, four airliners were hijacked; two were used as missiles to take out the World Trade Centers and of the remaining two, one crashed into the US Pentagon and the other was diverted and crashed by the passengers. Thousands of people were killed by:
> In 2002 the United States fought a war in Afghanistan against:
> In 2002 reporter Daniel Pearl was kidnapped and murdered by:

The answer to every question is "d. Muslim male extremist between the ages of 17 and 40."

Now, I am not disputing the accuracy of these historical events, and, as a Bible-believing Christian, I am certainly not excusing the murderous actions of "Muslim male extremists," or defending in any way the Muslim religion—something that President Bush has done. What I do have a problem with is Christians using this to justify Bush and his war. These questions are usually followed by the statement that "Our country and our troops need our support." The idea being that the bombing, maiming, and killing that our troops are doing in Iraq is okay since, after all, they are just "Muslim male extremists" who are being bombed, maimed, and killed. This is a non sequitur of the worst sort. It is pure sophistry. We are supposed to believe that "Muslim male extremists" did all these things because they were "Muslim male extremists." The United States was just minding its own business in 155 regions of the world until "Muslim male extremists" attacked us for no other reason than that they were "Muslim male extremists."

Here is a little history test of my own. Which country overthrew the democratically elected leader of Iran in 1953 and installed a puppet dictator? Why, the United States did. No wonder Iranians took over the U.S. embassy in 1979 after they ousted the shah that we forced them to live under for twenty-five years!

Exhibit B is the most ridiculous piece of pro-war propaganda I have ever seen. It too has unfortunately circulated among Christians via e-mail. It consists of a series of "Did you know" questions that supposedly demonstrate how good things are going for the Iraqi people since we invaded their country and killed tens of thousands of them. Here is a sample from the 2005 version: "Did you know there are more than 1100 building projects going on in Iraq? They include 364 schools, 67 public clinics, 15 hospitals, 83 railroad stations, 22 oil facilities, 93 water facilities and 69 electrical facilities." The rest of the questions can be seen here, with comments by someone who felt compelled to respond. There is also a 2003 version here, with a response by an Iraqi here. All of the data about how wonderful things are in Iraq is supposedly verifiable on the website of that fair and impartial organization, the U.S. Department of Defense (strange, no link is ever provided). The reason we didn't know about these wonderful things was because of the "Bush-hating media."

Of course there are building projects going on in Iraq—we destroyed the place with bombs for three years and with sanctions for thirteen years before that. How Christians can be suckered by the likes of such absurd propaganda as this is a greater mystery than how the Pyramids were built. They must want to believe it.

They are beam Christians.

These beams can take many forms. For some the beam is President Bush. Because they are so blinded to Bush's pseudo-Christianity, some

Christians actually believe that Bush is "God ordained" or "God's anointed" or "one of us." For others the beam is conservatism. Christians who are theologically conservative have made a terrible mistake in identifying with the conservative movement, with is propensity for nationalism and power at the expense of liberty. For some the beam is the Republican Party. They know the Democratic Party is too far to the left to even consider. But in spite of the bones it throws to the free market, the Republican Party is no better. It is the party of militarism, big government, plunder, compromises, and sellouts. For others the beam is the military. They actually think that the Department of Defense is defending our freedoms by meddling in the affairs of other countries all over the globe. The fact that the United States spends more on its military than Russia, China, Japan, Britain, Saudi Arabia, France, Germany, Brazil, India, Italy, South Korea, Iran, Israel, Taiwan, Canada, Spain, Australia, the Netherlands, Turkey, and Singapore put together doesn't seem to raise a red flag with these people. In some cases it is the U.S. government that is the beam which blinds these Christians. They can be spotted by the sound of their mantra: "obey the powers that be." They want so much to believe that the U.S. government is a force for good in the world instead of the force for evil that it currently is because of its military adventures and its interventionist foreign policy.

Beam Christians are shallow thinkers. They foolishly reason that because some outspoken liberals are opposed to this war then they should support it. These Christians have such a beam in their eye that it has gone into their brain and affected their thinking. It doesn't seem to have ever occurred to these people that it is the retired generals and groups like Veterans for Peace and Iraq Veterans against the War that oppose the war that anti-war Christians are in agreement with, not some Hollywood leftist who only opposes the war because a Republican president started it.

Some Christians are blinded by indifference. Don't ask them their view about Bush and his war—"What difference does it make?" is their only reply. Perhaps the greatest beam that blinds some Christians is pride. They will not publicly admit that they were deceived into supporting the war and were wrong about Bush, wrong about the conservative movement, wrong about the Republican Party, wrong about the military, and wrong about the government's foreign policy.

It is a terrible disgrace that, instead of the next military adventure of the U.S. government being denounced from every pulpit and pew of every church in the country, there are some beam preachers in the pulpit and some beam Christians in the pew who can be counted on to support it. Last, and certainly least, will be the bloodthirsty Christian e-mail debaters who drool piety while they recite their mantras and make apologies for the state and its wars. Although they would all claim to be Bible-believing Christians, they manifest their biblical ignorance when they imply that disrespect for the government is a grave sin. On this they are against the Founding Fathers, Christian or otherwise, and all of their Christian forefathers.

When Hermann Goering was interviewed by Gustave Gilbert in his cell at the Nuremberg jail in 1946 (published in *Nuremberg Diary*), he made a profound statement about war that is still relevant sixty years later. Here is the relevant part of the interview:

> Gilbert: We got around to the subject of war again and I said that, contrary to his attitude, I did not think that the common people are very thankful for leaders who bring them war and destruction.
>
> Goering: Why, of course, the people don't want war. Why would some poor slob on a farm want to risk his life in a war when the best that he can get out of it is to come back to his farm in one piece. Naturally, the common people don't want war; neither in Russia nor in England nor in America, nor for that matter in Germany. That is understood. But, after all, it is the leaders of the country who determine the policy and it is always a simple matter to drag the people along, whether it is a democracy or a fascist dictatorship or a Parliament or a Communist dictatorship.
>
> Gilbert: There is one difference. In a democracy the people have some say in the matter through their elected representatives, and in the United States only Congress can declare wars.
>
> Goering: Oh, that is all well and good, but, voice or no voice, the people can always be brought to the bidding of the leaders. That is easy. All you have to do is tell them they are being attacked and denounce the pacifists for lack of patriotism and exposing the country to danger. It works the same way in any country.

Unfortunately, and to their shame, it works the same way with Christians as well. From the discord-sowing, self-proclaimed champion e-mail debater to the indifferent, washed-up evangelist, to the blind government-respecting employee of a Christian ministry—it works the same way every time. They are all beam Christians.

* * * * *

CHRISTIANITY AND THE WAR

This talk was delivered, at the request of Congressman Ron Paul, to Republican and Democratic staff aides of the US House of Representatives in Washington, DC, on May 25, 2006.

Never in my life did I ever think that I would find myself agreeing with Senator Ted Kennedy on anything. But what he recently said about the war in Iraq is right on:

> In his march to war, President Bush exaggerated the threat to the American people. It was not subtle. It was not nuanced. It was pure, unadulterated fear-mongering, based on a devious strategy to convince the American people that Saddam's ability to provide nuclear weapons to Al Qaeda justified immediate war.

I find myself agreeing with more and more Democrats now-a-days, at least in their criticisms of the Bush administration's Iraq policy. Democratic Representative John Murtha, a decorated Vietnam War veteran, has called for the pullout of U.S. troops from Iraq, labeling the president's Iraq policy "a flawed policy wrapped in illusion." Another Democrat, Representative Dennis Kucinich, has strongly criticized the president for being responsible for the death and destruction that has taken place in Iraq.

Are these Democratic criticisms of the president just the result of the usual partisan politics that we see everyday on the House and Senate floor? Perhaps. I suspect that the Republicans would be leveling the same criticisms of the war as the Democrats if it was a Democratic president that had launched this war.

But politics or no politics—the war in Iraq is an unconstitutional, unnecessary, immoral, senseless, unjust, and unscriptural undertaking. It is unconstitutional because only Congress has the authority to declare war. It is unnecessary because Iraq was no threat to the United States. It is immoral because it was based on lies. It is unjust because it is not defensive. It is senseless because over 2,400 U.S. soldiers have died in vain. But this war is also unscriptural, and, because I am a Christian—a conservative evangelical Christian—I intend this to be the focus of my remarks.

The percentage of Americans who identify their religion as Christianity is higher than that needed in Congress to pass a constitutional amendment or override a presidential veto. The percentage of members of Congress who identify themselves as Christian is even higher. But as we have now passed the third anniversary of the invasion of Iraq, support for the war among Christian Americans continues, funding for the war by a Christian Congress continues, and justification for the war by a Christian president continues. And we wonder why Muslims hate us?

The subject I want to address is Christianity and the war. What does Christianity have to say about this war? What should the attitude of Christians be toward this war?

If there is any religion that should be opposed to war it is Christianity. And if there is any group of people in America that should be opposed to war it is Christians. All wars are, in the words of George Washington, a "plague of mankind," but this war in particular is a great evil. Waging the war is against Christian "just war" principles. Conducting the war is contrary to the whole spirit of the New Testament. Fighting the war is in opposition to the practice of the early church. Participants in the war violate the express teaching of the sixth commandment: "Thou shalt not kill." Supporters of the war violate the first commandment: "Thou shalt have no other gods before me."

Waging this war is against every Christian "just war" principle that has ever been formulated. A just war must have a just cause, be in proportion to the gravity of the situation, have obtainable objectives, be preceded by a public declaration, be declared only by legitimate authority, and only be undertaken as a last resort. If there was ever a war that violated every one of these principles it is this war.

The only just cause for war is a defensive one, but this war is clearly both preemptive and offensive. Governments never find this to be a problem, however, and routinely offer up a myriad of reasons why their particular cause is just. Propaganda and demonization of the enemy play a large part in garnering public support for the war. But contrary to government propaganda, it really is just as simple as G. K. Chesterton once said: "The only defensible war is a war of defense."

The "shock and awe" campaign waged by American forces is certainly out of proportion to the gravity of the situation considering that Iraq—a country with no navy or air force and an economy in ruins after a decade of sanctions—was never a threat to the United States. Iraq was merely the new enemy the U.S. military/industrial complex selected after the end of the Cold War.

What were our objectives in this war? Finding weapons of mass destruction? Removing Saddam Hussein? Enforcing UN resolutions? If one stated objective was found to be a lie another could quickly be offered in its place. The number and scope of these objectives shows that there were no legitimate objectives. So why did we invade and occupy Iraq? A student at the University of Illinois documented 27 reasons put forth by the Bush administration or war hawks in Congress before the war began. There have been even more since then. A report issued by the U.S. House of Representatives Committee on Government Reform found that Bush, Cheney, Rumsfeld, Powell, and Rice made a total of 237 misleading statements in a two-year period about the threat posed by Iraq. And unlike some members of Congress who do not read the bills they vote on, I have read the report.

A public declaration is for the purpose of giving fair warning and an opportunity for conflict resolution—not a rubber stamp on something that was already in the works.

Was the Iraq war declared by legitimate authority? Since when does Congress have the authority to delegate its congressional war-making authority to the president? As the "father of the Constitution," James Madison, has said: "The Constitution expressly and exclusively vests in the Legislature the power of declaring a state of war [and] the power of raising armies. A delegation of such powers [to the president] would have struck, not only at the fabric of our Constitution, but at the foundation of all well organized and well checked governments." And is our authority to go to war the Constitution or the United Nations? The "Joint Resolution to Authorize the Use of United States Armed Forces Against Iraq" that was issued in October of 2002 mentions the UN twenty-one times but the U.S. Constitution only twice.

Was the war in Iraq undertaken as a last resort? Hardly. As I just said, it was in the works. All that was needed was the "Pearl Harbor" of September 11th to give it some semblance of credibility.

But not only is this war against Christian "just war" principles, conducting this war is contrary to the whole spirit of the New Testament. Although the Bible likens Christians to soldiers, and the Christian life to a battle, the Christian's weapons are not carnal and his battle is a spiritual one. The Christian is admonished to "put on the whole armor of God." His only weapon is "the sword of the spirit, which is the word of God." Avoiding conflict and strife and seeking to do good are recurrent themes in the New Testament; for example: "See that none render evil for evil unto any man; but ever follow that which is good." If there was anything at all advocated by the early Christians it was peace, as we again read in the New Testament: "Live peaceably with all men."

These themes used to be on the lips of Christian ministers. Back before the Civil War, a Baptist minister writing in the *Christian Review* demonstrated that Christian war fever was contrary to the New Testament:

> Christianity requires us to seek to amend the condition of man. But war cannot do this. The world is no better for all the wars of five thousand years. Christianity, if it prevailed, would make the earth a paradise. War, where it prevails, makes it a slaughter-house, a den of thieves, a brothel, a hell. Christianity cancels the laws of retaliation. War is based upon that very principle. Christianity is the remedy for all human woes. War produces every woe known to man.

Another Baptist minister, writing in the same publication, lamented about the terrible truth of Christian participation in war:

> War has ever been the scourge of the human race. The history of the past is little else than a chronicle of deadly feuds, irreconcilable hate, and exterminating warfare. The extension of empire, the love of glory, and thirst for fame, have been more fatal to men than famine or pestilence, or the fiercest elements of nature. The trappings and tinsel of war, martial prowess, and military heroism, have, in all ages, been venerated and lauded to the skies. And what is more sad and painful, many of the wars whose desolating surges have deluged the earth, have been carried on in the name and under the sanction of those who profess the name of Christ.

One of the most celebrated preachers of all time, the Englishman Charles Spurgeon, known as "the prince of preachers," remarked about Christianity and War:

> The Church of Christ is continually represented under the figure of an army; yet its Captain is the Prince of Peace; its object is the establishment of peace, and its soldiers are men of a peaceful disposition. The spirit of war is at the extremely opposite point to the spirit of the gospel.

If there is any war in history that is contrary to the whole spirit of the New Testament it is this one. All adherents of Christianity, of any creed or denomination, should be opposed to this war. So why aren't they? Much of the blame must be laid at the feet of the pastors, preachers, and priests who have failed to discern the truth and educate their congregations. We need ministers who are as concerned about killing on the battlefield as they are about killing in the womb.

But not only is this war against Christian "just war" principles and contrary to the whole spirit of the New Testament, fighting this war is in opposition to the practice of the early church. Not only did the early

Christians, following the example of the Lord himself, refuse to advance their ideals by political or coercive means, they condemned war in the abstract and did not participate in the state's wars. Lactantius describes Christians as "those who are ignorant of wars, who preserve concord with all, who are friends even to their enemies, who love all men as brothers, who know how to curb anger and soften with quiet moderation every madness of the mind." According to John Cadoux, the author of the definitive investigation of the early Christian attitude toward war and military service:

The early Christians took Jesus at his word, and understood his inculcations of gentleness and non-resistance in their literal sense. They closely identified their religion with peace; they strongly condemned war for the bloodshed which it involved; they appropriated to themselves the Old Testament prophecy which foretold the transformation of the weapons of war into the implements of agriculture; they declared that it was their policy to return good for evil and to conquer evil with good.

The early Christian aversion to war was revived and amplified in the Reformation age by the celebrated Dutch humanist, Erasmus. Although he lived many centuries ago, Erasmus's age was not unlike our own. Wars and international conflict were the order of the day. Contention was brewing between the West and the Muslim world. According to Erasmus, the only just and necessary war was a "purely defensive" one to "repel the violence of invaders." And because he believed that war is by "nature such a plague to man that even if it is undertaken by a just prince in a totally just cause, the wickedness of captains and soldiers results in almost more evil than good," Erasmus insisted that "all other expedients must be tried before war is begun; no matter how serious nor how just the cause." He chastised Christians for reproaches vomited out against Christ by nations of unbelievers "when they see his professed followers" warring "with more destructive instruments of mutual murder than pagans could ever find in their hearts to use." Erasmus also recognized that rulers incite war "to use it as a means to exercise their tyranny over their subjects more easily." As our Founding Father James Madison has said: "If tyranny and oppression come to this land, it will be in the guise of fighting a foreign enemy." The authority of the legislature and the force of law that thwart government power in peacetime quickly diminish during times of war. "Once war is declared," says Erasmus, "the whole business of the state is subject to the will of a few." He even noted how the issues of national security and public safety were used by the government to elicit support for war. Although Erasmus had never heard of George W. Bush, he nevertheless remarked in his *The Education of a Christian Prince* that "it happens sometimes that princes enter into mutual agreements and carry on a war on trumped-up grounds so as to reduce still more the power of the people and secure their own positions through disaster to their subjects." Here again is Madison: "Of all the enemies to public liberty, war is perhaps the most to be dreaded because it comprises and develops the germ of every other. War is the parent of armies; from these proceed debts and taxes; and armies, and debts, and taxes are the known instruments for bringing the many under the domination of the few." Would the Founding Fathers even recognize the bloated monstrosity we call the federal government—a government that spies on its citizens, confiscates 30 to 40 percent of their income, and regulates every part of their life?

Participants in this war violate the express teaching of the sixth commandment: "Thou shalt not kill." I have been told that this commandment does not apply to killing in war. Not to killing in a just war or a defensive war, but to killing in war. The result of this warped reasoning is the teaching that even if the war in Iraq is unconstitutional, senseless, immoral, and unnecessary, Christians can still in good conscience join the military and go to Iraq to bomb, maim, interrogate, and kill for the state simply because the state says so. U.S. soldiers killing for the state in Iraq cannot claim to be acting in self-defense because the war itself was not for self-defense. It was an act of naked aggression that was supposed to be a cakewalk, but it backfired with disastrous results for the United States. Is killing someone in a foreign country instead of on U.S. soil what distinguishes killing from self-defense and murder? Or is it the wearing of a uniform?

There has persisted throughout history, quite unfortunately, the idea among some Christians that mass killing in war is acceptable, but killing of one's neighbor violates the sixth commandment. I have termed this the Humpty Dumpty approach. We can see this attitude in the ancient Romans. The aforementioned Lactantius said of the Romans of his day:

> The more men they have afflicted, despoiled, and slain, the more noble and renowned do they think themselves; and, captured by the appearance of empty glory, they give the name of excellence to their crimes. Now I would rather that they should make gods for themselves from the slaughter of wild beasts than that they should approve of an immortality so bloody. If any one has slain a single man, he is regarded as contaminated and wicked, nor do they think it right that he should be admitted to this earthly dwelling of the gods. But he who has slaughtered endless thousands of men, deluged the fields with blood, and infected rivers with it, is admitted not only to a temple, but even to heaven.

Writing before Lactantius, Cyprian speaks of the idea held by some that "homicide is a crime when individuals commit it, but it is called a virtue, when it is carried on publicly." Erasmus addressed his fellow Christians about this same thing, and Charles Spurgeon has likewise said:

> If there be anything which this book denounces and counts the hugest of all crimes, it is the crime of war. Put up thy sword into thy sheath, for hath not he said, "Thou shalt not kill," and he meant not that it was a sin to kill one but a glory to kill a million, but he meant that bloodshed on the smallest or largest scale was sinful.

Supporters of this war also violate the first commandment: "Thou shalt have no other gods before me." Many American Christians have a warped "God and Country" complex which inevitably elevates the state to the level of God Almighty. If the state dictates that an intervention, invasion, or war is necessary then by God we must support the president and the troops no matter what. But the government of the United States and Christianity is a most unholy alliance. It has been soundly argued by the Foundation for Economic Education president, Richard Ebeling that "there has been no greater threat to life, liberty, and property throughout the ages than government. Even the most violent and brutal private individuals have been able to inflict only a mere fraction of the harm and destruction that have been caused by the use of power by political authorities."

When it comes to defending, believing in the legitimacy of, and carrying out the evil dictates of the state, Christians are under a higher authority. There are numerous examples of this in the Bible that the Christian can look to, like the Hebrew midwives, who were commanded by the state to kill any newborn sons, but because they "feared God," they disregarded the command of the king.

Christian warmongers are idolaters, as the famed Austrian economist Ludwig von Mises wrote in *Omnipotent Government*:

> Modern war is not a war of royal armies. It is a war of the peoples, a total war. It is a war of states which do not leave to their subjects any private sphere; they consider the whole population a part of the armed forces. Whoever does not fight must work for the support and equipment of the army. Army and people are one and the same. The citizens passionately participate in the war. For it is their state, their God, who fights.

The attitude of the Christian toward the state should be no different now than it was in the days of the apostles. Peter and John were brought before the authorities and asked: "Did not we straitly command you that ye should not teach in this name? And, behold, ye have filled Jerusalem with your doctrine, and intend to bring this man's blood upon us." It was then that the apostles uttered that immortal line: "We ought to obey God rather than men."

There is much more that could be said in opposition to this war besides the fact that it is contrary to every precept of Christianity. It was based on lies. It has created more terrorists than existed before the war. It has increased religious tension around the globe. It has done irreparable harm to the Middle East peace process. It has increased the hatred of America and Americans the world over. It has cost the taxpayers of this country over $200 billion, plus billions more for the forgotten war in Afghanistan. It has hurt the reputation of evangelical Christianity among non-Christians because of Christian support for the war. It is against the noninterventionist foreign policy of the Founding Fathers. It has wasted the lives of over 2,400 American soldiers. It has horribly wounded thousands more American soldiers. It has caused American families untold grief over their dead loved ones.

There can be no doubt whatsoever that this war is abhorrent to Christianity. The attitude of each individual Christian toward this war should be likewise. Unfortunately, however, this is not the case. Why? Why do some Christians continue to defend, tolerate, or make excuses for this unjust, immoral, and unscriptural war?

Here are five reasons why I think some Christians continue to support this war.

First, the September 11th terrorist attacks. Some Americans, including Christians I have talked to, continue to believe that Iraq was behind the September 11th attacks—even though the president himself now says otherwise.

Second, support for the nation of Israel. Evangelical Christians, as am I, are typically supporters of Israel, as am I. But what they fail to realize is that the nation of Israel is not the government of Israel—a corrupt government propped up by billions of dollars in U.S. foreign aid. And Iraq was no threat to Israel anyway.

Third, the religion of Islam. Some Christians are indifferent toward the war because it is just Muslims who are being killed. But what about the blood of over 2,400 dead American soldiers? Does killing Muslim infidels make their sacrifice worth it?

Fourth, the military. There is an unholy alliance between evangelical Christians and the military. Yet, the military *in its present form* does little to actually defend the country. Why isn't the U.S. military guarding *our* borders and patrolling *our* coasts instead of guarding the borders and patrolling the coasts of other countries? The president recently called for the stationing of some National Guard troops along our border with Mexico. It is too bad these troops sent to guard the Mexican border weren't taken out of Iraq.

And fifth, the conservative movement and the Republican Party. Many Christians, who by nature are conservative people, are in bed with the conservative wing of the Republican Party. But this is clearly a case of spiritual adultery. I am sorry to say that Conservatives have of late been known for their readiness to engage in military adventure throughout the world and the fact that they never met a federal program they didn't like as long as it furthered their agenda. Conservatism is fast becoming a movement that puts love of the state and its leader above all else, including liberty. Lew Rockwell, president of the Ludwig von Mises Institute in Auburn, Alabama, has brilliantly summarized what is wrong with modern conservatism:

> The problem with American conservatism is that it hates the left more than the state, loves the past more than liberty, feels a greater attachment to nationalism than to the idea of self-determination, believes brute force is the answer to all social problems, and thinks it is better to impose truth rather than risk losing one soul to heresy. It has never understood the idea of freedom as a self-ordering principle of society. It has never seen the state as the enemy of what conservatives purport to favor. It has always looked to presidential power as the saving grace of what is right and true about America.

The Republican Party has historically been the party of militarism, big government, plunder, compromises, and sellouts. Not in his wildest dreams could Lyndon Johnson have ever imagined his Democratic-controlled Congress increasing total spending or the rate of increase in spending as much as George Bush and his Republican-controlled Congress have done. And he too was fighting a war.

I do believe that the support of Christian evangelicals for the president and his war is waning. Perhaps it is not out of principle, but at least support for this war has diminished somewhat (although gullible Christians can be counted on to support the *next* intervention or war if a Republican president undertakes it). But it is a blight on Christianity that many of those who continue to support Bush and his war are evangelical

Christians. To their everlasting shame, I suspect that it is evangelical Christians who will support Bush until the bitter end—no matter how many more U.S. soldiers are killed, no matter long the war continues, no matter how many more billions of dollars are wasted, and no matter what outrages the president commits against the Constitution, the rule of law, and Christianity itself.

What, then, should be done? We should immediately withdraw our forces from Iraq, not because the war is not going as planned, not because we have suffered too many casualties, not because we have removed Saddam Hussein, not because we have accomplished our mission, not because there are too many insurgents, and not because Iraq had an election. We should withdraw our troops because the war was a monstrous wrong from the very beginning. How many more dead American soldiers and billions of dollars will it take before we finally say enough is enough? How many more dead American soldiers and billions of dollars will it take before the members of Congress say enough is enough? King Solomon, the wisest man who ever lived, said that there was "a time of war." This, my fellow Americans, is not the time.

* * * * *

THE CHRISTIAN AXIS OF EVIL

> "North Korea is a regime arming with missiles and weapons of mass destruction, while starving its citizens. Iran aggressively pursues these weapons and exports terror, while an unelected few repress the Iranian people's hope for freedom. Iraq continues to flaunt its hostility toward America and to support terror. . . . States like these, and their terrorist allies, constitute an axis of evil, arming to threaten the peace of the world." ~ President George W. Bush, State of the Union Address, January 29, 2002.

> "Beyond the axis of evil, there are other rogue states intent on acquiring weapons of mass destruction—particularly biological weapons. . . . In addition to Libya and Syria, there is a threat coming from another BWC signatory, and one that lies just 90 miles from the U.S. mainland—namely, Cuba." ~ U.S. Ambassador to the UN John R. Bolton, Remarks to the Heritage Foundation, May 6, 2002.

Bush and Bolton chose their words carefully. The term "axis of evil" was deliberately designed to invoke images of the Axis Powers in

World War II, which, of course, included Nazi Germany. Saddam Hussein was then said to be another Hitler, and the U.S. invaded Iraq. Now it is the president of Iran who is being compared to Hitler, by the Bush administration and others.

And who will be among the first to support the president's next military adventure? Why, the same ones that will support his current endeavor until the bitter end: Christians who try to serve two masters—Christ and the state (as long as it is controlled by "conservatives" or the Republican Party).

It is a disgrace—no, it is a moral outrage—that many Christians continue to support Bush and his war. Christian "leaders" are leading their followers astray. The blind are leading the blind. It is Christian "leaders" who moonlight as apologists for Bush and his war that make up the true axis of evil. To match the six members of Bush and Bolton's axis of evil, here are six members of the Christian axis of evil.

The first member of the Christian axis of evil is the Baptist pastor Jerry "God is pro-war" Falwell. It was bad enough when Falwell made a ridiculous, feeble attempt to justify, with Scripture, Bush's invasion of Iraq in a horrendous 2004 *WorldNetDaily* article titled "God is Pro-war." (I have critiqued this article here). On FOX News' Hannity & Colmes show on February 11, 2005, Rev. Falwell appeared opposite Rev. Wallis of *Sojourners* and tried to deny that many evangelical Christians were opposed to the Iraq war. Falwell's claim that the anti-war Christian movement could fit into a phone booth shows just how out of touch with reality he is. Falwell's Liberty University (supposedly a Baptist institution) then gave Hannity (a Roman Catholic) an honorary doctorate, and had him deliver the university's commencement address on May 14, 2005. Senator John McCain, said by Liberty to be "a practicing Christian," delivered the commencement address this year.

The second member of the Christian axis of evil is Pat "take out Chavez" Robertson. He is another Christian apologist for the Republican Party who has supported this war from the beginning. Robertson, who actually believes the war is being fought on Christian principles, considers criticism of the war to be treason. It should be noted that Robertson's "faith-based initiative," Operation Blessing, receives millions of dollars in federal grants every year.

The third member of the Christian axis of evil is the psychologist and author James "just war" Dobson of Focus on the Family. Back on March 31, 2003, soon after the invasion of Iraq, Dobson expressed his support for the war on his national daily radio broadcast. America entered Iraq "as a liberator—not as a conqueror." After equating Saddam Hussein with Stalin and Hitler, Dobson labeled Hussein another brutal tyrant who "must be stopped" because the United States has a "moral obligation" to stop evil and tyranny. Invoking the Neville Chamberlain argument, Dobson insisted that "appeasement of tyrants is never successful!" Just before this broadcast, in the March 27, 2003, issue of *Boundless* (a webzine published by Focus on the Family), a two-part column by Jay Budziszewski (Professor Theophilus) was interrupted in the "Office Hours" section to reprint one of his "classic" columns from the April 29, 1999, issue titled "Can War Be Justified?" His answer was, of course, yes, even if the war is not for self-defense.

That was three years ago. Perhaps Dobson has changed his mind?

Since phone calls and e-mails to his organization yield no response to this important question, we will have to rely on Focus on the Family publications, including its website. In the March 2006 issue of *Citizen* magazine, there is a pro-war article titled "Worth the Sacrifice." The author, Karl Zinsmeister, believes the war is justified because of how we are helping the children of Iraq. He believes that the United States has been "fighting a war of principle, for self-determination, to make a grim part of the world more humane and thereby less threatening, so that our children and Iraq's can grow up to enjoy God's dignity and freedom." In the same issue of *Citizen*, there is an interview conducted by associate editor Stephen Adam with Daniel Ayalon, the Israeli ambassador to the United States. The interview is headlined "Israel, Iran and the Global War on Terror." In reply to the question: "Do you agree with President Bush's approach to the global war on terror?" the Israeli ambassador said:

> Absolutely. Absolutely. We have to realize it's a war—and it's a total war—and once you realize it, that you're in a war, you cannot fight with one hand tied behind your back. The terrorists do not do that. They would use any vulnerability and everything in their power to destroy us. So, we have to be prepared for that. We have to take the war into their camp. If you play defensive, you know, things like 9/11 can happen again. You have to go after them to frustrate their organization, to go after their leaders, after everybody who gives them shelter as well.

A broadcast CD is available for sale from the Focus Resource Center titled "Supporting Operation Iraqi Freedom." It is described on the website with these words: "Dr. and Mrs. Dobson, along with co-host John Fuller, express their support for America's military, discuss the atrocities taking place under Iraq's evil regime, and emphasize the need for our nation to unite in prayer." There is no date given for when the broadcast was aired, but that is irrelevant since it is still for sale on the website. On April 19th and 20th of this year, Dobson interviewed on his radio program Admiral Timothy Keating, the current Commander of NORAD and NORTHCOM at Peterson Air Force Base in Colorado. Obviously, this was not to criticize the war.

The fourth member of the Christian axis of evil is the prophecy guru Hal "I'm on my fourth wife" Lindsey, who recently claimed in a column for *WorldNetDaily*, contrary to the Bush administration, that "it is now evident to all but the blindest partisans that the intelligence was correct and that Saddam not only had weapons of mass destruction, but that he worked directly with al-Qaida." Incredibly, after saying in his article that "Lenin is reputed to have referred to blind defenders and apologists for the Soviet Union in the Western democracies as 'useful idiots,'" Lindsey, one of the blindest apologists for this war that Bush could ever hope for, labels opponents of Bush's war as the "useful idiots."

The fifth member of the Christian axis of evil is Cal "I have a long list of favorite patriotic movies" Thomas. Back before the Iraq war formally started in March of 2003, Thomas, invoking Scripture, wrote in a column dated February 19, 2003, that "if ever there was a 'time for war' (Ecclesiastes 3:8), surely this is it." This was just after he wrote in a column dated February 6, 2003, about Colin Powell speaking to the U.N. Security Council and making "so strong a case that Iraqi dictator Saddam Hussein is in material breach of U.N. resolutions that only the duped, the dumb and the desperate could ignore it." This is the speech that Lawrence Wilkerson, a former colonel in the U.S. Army, a decorated Vietnam vet, and a life-long Republican who served as chief of staff to former Secretary of State Colin Powell, has recently stated was "a hoax on the American people, the international community, and the United Nations Security Council." This is the speech that Powell himself said, in a February 2005 interview with Barbara Walters on the ABC News 20/20 program, was a "blot" on his record. Did Thomas learn from his mistake? His most recent statement about the war is his most radical one yet: "This war should be stepped up and fought like World War II." And this man is "the most widely published op-ed writer in the world"?

The sixth member of the Christian axis of evil is Pat "I wanna get in the Rock N' Roll Hall of Fame" Boone. Although he has been in the news of late for rebuking the Dixie Chicks because they refuse to respect a president who lied the country into war, Boone was a full-fledged Christian warmonger and Bush apologist long before then. But that hasn't stopped him from being an embarrassment to the president:

> Boone: "More 9-11s are gonna happen unless we try to take the battle to them on their turf instead of letting 'em bring it to us on ours."
>
> Bush: "We have no evidence that Saddam Hussein was involved with September the 11th."
>
> Boone: "Pre-war intelligence about Saddam's WMDs was correct all along."
>
> Bush: "It is true that most of the intelligence turned out to be wrong."

Boone is part of a desperate group of diehard Republican armchair warriors who maintain that Iraq's weapons of mass destruction were smuggled across the border into Syria. But being the champion warmonger that he is, Boone further maintains that "they may still be there, waiting to be used against us." First it was said to be an unnamed number of trucks that transferred the weapons to Syria in February and March of 2003. Now it is said to be converted 747 passenger jets that transported the weapons into Syria in 2002. The latter claim (examined here) is based on the word of former Iraqi general Georges Sada (examined here), who claims that the two pilots (unnamed) of the two airliners that moved the weapons on fifty-six flights told him about it (he was not an eyewitness). Syria? According to Stephen Zunes (Middle East editor for Foreign Policy In Focus, and author of *Tinderbox: U.S. Middle East Policy and the Roots of Terrorism* (Common Courage Press, 2002):

> Syria, despite being ruled by the Baath Party, has historically been a major rival of Iraq's Baath regime. Syria was the only Arab country to back Iran during the Iran-Iraq War. It was one of the only non-monarchical Arab states to have backed the United States against Iraq during the first Gulf War. Iraq and Syria backed rival factions in Lebanon's civil war. As a member of the United Nations Security Council, Syria voted this past November in favor of the U.S.-backed resolution 1441 that demanded full cooperation by the Baghdad government with United Nations inspectors, with the threat of severe consequences if it failed to do so.

But as I have previously showed in my article "Weapons of Mass Distraction," it doesn't matter whether Iraq had weapons of mass destruction. There is still absolutely no reason why the United States would be justified in attacking and invading a sovereign country—no matter what we thought of that country's ruler, system of government, economic policies, religious intolerance, or human rights record.

Poor Pat Boone doesn't know if he wants to be a consecrated Christian or a rock star; he hasn't decided whether he should be a singer or a political commentator.

I suppose that since the publisher of *WorldNetDaily*, Joseph "I believe I am the only serious daily news columnist on the Internet" Farah, published the articles I referenced by Falwell, Lindsey, and Boone, and, judging by the things he himself has written, believes what those gentlemen have written, that he will have to be added to the Christian axis of evil as well. But that would make seven members, and since I have limited the group in this article to six, I won't include him—this time.

Anyone who is familiar with my writings knows that I do not write these criticisms as an outsider. I am willing to match my Christian, Protestant, conservative, evangelical, fundamentalist, Baptist credentials up against anyone. And yes, I know all about the doctrines of Islam and the dangers of "Islamofascism." But I also know all about the insidious nature of a U.S. foreign policy that sows discord, stirs up strife, intensifies hatred, and creates terrorists.

There is no telling how many thousands of Christian Americans that Bush administration lapdogs Falwell, Robertson, Dobson, Lindsey, Thomas, and Boone have influenced. I am sure there are many other Christian leaders and wannabe leaders who, because they likewise serve as cheerleaders for the president, the war, and the military, are candidates for membership in the Christian axis of evil. Identify them, mark them, avoid them—and speak out against them if you can. It is only when Christians learn to look behind the façade of religious piousness that cloaks these Christian warmongers that the influence of the Christian axis of evil will be destroyed.

* * * * *

THE HYPOCRISY OF CHRISTIAN WARMONGERS

We must impose sanctions. We must attack. We must invade. We must launch a preemptive strike. This country has attacked one of our ships. This country has numerous weapons of mass destruction, including a sophisticated nuclear capability. This country is one of only four countries that have not ratified the Nuclear Non-Proliferation Treaty. This country has attacked the infrastructure of a sovereign country. This country has a government that is propped up by billions of dollars of foreign aid taken from U.S. taxpayers. This country has spied on the United States, and obtained classified information. This country has a powerful lobby in the United States that many feel exercises undue influence over the U.S. government. And now, this country has bombed civilians in Christian areas of a sovereign country.

We have no choice; it is inevitable: The U.S. government must go to war against Israel.

Now wait a minute, Mr. Vance, says the Christian warmonger. I thought you were an evangelical Christian? I thought you were a supporter of Israel? I thought you were one of those dispensationalists? I thought your theology was premillennialism?

I don't like it any more than you do, Mr. Christian warmonger, but if the U.S. government goes in that direction we must support the government. We must obey "the powers that be" (Romans 13:1). We must "obey magistrates" (Titus 3:1). We must submit "to every ordinance of man for the Lord's sake" (1 Peter 2:13). So, if the U.S. government goes to war against Israel then we should support our president. We should support the troops. After all, they will be defending our freedoms. We should encourage every young person to join the military. What could be more honorable than to serve in the U.S. military and kill in the name of the U.S. government? How could it be anything but a just war since the goal would be to restore peace to the Middle East?

But Mr. Vance, you can't be serious. Even if all those things you say about Israel are true, the United States can't attack Israel. The Jews are God's chosen people. What about God's promises to Abraham? Don't Christians and Jews worship the same God? And what about Bible prophecy? There comes a point when we must "obey God rather than men" (Acts 5:29).

Exactly.

Christian warmongers don't really believe their own mantras. When they chant "obey the powers that be," "obey magistrates," and "submit yourselves to every ordinance of man," it doesn't actually mean anything. Since the war in Iraq began, Christian warmongers have turned these portions of Scripture into their mantras in order to justify the war. None of them actually believe that a Christian should always accept the latest government pronouncement, support the latest government program, or obey the government in every respect. It was all a ruse to justify an unjust war. If the government commands one of these Christians to shoot his neighbor and destroy his property, he will choose to disobey and suffer the consequences—just like if the government commands one of these

Christians to shoot an Israeli and destroy his property.

So, if a Christian warmonger doesn't really believe that Christians should always obey the state, then why does he lie and say that they should? Christian warmongers hide behind their mantras because they are trying to defend a president, a party, and a movement that are undefendable. Should a Christian have served in Hitler's army? What about Stalin's? Why not? Should a Christian have participated in the Holocaust or in one of the Russian czar's pogroms? Why not? Christian warmongers are very selective about which governments they think Christians should obey. Despite their rhetoric, they really don't think that everyone should blindly follow whatever the president or the government says. The bottom line is that the command for the New Testament Christian to "be subject unto the higher powers" (Romans 13:1) is not absolute.

Evangelical Christians who support U.S. intervention in the Middle East and defend everything done by the government of Israel have been duped by neoconservatives who do not share their views of Bible prophecy. They need to realize that the government of Israel is not the people of Israel. And if the government of the "Christian" United States is corrupt from top to bottom, why would any Christian think that the government of Israel is any less corrupt?

Some evangelical Christians have departed so far from the faith that they need to drop the evangelical prefix. Christians United for Israel (CUFI), the brainchild of megachurch pastor John Hagee of Cornerstone Church in San Antonio, recently held a "Washington/Israel summit" in Washington D.C. on July 18 & 19 "for the purpose of introducing the association to Senators and Congressmen, expressing our concerns for Israel's security and our support of Israel's right to the land by Biblical Mandate." That is all well and good, but they are forgetting one thing—one very important thing. Christians in the Bible were involved in Jewish evangelism. According to the conservative Jew David Brog, the former chief of staff for Sen. Arlen Specter, and now executive director of CUFI:

> All activities of CUFI are strictly non-conversionary. Christians who work with Jews in supporting Israel realize how sensitive we are in talking about conversion and talking about Jesus. So those who work with us tend not to talk about Jesus more, but talk about Jesus less. They realize it will interfere with what they are trying to do—building a bridge to the Jewish community to insure the survival of Judeo-Christian civilization.

Other evangelical Christians have likewise exchanged evangelism for dialogue. Another megachurch pastor, Rick Warren, of Saddleback Church in Southern California, spoke this past June 16 at Sinai Temple, a Jewish synagogue, during "Friday Night Live Shabbat services." According to Rob Eshman, the editor-in-chief of the *Jewish Journal of Greater Los Angeles*: "Warren managed to speak for the entire evening without once mentioning Jesus—a testament to his savvy message-tailoring." Warren also told Ron Wolfson, the Rabbi who invited him, that "his interest is in helping all houses of worship, not in converting Jews."

And Hagee and Warren are supposed to be evangelicals?

A group of Baptists in Massachusetts who were impressed with his views on religious liberty once sent President Thomas Jefferson a 1,235-pound cheese measuring 4 feet in diameter and 17 inches in height. Painted on the red crust was the inscription: "Rebellion to tyrants is obedience to God." The Bible says to pray for those in authority, not to campaign for them, vote for them, bomb for them, or kill for them. Christians need to wake up and read the cheese.

Disclaimer: Although it should be quite obvious, for those dense Christian warmongers who are prone to smear as anti-Semitic the slightest criticism of Israel's government, I should say that much of this article was written tongue-in-cheek. I am not in favor of the United States attacking Israel (or any other country). But I am also not in favor of the United States propping up any government with foreign aid pilfered from the taxpayers.

* * * * *

THE UNHOLY DESIRE OF CHRISTIANS TO LEGITIMIZE KILLING IN WAR

> "People want to kill people, and they want biblical permission to do so." ~ Wilma Ann Bailey

It is bad enough to hear the Bush Administration, the neocons, the Randians, most Republicans in Congress, the right-wing talk show hosts, and some assorted libertarians still defend the war in Iraq, but it is even worse when Christians do the same.

Never at any time in history have so many conservative, evangelical Christians held such unholy opinions.

The adoration that many of these Christians have toward President Bush is unholy. The association of many of these Christians with the Republican Party is unholy. The alliance between evangelical Christianity and the military is unholy. The idolatry that many of these Christians manifest toward the state is unholy. But what continues to amaze me the most is the unholy desire on the part of many of these Christians to legitimize killing in war.

The Sixth Commandment

Although the attempt to legitimize killing in war is done in a number of ways, watering down the sixth commandment's prohibition against killing is always one of them. If someone is in the military or otherwise in the killing business for the state, then (so we are told) the commandment doesn't apply. Many Christians would go further and say that the commandment never applies to killing in war, period, or at least it doesn't apply to American troops. Others have the crazy idea that the commandment must be interpreted in light of the September 11th attacks. And although they would never say it publicly, some Christians believe that the commandment doesn't apply to the killing of Muslim infidels because they're not "innocent."

The simplest way to water down the prohibition against killing is to redefine it. Since killing in the sixth commandment obviously doesn't mean "the taking of any life," it has been limited by some Christians to murder because, as everyone knows (so we are told), it is not murder to kill a man on the battlefield. Therefore, Christians can in good conscience enlist in the military knowing that they might be expected to travel halfway around the world and bomb, maim, "interrogate," and kill for the state. No Christian need fear any negative consequences by God at the Judgment because he can't be faulted for "following orders" or "obeying the powers that be." End of story. Case closed. Christians can join the military or the National Guard and kill heartily in the name of the Lord. We should support the troops. They are not responsible for anyone they kill during a war. We should support conscription if the state says it needs more troops. We should ask God to bless our troops.

On the phrase "Thou shalt not kill" in the sixth commandment, here is Kenneth C. Davis, author of *Don't Know Much About the Bible: Everything You Need to Know About the Good Book but Never Learned* (William Morrow, 1998):

> This is another critical King James Version mistranslation of the original Hebrew. The correct reading is "You shall not murder" (NRSV, JPS, and others). As the rest of the Hebrew scriptures clearly indicate, God had no problem with certain forms of killing.

So, Kenneth Davis, who couldn't recite the Hebrew alphabet if his life depended on it, tells us that the most widely accepted Protestant version of the Bible mistranslates "the original Hebrew."

Where, then, is Davis getting his information? Evangelicals Robert Morey, in his book *When Is It Right to Fight?* (Christian Scholars Press, 2002, originally Bethany House, 1985), and Loraine Boettner, in his book *The Christian Attitude Toward War*, (Presbyterian and Reformed, 3rd ed., 1985), say basically the same thing. Morey mentions, but does not otherwise refer to, the definitive work of C. John Cadoux, *The Early Christian Attitude to War: A Contribution to the History of Christian Ethics* (Headley Bros., 1919), in arguing that the early church did not reject war and military service for Christians. Boettner, manifesting a profound ignorance of American history, believes that "America is not and never has been a militaristic nation."

A noted evangelical recently wrote:

> Previously we examined five ways in which God revealed that murder violates and perverts His moral absolutes and fixed order of moral law. The fifth way was through God giving Israel the following commandment: "You shall not murder" (Ex. 20:13). Some versions of the Bible use the word *kill* instead of *murder*. But since the Bible indicates that some killings are not murder but are permissible and, in some cases, required by God, "You shall not murder" is "a more precise reading than the too-general . . . 'thou shalt not kill'" [quoting the *Theological Wordbook of the Old Testament* (Moody, 2003)].

He goes on to quote from volume 13 of the *Theological Dictionary of the Old Testament* (Eerdmans, 2004) regarding the Hebrew word for *kill* in Exodus 20:13: "It is noteworthy that *rsh [rasah]* is never used for killing in battle or for killing in self-defense. Neither is it used for suicide."

Even Norman Geisler, in his valuable book, *Christian Ethics: Options and Issues* (Baker, 1989), tells us that the prohibition against killing in Exodus 20:13 "is translated correctly by the New International Version: 'You shall not murder.'"

Thus, the general evangelical consensus is that the Hebrew word underlying the word *kill* in the sixth commandment means "murder." Most of the Christians who make this argument do so, not because they know anything about biblical Hebrew or Bible translation, but because they are trying to justify Christians killing for the state in Iraq, Afghanistan, or wherever else the government has sent or will send its soldiers. This gives them something to fall back on when the recitation of their "obey the powers that be" mantra doesn't quite do the job.

This ideological desire to legitimize killing in war is an unholy one, and every Christian who attempts to do so should be ashamed of himself and repent "in sackcloth and ashes" (Matthew 11:21).

Kill or Murder?

Fortunately, Christians who are beginning to question the lies of the Bush Administration and distrust the latest pronouncements of their "leaders" have some help.

Wilma Ann Bailey, an associate professor of Hebrew and Aramaic Scripture at Christian Theological Seminary in Indianapolis, has penned a small (94 pages) book called *"You Shall Not Kill" or "You Shall Not Murder"? The Assault on a Biblical Text* (Collegeville: Liturgical Press, 2005).

I do not know Ms. Bailey, and doubt seriously that we could have much fellowship around any other thing than the subject of her book. She would probably consider me to be a fundamentalist, and I would probably consider her to be a liberal. I strongly disagree with her approach to Scripture (she believes that the source of Exodus 20 and 21 may be different because the vocabulary is different and Exodus 20 is apodictic law while Exodus 21 is casuistic law). I strongly disagree with her interpretation of Scripture (she denies that God sanctioned war, killing, and capital punishment in the Old Testament). I also strongly disagree with her political philosophy (she is in favor of gun control).

Nevertheless, Bailey has written an important work that I highly (but reservedly) recommend to anyone (Christian or not) who believes or is familiar with the "sixth commandment only prohibits murder" argument.

I have written briefly about this issue in my article "Humpty Dumpty Religion." There I showed that it was wrong to limit the sixth commandment to just prohibiting murder. I have also explained in my article "Is It or Isn't It?" that even if we grant that it is only murder which is prohibited by the sixth commandment, Christian warmongers are still responsible for explaining how U.S. soldiers killing for the state in Iraq is anything but murder. But because this is the first book on the subject that I have seen, the whole idea needs to be revisited and expanded upon.

Bailey's book focuses on "the meaning of the Hebrew word used in Exod 20:13 and the altering of the English translation of the commandment in several large traditions during the twentieth and twenty-first centuries." The book contains six short chapters and two short appendixes.

The first chapter is an analysis of the Hebrew word underlying the prohibition against killing in the sixth commandment. This chapter is not only the longest; it contains the meat of the book. The next four chapters survey this commandment in Evangelical Protestantism, Mainline Protestantism, Judaism, and Roman Catholicism. The final chapter is her explanation of why "killing is not the solution to the problem of killing." The first appendix is a helpful list of the major translations of the Bible with an indication of whether they use *kill* or *murder* in the sixth commandment. The second appendix is a technical study of the Hebrew word underlying the prohibition against killing in the sixth commandment. It is basically an expansion of the first chapter for scholars. All Hebrew words in the book are transliterated, except for those in the second appendix. (Bailey transliterates the Hebrew root in question as *rtsh*. Other acceptable transliterations are *rsh*, *rasah*, and *ratsach*, which is the form I have used in previous articles.)

We need not read far into the preface to see the direction in which Bailey is headed:

> The sixth commandment is perhaps the most disturbing of all the commandments. This is evidenced by the lengths to which scholars and church folk go to explain it away. Most killing throughout history has taken place within the context of what is legal (e.g., war, capital punishment) and therefore exempt from this commandment in the minds of many people. Interpreters narrow the prohibition to what relatively few people do, a criminal act—a person illegally killing another person—while allowing for the bulk of killing that takes place in the world to continue.

"This commandment," she continues, "exposes the true moral substance or vacuity of its interpreters. The Quaker Elton Trueblood once observed: 'The ultimate moral principles of a people are revealed, not by what they *do* but by the way in which they defend their actions.'"

Bailey argues four things in her first chapter:

- The English word "murder" is too limited and too varied a legal term to function adequately as the translation for the Hebrew word *rtsh*.
- The use of *rtsh* in other biblical texts indicates that the word is meant to be translated more broadly.
- The verbal form of *rtsh* often appears in a list or an ambiguous phrase that makes it impossible to determine a precise meaning.
- Murder is too rare a crime to merit Ten Commandment status.

She first shows that "the word 'murder' is a legal term," with a variety of meaning "from one jurisdiction to another." The fifty states each have their own legal code that defines what a murder is. Bailey then undertakes an exhaustive study of the Hebrew word *rtsh* in the Old Testament. Among other things, she points out that when this word is used in a list, "it is impossible to determine its precise meaning," Ahab is said to have killed (*rtsh*) Naboth (1 Kings 21), but never actually killed anyone, and a lion can kill (*rtsh*) someone, but would never be considered a murderer.

She concludes in chapter one:

> This chapter has presented a biblical argument against the automatic assumption that the commandment "You shall not kill" must be understood as "You shall not murder." First, it is clear that the Hebrew word *rtsh* does not mean 'murder' everywhere it is found in the Bible. Second, it is inappropriate to harmonize Scripture rather than letting the various theological traditions in the Bible speak for themselves. The English word 'murder' is a restricted legal term. Last, the Ten Commandments are meant to be general and not to refer to one particular, rarely committed crime.

After refuting the arguments for the translation "murder" in the sixth commandment using the biblical data, Bailey turns to how that commandment has been interpreted and translated in the various theological traditions: Evangelical Protestantism, Mainline Protestantism, Judaism, and Roman Catholicism.

The second chapter, "The Sixth Commandment in Evangelical Protestantism," is the most important of these because of the unholy alliance that exists today between evangelical Christianity and the military. Bailey shows that evangelicals were pacifistic during the period between the world wars, but notes that "by the 1960s the argument that the word 'kill' in the Ten Commandments really means 'murder' was being used by evangelicals even though the primary Bible translation used by evangelicals, the King James Version, did not read 'murder.'" This is no doubt due in a large measure because "in the latter half of the twentieth century being patriotic in the United States started to mean being pro-military and pro-war." In this chapter Bailey chronicles the shift in the rendering of the sixth commandment in the Bible translations of evangelicals from *kill* to *murder*. This change was accepted because of the "melding of evangelicalism, patriotism, and militarism."

"Although," as Bailey says, "a major American mainline translation did not read 'murder' until the publication of the *New Revised Standard Version* in 1989," the notion "began appearing in commentaries and sermons much earlier." Why have mainline Protestants, who would be most open to critical scholarship, also produced a translation that reads "murder"? Bailey bluntly replies: "People want to kill people, and they want biblical permission to do so. The translators of the NRSV and the other translations of the late twentieth century gave them that permission."

English translations of the Old Testament made by Jews did not appear until the middle of the nineteenth century. The earliest, that of Isaac Leeser in 1853, reads "kill," but this was changed in the Jewish Publication Society's 1917 translation to "murder." Thus, Bailey acknowledges, the translation of *murder* has a longer history in Judaism than Protestantism, but, as she also shows, "it is not an unchallenged reading."

In her chapter on the commandment in Roman Catholicism, Bailey finds that "all of the English translations produced in the Roman Catholic tradition have been consistent in the translation of the commandment." Yet, she believes that "the church developed 'just war' theory in order to theologically cope with the incongruity between biblical teachings (particularly New Testament teachings) and the desire of the state to wage war. Wars that were declared to be just, however, tended to be wars the state wanted to fight."

In her concluding chapter, Bailey summarily restates her objection to the "movement away from the traditional wording of the sixth commandment" in the late twentieth century and into the twenty-first century: "This would be appropriate if it more accurately reflected the meaning of the biblical text, but it does not." Her argument in the end is that rather than being more precise, *murder* is much too narrow of a translation. The ambiguity of the word *kill* in English matches that of *ratsach* in Hebrew. And since "the vast majority of violent and unnatural deaths during the last century were not the result of murder, but actions that in English are covered by the word 'kill,'" to limit "the scope of the commandment to illegal one-on-one killing exempts the primary causes of unnatural deaths in the twentieth and early twenty-first centuries."

There is no disputing the fact that many modern versions of the Bible narrow the prohibition against killing in the sixth commandment to murder. There is also no disputing the fact that many Christians appeal to the sixth commandment, not to condemn killing in war, but to countenance it. But does the first fact necessarily have to lead to the second? Has the change in the sixth commandment from *kill* to *murder* in recent translations of the Bible contributed to some Christians turning into

Christian warmongers? I think not. And neither does Bailey. She is merely saying that the change was accepted and even welcomed by those seeking biblical permission to legitimize killing in war. Does she put too much emphasis on this change in translation? I think so, and for four reasons. First, the earliest major modern Bible translation to make the change from *kill* to *murder* was the Revised Version of 1885. This is much too early to substantiate Bailey's thesis. Second, the venerable King James Version of the Bible (but not the New King James Version), which is the only Bible used by some conservative Christian warmongers, contains the familiar reading "thou shalt not kill." But this hasn't stopped these Christians from defending the death and destruction meted out by "Christian" U.S. soldiers in Iraq. Third, a reviewer of Bailey's book from Denmark pointed out that "the Danish Bible changed from 'kill' to 'murder' in the late 1990s, but neither is capital punishment favored in the Danish society nor is there a growing positive attitude to (just) war but rather to the contrary." And then there is the matter of the 1917 Jewish Publication Society translation—obviously not even the work of Christians—which also reads "murder."

I have some other problems with Bailey's book as well. She does not address the implications of an absolute prohibition against killing that she seems to be sanctioning. Also, she unfortunately does not interact with the New Testament references to the sixth commandment (Matthew 5:21, 19:18; Mark 10:19; Luke 18:20; Romans 13:9). The strength of Bailey's book clearly lies in the first chapter where she shows that the Hebrew word for *kill* in the sixth commandment doesn't mean murder in many contexts. Therefore, Bible versions that use the translation *murder* are wrong to narrowly focus the word.

The Unholy Desire to Legitimizing Killing in War

Christians who desire to legitimize killing in war will attempt to do so no matter what any Bible says. Most, however, want some kind of biblical permission for their unholy desire.

If their Bible reads "murder" in the sixth commandment, then Christians will repeat the old canard that "All murder involves the taking of life, but not all taking of life is murder" and say that killing in war is not murder. And not only is it not murder, to kill for your county—regardless of the location of the war—is the quintessence of patriotism. To kill for your country—regardless of the cause of the war—is always the right thing to do. To kill for your country—regardless of the nature of the war—is a perfectly okay thing for a Christian to do.

If their Bible reads "kill" in the sixth commandment, then Christians can simply redefine it as "murder" and treat the text as if that is what it actually says. Therefore, everything said in the previous paragraph would then apply.

But just because the sixth commandment prohibited murder doesn't necessarily mean that it allows for killing in war. Would anyone say that manslaughter is acceptable because the commandment only condemns murder? Why, then, do people appeal to the sixth commandment to justify killing in war unless they have an ideologically desire to legitimize killing in war?

There are, of course, other attempts by Christians to legitimize killing in war by distorting the sixth commandment. They reason that one cannot apply the sixth commandment to killing in war:

> Because the prohibition against killing in the commandment obviously doesn't mean the taking of any life.
>
> Because God commanded the Jews in the Old Testament to go to war against other nations.

Every Christian I have ever talked to or read who made these statements did so, not because of his concern to correctly interpret the Scripture, but because of his desire to justify Christians killing for the state in Iraq. In reply to the former reason I would point out that it is unlawful killing that is condemned in the sixth commandment. Killing in self-defense, animal sacrifices, and capital punishment were all permitted by God in the Old Testament because they were lawful killings. There is nothing lawful about an American soldier traveling thousands of miles away and killing an Iraqi in his own house. In reply to the latter reason I would remind the desperate Christian warmonger who uses it that no nation or group of people can claim today to enjoy the privileged position that was occupied by the nation of Israel in the Old Testament. And that goes for the United States as well.

The desire to legitimize killing in war is an unholy one. Of all people, it is conservative, evangelical Christians who ought to be the first to denounce the state's latest pretext for war instead of defending it and in many cases supplying the state with a fresh supply of cannon fodder in the form of their young people. It is a terrible blight on Christianity that many non-Christians are not so blindly in love with the state that they defend its president, its military, and its wars.

* * * * *

WAR, FOREIGN POLICY, AND THE CHURCH

This talk was delivered on June 3, 2007, at the Future of Freedom Foundation's Conference on "Restoring the Republic: Foreign Policy and Civil Liberties."

It is fitting that today is a Sunday because I would like to speak this afternoon about what the Church should be saying about war and foreign policy. This war, like all of the other foreign wars the United States has been involved in, is a consequence of our interventionist foreign policy.

Although the foreign policy of the current administration has been referred to as "the Bush Doctrine" and "this great mission," it is not much different from the foreign policy of most previous administrations. Gunboat diplomacy may have given way to cowboy diplomacy, but U.S. foreign policy is still aggressive, reckless, belligerent, and meddling. The history of U.S. foreign policy is the history of hegemony, nation building, regime change, and jingoism. In a word, it is a history of interventionism, with its stepchildren imperialism and empire.

Although Donald Rumsfeld claims that "we don't seek empires" and "we're not imperialistic," I don't hesitate to use the terms. Not only did the 9/11 Commission Report conclude that "the American homeland is the planet," it referred to the Department of Defense as "the behemoth among federal agencies. With an annual budget larger than the gross domestic product of Russia, it is an empire." The extent of the U.S. global empire is almost incalculable. The Department of Defense's "Base Structure Report" states that the Department's physical assets consist of "more than 600,000 individual buildings and structures, at more than 6,000 locations, on more than 30 million acres." There are over 700 U.S. military bases on foreign soil. There are U.S. troops stationed in 159 different regions of the world in every corner of the globe. There are 285,000 U.S. troops stationed in foreign countries, not counting the 200,000 troops in Iraq and Afghanistan. There are 100,000 U.S. soldiers in Europe to face a non-existent Soviet Union. The United States has commitments to provide security to over 35 countries. The United States still maintains 64,000 troops in Germany, 33,000 troops in Japan, and 10,000 troops in Italy—sixty years after World War II. We have, in fact, never stopped mobilizing for war since World War II, manufacturing enemies where we could find none. In addition to military personnel, the Department of Defense employs 675,000 people worldwide, including thousands of foreign nationals. But instead of all of this being an example of imperialism and empire, we are told by neoconservative intellectuals that the United States is merely exercising "benevolent hegemony."

Because the United States seems to have none of the benefits of an empire—but all of its drawbacks—some imperialists—those who believe that it is in the national interest of the United States to intervene in conflicts around the globe, attempt to control foreign governments, and spread our political and economic systems to other countries by force—argue that we are not an empire because we haven't annexed any country's soil in over a hundred years. But America's unprecedented global presence of troops, bases, and ships clearly says otherwise. We may not be an empire in name, but we are an empire in denial. A noted British historian has remarked that "the greatest empire of modern times has come into existence without the American people even noticing." Well, some of us have noticed and we don't like what we see. Besides the obvious—an empire of troops, bases, and ships—we see an empire of influence, domination, and occupation; we see an empire maintained by bribes, threats, and coercion. We see an empire sustained by nationalism, militarism, and jingoism.

America spends more on defense than the next twelve countries combined. This can't be because we have more people—China and India have a greater population; or because we have a larger land area to protect—Russia and Canada have more territory. With an official budget for fiscal year 2008 that is over $538 billion, Pentagon spending accounts for about 40 percent of total world military spending. Yet, economist Robert Higgs has estimated that the true amount spent by the United States on defense will actually top $1 trillion for the first time in history. This means that defense-related spending will account for about one-third of the total federal budget. But, some would say, that is a small price to pay for our security: This is a dangerous world we live in, and the United States faces a variety of threats from terrorists and rogue nations—there is no price too high to pay for our security. There is no disputing that there are a number of countries in the world that hate the United States. And that number would be even higher if we turned off the foreign aid spigot. But instead of reserving to ourselves the right of preemptive strikes and saying of potential foreign aggressors, like President Bush did, "bring them on," shouldn't we be asking some serious questions about our foreign policy? Why do they hate us? Why do they burn our flag? Why do they demonstrate against us? Why did they bomb our embassies? Why did they try to blow up one of our ships? Why did they take out the Twin Towers? I think we will find that in most cases the answer is because of our foreign policy.

Many Americans have begun to wonder why, if the mission of the Defense Department is to defend the country, we need a Department of

Homeland Security. The truth of the matter is that the Department of Defense, which couldn't defend its own headquarters, is misnamed. Rather than guarding our borders, patrolling our coasts, and protecting our citizens, the DOD is focused on invading the next country and fighting the next foreign war. Foreign military bases are for offensive military actions, not defensive ones. And likewise for the stationing abroad of thousands of military troops. There is no better example, of course, of the true mission of the Department of Defense than the current war in Iraq—an unconstitutional, unnecessary, immoral, senseless, and unjust war if there ever were one. It is unconstitutional because only Congress has the authority to declare war. It is unnecessary because Iraq was no threat to the United States. It is immoral because it was based on lies. It is unjust because it is not defensive. It is senseless because 3,400 U.S. soldiers have died in vain. The war in Iraq is also terribly expensive, costing the American taxpayers over $200 million a day. The final cost of the war is projected to be as high as $2 trillion. That is a far cry from the $50 billion that then Secretary of Defense Rumsfeld said the war would cost.

So rather than America's military heritage being one of how the military has defended the country from attack, it is instead one of invasion, destabilization, occupation, subjugation, oppression, death, and destruction. Instead of the U.S. military defending our freedoms, the military has been at once the world's policeman, fireman, social worker, bully, and busybody. Rather than the presence of the U.S. military guaranteeing peace and stability throughout the world, the presence of the U.S. military more often than not is the cause of war and instability around the globe. Instead of existing to defend the country, U.S. troops exist to serve as the president's personal attack force, ready to obey his latest command to deploy to any country for any reason.

Yet, after the historical record has been laid bare, some people just don't get it. After the United States invaded Mexico under false pretenses; after we helped to overthrow the existing monarchy in Hawaii; after we seized Cuba, Puerto Rico, the Philippines, and Guam from Spain during the Spanish-American War; after the United States intervened militarily in Nicaragua, Panama, Honduras, the Dominican Republic, Korea, Cuba, China, and Mexico before World War I; after we sent troops to Cuba, the Dominican Republic, Russia, Panama, Honduras, Yugoslavia, Guatemala, Turkey, and China between the world wars; after we engaged in a hundred additional military actions following World War II—after all this, some people still can't see (or perhaps don't want to see) the insidious nature of U.S. foreign policy.

Writing in the *Weekly Standard* in 2001 soon after the September

11th attacks, neoconservative CFR Senior Fellow Max Boot maintained that rather than the attack being a "payback for American imperialism," it "was a result of insufficient American involvement and ambition; the solution is to be more expansive in our goals and more assertive in their implementation." Contrast this with the opinion of Chalmers Johnson, who has written a trilogy of books on the true nature of U.S. foreign policy: "The suicidal assassins of September 11, 2001, did not 'attack America,' as political leaders and news media in the United States have tried to maintain; they attacked American foreign policy." The world doesn't hate us for our wealth, our freedoms, and our culture, it hates us for our foreign policy. Although militant Islamists may want to convert Americans to Islam, outlaw pornography, jail homosexuals, ban alcohol, cover up women's midriffs, and clean up our decadent culture, they have consistently maintained and demonstrated that it is the U.S. presence in the Middle East, blanket support for Israel, years of aggression against Iraq, and support for corrupt Arab governments for which they are willing to resort to terrorist attacks. Terrorist attacks against the West are political in nature, not cultural or religious.

Max Boot has further said that U.S. imperialism "has been the greatest force for good in the world during the past century." This thinking has even pervaded the highest office in the land. Echoing the inscription on the Liberty Bell, President Bush closed his Second Inaugural Address with the statement that "America, in this young century, proclaims liberty throughout all the world, and to all the inhabitants thereof." But rather than receiving a proclamation of liberty, what many people in foreign countries receive instead are threats, bombs, and bullets.

It is no wonder former U.S. Attorney General William Ramsey Clark has said that "the greatest crime since World War II has been U.S. foreign policy." And Murray Rothbard, who was at once the twentieth century's greatest proponent of liberty and opponent of the state, was perfectly justified in saying that "empirically, taking the twentieth century as a whole, the single most warlike, most interventionist, most imperialist government has been the United States."

From a Christian perspective there is only one way to describe U.S. foreign policy: it is evil. It was evil before the United States invaded Iraq, and it would still be evil if the United States withdrew all its forces from Iraq tomorrow. It is because of our foreign policy that the U.S. military has become—through its wars, interventions, and occupations—the greatest force for evil in the world. U.S. foreign policy sows discord among nations, stirs up strife where none existed, intensifies the hatred that many foreigners around the world have for Americans and each other, and creates terrorists faster than we can kill them.

The United States has pressured, destabilized, undermined, manipulated, and overthrown governments, including democracies. We have assassinated or attempted to assassinate foreign leaders. We have destroyed industry, culture, and infrastructure. We have helped install autocrats and dictators. We have sponsored regime changes in countries that no longer favored U.S. corporate interests. We have backed and engineered military coups. We have been involved with torturers, death squads, drug traffickers, and other "unsavory persons." We have allied ourselves with murderous regimes. We have downplayed massive numbers of civilian casualties by dismissing them as collateral damage. We have labeled violence perpetrated by our opponents as terrorism, atrocities, ethnic cleansing, and genocide while minimizing or defending the same actions committed by the United States or its allies. We have engaged in thousands of covert actions. We have undertaken massive propaganda campaigns to deceive foreigners about their own country. We have kidnapped foreign citizens in their own country. We have transported insurgents and detainees to torture-friendly countries. We have looted and confiscated government documents from foreign countries. We have selectively intervened in countries for dubious humanitarian concerns while ignoring real suffering and death in other countries. We have used humanitarian interventions as a guise for imperialism. We have encouraged favored governments to engage in human rights violations. We have supported corrupt and tyrannical governments. We have crushed populist and nationalist movements struggling against tyrannical regimes. We have trained foreign soldiers and police to suppress their own people. We have influenced, sabotaged, financed, and otherwise interfered with elections in other countries. We have taken sides or intervened in civil wars. We have recklessly tested and knowingly used chemical and biological weapons on both U.S. citizens and foreigners in their countries. We have encouraged the use of chemical and biological weapons by other nations, and trained foreign nationals to do the same. We have downplayed the slaughter of civilians killed in civil wars if they were on the side we didn't agree with. We have provided military hardware to and trained the paramilitary forces of foreign countries. We have engaged in provocative naval actions in international waters under the guise of protecting freedom of navigation. We have bribed, blackmailed, and bullied our way around the world. Say what you will, believe what you will about the nuclear programs of Iran and North Korea, the fact remains that the United States is the only country to have ever used nuclear weapons on people—and we did it twice.

The United States is an overextended, out-of-control, rogue nation. Yet, the mere mention of the evil that the United States has perpetrated throughout the world upsets and angers many Americans because they have the mindset that a terrorist is someone who detonates a bomb but doesn't wear an air force uniform. But because we live in an imperfect world of nation-states that is not likely to change anytime in the near future, the question of U.S. foreign policy cannot be ignored. Randolph Bourne's observation almost one hundred years ago that "war is the health of the State" has never been more relevant than right now. Those who disparage the welfare state while turning a blind eye to the warfare state are terribly inconsistent. There is an intimate connection between foreign policy and domestic policy, as I will point out in my conclusion.

If there is any religion that should be opposed to the evils of war it is Christianity. And if there is any group of people in America that should be opposed to a militaristic foreign policy it is Christians. Yet, in the Church will be found some of the greatest supporters of the state, its president, its military, and its wars.

The question before us, then, is what should the Church be saying about war and foreign policy? Before answering that question, I would like to point out not only what things the Church is saying now about war and foreign policy, but why I believe these things are being said.

So what is the Church saying now about war and foreign policy? Unfortunately, the Church is either saying things that are wrong or is not saying enough about what is wrong. In the Church's conservative, evangelical, and fundamentalist circles—and I identify loosely with all three—much of what is being said is not just wrong, it is evil, immoral, hypocritical, shameful, and more importantly, unscriptural. But the Church is also not saying enough. It is not saying enough about the defective Christianity of the president. It is not saying enough about the evils of war. It is not saying enough about our overgrown military establishment. It is not saying enough about our interventionist foreign policy. It is not saying enough about the warfare state.

President Bush has mastered the art of using religious rhetoric to capture the support of gullible Christians for his aggressive, militaristic, interventionist foreign policy he terms "this great mission." As seminary professor emeritus Walter Wink has well said: "Evil never feels safe unless it wears the mask of divinity." The biggest foreign policy blunder of the Bush administration is, of course, the war in Iraq. This war in particular is a great evil, for a just war, rather than being an offensive, preemptive, open-ended, "shock and awe" campaign, must have a just cause, be in proportion to the gravity of the situation, have obtainable objectives, and only be undertaken as a last resort. If there was ever a war that violated every one of these principles it is the Iraq war.

But the problem is not just that waging this war is against every Christian "just war" principle that has ever been formulated. Conducting the war is contrary to the whole spirit of the New Testament. Fighting the war is in opposition to the practice of the early church. Participants in the war violate the express teaching of the sixth commandment: "Thou shalt not kill." Supporters of the war violate the first commandment: "Thou shalt have no other gods before me." Although the Bible likens Christians to soldiers, and the Christian life to a battle, the Christian's weapons are not carnal and his battle is a spiritual one. The Christian is admonished to "put on the whole armor of God," not a military uniform. His only weapon is "the sword of the spirit, which is the word of God," not an M16.

An overwhelming majority of Americans identify themselves as Christians. The same can be said of soldiers, sailors, airmen, and Marines in the military. The percentage of congressman who identify their religion as Christianity is higher than that needed to override a presidential veto. The president has been very vocal about his faith. But now that we have passed the fourth anniversary of the U.S. invasion of Iraq, support for the war among Christian Americans continues, bombing and killing by Christians in the military continues, funding for the war by a Christian Congress continues, and justification for the war by a Christian president continues. And we wonder why Muslims hate us?

It is appalling that many defenders of the war in Iraq are Christians; it is even worse when they appeal to Scripture to excuse or justify a senseless war that has now resulted in the deaths of 3,400 U.S. soldiers and the wounding of countless thousands more, not to mention the tens of thousands—and perhaps hundreds of thousands—of Iraqis. To their everlasting shame, I suspect that it is the most conservative of Christians who will support the war until the bitter end—no matter how many more U.S. soldiers die for a lie, no matter how many more young American men (and women) are disabled for life, no matter how many more years the war continues, no matter how many more billions of dollars are wasted, and no matter what outrages the government commits against the Constitution, civil liberties, and the rule of law.

As a Christian, an American, a father, and a taxpayer, I have not only opposed this war from the beginning, I have vehemently denounced it as well. I have never wavered in my contempt for those who sought it, my disagreement with the president who instigated it, my disgust for the Congressmen who fund it, my loathing for the conservatives who promote it, my abhorrence of the Christians who defend it, and my pity for the soldiers who were duped by military recruiters to participate in it. I believe that Christian support for the president and his war has diminished somewhat. Unfortunately, however, this is generally not out of principle, but only because defending the war has become such an embarrassment.

Christian leaders—many of whom I have said make up the Christian Axis of Evil—are some of the most vocal apologists for the president, his party, his aggressive foreign policy, and his war. Televangelist Pat Robertson wanted the U.S. government to assassinate the leader of another country. But what should we expect from someone who thinks the war in Iraq is being fought on Christian principles, and who considers criticism of the war to be treason? Catholic Radio and television personality Sean Hannity maintains that America has a "moral obligation" to fight for the security "of any oppressed nation." But what do we do when we are the oppressors? Watergate conspirator turned prison minister Chuck Colson thinks the preemptive war against Iraq was self-defense. Conservative columnist and evangelical Cal Thomas wants the war in Iraq to be "stepped up and fought like World War II." I guess that means he is in favor of firebombing Iraqi cities and then nuking a couple more for good measure. The late Republican apologist and Baptist preacher Jerry Falwell, who ranked George Bush with Ronald Reagan "as one of America's greatest presidents," believed the invasion of Iraq was just and right because "God is pro-war." What Falwell means, of course, is that God is pro-American wars. Prophecy guru and fanatical warmonger John Hagee wants the United States to go to war against Iran—and the sooner the better. The Friends of Israel Gospel Ministry regards the president of Iran as worse than Hitler. Not only does he wish to destroy Israel, his "next move is westward to Europe and then on to finish off the hated United States." But these so-called Christian leaders are not alone. They still command the attention and respect of thousands of Christians in the pew. Their ministries are not hurting for money or followers. And it will remain that way until Christians are as concerned about killing on the battlefield as they are about killing in the womb.

Why are Christians saying these things? There is no doubt that this war is abhorrent to Christianity. If there is any war in history that is contrary to the whole spirit of the New Testament it is the current one. All adherents of Christianity, of any church, creed, or denomination, should be opposed to this war of aggression. So why aren't they? Why do Christians who don't agree with President Bush's domestic policies—and think even less of his Christianity—remain silent about his unjust, immoral, and unscriptural war, and his reckless, interventionist foreign policy that increases hatred for America and Americans and therefore undermines Christian mission work around the world?

The first reason why Christians are saying these things is the September 11th terrorist attacks. Even though the president himself now says otherwise, many Christians continue to believe that Iraq was behind those attacks. Few have stopped their thirst for revenge long enough to realize that the 9/11 attacks were themselves an act of revenge for over a decade of abuses. The attacks were a guerilla action against the United States for what Arabs and Muslims see as our invasion and interference in their homelands. The attacks were in retaliation for anger and resentment over U.S. foreign policy. Surely Christians are aware of the scriptural principle that "whatsoever a man soweth that shall he also reap"?

The second reason why is Saddam Hussein. We have continually been told that Hussein was a corrupt, evil ruler. Although that assessment is certainly correct, every country has its share of corrupt, evil rulers—just look at the United States. The world has always been full of corrupt, evil rulers, and it always will be until Jesus Christ returns to rule and reign in righteousness. But wasn't Saddam Hussein the same oppressive dictator in the 1980s who brutalized his own people? Why is it, then, that he was our friend up until the Persian Gulf War? And wasn't he a greater "threat" to U.S. interests under the first George Bush? If Hussein was so bad, any Iraqi could have put a bullet in his head and gone down in history as a hero. Don't evil dictators ever sleep or go to the bathroom? But not only has Hussein been deposed, he has been executed. So why are U.S. troops still in Iraq? What happened to "Mission Accomplished?" And if Hussein was an oppressive dictator who was hated by his people, then how does that justify making war on an entire country of people who were his enemies? But have not the Iraqis killed, injured, or maimed thousands of U.S. soldiers? Of course they have. We would do the same thing to foreign troops that invaded our soil. Ridding Iraq of Saddam Hussein was not worth the life of one American.

The third reason why is Islam. Some conservative Christians dismiss the thousands of Iraqi civilian deaths as collateral damage because they are Muslims. Some of the same Christians who never hesitate to criticize the role of the Catholic Church in the Crusades view the war in Iraq as a modern-day crusade against Muslims. Although President Bush thinks that Muslims and Christians worship the same God, conservative Christians consider Islam to be false religion. But there are a lot of false religions in the world, and the God of the Bible never called, commanded, or encouraged any Christian to kill, make apologies for the killing of, or excuse the killing of any adherent of a false religion.

The fourth reason why is Israel. For biblical reasons, evangelical Christians are typically supporters of Israel. Unfortunately, however, some of them thought that Iraq was a threat to Israel, and therefore the U.S. was justified in invading Iraq and overthrowing Saddam Hussein. But with enough assorted weaponry to destroy Iraq many times over, Israel was not in danger from Iraq. Rather than protecting Israel by invading Iraq, the opposite has occurred. The continued presence of the U.S. military in the Middle East increases Muslim hatred of both America and Israel and therefore increases terrorism. Gullible evangelical Christians have been used by neoconservatives who care not a whit about Bible prophecy.

The fifth reason why is the Republican Party. It is bad enough when most Republican members of Congress and the Republican Party faithful continue to blindly follow the leadership of a Republican president who will go down in history as doing more to expand the power of government than any other Republican president since Abraham Lincoln, but it is even worse when conservative Christians go along with them. Too many Christians are in love with the Republican Party. But this is clearly a case of spiritual adultery. The Republican Party has not only historically been the party of big government, its members have of late taken to supporting pre-emptive war, bloated defense and intelligence budgets, secret military tribunals, torture of "enemy combatants," extraordinary renditions, an increasingly militarized society, the violation of basic civil liberties, undue government secrecy, and domestic spying programs. Just like the Democratic Party, the Republican Party never met a federal program it didn't like as long as it furthered the party's agenda. I suspect that the Republicans would be leveling the same criticisms of the Iraq war as the Democrats if it were a Democratic president who had launched the war. According to Representative John Duncan of Tennessee, a rare Republican opponent of the Iraq war from the beginning, "Eighty percent of House Republicans voted against the bombings in the former Yugoslavia under President Clinton. I am convinced that at least the same percentage would have opposed the war in Iraq if it had been started by a Democratic president."

The sixth reason why is the U.S. military. Christians will generally agree with you if you denounce some of the more outrageous abuses of the government, most will concur if you condemn the welfare state, many will go along with you if you disparage one of the presidents, some will put up with you if you criticize the U.S. global empire, a few will even tolerate you if you denigrate the warfare state, but once you question the military in any way—its size, its budget, its contractors, its bureaucracy, its efficiency, its purpose, and especially its acts of death and destruction as the coercive arm of the state—many Christians will brand you as a pacifist, a liberal, a leftist, a Quaker, a communist, a coward, an appeaser, and even a traitor or an America-hater. There is an unholy alliance between conservative Christians and the military. But this too is an illicit affair. It is contrary to the tenor of the New Testament. It is an affront to the Savior. It is a blight on Christianity. Some Christians have practically elevated military "service" to the level of the Christian ministry, believing that the U.S. military is the Lord's army that fights against the Muslim infidel. It is a terrible disgrace that, instead of the next military adventure of the U.S. government being denounced from every pulpit and pew of every church in the country, there are many preachers in the pulpit and many Christians in the pew who can be counted on to support it. Even Christians who oppose Bush's pseudo-Christianity, his socialist domestic policies, and his interventionist foreign policies can be found encouraging (or else not discouraging) the young men in their church to join the military and then "obey the powers that be" when it comes to bombing, interrogating, maiming, and killing for the state in some foreign war that has nothing to do with defending the United States. Our support for the troops should be limited to praying for them. But how should we pray for them? Should we pray that God bless the troops while they drop their bombs, throw their grenades, launch their missiles, fire their mortars, and shoot their bullets? Should we pray that the troops are protected while they injure, torture, maim, and kill others? Should we pray that the troops are successful when they drive their tanks into a city and reduce it to rubble? I think rather that we should pray that the troops come home now so that not one more drop of blood from an American soldier is shed on foreign soil.

The last reason why Christians are saying these things is the state itself. Many Christians are in love with the state. They have a warped "God and Country" complex which inevitably elevates the state to the level of God Almighty. Sure, they may complain about paying their taxes, obeying a frivolous law, or complying with some regulation; they may get upset with Supreme Court decisions about abortion, and even get outraged about government grants used to fund pornographic art exhibits. But when it comes to the subject of war and the military they lose their minds. Bombing, maiming, interrogating, and killing are okay as long as it is done in service for the state. The military and the CIA are great employment opportunities for Christian young people. I have never heard or read of any president that has received as much adoration as the current president. If he dictates that an intervention, invasion, or war is necessary then the typical Christian response is trust, no need to verify. But the government of the United States and Christianity is a most unholy alliance. It has been argued by the Foundation for Economic Education president Richard Ebeling that "there has been no greater threat to life, liberty, and property throughout the ages than government. Even the most violent and brutal private individuals have been able to inflict only a mere fraction of the harm and destruction that have been caused by the use of power by political authorities." The U.S. government is no exception. The Bible says to pray for those in authority, not to campaign for them, vote for them, bomb for them, or kill for them. When it comes to defending, believing in the legitimacy of, and carrying out the evil dictates of the state, Christians are under a higher authority. Since when was blind obedience to the state a tenet of New Testament Christianity? The attitude of the Christian toward the state should be no different now than it was in the days of the early Church. The apostles Peter and John were brought before the authorities and asked: "Did not we straitly command you that ye should not teach in this name? And, behold, ye have filled Jerusalem with your doctrine, and intend to bring this man's blood upon us." It was then that the apostles uttered that immortal line: "We ought to obey God rather than men."

All of these things being said, I would now at long last like to give you ten things the Church should be saying about war and foreign policy. But instead of appealing to the latest pronouncement of one of our self-anointed Christian "leaders" who moonlights as a cheerleader for the Bush administration, I appeal to the Scripture. To the U.S. government the Church should be saying ten things.

1. Ephesians 4:29: "Let no corrupt communication proceed out of your mouth." The communication that comes forth from U.S. government officials is routinely corrupt communication. In response to the charge that more than a half a million children in Iraq died as a result of U.S. sanctions, soon-to-be Secretary of State Madeleine Albright responded that the price was "worth it." Commenting on new interrogation techniques he approved that included forcing prisoners to stand for four hours at a time, then Secretary of Defense Rumsfeld arrogantly wrote: "I stand for 8-10 hours a day. Why is standing limited to 4 hours?" On the eve of the Persian Gulf War, the senior President Bush stated: "And so to every sailor, soldier, airman, and marine who is involved in this mission, let me say you're doing God's work." He also remarked once when he was the vice-president: "I will never apologize for the United States of America. I don't care what the facts are." This corrupt communication has increased under the current president, as this statement from George W shows: "No

act of America explains terrorist violence, and no concession of America could appease it." Like father like son.

2. Romans 12:17: "Provide things honest in the sight of all men." Dishonesty is the rule when it comes to the U.S. government. Who can forget FDR on the eve of U.S. intervention into World War II: "I have said this before, but I shall say it again and again and again: Your boys are not going to be sent into any foreign wars. They are going into training to form a force so strong that, by its very existence, it will keep the threat of war far away from our shores." And what about LBJ campaigning for president in 1964: "We are not about to send American boys nine or ten thousand miles away from home to do what Asian boys ought to be doing for themselves." And then there is our current president: "Iraq has attempted to purchase high-strength aluminum tubes and other equipment needed for gas centrifuges, which are used to enrich uranium for nuclear weapons."

3. 1 Thessalonians 5:15: "Ever follow that which is good." Although Madeleine Albright once made the claim: "The United States is good," we have not ever followed that which is good. The Scripture says that "righteousness exalteth a nation, but sin is a reproach to any people." The United States could and should be the moral leader of the world. Old Right senator Robert Taft once remarked that "if we confine our activities to the field of moral leadership we shall be successful if our philosophy is sound and appeals to the people of the world." The problem with this, as Taft also recognized, is that the United States wants to force on foreigners "through the use of American money and even, perhaps, arms, the policies which moral leadership is able to advance only through the sound strength of its principles." And as Old Right Republican congressman Howard Buffett explained: "Our Christian ideals cannot be exported to other lands by dollars and guns. Persuasion and example are the methods taught by the Carpenter of Nazareth."

4. Galatians 6:10: "As we have therefore opportunity, let us do good unto all men." Ms. Albright also said of the United States: "We try to do our best everywhere." This too is incorrect for the United States does not do good unto all men. In many cases we do just the opposite. Just ask those who have lost loved ones, limbs, or property from U.S. mines, bombs, and bullets. In a speech at a NATO summit before the invasion of Iraq, President Bush said: "Great evil is stirring in the world." Although the president would disagree, more often than not, it is the United States that commits evil deeds or stirs up evil in the world.

5. Ephesians 5:11: "Have no fellowship with the unfruitful works of darkness." The U.S. government, through the CIA, the military, and the

state department, has regularly maintained cozy relationships with dictators, thugs, strongmen, and other corrupt rulers who commit works of darkness, as well as committing numerous works of darkness. Donald Rumsfeld should forever be haunted by the picture of him and Saddam Hussein taken in 1983 when he was sent to Iraq as a special envoy of President Reagan. Although the United States restored formal relations with Iraq in 1984, we had already begun, even before Rumsfeld made his trip, to secretly provide Iraq with intelligence and military support, contrary to our official neutrality in the Iran-Iraq War, and knowing that Iraq had used chemical weapons. The United States has committed numerous works of darkness, including assassinations, propaganda campaigns, regime changes, and covert actions.

6. Romans 12:17: "Recompense to no man evil for evil." The world is full of evil. Always has been; always will be. I believe it was Edward Gibbon who said: "History is, indeed, little more than the register of the crimes, follies, and misfortunes of mankind." When evil is committed against the United States, we should first seek to discover why it happened before we recompense evil for evil by sending in the Marines. As much as it pains me to say it, most of the evil perpetrated against the United States is in response to our interventionist foreign policy.

7. 1 Peter 4:15: Don't be "a busybody in other men's matters." No one likes a busybody. People universally prefer that others mind their own business. The United States is a global busybody—a global busybody with bombs. Supposedly sovereign countries can't even have an election without the United States intervening in one way or another. Fraud or no fraud, foreign elections are none of our business. How would we feel if China or Russia sent "observers" to monitor our elections because of the recent cases of fraud? We would be furious. And as much as many Americans loathe George W. Bush, how would we feel if another country said that we needed to submit to a regime change? We would likewise be outraged. Most of what happens in the world is none of our concern and certainly none of our business. Why do we wonder that the rest of the world objects to us sticking our nose in their business?

8. 1 Timothy 5:21: "Doing nothing by partiality." Instead of doing nothing by partiality, the United States regularly does just the opposite. In fact, the history of U.S. foreign policy is the history of showing partiality to one country over another or being partial to a country if it serves some policy objective—even if it means turning a blind eye to that country's ruler, system of government, human rights violations, treatment of women, economic policies, or religious intolerance.

9. Romans 12:18: "Live peaceably with all men." Even though

there is an abundance of evil in the world, there is no reason why the United States cannot live peaceably with the rest of the world. When the Scripture simply says to live peaceably, it doesn't imply that you should make your opponents die so you can live peaceably. The Scripture also says to live peaceably with all men. That would include countries that are communist or Muslim. It doesn't matter what form of government, type of ruler, or national policies a country has. We can live peaceably by recognizing that there is nothing we can do about most of the evil in the world. We can live peaceably by realizing that we cannot remake the world in our image. And most importantly, we can live peaceably by not being the cause of evil in the world.

10. Exodus 20:13: "Thou shalt not kill." God only knows how many people around the world have been killed as a direct result of U.S. foreign policy. No, I am not equating the United States with Nazi Germany, Soviet Russia, or Red China. With the exception of Indians, the United States generally kills foreigners, not American citizens. We killed at least two million Vietnamese and Cambodians in a war that was both undeclared and unnecessary. We have now killed or been responsible for the deaths of perhaps half a million people in Iraq. From the beginning of the Iraq War, I have maintained that participants in this evil war violate the express teaching of the biblical commandment against killing. Christian apologists for war say that either the commandments don't apply to the state, and therefore killing done in service for the state is permissible, or else that the sixth commandment is limited to murder, and therefore killing done in wartime is permissible. Therefore, just as Calvary covers it all, my past with its sin and shame, so the wearing of a uniform covers it all, my military service with its death and destruction. Thus, killing someone you don't know, and have never seen, in his own territory, who was no threat to anyone until the United States invaded his country, is not murder if the U.S. government says that he should be killed. No soldier is responsible for the death and destruction he inflicts in a foreign country as long as it is state-sanctioned death and destruction. I reject this ghastly statolatry.

There is an unholy desire on the part of some Christians to legitimize killing in war. They have the attitude that what is required conduct for individuals, is not required conduct for nations. In the minds of some Christians, it is okay for someone to put on a uniform and kill someone half way around the world, but it is murder if the same person killed someone here in the United States. Although it was Oliver Cromwell who said that "there are great occasions in which some men are called to great services in the doing of which they are excused from the common rule of morality," even a nominal Christian like Thomas Jefferson spoke against this mindset, writing in a letter to James Madison in 1789: "I know but one code of morality for men, whether acting singly or collectively. He who says I will be a rogue when I act in company with a hundred others, but an honest man when I act alone, will be believed in the former assertion but not in the latter." A man does not throw his morality out the window just because he puts on a uniform.

There is nothing inherently "religious" about what the Church should be saying about war and foreign policy. It is merely aversion to war and the noninterventionist foreign policy of the Founding Fathers. A noninterventionist foreign policy is not just an Old Right foreign policy, a libertarian foreign policy, or a paleoconservative foreign policy, it is a Jeffersonian foreign policy. Jefferson believed in no judgment, no meddling, no political connection, no partiality, no war, and no entangling alliances. What is wrong with the wisdom of Jefferson? How much wiser were the Founding Fathers than Bush, Cheney, Rumsfeld, Wolfowitz, Perle, Powell, Rice, and the other architects of the Iraq war!

What would a noninterventionist foreign policy look like? We haven't had one in so long that it might be hard to imagine what it would be like. Perhaps it would be better to consider what a noninterventionist foreign policy would not look like. Having a noninterventionist foreign policy doesn't mean that the United States should refuse to participate in the Olympics, refuse to make treaties, refuse to issue visas, refuse to trade with other countries, refuse to allow foreign investment, refuse to extradite criminals, refuse to mediate disputes, refuse to exchange diplomats, refuse to allow cultural exchanges, refuse to allow travel abroad, or refuse to allow immigration.

A noninterventionist foreign policy would not be an isolationist foreign policy. The word isolationism is a pejorative term of intimidation used to stifle debate over foreign policy. No advocate of nonintervention in foreign affairs wants to "build a fortified fence around the United States and retreat behind it"—as Clinton's national security adviser Sandy Berger smeared opponents of an interventionist U.S. foreign policy. In his 2006 State of the Union speech, President Bush did the same thing, thrice warning us of the danger of retreating into isolationism.

A noninterventionist foreign policy is a policy of peace, neutrality, and free trade. A noninterventionist foreign policy would mean no more invasions, no more threats, no more sanctions, no more embargoes, no more spies, no more meddling, no more bullying, no more foreign entanglements, no more entangling alliances, no more military advisors, no more troops and bases on foreign soil, no more NATO-like commitments, no more trying to be the world's social worker, fireman, and policeman, no more nation building, no more peacekeeping operations, no more spreading democracy at the point of a gun, no more regime changes, no more covert actions, no more forcibly opening markets, no more enforcing UN resolutions, no more liberations, and no more shooting, bombing, maiming, and killing. A noninterventionist foreign policy would also mean no foreign aid, no humanitarian aid, no disaster relief, and no payments to the United Nations, the International Monetary Fund, or the World Bank. Would a noninterventionist foreign policy mean that individual Americans could not or would not help foreigners? Of course not. But those who desire not to provide assistance should not be forced to pay for it with their tax dollars.

The United States cannot police the world. We have no right to police the world. It is the height of arrogance to try and remake the world in our image. Most of what happens in the world is none of our concern and certainly none of our business. It is not the responsibility of the United States to remove corrupt rulers and oppressive dictators from power. The kind of government a country has and the type of leader it has is the sole responsibility of the people in that country. There is absolutely no reason why the United States would be justified in attacking and invading a sovereign country—no matter what we thought of that country's ruler, system of government, treatment of women, economic policies, religious intolerance, or human rights record. If the people in a country don't like their ruler, then they should get rid of him themselves and not expect the United States to intervene. The truth of the matter is that the handful of men who hold political power in a country cannot in and of themselves compel that country's citizens to obey them in every respect. They have to have the cooperation of the people. If an individual American feels so strongly about one side in a civil war or border dispute, then he can send money to the side he favors, pray for one side to be victorious, or enlist in the army of his preferred side; that is, anything but call for sending in the U.S. Marines. How strange it is that advocates of U.S. military interventions consider us noninterventionists to be unpatriotic and anti-American when we are the ones concerned about the life of even one American being used as cannon fodder for the state. We never considered the shedding of the blood of even one American to be "worth" the latest lie that U.S. troops are dying for.

So what should the United States do? In the words of the late Murray Rothbard, the United States should "abandon its policy of global interventionism," "withdraw immediately and completely, militarily and politically, from everywhere," and "maintain a policy of strict political 'isolation' or neutrality everywhere." Political isolation is the only isolation we desire. Once we bring the troops home from around the globe, strict limits should be set to keep them home. Marine Corps Major General Smedley Butler recommended a Peace Amendment that would prohibit the removal of the Army from U.S. soil, limit the distance that Navy ships could steam from our coasts, and limit the distance that military aircraft could fly from our borders.

I would like to say something in conclusion about civil liberties. Intervention abroad cannot but follow intervention at home. There is no way a country can have hundreds of foreign bases and thousands of troops stationed overseas without a massive and oppressive bureaucracy at home. Conservative godfather and Cold Warrior William F. Buckley admitted as much back in the early 1950s: "We have to accept Big Government for the duration—for neither an offensive nor a defensive war can be waged given our present government skills except through the instrumentality of a totalitarian bureaucracy within our shores." Buckley went on to recommend that we support "large armies and air forces, atomic energy, central intelligence, war production boards and the attendant centralization of power in Washington." William Jennings Bryan articulated a better idea over one hundred years ago: "We assert that no nation can long endure half republic and half empire, and we warn the American people that imperialism abroad will lead quickly and inevitably to despotism at home."

The state uses war to strip its citizens of their liberties. The authority of the legislature and the force of law that, at least in principle, thwart government power in peacetime quickly diminish during times of war. The "father of the Constitution," James Madison, said about the relationship between war and civil liberty: "If tyranny and oppression come to this land, it will be in the guise of fighting a foreign enemy."

Throughout the twentieth century, interventionism was the guiding principle of U.S. foreign policy under either political party. The 9/11 attacks were just the beginning of a worldwide revolt against U.S. imperialism and empire. Of all people, Christians should know the truth and speak the truth about the evils of U.S. wars and foreign policy. They should see Bush's rhetoric about extending "the benefits of freedom across the globe" and enlarging "the realm of liberty" for what it is: plain, old-fashioned interventionism, pure and simple. Only a Jeffersonian foreign policy of peace, commerce, friendship, and no entangling alliances can cut the tentacles of U.S. global interventionism. Can any Christian honestly say that Bush's principles are better than Jefferson's principles?

* * * * *

WHAT HAPPENED TO THE SOUTHERN BAPTISTS?

> "We can see no just ground for the enormous military and naval establishment now being built up and maintained by our government." ~ Southern Baptist Convention, 1936

> "We express pride and strong support for our American military." ~ Southern Baptist Convention, 2004

What happened to the Southern Baptists?

The Southern Baptist Convention (SBC) is the largest Protestant denomination in the United States. The annual meeting of the SBC was held this year in San Antonio, Texas, on June 12 & 13. President Bush addressed the crowd of thousands of messengers via satellite with a nine-minute speech on the closing day "to multiple lengthy applauses and standing ovations," according to Baptist Press, the official news agency of the SBC.

Although he is not a Southern Baptist, Bush has addressed the SBC annual meeting, either by satellite or videotape, every year since 2002. The only exception was last year, when Secretary of State Condoleezza Rice, who is also not a Southern Baptist, spoke to the SBC messengers in person in Greensboro, North Carolina, because Bush made a secret trip to Iraq during the time of the SBC annual meeting in 2006.

Like he did in 2004 and 2005, the president mentioned Southern Baptist support for the military in his recent comments to the SBC messengers:

> I also appreciate the fact that Southern Baptists are supporting our brave men and women in uniform, and their families. I know you pray for their safety as they defend our people and extend the hope of freedom to the oppressed across the globe. I appreciate the fact you've sent care packages, and tend to the spiritual needs as military chaplains or kneel in prayer. I thank you as you support those who volunteer to serve our nation.

If the president were honest, he would have thanked the pastors at the annual meeting for supplying cannon fodder for the state in the form of their young men that they encouraged to join the military.

Southern Baptists have been some of the greatest supporters of Bush and his war. Richard Land, head of the SBC's Ethics & Religious Liberty Commission, "the public policy arm of the Southern Baptist Convention," is the author of the infamous "Land Letter" to President

Bush in October of 2002 which agreed that Bush's "policies concerning the ongoing international terrorist campaign against America are both right and just," and that Bush's "stated policy concerning using military force if necessary to disarm Saddam Hussein and his weapons of mass destruction is a just cause." The letter was also signed by other warvangelical, Republican Party operatives like Chuck Colson, Bill Bright, and D. James Kennedy.

And just recently, LifeWay Christian Resources (Southern Baptist) and Holman Bible Outreach International (an entity of LifeWay) joined with Task Force Patriot USA to sponsor a Memorial Day weekend tribute to active duty U.S. troops, veterans, and their families at Georgia's Stone Mountain Park. The tribute was called "Task Force Patriot Salute to the Troops." One of the many "military and civilian motivational speakers" was Bobby Welch, a former president of the SBC and a decorated Vietnam War veteran.

What was different about the SBC annual meeting this year is that there was no resolution passed expressing an opinion or concern about the president, the military, the wars in Iraq and Afghanistan, or the war on terrorism. However, this does not mean that the messengers to the SBC annual meeting are now anti-war activists. None of the pro-war/pro-military resolutions issued from 2002 to 2006 were repudiated in a resolution like the 1996 resolution that apologized to Blacks for "condoning and/or perpetuating individual and systemic racism in our lifetime."

In 2006 a resolution was passed "On Prayer for The President and The Military," which states in part that whereas:

- Our nation is currently engaged in a global war on terrorism, and our military is fighting against a determined and fanatical enemy that is threatening the liberty and security of our nation and of the world; and
- The determined efforts of President George W. Bush and the sacrificial actions of our military personnel have resulted in Afghanistan, formerly under an oppressive regime, and Iraq, formerly under a brutal dictatorship, holding free and democratic elections and developing their own constitutional governments;

It is resolved:

- That we also express our appreciation for the military chaplains,

who encourage service personnel to seek God in prayer;
- That we encourage all Southern Baptists to pray without ceasing for the president and all of our military personnel, especially those who are serving in areas of great danger (1 Thessalonians 5:17);
- That we not only continue praying for all our military families, but that we also continue ministering to them in the name of Jesus, especially those grieving families of military personnel who have paid the ultimate price for our national freedom, remembering that Jesus laid down His life for us and paid the ultimate price for our spiritual freedom (John 15:13).

In 2005 a resolution was passed "On Appreciation of Our Troops and President," which states in part that whereas:

- Members of the United States military and allied forces continue to be aggressively engaged in the ongoing global war on terror;
- Our troops play a vital role in preserving and protecting freedom in the United States and throughout the world;
- The sacrificial efforts of our military personnel have made it possible for some nations formerly ruled by dictators to hold democratic elections, ushering in a new era of freedom for the people of those nations;

It is resolved:

- That the messengers to the Southern Baptist Convention meeting in Nashville, Tennessee, June 21–22, 2005, express appreciation to our servicemen and servicewomen in all branches of the military who are serving faithfully and honorably, both at home and abroad;
- That we encourage Southern Baptists to pray for the safety and well-being of our military personnel at all times;
- That we express pride and strong support for our American military and eagerly anticipate the day our troops return home upon successful completion of their missions;
- That we express deepest gratitude and respect for our president in light of the gravity of the decisions he must make and the leadership role he fills;
- That we encourage all Southern Baptists to pray regularly for our president and to stand with him in opposing global terrorism

as he makes decisions that potentially impact the entire earth.

In 2004 a resolution was passed "On Appreciation of Our American Military," which states in part that whereas:

- Members of the United States military serve our country faithfully, both at home and abroad, maintaining peace throughout the world, and are aggressively engaged in the global war on terror;
- Each of our service personnel plays a vital role in preserving freedom in the United States and throughout the world;
- Each American service man and woman is called upon to protect and preserve the freedom we hold dear;

It is resolved:

- That the messengers to the Southern Baptist Convention meeting in Indianapolis, Indiana, June 15–16, 2004, express appreciation to our service men and women in all branches of the military who are serving faithfully and honorably, both at home and abroad;
- That we encourage Southern Baptists to pray for the safety and well-being of our military personnel at all times, with particular attention to those who are in harm's way;
- That we express pride and strong support for our American military.

In 2003 a resolution was passed "On the Liberation of Iraq," which states in part that whereas:

- The Iraqi people have suffered for decades under the oppressive and autocratic regime of Saddam Hussein;
- The Iraqi regime was marked by repression, intimidation, mass murder, and extreme hostility to the most basic human rights of its people;
- Saddam Hussein repeatedly defied the demands of the international community to verify Iraqi compliance with United Nations resolutions against the proliferation of weapons of mass destruction;
- We believe Operation Iraqi Freedom was a warranted action based upon historic principles of just war;

It is resolved:

- That the messengers to the Southern Baptist Convention meeting in Phoenix, Arizona, June 17–18, 2003, affirm President George W. Bush, the United States Congress, and our armed forces for their leadership in the successful execution of Operation Iraqi Freedom;
- That we commend the valiant and sacrificial service of the men and women of our armed forces and the ministry of our chaplains;
- That we call on Southern Baptists to pray for our troops and our diplomatic leaders as they aid in the rebuilding of the nation of Iraq;

In 2002 a resolution was passed "On the War on Terrorism," which states in part that whereas:

- Following the ruthless and wicked attack on America on September 11, 2001, our nation was forced to respond in self-defense with a war on international terrorism;
- It has become increasingly clear that a vast, international terrorist network exists, which is allied with regimes that sponsor and support its evil goals;
- Terrorist groups and their state sponsors threaten to continue their assault on innocent people and to escalate this terror through the use of instruments of mass destruction-including chemical, biological, and nuclear weapons;

It is resolved:

- That the messengers to the Southern Baptist Convention meeting in St. Louis, Missouri, June 11–12, 2002, declare our abhorrence of these horrific acts of international terrorism;
- That we applaud the moral clarity of the President of the United States in his denunciation of terrorist groups as "evildoers" who must be resisted;
- That we wholeheartedly support the actions of the United States government, its intelligence agencies, and its military, in the just war against the terrorist networks and their state sponsors;
- That we urge our President, our congressional leaders, and our military authorities, in a renewed spirit of American unity, to

> address the growing threat of terrorist-supportive nations and the vicious quest to attain weapons of mass destruction;

What happened to the Southern Baptists?

None of the resolutions having anything to do with war or the military issued by the Southern Baptists at their annual meeting since they began the practice in 1845 read anything like the resolutions on those subjects passed since 2002. Even when the United States was fighting "real wars," the SBC was a voice for peace and against militarism.

During the midst of the so-called Civil War, although a resolution was passed in 1863 which expressed support for the Confederacy and the "just and necessary war," the Southern Baptists also stated that they deplored "the dreadful evils of the war" and that they earnestly desired peace. They further acknowledged that their "sins have deserved the terrible calamities that God has sent upon us."

The Southern Baptists passed no resolutions related to the president, the war, or the military during the Spanish-American War or its aftermath.

In 1907 a resolution on world peace was passed which resolved:

> That we look with devout gratitude to Almighty God upon the advance throughout the wide world of the cause of peace, for "Peace hath her victories no less renowned than war"; and we desire and will pray for the day to hasten when all nations will settle their difficulties by arbitration rather than the resort to arms; and the song of the angels at the advent of Christ be fully realized—"Peace on earth, good will to men."

In 1911 another resolution on peace was issued which not only stated that "no good nor satisfactory reasons can be found for war between civilized and Christian nations," but also that "war is a scourge, is wrong in principle and morally corrupting." It was resolved that "as Southern Baptists we will talk up peace and talk down war; that we will pray God for universal peace."

After the United States entered World War I in 1917, although the Southern Baptists passed a resolution which resolved that they "pledge to our President and government, our prayers, our loyal and sacrificial support in the war in which we are engaged," the same resolution also stated that "there has come upon earth a spirit which has plunged the nations that have been considered foremost in the lines of advancing civilization into a war more ruthless and more destructive of human life and human happiness than the world has ever before known." Three things were then resolved:

- That we deeply deplore this awful and sorrowful calamity which has caused these leading nations to drench the earth in the precious blood of their own loyal citizens.
- That we reaffirm our faith in the righteousness of the Sermon on the Mount, and our confidence and infallible wisdom of him who has taught us to love our enemies, to bless them that curse us, and to do good to them that despitefully use and persecute us.
- That we desire a stronger faith in the God who maketh wars to cease even unto the ends of the earth, and we shall rejoice if our own people, and all of every name who love the Lord Jesus Christ, in sincerity, shall find it in their hearts to pray for kings and for all that are in authority that we may live quiet and peaceable lives in all godliness and honesty.

After the Great War, a resolution on peace and disarmament was issued in 1921 which, after recognizing that "the matter of the reconstruction of the world upon a permanent peace basis, is the supreme question of the present," resolved "that, as a Convention of Christians, we are glad to join other bodies in an endorsement of this seemingly, practical movement toward disarmament with the hope and prayer that our torn and bleeding world may be restored to peace under the guidance and benediction of the Prince of Peace."

In 1929 a Social Service Committee Recommendation was adopted which resolved:

> That we approve and commend the action of the United States Senate in ratifying the multilateral Briand-Kellogg Peace Treaty; that we rejoice in the outlawry of war embodied in this treaty; that we condemn recourse to war for the solution of international controversies and we pledge our support to the government in this renouncement of war and in seeking by every worthy and legitimate means to promote and maintain permanent international peace.

In 1932 another Social Service Committee Recommendation was adopted which resolved:

> That we oppose the continued large expenditure by the Government for military and naval equipment; that we oppose military

> training in the schools and colleges, whether denominational or state; and that we favor full and complete disarmament as rapidly as it can possibly be accomplished, except such armament as may be absolutely necessary for police duty within our own territory and on our borders. Moreover, we reaffirm our hearty approval of the international agreement to renounce war as a national policy and our gratitude at the growing conviction among Christians of the incompatibility of war with the ethical principles of our Lord Jesus Christ.

In 1933 the first of several major peace resolutions was issued. Among other things, it resolved:

- That we pledge anew our devotion to the cause of International Good Will and World Peace and that we urge upon our pastors and people the obligations of their stewardship, both as the advocates and as the exemplars of the spirit of peace and good will toward all men.
- That we again declare our unwavering belief that the United States Senate ought to ratify without further delay the protocol of the International Court of Justice, commonly known as the World Court, so that our government may have official representation on that Court and may contribute directly and officially to the maintenance and promotion of World Peace. This has been recommended repeatedly by several Presidents, has been concurred in by each of the major political parties, and is demanded we believe by a great majority of the American people. We can see no sound reason for continued delay by the Senate and we urge prompt action.

Another was issued in 1935, which resolved:

- That we hereby declare our unalterable opposition to war and our devotion to the maintenance of peace among the nations of the world.
- That we approve of the investigation of the operations and methods of armament and munition manufacturers, conducted by a committee of the United States Senate headed by Senator Nye, with a view to formulating legislation which shall end the military racket and take the profit out of war; we desire to see this investigation carried to completion and to see it result in appropriate and effective legislation.

A major statement on war, peace, and the military was published in 1936. Its five points were:

- That we reaffirm our belief in and devotion to international peace and to the spirit of peace both for individuals and nations as embodied in the teachings and exemplified by the spirit of Christ our Lord.
- That we reaffirm also our utter opposition to and hatred of war as the most inexcusable and insane policy that could be pursued by the nations of the earth in their dealings with one another, destructive not only of human life and treasure but of all that is high and worthy in human ideals and objectives.
- That we pledge ourselves as citizens and Christians that we will not support our government in any war except such as might be necessary to repel invasion of our land or to preserve fundamental human rights and liberties.
- That we can see no just ground for the enormous military and naval establishment now being built up and maintained by our government at the expense of approximately one billion dollars a year, and that we look with disfavor both upon this establishment as being in the nature of a challenge to other countries and contributing to the war spirit and upon the huge and unnecessary tax burden laid upon the shoulders of people already overburdened with taxation.
- That we again express our belief that the Protocol of the Court of International Justice, commonly known as the World Court, with the reservations already made by the United States Senate, should be ratified by the Senate and that we all give our influence to that end.

In a 1937 resolution on war and peace, it was first stated:

- That we believe that the great world powers having outlawed war by treaty and having committed themselves to the policy of the peaceful settlement of all international disagreements can and ought to find solution of all their problems without the arbitrament of arms.
- As citizens of the United States we will do everything possible to keep our nation out of war, and we reaffirm our opposition to all aggressive war at home or abroad.

And then it was resolved, regarding international relationships:

- We recognize that a warless world is the Christian ideal and that we Christians should throw all our weight and power into the balance for peace.
- That we petition the President of the United States to consider the advisability of calling a conference of world powers to consider the possibility of disarmament, believing that this would do much to relieve strained international relationships which are endangering world peace at the present time.

A resolution was issued in 1939 that expressed a "deep sense of regret and dissatisfaction with the large part American manufacturers and merchants are having in the revolting, inhuman and barbaric invasion and spoliation of China by Japan." The messengers to the 1939 SBC annual meeting were "especially concerned over the fact that Americans are sharing so largely in this unholy work and without interference by the American Government." The members of the SBC churches were enjoined to "write to their representatives in both Houses of Congress, earnestly urging action to stop American participation in this war of conquest." And regarding international relations, the messengers pledged themselves "anew to the spirit of peace and to the cultivation of that spirit among our people and in our relation to all other peoples." It was even suggested that SBC churches set up and maintain peace committees "for the dissemination of information and the cultivation of the spirit of peace."

After World War II had begun in Europe, a strong anti-war statement was issued in June of 1940 which, among other things, resolved:

- That we hereby express our utter abhorrence of war as an instrument of International policy and our profound conviction and belief that all International differences could and of a right ought to be composed by peaceful diplomatic exchanges, and, when these fail, by arbitration.
- That the continued sacrifice of human treasure and human blood in International war is a wanton and wicked waste for which nations, and particularly their rulers who declare and prosecute war, must give an account to the All Wise and All Just Judge of all the earth.
- That the extremes of human slaughter to which the present mechanized war has gone staggers human belief and is a sad

illustration of how all scientific knowledge and development, which should contribute only to human welfare, can be debased and devoted to human destruction.

- That while we acknowledge the right of national self-defense, our utter abhorrence of war and its attendant evils compels us to voice the conviction that even a defensive war should be waged only as a last resort after every effort has been made to reach a settlement of international problems in fairness to all the nations involved.

Also included was a lengthy statement about supporting conscientious objectors:

> Baptists have always believed in liberty of conscience and have honored men who were willing to brave adverse public opinion for the sake of conscientious scruples. A considerable number of members of churches of our Convention, through their interpretation of the moral teachings of Christ, have reached the position of a conscientious objection to war that prohibits them from bearing arms.
>
> The Convention ought to accord to them the right of their convictions as it accords to others the right to differ from them, and ought to protect them in that right to the extent of its ability. Therefore,
>
> Be it RESOLVED, That the Convention go on record as recognizing such right of a conscientious objection, and that the Convention instruct the Executive Committee to provide facilities for their registration with the denomination, in order that the Executive Committee may be able to make accurate certification to the government concerning them at any time it should be called for.

Included in this 1940 resolution was also this notable closing statement:

> Because war is contrary to the mind and spirit of Christ, we believe that no war should be identified with the will of Christ. Our churches should not be made agents of war propaganda or recruiting stations. War thrives on and is perpetuated by hysteria, falsehood, and hate and the church has a solemn responsibility to make sure there is no black out of love in time of war. When men and nations are going mad with hate it is the duty of Christ's ministers and His churches to declare by spirit, word, and conduct

> the love of God in all men. In time of war it is our Christian responsibility to prepare for peace. We would, therefore, urge our churches to think and work toward a Christian social order in which a just and lasting peace can be realized.

On the eve of U.S. involvement in World War II, the longest peace resolution the Southern Baptists ever published was issued in 1941. At this meeting in Birmingham, Alabama, it was resolved:

- That we declare our abhorrence of war and all its insanity and brutality. We are a peace-loving people and we know of no issues, national or international, which could not be settled in fairness and equity by the orderly processes of civilized society if only the leaders of the nations were willing to practice the principles of justice, truth, and righteousness. We sincerely believe that the rank and file of our denomination, even as the rank and file of our nation and the other nations as well, much prefer that all international disputes and conflicting interests be composed by the processes of peace rather than by the arbitrament of war.
- That with one accord we turn to Almighty God, through Christ his Son, in humble petition for the forgiveness of whatever measure of corporate guilt may be ours with regard to the present international conflict, and, that our nation, through repentance and faith in the Lord Jesus Christ may be so yielded to the Divine Plan, that we may be effectively used in helping to bring to the nations of the world a just and righteous peace.
- That we invite the membership of our churches and all Christian believers throughout the world, to pray daily at a given hour, both in public and in private places, to the end that such a "just and righteous peace" may be speedily achieved.

The messengers to this SBC annual meeting made a pledge

> as Christian patriots to pray earnestly unto our God and Saviour that a righteous peace may soon be granted unto all the warring nations: that our own nation may be spared the horrors of war, if that be the divine will, and that our nation may be used as a mighty instrument of peace and truth and righteousness and brotherhood; that Almighty God will, in the power of his might, take charge of the nations and overrule their folly and sin to the praise of his great and holy name.

It was also recognized that "there may be honest differences of opinion about the issue in the present conflict, but we are deeply resolved that any difference shall not cause any breach in our fellowship." Contrast this attitude with that of the modern Christian Right. In some circles, if one opposes Bush and his war then he is said to part of the "blame-America-first crowd," and ridiculed with epithets like traitor, defeatist, defeatocrat, appeaser, communist, liberal, Quaker, pacifist, and peacenik.

Because this resolution mentioned the evils that were then occurring in the world, desired the U.S. government "to work out the wisest and most effective means to aid England, our national ally, in this titanic struggle," and urged the government "to quicken rather than slacken all measures needed to strengthen the defenses of the Western Hemisphere against all kinds of aggression from any and all powers which seek to undermine and to overthrow our peaceful and democratic ways of life," a clarifying statement was added disavowing militarism: "The aforesaid resolution may be misinterpreted by some as a committal to the principle of militarism, Therefore, be it resolved that the aforesaid resolution, in no way commits the Southern Baptist Convention to an approval of war, as a recognized principle in settling international differences."

Although the United States entered World War II at the end of 1941, the Southern Baptists throughout the war issued no resolutions expressing support for the president or the troops. Surprisingly, there was no resolution having anything to do with the war that was published in 1942 and 1945. In 1943, although it was acknowledged that "Southern Baptists as loyal citizens of the United States are cooperating and participating in all branches of the present war, including the Army, the Navy and the Air Corps," it was also stated that "the prosecution of the war for the maintenance, perpetuation and extension of the four freedoms, well known and enjoyed by American citizens in our Constitutional Democracy, may not accomplish the purposes for which it is fought, unless a just and righteous peace follows the termination of the war." In 1944, instead of expressing support for the troops, the Convention resolved to support conscientious objectors working in civilian camps under the supervision of the National Service Board.

Between World War II and the Vietnam War, the Southern Baptists issued numerous resolutions that advocated world peace, reaffirmed the basic incompatibility of war with the moral principles and purposes of Christianity, denounced the moral conditions in American military camps abroad, condemned militarism, expressed support for conscientious objectors and exempting religious teachers from conscription, and expressed opposition to peacetime conscription, not only in the United States, but worldwide.

After the escalation of U.S. involvement in Vietnam, peace resolutions were issued during the years from 1966 to 1973. And instead of putting out resolutions during the Vietnam years in appreciation of the president and the troops, support for conscientious objectors was reaffirmed. In 1969 a resolution was issued which stated that "those who for reasons of religious conviction are opposed to military service should be exempted from forced military conscription." In 1972 the Southern Baptists acknowledged support for "both our youth who, as a matter of conscience, choose to participate in war and those who, as a matter of conscience, object to participation in war, extending them assistance in exercising their rights and privileges as permitted under law."

The Southern Baptists issued another peace resolution in 1974. In 1977 an anti-torture resolution was issued that condemned "any use of torture as a sin against God and a crime against humanity." It was further affirmed that "torture demonstrates the very opposite of love and violates the will of God revealed in Jesus Christ." It is too bad that no such resolution was produced after the Abu Ghraib scandal. Various resolutions supporting arms control were issued by the Southern Baptists from 1978 to 1983.

Things began to change in 1991. You will recall that that was the year in which the United States invaded Iraq the first time. Although the war had ended long before the SBC annual meeting in June, a resolution was still issued which resolved:

- That we the messengers to the Southern Baptist Convention meeting in Atlanta, Georgia, June 4–6, 1991, commend and salute the President of the United States as Commander-in-Chief of the Armed Forces, the Joint Chiefs of Staff, the commanders in the field, and the men and women of every military rank for their preparedness and resolve, their commitment to duty and to country, their fortitude in the face of danger, and their overwhelming victory in Operation Desert Storm;
- That we especially honor those who died in the conflict for their ultimate sacrifice in the cause of freedom and that we offer our heartfelt sympathy and gratitude to their families;
- That we express reverent thanksgiving to Almighty God, the Judge of all nations, who is mightier than all armies and who alone is able to save, for His guidance, His mercy, and His blessing on our nation in Operation Desert Storm.

What happened to the Southern Baptists? Their overwhelming support for the U.S.-initiated Persian Gulf War shows that they fully accepted the government's new enemy after the end of the Cold War: Saddam Hussein. Thus began their descent down the slippery slope of militarism, presidential aggrandizement, and statolatry. The transformation was made complete in 2001.

What happened to the Southern Baptists? The events of September 11, 2001, apparently "changed everything." Yet, after the fiasco that is the war in Iraq has been scrupulously exposed many times over, no change in opinion has been forthcoming from the SBC. Instead, the man most responsible for the war is welcomed with applause and ovation. But there is one thing that the events of September 11th didn't change-the reckless, belligerent, and meddling U.S. foreign policy responsible for the blowback we suffered on that date, and will inevitably experience again since our militaristic, interventionist foreign policy likewise shows no sign of changing.

* * * * *

THE DOCTRINE OF A CHRISTIAN WARMONGER

I have maintained throughout the war in Iraq that, even though it is Christianity above all religions that should be opposed to the evils of war, in the Church will be found some of the greatest supporters of the current war. I have also maintained that much of the blame for Christian support for Bush and his war must be laid at the feet of the pastors, preachers, and priests who have failed to discern the truth and educate their congregations.

Yes, Christians are ultimately responsible for their support for or indifference to the latest government war. Yes, Christians should not blindly follow their governmental and religious leaders. Yes, Christians should be following the biblical admonition to "prove all things" (1 Thessalonians 5:21). And yes, Christians should be accessing the abundance of alternative news sources that are available. But it is Christian leaders—many of whom could double as Republican Party operatives without changing their sermons—that bear special responsibility for the attitudes of love for the military, respect for the government, adoration of the president, and contempt for human life that exists among many Christians in the pew.

A typical example of a Christian leader who spouts pro-war propaganda from the pulpit is Pastor Tod Kennedy of the Spokane Bible

Church in Spokane, Washington. His attempt to justify Bush and his war can be seen in the seventeen-proposition presentation he calls "The Doctrine of God and War." A better title would be "The Doctrine of a Christian Warmonger."

Kennedy's First Proposition: Three Sources of War

Kennedy does not get off to a good start. His three sources of war turn out to be just two: man and Satan. "Man has a sinful nature," and Satan is "the temporary ruler of this world" and has "his own world system which he promotes." Kennedy's third source of war should have been God himself. How could he forget that "The LORD is a man of war" (Exodus 15:3)? What a perfect verse to bring up so that it could be twisted to justify the Iraq War! Jerry Falwell did exactly that. True, God brought the Jews "out of the land of Egypt by their armies" (Exodus 12:2), and true, God commanded the nation of Israel in the Old Testament to fight against heathen nations (Judges 6:16), but George Bush is not God, and America is not the nation of Israel. So, even if Kennedy were smart enough to include God as a source of war, it still would not follow that God sponsored the war in Iraq and that we should pray that he would bless our troops. It would not follow unless, of course, one was a Christian apologist for Bush and his war.

Kennedy's Second Proposition: War: A Continuing Fact of Life

Kennedy correctly states that "wars will continue to be fought and rumors of wars will continue to spread throughout the world until Jesus Christ personally rules the earth in the Millennial Kingdom." True, but what is implied here is that Christians shouldn't oppose the war in Iraq. But just because wars have been fought since the beginning of time and will be fought until the end of time doesn't mean that Christians should advocate them, defend them, or participate in them. Many evil things are continuing facts of life: murder, adultery, theft, assault. Should Christians just excuse them as inevitable and never speak out against them? Should Christians justify participation in them because they are expected? Obviously not. So why is war treated differently? Why do some Christians with an otherwise "sound mind" (2 Timothy 1:7) turn into babbling idiots when it comes to the subjects of war, the military, and killing for the state?

Kennedy's Third Proposition: Only Spiritual Peace Is Possible Now

Once again Kennedy makes a correct statement: "There will be no world peace before Christ returns, but there can be spiritual peace." But once again it is obvious—based on the design of his whole presentation—that he is implying that Christian indifference to, defense of, and participation in war is acceptable because there will be no world peace before Christ returns. Not only should Kennedy have pointed out that "being justified by faith, we have peace with God through our Lord Jesus Christ" (Romans 5:1), he should have pointed out that, even though there will be no world peace until the return of Christ, Christians are admonished in the New Testament about how they can and should live in peace:

- Blessed are the peacemakers (Matthew 5:9)
- Live peaceably with all men (Romans 12:18)
- Follow peace with all men (Hebrews 12:14)

True, there will be no world peace before Christ returns, but this doesn't mean that Christians should contribute to the lack thereof.

Kennedy's Fourth Proposition: Preparation for War Reduces Warfare

History has shown that it is in fact the exact opposite that is true: Preparation for war increases warfare. Kennedy comments: "War is an unwanted but real part of human history, and those who recognize this and prepare for war will have more freedom, more prosperity, and more peace than those who do not prepare and try to avoid war at any price (Numbers 10.9; Judges 3.1–2; Ecclesiastes 3.8; Nehemiah 4.7–22; Psalm 144.1; Proverbs 20.18; Proverbs 24.6)." The U.S. government is preparing for war more now than at any time in history. After a study of Bush's budget proposals for fiscal year 2008, economist Robert Higgs reported that "for now, however, the conclusion seems inescapable: the government is currently spending at the rate of approximately $1 trillion per year for all defense-related purposes." It is preparing for defense that reduces warfare—just look at Switzerland. Has the United States preparing for war brought us more freedom? Mr. Kennedy must never have flown on an airplane in the last few years. The U.S. government has worked overtime to destroy our freedoms since the adoption of the tyrannical USA PATRIOT Act in 2001. American freedom, prosperity, and peace diminish the more that the U.S. government prepares for war.

Kennedy's Fifth Proposition: To Kill in Battle Is Not Murder

This is one of Kennedy's most dangerous propositions. Yes, to kill in battle is not murder according to federal and state legal codes, but this is not what he is saying. Kennedy is trying to sanctify killing for the state. His first comment about his fifth proposition makes this clear: "The killing of the enemy in war is not murder, nor a sin of any kind. Exodus 20.13 refers to murder." To prove that the sixth commandment is limited to just murder, Kennedy, like all Christian warmongers, refers to the Hebrew word underlying the prohibition against killing in the sixth commandment: "The Hebrew word RATSACH, Strong #7523 means murder or manslaughter." [I should point out that "Strong" is a reference to Strong's Concordance, which contains dictionaries of Hebrew and Greek words used in the Bible.] Since I have examined in great detail the "sixth commandment only prohibits murder" argument in a previous article, "The Unholy Desire of Christians to Legitimize Killing in War," I would refer the reader to it, and also to the articles "Humpty Dumpty Religion" and "Is It or Isn't It?" But what of Kennedy's ghastly proposal that it is not "a sin of any kind" to kill someone in war? He did not say killing in a just war or a defensive war (as if there's a difference) was not a sin, he said "in war." He did not specify whether the "enemy" one could kill was real or merely a creation of the U.S. government. Is Kennedy saying that it is not a sin to travel thousands of miles from U.S. soil and kill someone who was not a threat to any Americans until the United States invaded his country because the government says he is the enemy and must be killed? I believe he is. But if killing the enemy in war is not a sin, then Iraqis who kill American soldiers are not sinning either. After all, they are fighting a defensive war against a real enemy who invaded them. Contrary to Kennedy, I believe that killing someone in a preemptive war is a grave sin, even if that someone is a Muslim infidel.

Kennedy's Sixth Proposition: OT Biblical Words for Kill

Here Kennedy lists three Old Testament Hebrew words that refer to killing:

- NAKAH, Strong #5221 legitimate killing in battle, to smite, sometimes with penalty.
- RATSACH, Strong # 7523 command against murder. Also used for nonpremeditated killing.
- HARAG, Strong #2026, to kill by intention or accident.

And his point is? Although his intention is probably to show that "the original Hebrew" makes it clear that there are different types of killing in the Bible, Kennedy, like all wannabe Hebrew scholars, is saying nothing but look at how smart I am since I mentioned some Hebrew words.

Kennedy's Seventh Proposition: NT Biblical Words for Kill

Here Kennedy lists two New Testament Greek words that refer to killing:

- PHONEUO, Strong #5407, murder.
- APOKTEINO, Strong #615, to kill, slay, put to death.

Once again, Kennedy is trying to impress us with his knowledge of the original languages. And once again he is saying nothing. In fact, he forgot to mention the other Greek words in the New Testament for kill: *anaireo, thuo, thanatoo, diacheirizomai,* and *sphazo.*

Kennedy's Eighth Proposition: God Is Not Anti-War

This is a very vague and misleading statement. If God is not anti-war, then would it not mean that he would approve of China warring against Taiwan, India warring against Pakistan, and Russia warring against Chechnya? I presume it would also mean that God has not had a problem with any war that has ever been fought since he created man. Obviously, this is not what Kennedy means. So why doesn't he just come out and say that he thinks God approves of the war in Iraq? Or if he really wanted to be honest, he could say that he believes God endorses all American wars. But did not Kennedy begin his presentation with the proposition that war occurs because "man has a sinful nature" and Satan rules the world and promotes his world system? How, then, can he claim that God is not anti-war? Kennedy's proof that God is not anti-war is that he "sponsors just wars" in the Old Testament to:

- Remove degenerate nations (Jericho—Joshua 5.13–Joshua 6; Ai—Joshua 8)
- To defeat the enemies of Israel (Hagrites—1 Chronicles 5.18–22)
- To protect families and nations (Nehemiah 4)
- To gain peace (Ehud and Moabites—Judges 3.26–30)

Although God sponsored these wars, and used his chosen nation (Deuteronomy 7:6–7) to conduct them, it does not follow that God sponsors American wars or that America is God's chosen nation. It does not follow unless, of course, one is a Christian apologist for the U.S. government and its wars.

Kennedy's Ninth Proposition: Military Service Is Necessary

Necessary for what? Necessary for whom? All Kennedy says is this: "It is necessary to gain national freedom, then to preserve national freedom (Numbers 1.2–3; Numbers 31.1–5; Joshua 1.6–11; 11.23; Judges 8.1; 1 Chronicles 5.22; Psalm 18.34; Luke 14.31)." First of all, the fact that Kennedy listed a number of Scripture references here means absolutely nothing. Satan quoted Scripture when he tempted the Lord (Matthew 4:5). The first five Old Testament references given by Kennedy all concern the necessity of military service for certain members of the nation of Israel. The verse in First Chronicles simply states that a particular war "was of God." The verse in Psalms concerned King David personally. The lone reference in the New Testament was to an illustration given by the Lord in which he mentioned a king warring against another king. Kennedy is "handling the word of God deceitfully" (2 Corinthians 4:2). Americans have only twice in their history served in the military to "gain national freedom": the Revolutionary War and the War for Southern Independence. One of the greatest myths in America today is that the U.S. military exists to "preserve national freedom." The U.S. military is focused on fighting foreign wars, peacekeeping operations, regime changes, nation building, providing security for factions in foreign countries, humanitarian concerns, disaster relief, enforcing UN resolutions, and otherwise intervening in the affairs of other countries-anything but defending our freedoms. It is not necessary for any American Christian to join the U.S. military for any reason-except, of course, to get money for college.

Kennedy's Tenth Proposition: Military Service Is Honorable

Kennedy is on shaky ground here. He begins with the statement: "There is nothing in the New Testament prohibiting military service, training, or war." Well, there is nothing in the New Testament prescribing them either. Just like there is nothing in the New Testament condemning or commending abortion or smoking marijuana. Kennedy continues:

"Christ, Luke, and Paul assume that military service is an honorable profession; they accept the normal function of the military for national readiness, defense, and waging of legitimate war."

- Christ (Matthew 8.5–10; Luke 14.31)
- Luke (Acts 10.1–3, 22–25)
- Paul (Acts 23.11–35; 1 Corinthians 9.7; 2 Timothy 2.3–4)

The bare fact that Christ, Luke, and Paul mentioned soldiers and warfare does not necessarily mean that they considered military service to be an honorable profession. Christ elsewhere referred to publicans and harlots (Matthew 21:31). Does Kennedy consider them to be honorable professions? Likewise, Solomon in the Old Testament mentioned the drunkard and the glutton (Proverbs 23:21). Should we aspire to be like them? In the above Scripture passages, Christ and Paul each cite warfare in a neutral sense when giving an illustration. Paul additionally refers to spiritual soldiers of Christ. We know from Paul elsewhere that the weapons of these soldiers are not carnal (2 Corinthians 10:4), and that they are armed with "the sword of the spirit, which is the word of God" (Ephesians 6:17). But what about the actual soldiers described by Christ, Luke, and Paul? These are centurions. There are at least eleven of them mentioned in the New Testament. They are generally spoken of in a positive or neutral sense, except for the one who stood by when Paul was beaten (Acts 22:25) and the one who "believed the master and the owner of the ship, more than those things which were spoken by Paul" (Acts 27:11). I wonder why Kennedy didn't bring up some other soldiers in the New Testament, like the ones who mocked, stripped, spit on, smote, and crucified the Lord Jesus (Matthew 27:27–35), the ones who cast lots for his garments (John 19:23–24), the ones who took bribes to say his body was stolen (Matthew 28:12–15), and the one who thrust a spear in his side (John 19:34)? Kennedy is very selective about which soldiers are honorable. If military service is an honorable profession, then was serving as an SS officer an "honorable profession"? What about serving as a guard at Auschwitz? Kennedy is implying that it is honorable to serve in the U.S. military. But regardless of whether it was at one time honorable to serve in the military of some country, and regardless of whether it was at one time honorable to serve in the military of the United States, it is certainly not honorable now to serve in the U.S. military in any capacity. Moreover, is it "normal" for a nation's military to station its military in three fourths of the world's countries? What do U.S. troops overseas in 150 different regions of the world have to do with "national readiness, defense, and waging of legitimate war"? Kennedy also remarks that "God even commends those who wage war against aggressors (Hebrews 11.22–34)." Does he think that no one will bother to check the Scripture passages he lists to buttress his propositions? Hebrews 11:22–34 is part of a series in which is mentioned instances of the faith of some famous Old Testament characters. Hebrews 11:22 is about Joseph and his bones. Hebrews 11:23–27 concerns Moses being hid when he was born, refusing to be called Pharaoh's grandson, choosing to suffer with his people, forsaking Egypt, and keeping the Passover. Hebrews 11:29 refers to the nation of Israel going through the Red Sea. Hebrews 11:30 tells about the walls of Jericho falling down. Hebrews 11:31 brings up the harlot Rahab receiving spies with peace. Hebrews 11:32 mentions the names of Gideon, Barak, Samson, Jephthah, David, Samuel, and "the prophets." It is only when we get to Kennedy's last two verses that we see something that is remotely related to someone waging "war against aggressors." Hebrews 11:33–34 tells us that these individuals "subdued kingdoms," "waxed valiant in fight," and "turned to flight the armies of the aliens." True, they did wage war against aggressors, but that is not the whole story. They were Jews who waged war against the people that God told them to wage war against. They were not Christians fighting a crusade against Islamofascism. And by no stretch of the imagination do their actions imply that God wants the U.S. military to wage war against Iraqis. If God "commends those who wage war against aggressors," then he should be pouring out his blessings on Iraq since it is the United States that is clearly the aggressor. Does this mean that Iraqis are justified in killing U.S. soldiers? It would have to. So Kennedy is not only dishonest, he is once again "handling the word of God deceitfully" (2 Corinthians 4:2).

Kennedy's Eleventh Proposition: Jesus Christ is a Battlefield Commander

This proposition seems to be provocative, but is nevertheless true, as Kennedy explains:

> Jesus Christ has in the past and will in the future serve as a battlefield commander. He is called "LORD of Hosts" or "LORD of the Armies" and "a warrior." He has killed thousands of enemy soldiers and will do so in the future (Exodus 14.13–14, 25; 15.3; Isaiah 37.33–37; Zechariah 14.1–5; Revelation 19.11–15).

The enemy soldiers referenced in the past are the Egyptians and the Assyrians; the ones in the future are rebellious nations at the Second

Advent of Christ. The problem here is a simple one: American military officers are not surrogates for Jesus Christ. Whatever Jesus Christ did or will do has absolutely no relevance to what the U. S. military does in Iraq or anywhere else, except, of course, in the depraved mind of a Christian warmonger. The Bible says that "in righteousness" Jesus Christ "doth judge and make war." There is nothing righteous about the actions of U.S. battlefield commanders.

Kennedy's Twelfth Proposition: Bully Nations and Aggressors

Here Kennedy makes a true statement: "Bully nations and aggressors use propaganda to persuade other nations not to resist their attacks. The propaganda appeals to the cowards and 'peace at any price people' (Isaiah 36–37)." The chapters he references in Isaiah concern Sennacherib the king of Assyria and Hezekiah the king of Israel. Assyria was the bully and aggressor nation, and did use propaganda. However, Hezekiah prayed to the Lord and the angel of the Lord smote the Assyrians, not the Israeli army, so no parallel can be drawn to the U.S. military fighting against bully and aggressor nations. And regarding bully nations, with hundreds of bases on foreign soil and troops in 150 different locations around the world, it is the United States that is the biggest bully on the block. We are the largest and most dangerous aggressor nation-just ask two million dead Vietnamese and Cambodians if you ever get the chance.

Kennedy's Thirteenth Proposition: Unjust Aggression Is Wrong

Since Kennedy remarks here: "The Lord is against unjust aggression," he ought to be speaking out about how God is against the United States since the Iraq War is nothing but unjust aggression. But like many pastors, preachers, and priests, Kennedy is saying just the opposite. He simply doesn't believe that the United States commits unjust aggression. How could he? If the war in Iraq is not unjust aggression, then nothing the United States has ever done, or will do in the future, could possibly be labeled unjust aggression.

Kennedy's Fourteenth Proposition: Anti-War People Misuse Scripture

This is an incredible proposition since it is Kennedy who has misused Scripture throughout all of his propositions thus far. He comments: "There are certain passages that anti-war people use to try to condemn all warfare. Each passage can be explained. None say that military service, war, or killing the enemy in battle is wrong." Kennedy cites Exodus 20:13, Isaiah 2:4 with Joel 3:9–10, and Matthew 5:9, 43–44. Well, since none say these things are right either then Kennedy has not proved his point. Exodus 20:13 is, of course, the sixth commandment: "Thou shalt not kill." I have discussed this above under Kennedy's fifth proposition, "To Kill in Battle Is Not Murder." The references in Isaiah and Joel are prophetic passages about people beating swords into plowshares and plowshares into swords. I may have missed something, but I am not aware of any "anti-war people" misusing these passages to condemn all warfare. The verses in Joel can actually be used to their advantage by "pro-war people." The verses in Matthew are part of the well-known Sermon on the Mount. Kennedy doesn't like them because they talk about being a peacemaker and turning the other cheek. But I, one of the "anti-war people" that Kennedy speaks about, would be among the first to acknowledge that they would not prevent a nation from waging a just; that is, a defensive war. On the Sermon on the Mount, see my article "The Warmonger's Beatitudes."

Kennedy's Fifteenth Proposition: Warfare and the New Testament

Kennedy asks and then answers a good question. He asks: "Why does the New Testament not emphasize physical warfare?" He answers: "New Testament [is] addressed primarily to believers, residents of God's spiritual kingdom, who engage in spiritual warfare. The spiritual battle is still set within context of nations in conflict, nations who continually replay the story, begun by Satan, of pride and rebellion." It would have been better, of course, if Kennedy had said that the New Testament doesn't emphasize physical warfare because it is contrary to the tenor of the New Testament, an affront to the Savior, and a blight on Christianity.

Kennedy's Sixteenth Proposition: Just War Doctrine

Kennedy's sixteenth proposition actually consists of five segments: a brief introduction to just war theory as articulated by Thomas Aquinas followed by four groups of quotes from Aquinas, Augustine, and Luther. Aquinas's three requirements for just war are stated to be:

- The leader of a nation has the authority and responsibility to wage war to protect the citizens from external enemies.

- A nation wages war to avenge an attack or a wrong inflicted.
- A nation must wage war to advance good or to avoid evil.

The quotes he gives by Aquinas and Augustine back up these requirements. There are two problems here. One, Kennedy begins with Aquinas and backs him up with Augustine instead of beginning with Paul and backing him up with Jesus; that is, he appeals to men instead of Scripture. And two, as I have previously pointed out:

> This war in particular is a great evil, for a just war, rather than being an offensive, preemptive, open-ended, "shock and awe" campaign, must have a just cause, be in proportion to the gravity of the situation, have obtainable objectives, and only be undertaken as a last resort. If there was ever a war that violated every one of these principles it is the Iraq war.

To supplement Aquinas and Augustine, Kennedy quotes Luther: "Without armaments peace cannot be kept; wars are waged not only to repel injustice but also to establish a firm peace." But since the American invasion of Iraq was itself a great injustice, and has done anything but establish a firm peace, nothing Luther said can be used to defend the actions of the United States in Iraq. Kennedy must have missed Luther's statement about a soldier obeying God rather than men and refusing to go to war if the cause is unjust.

Kennedy's Seventeenth Proposition: Protection of America

Kennedy's seventeenth proposition contains six segments: an introduction, two selections from the Constitution, three groups of quotes by President Bush, and a conclusion to the entire series of propositions that should have been his eighteenth proposition. He begins:

> The leader or leadership of a nation must protect that nation. The king, president, premier, constitution, or other authority has the God-ordained responsibility to protect the people under his authority. If an aggressor makes plans or does attack, the leadership must take military action to protect his nation. Failure to do so is failure to fulfill his biblical mandate (Romans 13.1–6).

With the exception of the last sentence (Romans 13 has nothing to do with national defense), there is nothing wrong with Kennedy's opening statement. However, he goes downhill from there. He next makes the claim that "the Constitution gives the President the responsibility and the authority, as commander in chief of the military, to wage war for the protection of the nation and its citizens." But this is not backed up by the two selections he makes from the Constitution. Kennedy quotes the passage from Article II, Section 2, where the president is designated the commander in chief of the armed forces. This he says to "compare with Article I, Section 8, "The Congress shall have power ... to declare war." It is Congress that has the responsibility and authority to "wage war for the protection of the nation and its citizens." Kennedy has the proverbial cart before the horse. The quotes from Bush are pathetic:

> We don't need anybody's permission [to defend our country]....I will not leave the American people at the mercy of the Iraqi dictator and his weapons.
>
> But [Saddam should disarm] in the name of peace and the security of the world. If he won't do so voluntarily, we will disarm him.
>
> I'm convinced that a liberated Iraq will be important for that part of the world.
>
> My faith sustains me because I pray daily, I pray for guidance and wisdom and strength....If we were to commit our troops—if we were to commit our troops I would pray for their safety, and I would pray for innocent Iraqi lives as well.

These statements are pathetic because, first of all, the United States was never in danger from the Iraqi dictator and his weapons. He was a monster of our own creation, contrary to the foreign policy of John Quincy Adams. Secondly, why don't we disarm China, Russia, Israel, or the other countries that have real weapons of mass destruction? Who are we to demand that Iraq disarm? And thirdly, that is some liberation job we did in Iraq. There are 500,000 dead Iraqis who care not a whit for our liberation of their country. Oh, and I wonder how many innocent Iraqi lives that Bush ever prayed for? Perhaps Kennedy should have quoted Bush on how Iraq was not responsible for the September 11th attacks, and how most of the intelligence he relied on turned out to be wrong.

The last part of Kennedy's seventeenth proposition asks the question: "So What does this mean to me?" He answers:

- Military service is honorable.
- It is not sin or wrong to kill the enemy in war; it is right and it

is my duty.

- Just wars must be fought to protect and preserve life and freedom.
- Aggressors who threaten our life and freedom must be removed-most often by death in war.
- Those who refuse to fight or support our military in just wars are either cowards or confused.
- The President of the United States has a responsibility to seek out and kill those who attack us.
- I am responsible to pray for my President and leaders.

I would rephrase this somewhat:

> Military service in the current U.S. military is not honorable. It is a sin and a wrong to kill an enemy in an unjust war that has been created by the government. It is not right and it is not the duty of any Christian to fight the state's unjust wars. We should stop giving aggressors who threaten our life and freedom just cause to aggress against us. But even this doesn't apply to Saddam Hussein since Iraq was no threat to our life and freedom. Those who refuse to fight or support our military in unjust wars like the war in Iraq are heroes and informed. I am responsible to pray for my President and leaders, but I should pray that he and they stop the unjust aggression that is the war in Iraq.

Conclusion

Following Kennedy's seventeenth proposition, he concludes with what he calls "Freedom's Call"—an excerpt from Patrick Henry's "Give me liberty, or give me death" speech. The implication is that the current war in Iraq is somehow on the same level as the American Revolutionary War. Nothing, of course, could be further from the truth.

Tod Kennedy may be a godly man, a dedicated pastor, and a gifted Bible teacher, but he is a terribly deceived Christian warmonger. He owes his congregation an apology for leading them astray because he is such an apologist for Bush and his war. The presentation by Pastor Kennedy that I have critiqued is dated 2003. Perhaps he has changed his views. If he has then he should change his presentation or remove it from his church's website. But even if he has changed his mind about Bush and the war, many other evangelicals haven't, and would make the same arguments that Kennedy has made. A recent poll conducted by Christianity Today magazine asked the question: "Do evangelicals need a time of repentance for the Iraq war?" I am sorry to have to report that 38 percent of respondents (a plurality) answered: "No. The war in Iraq was necessary and justified." Such is the doctrine of Christian warmongers.

* * * * *

WHAT ABOUT HITLER?

> "I think that we desire war. We want war to be permissible without sacrificing all the values we hold most dear. As a result, we endeavor to manipulate and twist those values and moral principles to accommodate that desire rather than recognize war as the moral offense it is." ~ Robert Brimlow

Adolf Hitler is alive and well, and especially among neocon warmongers, conservative interventionists, Christian armageddonists, and other advocates of perpetual war for perpetual peace.

The original President Bush and the current incarnation have both all but compared Saddam Hussein to Hitler. Now it is the president of Iran who bears the Hitler label. Indeed, as Glenn Greenwald has well said: "Whoever is next on the War List is always The New Hitler and the country they lead is always The New Nazi Germany." But it is not incarnate in these mischaracterizations that Hitler lives today.

When all else fails, proponents of the war in Iraq inevitably retreat to the Hitler question. Okay, maybe life in Iraq under Saddam Hussein was better than the situation in Iraq now, but what about Hitler? Perhaps the United States shouldn't have invaded Iraq, but what about Hitler? Yes, it is tragic that almost 4,000 U.S. soldiers have died in Iraq, but what about Hitler? Perhaps the troop surge was a bad idea, but what about Hitler?

But it's not just those who champion the war in Iraq that invoke the Hitler question. The same thing is done by those who are adamantly opposed to this U.S. military adventure, but not some previous one. Failure to receive a satisfactory answer to the Hitler question is certainly one of the main reasons why many who recognize the folly of war hesitate to label themselves as anti-war.

The Hitler question is something that Robert Brimlow, a philosophy professor at St. John Fisher College in New York, has pondered for many years. After a series of outlines, drafts, and proposals (which, it should be noted, began before 9/11), he has collected his thoughts in *What about Hitler? Wrestling with Jesus's Call to Nonviolence in an Evil World* (Brazos Press, 2006). The book is part of the publisher's series on The

Christian Practice of Everyday Life, a series which "seeks to present specifically Christian perspectives on some of the most prevalent contemporary practices of everyday life."

This work came about in part due to the persistent asking of the Hitler question whenever the author made "an argument for pacifism in his philosophy classes." Brimlow believes that Christians "are not called to be pacifists; we are called to be Christians, and part of what it means to be Christian is to be peacemakers." But Hitler or no Hitler, the author doesn't believe that so-called just war theory is the answer to limiting war. The book, in fact, stands just war theory on its head, arguing that it is used to justify war. It also contains some painful rebukes to Christian defenders of war that I wish I had uttered himself.

But first, the negative. Each chapter of the book is prefaced by a Scripture passage and the author's meditation upon it followed in most cases by a prologue. But since the meditations are not directly related to the subject of the chapters, and the prologues, which are basically personal experiences, are generally irrelevant as well, they can all be safely passed over. The last three chapters (7, 8, & 9), which present the Christian response to the Hitler question, an elaboration, and an elaboration on the elaboration, should really be combined, especially since chapter 7 contains only a one-page response after a four-page meditation. Along with the lack of an index, these are minor quibbles we can live with in a book that so boldly and powerfully tackles just war theory and the Hitler question.

Brimlow doesn't waste any time, striking at the root of just war theory with an assault on Augustine in the first chapter: "Augustine is a saint, a father of the church, a good theologian, and a wonderful philosopher. He is also wrong." And not only is it the Church Father Tertullian that we should look to: "The basis of Tertullian's objection to Christian involvement with the military should be obvious to anyone with even a cursory knowledge of the gospel."

Brimlow then demolishes the finer points of just war theory itself, even taking on the theologian Thomas Aquinas. The author considers just war theory, "as developed and defended both by church theologians and secular philosophers," untenable, and for three reasons:

- Just war theory is untenable because it is difficult to know with sufficient confidence whether all of its conditions have been met.
- Just war theory is untenable because some of its tenets are impossible to realize.
- Just war theory is untenable because it is used to justify rather

than to prevent war.

First, there is the knowledge problem:

> It is not often easy to determine when a just cause for war exists or what criteria a state may use in reaching the determination that a just cause is operative.

> One of the primary difficulties with the just war requirements should be apparent: it is not very clear when the conditions of just cause and last resort have been satisfied.

> As soon as just war theory adapts to accommodate and allow preemptive attacks by a threatened state, it is no longer clear either how much solid evidence is required or how much discussion or negotiation would be prudent.

Second, the carrying out of the *jus in bello* principle of discrimination between the civilian population and enemy combatants is impossible. Says Brimlow: "It is obvious that a war, in order to be just, must not inflict harm or death or injury on innocent persons, or else it is no better (except, perhaps, quantitatively) than the original aggression. The problem facing those who wish to justify war is that it is impossible to conduct a war without harming some innocents. It is in the very nature of war that innocents will die."

And third, just war theory in practice is used for something entirely opposite its stated purpose: "Another difficulty with the just war criteria, at least to this point and taken as a whole, is that they seem able to justify almost all wars rather than to provide a means to limit the number of wars that would be considered just." Indeed, under just war theory, "a state may initiate hostile military action against another state that poses no direct threat to it. Using just war theory, Brimlow even makes the case that "Nazi Germany's initiation of World War II in the European theater—as well as the events that led up to it—satisfy the criteria for just cause as well as any other."

I might also add that it is the state that decides to go to war, not the people, most of whom want nothing to do with war; that is, until the state sufficiently propagandizes its citizens, as Hermann Goering explained. The state always claims that it is acting defensively, has the right intention, has the proper authority, is undertaking war as a last resort, has a high probability of success, and that a war will achieve good that is proportionally greater than the damage to life, limb, and property that it will cause.

Brimlow concludes about just war theory:

> The criteria set out and developed by just war theory are simply too flaccid and flexible to yield an outlawing of some of the most immoral and heinous activities of the last century.
>
> Just war theory is untenable. Among other things, just war theory contradicts itself in that it sanctions the killing of innocents, which it at the same time prohibits. In addition, just war theory can also be used effectively to justify all wars.

It is no wonder that "the Christian concerns about justifying warfare set the tone for subsequent secular justifications." Indeed, just war theory "has become fundamentally a secular doctrine." Brimlow argues that "this must be so, because no Christian could justify war without leaving Jesus and the gospel out of it."

But even if Brimlow's indictment of just war theory is correct, and even if "almost all the wars that have been fought over the millennia were wrong on both philosophical and theological grounds," and even if "pacifism might be what is called for in the vast majority of cases," there is one thing will abrogate every vestige of morality and turn the ardent pacifist into a crazed warmonger: the so-called supreme emergency.

The greatest example of the supreme emergency is, of course, Hitler. The Nazi regime "provides the paradigmatic example of a special case that justifies using extraordinary means to defeat an enemy" even if it means violating the rights of the innocent. Because Hitler is "the embodiment of hatred, murder, death, and destruction," he has become "a symbol for all those threats to us that appear immune to rational discourse, pragmatic calculation and bargaining, and appeals to self-interest or moral goodness."

Brimlow doesn't buy the supreme emergency argument, and certainly not as articulated by contemporary just war theorist Michael Walzer, author of *Just and Unjust Wars* (Basic Books, 2000). Brimlow points out that not only does Walzer assert that "even the lives of innocent may be sacrificed, with justification, in the case of supreme emergencies," he maintains that when the rights of neutrals, innocents, and noncombatants are overridden, they have not been "diminished, weakened, or lost." Brimlow concludes that the supreme emergency argument suffers from the same knowledge problem as just war theory: "It is difficult to determine with any precision when a supreme emergency begins or when it ends, even retrospectively."

Brimlow finds it curious that "we take Hitler as the figure and symbol for the embodiment of the utmost evil." It is Stalin, "at least in terms of sheer numbers of innocents intentionally and directly slaughtered," whose "record of murders supersedes Hitler's." It is Stalin—our ally in World War II—who not only initiated pogroms, purges, and persecutions (like Hitler), but used starvation and terror as a weapons. Stalin "appears to be more bloodthirsty than Hitler." He could even be "the greatest monster of the twentieth century."

In the end, Brimlow maintains that the Hitler question is a dishonest one:

> It assumes that Christians and the church have no involvement and no responsibility prior to some arbitrary date in the early 1940s. If the question is asking how a pacifistic church should have responded to the horrors of the Holocaust, the answer surely lies in being a peacemaking church long before the Holocaust ever began. The church should have preached and lived a love of the Jews for many centuries before the twentieth; the church should have formed Christians into the kind of people who do not kill Jews, or homosexuals, or gypsies, or communists, or other Christians, or Nazis, or whoever else was victimized by the war. The church should have lived and taught in such a way that the First World War would have been incomprehensible in a largely Christian Europe and, failing that, should have railed against the Versailles Treaty and the vengeance it embodied in favor of forgiveness and reconciliation. The failure of the church and of Christians to be peacemakers in 1942 is horrible precisely because it is a result and culmination of centuries of failure. Antisemitism, violence, warfare, strife, hatred, and intolerance have been and continue to be acceptable practices for Christians—usually in the name of politics, nationalism, or even religious truth.

Brimlow courageously concludes: "Given the stature of a Stalin, why is it that Hitler is the one who provides the standard by which we measure evil and analogize the worst behavior of leaders and states?"

We can even take this a step further. It was not Hitler who boycotted Jewish businesses. It was not Hitler who enforced the Nuremberg laws. It was not Hitler who participated in the Krystalnacht. It was not Hitler who transported Jews to death camps. It was not Hitler who killed American, British, Russian, and French soldiers during World War II. And it was not Hitler who killed the millions of civilians who died during the "Good War." And neither did Hitler put a gun to anyone's head and force them to do any of these things. Was Hitler evil? Yes. Was Hitler a despicable human being? Certainly. Would the world have been better off if someone had put a bullet in his head? Of course. Nevertheless, Hitler is given too much credit for what transpired during the Nazi regime (and yes, for those who question my hatred of Nazism: it was an evil, brutal regime, and so was Stalin's).

The problem with Hitler is that the great evil that he personifies has been imputed to Osama bin Laden, al Qaeda, "bad" Muslim leaders (as opposed to the "good" Muslim leaders that are our allies), and Islamic terrorists in general. Brimlow doesn't buy this argument either. He believes it "more appropriate to consider the actions of Al Qaeda and other terrorists to be criminal rather than aggressive in the traditional sense." Although certainly not defending the actions of bin Laden and al-Qaeda, Brimlow recognizes the part that an interventionist U.S. foreign policy has played in stirring up anti-Americanism in the Muslim world. When the United States responded to the 9/11 attacks, it was responding to "an attack that was, in itself, a response to an attack." In analyzing the complaints against America in the "Letter to America" attributed to bin Laden, Brimlow remarks that "our allies and many others in the international community have leveled similar charges against us for decades, and even a cursory examination of our history in many parts of the world, especially Latin America, gives considerable credence to his views." This is because "the American government and the American people have been and continue to be curiously blind to the cumulative effect our policy decisions have on other people around the world."

Brimlow argues that "just war theory and supreme emergencies cut both ways." If they are "sufficient to sanction the killing and destruction inherent in conventional and total wars, then they are sufficient to sanction terrorism as well." Indeed, to "accept one as right and proper is to accept the other, and this means we have no moral basis to object to what Al Qaeda and other terrorist organizations are doing."

Brimlow's solution for the individual Christian to the Hitler problem will not be too well-received in the Christian community, especially among warvangelicals:

> We must live faithfully; we must be humble in our faith and truthful in what we say and do; we must repay evil with good; and we must be peacemakers. This may also mean as a result that the evildoers will kill us. Then, we shall die.
>
> Our call to follow Jesus and be peacemakers means that we will die. We don't like this message, so we recoil from it and consider it incomprehensible; and we find ways to reinterpret the gospel or

> to understand the "real" meaning of Jesus's message in order to obfuscate and avoid this conclusion. He could not have meant what he said; "death" must be a metaphor for something else.

The author began his study of just war theory by wondering "how the church arrived at the position that some wars can be considered not only justifiable but also consistent with the demands of the gospel." Because this position is so entrenched in certain sectors of Christendom, we can only hope and pray that Brimlow's book causes some to rethink their position.

What about Hitler? Yeah, what about him?

* * * * *

CHRISTIANITY AND WAR

This talk was delivered on June 8, 2008, at the Future of Freedom Foundation's conference on "Restoring the Republic: Foreign Policy and Civil Liberties."

I would like to speak to you today about Christianity and War. I don't suppose there is anything I write and speak about with more fervor than the biblical, economic, and political fallacies of religious people. This is especially true regarding the general subject of Christianity and war. If there is any group of people that should be opposed to war, torture, militarism, the warfare state, state worship, suppression of civil liberties, an imperial presidency, blind nationalism, government propaganda, and an aggressive foreign policy it is Christians, and especially conservative, evangelical, and fundamentalist Christians who claim to strictly follow the dictates of Scripture and worship the Prince of Peace. It is indeed strange that Christian people should be so accepting of war. War is the greatest suppressor of civil liberties. War is the greatest destroyer of religion, morality, and decency. War is the greatest creator of fertile ground for genocides and atrocities. War is the greatest destroyer of families and young lives. War is the greatest creator of famine, disease, and homelessness. War is the health of the state.

But Christianity is in a sad state. In the Church can be found some of the greatest supporters of the state, its leaders, its military, and its wars. Christians who are otherwise good, godly, disciples of Christ often turn into babbling idiots when it comes to the subjects of war, the military, and killing for the state. There is an unholy desire on the part of a great many Christians to legitimize killing in war. There persists the idea among too many Christians that mass killing in war is acceptable, but the killing of one's neighbor violates the sixth commandment's prohibition against killing. Christians who wouldn't think of using the Lord's name in vain blaspheme God when they make ridiculous statements like "God is pro-war." Christians who try never to lie do so with boldness when they claim they are pro-life, but refuse to extend their pro-life sentiments to foreigners already out of the womb. Christians who abhor idols are guilty of idolatry when they say that we should follow the latest dictates of the state because we should always "obey the powers that be." Christians who venerate the Bible handle the word of God deceitfully when they quote Scripture to justify U.S. government wars. Christians who claim to have the mind of Christ show that they have lost their mind when they want the full force of government to protect a stem cell, but have no conscience about U.S. soldiers killing for the government.

There is an unseemly alliance that exists between certain sectors of Christianity and the military. Even Christians who are otherwise sound in the faith, who are not fooled by Bush's pseudo-Christianity and faith-based socialism, who believe that the less government we have the better, who don't support the war in Iraq, and who oppose an aggressive U.S. foreign policy get indignant when you question the institution of the military. Some churches would have no trouble doubling as military recruiting centers. There are Christian colleges that even offer Army ROTC. Most churches fawn over current and former members of the military, not just on Veterans Day, but on other holidays like Memorial Day, Armed Forces Day, and the Fourth of July, and also on special "military appreciation" days that they designate. Well, like those in foreign countries on the receiving end of a U.S. military intervention, I don't appreciate most of what the military does today, as I will explain later.

Much of the blame for Christian support for war must be laid at the feet of the pastors, preachers, and priests who have failed to discern the truth themselves so they can educate their congregations. It is tragic that many so-called Christian "leaders" moonlight as apologists for Bush, the Republican Party, and Bush's Republican-supported war. In fact, some of them could double as Republican Party operatives without changing their sermons. Too many pastors are cheerleaders for war, bloodshed, death, and destruction; since, after all, Iraqis are all just a bunch of dumb ragheads, Muslim heathens, or incorrigible terrorists. We hear more from the pulpit today justifying military intervention in the Middle East than we do about the need for missionaries to go there. It is appalling that instead of the next military adventure of the U.S. government being denounced from every pulpit in the land, it will be preachers who can be counted on to defend it—and more so if it is another Republican war. To compound all of this, many of the church and denominational leaders who don't follow the Republican Party line and don't support the war in Iraq are strangely silent. Not a word about the immorality of the Iraq War. Not a word about U.S. imperialism. Not a word about the lies of the U.S. government. Not a word about the pseudo-Christianity of the president. Not a word about Christians naïvely supporting the latest U.S. government pronouncement. Not a word about the CIA and the military being no place for a Christian young person. Not even a mild word of warning about the evils of the U.S. government. I don't buy the excuse that these leaders are merely preaching and teaching the Bible and choosing not to dabble in politics. They are not silent about the evils of rock music, trashy daytime television, abortion, and pornography, even though the Scripture doesn't mention these things, yet they are silent about the evils of war. Perhaps their churches contain too many current and former members of the military and they don't want to rock the boat. Perhaps they are veterans themselves and feel embarrassed to now criticize their former employer.

If there is any group within Christianity that should be the most consistent, the most vocal, the most persistent, and the most scriptural in its opposition to war and the warfare state, it is conservative Christians who look to the Bible as their sole authority. Yet, never at any time in history have so many of these Christians held such unholy opinions. The adoration they have toward President Bush is unholy. The association they have with the Republican Party is unholy. The admiration they have for the military is unholy. The thirst they have for war is unholy. The callous attitude they have toward killing foreigners is unholy. The idolatry they manifest toward the state is unholy.

If you doubt the truth of what I am saying about the sad state of Christianity, then look no further than the support that a theocratic warmonger like Mike Huckabee received in primary elections earlier this year held all over the South in the so-called Bible Belt. A church in my hometown of Pensacola, Florida, even had Huckabee in to preach on a Sunday evening during primary season. And this time the primaries down South weren't the usual case of Christians holding their noses and voting for what they perceived to be the lesser of two or more evils, for there was actually a principled conservative Christian on the ballot—Ron Paul. Much of the Christian antagonism toward Dr. Paul was on account of his opposition to the war in Iraq and the larger war on terror. Yet, Christians who chose Huckabee over Paul chose the greater evil that they hoped to avoid. They themselves are evil, not because they rejected Ron Paul, but because they love war, the military, and the warfare state. Huckabee not only supported the sending of more troops to their death in Iraq, he actually maintained that we should not withdraw from Iraq because "we are winning." If we are winning in Iraq when four thousand American soldiers are dead, thousands of physically and/or mentally disabled soldiers need a lifetime of care, a trillion dollars has already been spent, the morale and readiness of the military is at historic lows, the Guard and Reserve forces are decimated, military hardware and equipment are worn out, the reputation of America in the eyes of the world is at rock bottom, and new terrorists are being created faster than we can kill them, I hate to see what kind of condition we would be in if we started losing.

And then there is John McCain, whose foreign policy is based on a Beach Boys song. Although he has been harshly criticized by many Christians for not being conservative enough, he is rarely if ever condemned for being the most radical warmonger of all the presidential candidates. Christians may disagree with some of his proposals, but they generally consider him to be a decorated war hero instead of a dangerous mad bomber. I have already heard Christians talking about holding their noses in the November election and voting for McCain so we don't get one of those evil Democrats in the White House, as if McCain were any less evil than any Democrat who has ever held or run for the office.

I have made some shocking statements about religious people, perhaps even some provocative and incendiary statements. In fact, people that don't know anything about me might be inclined to believe that my remarks thus far have been an attack on Christianity. To the contrary, I am a Bible-believing Christian, as conservative as they come. Probably more conservative than many nominal Christians would feel comfortable with. True, I have spoken or written negative things about every religion, sect, and Christian denomination—including my own—but the difference between me and Christian apologists for Bush, the Republican Party, the military, war, and the state is that I worship the God of the Bible, not Mars, the god of war. Although I am not an ordained minister, I have preached in churches and other venues. I have earned degrees in theology. I have taught children in Sunday school and adults in Bible college. I will put my conservative Christian credentials up against anyone. I think I know Christianity and Christians as well as anyone. So, please understand that it is not Christianity I am criticizing; it is Christians who, by their persistent support for war, the warfare state, and the military, are giving Christianity a bad name.

The result of Christian support for war reminds me of a story in the Old Testament about two sons of the patriarch Jacob. In order to avenge the rape of their sister by some foreigners, the sons of Jacob told their leader that if his people consented to be circumcised, then both groups of people could intermarry and the rapist could have their sister to wife. However, after all the foreigners were circumcised, when they were sore, two sons of Jacob, Simeon and Levi, came and slew all the men who were incapacitated and spoiled their city. When their father Jacob heard about this, he told his sons: "Ye have troubled me to make me to stink among the inhabitants of the land."

Christian warmongers have made Christians to stink among the non-Christian inhabitants of the United States. After five years of this senseless war in Iraq, some of the war's greatest defenders continue to be Christians. A poll conducted last year by *Christianity Today* magazine asked the question: "Do evangelicals need a time of repentance for the Iraq war?" A plurality of respondents answered in the negative, and agreed with the proposition that the war in Iraq was necessary and justified. Sure, overall Christian support for the war has declined. Unfortunately, however, it is generally not out of a principled opposition to war and the warfare state, but only because the war didn't turn out as planned, the war is taking too long, the war has been mismanaged, the war is costing too much, or the war has resulted in too many dead and wounded American troops. The morality of going to war in the first place, as well as the number of dead and wounded Iraqis, is of absolutely no concern to most Christian Americans. Yet, every dead American solider is a hero. What a beautiful word is that word "hero"; the more hideous the death, the more beautiful the name it is necessary to find for it.

Christians have bought into a variety of American nationalism that has been called the myth of American exceptionalism. This is the idea that the government of the United States is morally and politically superior to all other governments; that America is a city on a hill—the redeemer nation, the Messiah nation, Rome on the Potomac, the "hope of all mankind," as President Bush termed it; that American values are the only true values; that the United States is the indispensable nation responsible for the peace and prosperity of the world; that the motives of the United States are always benevolent and paternalistic; that to accept American values is to be on the side of God, but to resist them is to oppose God; that other governments must conform to the policies of the U.S. government; that other nations are potential enemies that threaten U.S. safety and security; and that the United States is morally justified in imposing sanctions or launching military attacks against any of our enemies that refuse to conform to our dictates.

This is why U.S. foreign policy is aggressive, reckless, belligerent, and meddling. This is why U.S. foreign policy results in discord, strife, hatred, and terrorism toward the United States. This is why U.S. foreign policy excuses the mass murder of civilians in the Philippines, Germany, Japan, Korea, Vietnam, Laos, Cambodia, and Iraq as for the greater good. This is why the fruits of U.S. foreign policy are the destabilization and overthrow of governments, the assassination of leaders, the destruction of industry and infrastructure, the backing of military coups, death squads, and drug traffickers, imperialism under the guise of humanitarianism, support for corrupt and tyrannical governments, brutal sanctions and embargoes, and the United States bribing and bullying itself around the world as the world's policeman, fireman, social worker, and busybody. And because Americans are preoccupied with reconciling religious faith with national pride, they care little about the consequences of American foreign policy, preferring instead to view the world in Manichean terms of good (us) and evil (them).

People who are non-Christian or non-religious and oppose the actions of the warfare state should be concerned about the Christian attitude toward war. An overwhelming majority of Americans identify themselves as Christians. The same can be said of the members of the U.S. military. The percentage of congressman who identify their religion as Christianity is higher than that of the general population. If Christians at all levels of society were to withdraw their support for the war in Iraq, the war on terror, and the military, the war in Iraq would end tomorrow, the war on terror would be suspended, and the military would no longer receive a steady supply of cannon fodder from churches and Christian colleges. What a shame that non-Christians, including atheists, agnostics, infidels, pagans, and the irreligious, who oppose the genocide that the United States has unleashed in Iraq, have a moral code higher than that of many Christians. Non-Christian Americans should know that Christian enthusiasm for war and the warfare state is a perversion of Christianity, an affront to the Saviour whom Christians worship as the Prince of Peace, a violation of Scripture, contrary to the whole tenor of the New Testament, and an unfortunate demonstration of the profound ignorance many Christians have of history and their own Bible. God only knows how many non-Christians have been driven from Christianity because of Christian indifference toward or outright support of war.

The early Christians were not warmongers like so many Christians today. They did not idolize the Caesars like some Christians idolize President Bush. They did not make apologies for the Roman Empire like many Christians do for the U.S. Empire. They did not venerate the institution of the military like most Christians do today. They did not participate in the state's wars like too many Christians do today. If there was anything at all advocated by the early Christians it was peace. After all, they had some New Testament admonitions to go by:

- Blessed are the peacemakers (Matthew 5:9)
- Live peaceably with all men (Romans 12:18)
- Follow peace with all men (Hebrews 12:14)

Aggression, violence, and bloodshed are contrary to the very nature of Christianity. True, the Bible on several occasions likens a Christian to a soldier. As soldiers, Christians are admonished to "put on the whole armor of God." The Apostle Paul, who himself said: "I have fought a good fight," told a young minister to "war a good warfare." But the Christian soldier in the Bible fights against sin, the world, the flesh, and the devil. He wears "the breastplate of righteousness" and "the helmet of salvation." The weapons of the Christian are not carnal: his shield is "the shield of faith" and his sword is "the word of God." The New Testament admonishes Christians to not avenge themselves, to do good to all men, and to not render evil for evil. There is nothing in the New Testament from which to draw the conclusion that killing is somehow sanctified if it is done in the name of the state.

The Church Father Justin Martyr described the peaceful nature of the early Christians:

> And we who had been filled with war and mutual slaughter and every wickedness, have each one—all the world over—changed the instruments of war, the swords into ploughs and the spears into farming instruments, and we cultivate piety, righteousness, love for men, faith, and the hope which is from the Father Himself through the Crucified One.

> We who hated and slew one another, and because of differences in customs would not share a common hearth with those who were not of our tribe, now, after the appearance of Christ, have become sociable, and pray for our enemies, and try to persuade those who hate us unjustly, in order that they, living according to the good suggestions of Christ, may share our hope of obtaining the same reward from the God who is Master of all.

Unlike many Christians today who proudly serve in Caesar's army, the early Christians were critical of the Roman Empire and military service. Instead of being willing to die for the emperor and his empire, Christians declared "Jesus Is Lord" in direct opposition to Roman imperial claims.

The Church Father Lactantius explained that the Romans believed

> that there is no other way to immortality than by leading armies, devastating foreign countries, destroying cities, overthrowing towns, and either slaughtering or enslaving free peoples. Truly, the more men they have afflicted, despoiled, and slain, the more noble and renowned do they think themselves; and, captured by the appearance of empty glory, they give the name of excellence to their crimes. . . .
>
> If any one has slain a single man, he is regarded as contaminated and wicked, nor do they think it right that he should be admitted to this earthly dwelling of the gods. But he who has slaughtered endless thousands of men, deluged the fields with blood, and infected rivers with it, is admitted not only to a temple, but even to heaven.

Unfortunately, the nineteenth-century Quaker Jonathan Dymond similarly observed of Christians: "They who are shocked at a single murder on the highway, hear with indifference of the slaughter of a thousand on the field. They whom the idea of a single corpse would thrill with terror, contemplate that of heaps of human carcasses mangled by human hands, with frigid indifference." The famed church historian Adolf von Harnack described the features of military life that would have presented great difficulty to Christians:

> The shedding of blood on the battlefield, the use of torture in the law-courts, the passing of death-sentences by officers and the execution of them by common soldiers, the unconditional military oath, the all-pervading worship of the Emperor, the sacrifices in which all were expected in some way to participate, the average behaviour of soldiers in peace-time, and other idolatrous and offensive customs—all these would constitute in combination an exceedingly powerful deterrent against any Christian joining the army on his own initiative.

The aforementioned Lactantius describes Christians as "those who are ignorant of wars, who preserve concord with all, who are friends even to their enemies, who love all men as brothers, who know how to curb anger and soften with quiet moderation every madness of the mind."

And then came just war theory. This was the attempt by Augustine to reconcile Christian participation in warfare with the morality of New Testament Christianity by, among other things, distinguishing between soldiers' outwardly violent actions while waging war and their inwardly spiritual disposition. In its essence, just war theory concerns the use of force: when force should be used and what kind of force is acceptable. The timing of force relates to a country's justification for the initiation of war or military action; the nature of force relates to how military activity is conducted once a country commits to use force. The principle of the just war is actually many principles, all of which must be met for a war to be considered just. I agree with Christian philosopher Robert Brimlow, who views just war theory as untenable because it is difficult to know with sufficient confidence whether all of its conditions have been met, because some of its tenets are impossible to realize, because the criteria of just war theory are too flexible, because it contradicts itself in that it sanctions the killing of innocents, which it at the same time prohibits, and because it used to justify rather than to prevent war. Indeed, just war theory can be used effectively by all sides to justify all wars. I would add that just war theory is not even based on Scripture. It is, however, rooted in blind obedience to the state. It is the state that decides to go to war, not the people, most of whom want nothing to do with war; that is, until the state sufficiently propagandizes its citizens. The state always claims that it is acting defensively, has the right intention, has the proper authority, is undertaking war as a last resort, has a high probability of success, and that a war will achieve good that is proportionally greater than the damage to life, limb, and property that it will cause. Just war theory merely allowed Christians to make peace with war.

Then, of course, came the Crusades, followed by the continual wars among European Christians. The ultimate picture of the folly of war is the bloodbath perpetrated by the Christian nations in World War I. I have heard a lot lately about how most terrorists are Muslims, about how Islam is a violent religion, and about how Muslims are willing to kill in the name of their religion. That may all be true, but Christians who live in glass houses should be careful about throwing stones at Muslims. Yes, I am familiar with the tenets of the Muslim religion. And when I mentioned that I had said negative things about every religion I certainly meant to include Islam. But it was Christians who expelled the Jews from Spain in the fifteenth century, not Muslims. It was Christians who exploited and killed Africans by the millions in the Congo Free State in the late nineteenth century. It was Christians—Christian Americans—who slaughtered thousands of Filipinos in the so-called Philippine Insurrection at the turn of the twentieth century after we "liberated" them from Spain. And then, from 1914 to 1918, in battle after senseless battle, Christian soldiers in World War I shot, bombed, torpedoed, burned, gassed, bayoneted, and starved each other and civilians until twenty million of them were wounded and another twenty million lay dead.

And what did the Christians at home in the United States do and say before and during World War I? Their conduct was shameful. Challenged with the problem of arousing the patriotic spirit of the nation, government leaders must convince the populace of the absolute necessity of war, the utter wickedness of the enemy, and the supreme justness of the country's cause. To these ends the churches became willing servants of the state. They contributed to wartime hysteria and propaganda. Christianity became an adjunct to nationalism. Loyalty to one's country became the highest expression of the Christ-like life. Love of country exceeded love of mankind. God and country became synonymous. To give one's life for his country and its flag was to give it for God and his Kingdom. As Christ died to make men holy, so U.S. soldiers died to make men free. There was no difference between the pronouncements of patriotic organizations, government propaganda bureaus, and the edicts of Christian leaders. Religious organizations and nationalistic groups vied with each other in their flowery patriotic declarations. America's participation in the war was viewed as a missionary enterprise.

It is a blot on Christianity that many of the religious dissenters from the drive for war were unorthodox Christians—socialists, Unitarians, Universalists, Adventists, and Jehovah's Witnesses. Several members of this latter sect were sentenced to prison for circulating a book by their late leader with this particularly objectionable passage:

> Nowhere in the New Testament is patriotism (a narrowly minded hatred of other peoples) encouraged. Everywhere and always murder in its every form is forbidden. And yet under the guise of patriotism civil governments of the earth demand of peace-loving men the sacrifice of themselves and their loved ones and the butchery of their fellows, and hail it as a duty demanded by the laws of heaven.

What a shame that this statement was not on the lips of every so-called orthodox Christian.

Orthodox clergymen in the pulpit and their followers in the pew both succumbed to war psychology and societal pressure just as most other citizens. One Baptist pastor said that he looked "upon the enlistment of an American solider" as he did "on the departure of a missionary for Burma." A Presbyterian minister likewise remarked: "Every dollar and every service given to Uncle Sam for his army is a gift to missions." The dean of Oberlin College, who was also a Congregational minister, maintained that "the Christian soldier in friendship wounds the enemy. In friendship he kills the enemy." A Methodist preacher from Pittsburgh declared that he "would have gone over the top with other Americans." "I would have driven my bayonet into the throat or the eye or the stomach of the Huns without the slightest hesitation," he said, "and my conscience would not have bothered me in the least." An Episcopal minister wrote in the Atlantic Monthly that "the complete representative of the American Church in France is the United States Army overseas." Leaders in the Lutheran and Catholic churches had no trouble expressing their patriotism by a steadfast allegiance to the government.

One of the most notable Christian servants of the state during World War I was Ralph McKim, the rector of the Church of the Epiphany in Washington D.C. McKim made claims for Germany that were never ascribed to Hitler: "Germany seeks to control the whole world. Her ambition is to dominate mankind. Her aim is to bring all peoples and nations under the Hohenzollerns." To McKim, the conflict in Europe was a "crusade" and a "holy war." Because he believed that civilization was at stake, "and humanity—and Christianity itself," McKim maintained: "It is God who has summoned us to this war. It is His war we are fighting." Soldiers at the front were "marching to Calvary" to meet "the armies of Antichrist."

Other Christian ministers during World War I advocated restraints on anti-war speech and writing, the suppression of German-language newspapers, the purchase of war bonds, spying on American citizens, the death penalty for those who obstructed recruiting, harsh treatment of conscientious objectors, absolute loyalty to the government, hatred of the German people, torture of the German Kaiser, a one hundred-year boycott of German goods, and the mass sterilization of soldiers in Germany.

Para-church organizations were enlisted by the state as well. The YMCA was recruited to check morals, promote morale, and make men better fighters physically. Its secretaries exhibited the Bible as the greatest of all war books, and presented Jesus as a warrior thrusting his bayonet through a Hun in battle as example to others. Even the American Peace Society, whose members consisted largely of Christians, came to support the war. Religious journals donated advertising space for the sale of war bonds. Near the war's end, Christian Work magazine ran a full-page ad that read at the top of the page: "Kill the Hun, Kill his Hope." In the middle of the page was a picture of a bayonet and a $100 liberty bond. Underneath this was the reminder: "Bayonet and Bond—both Kill! One Kills the Hun, the Other Kills his Hope. Buy U.S. Government Bonds."

We hear much of the same now regarding the Iraq War, and without the massive government propaganda campaign that was undertaken during World War I. I guess Christians have gotten dumber. When Bush ordered the invasion of Iraq in March of 2003 with the announcement that our cause was just, Christians lined up in droves to support their president. They enlisted in the military. They put "W" stickers and yellow ribbons on their cars. They implored us in church to pray for the troops. They made heroes out of every dead American soldier. They began reciting their patriotic sloganeering, their God-and-country rhetoric, and their "obey the powers that be" mantra. They dusted off their books on just war theory. They denounced Christian opponents of the war as liberals, pacifists, traitors, and Quakers, usually preceded by the adjectives *unpatriotic* and *anti-American*.

Why? Why have so many religious people gotten it so wrong? As I have explained in many of my articles on Christianity and war over the years, there are many reasons: thinking that the war in Iraq was in retaliation for the 9/11 attacks, believing that Saddam Hussein was another Hitler, supposing that Iraq was a threat to the United States, seeing the war in Iraq as a modern-day crusade against Islam, assuming that the United States needed to protect Israel from Iraq, viewing Bush as a messiah figure, equating the Republican Party with the party of God, blindly following the conservative movement, deeming the state to be a divine institution instead of a lying, stealing, and killing machine, failing to separate the divine sanction of war against the enemies of God in the Old Testament from the New Testament ethic that taught otherwise, having a profound ignorance of history and primitive Christianity, reading too much into the mention of soldiers in the New Testament, adopting the mindset that brute force is barbarism when individuals use it, but honorable when nations are guilty of it, possessing a warped "God and Country" complex, holding a "my country right or wrong" attitude, and as I mentioned previously, accepting without reservation the myth of American exceptionalism.

But if I had to single out one thing that has caused Christians to be so accepting of war and the warfare state it would have to be the military. Americans love the military, and American Christians are no exception. It doesn't seem to matter the reason for each war or intrusion into the affairs of another country. It doesn't seem to matter how long U.S. troops remain after the initial intervention. It doesn't seem to matter how many foreign civilians are killed or injured. It doesn't seem to matter how many billions of dollars are spent by the military. It doesn't even seem to matter what the troops are actually doing—Americans generally believe in supporting the troops no matter what. Social activist Lee Griffith remarks in his book *The War on Terrorism and the Terror of God*:

> Currently, public support for military actions is virtually instinctive, especially so if troops have already been placed in harm's way.
>
> It is claimed that, to question the endeavor, to express less than enthusiastic support is to show callous disregard for the lives of the young women and men who face enemy bullets on our behalf. As if by magic, the charge of disregard for life is leveled against those who oppose placing troops on the battlefield while the potentates who placed them there are held immune.

Americans are repulsed by the serial killer who, to satisfy the basest of desires, dismembers his victims; but revere the bomber pilot in the stratosphere who, flying above the clouds, never hears the screams of his victims or sees the flesh torn from their bones. Killing women and children at a distance of five feet is viewed as an atrocity, but at more than five thousand feet it is a heroic act.

Christians of all branches and denominations have a love affair with the military. This alliance includes Catholic just-war theorists, evangelicals in and out of the military, Red-State Christian fascists, Reich-wing Christian nationalists, progressive Christians who oppose the war in Iraq, theocon Values Voters, Christians who are not part of the Religious Right, and even conservative Christians who oppose an aggressive, interventionist foreign policy. The superstitious reverence that many Christians have for the military in some cases borders on a fetish. Criticism of the military is strictly verboten. To question the military in any way—its size, its budget, its efficiency, its bureaucracy, its contractors, its weaponry, its mission, its effectiveness, its foreign interventions—is to question America itself. One can condemn the size of government, but never the size of the military. One can criticize federal spending, but never military spending. One can denounce government bureaucrats, but never military brass. One can deprecate the welfare state, but never the warfare state. One can expose government abuses, but never military abuses. One can label domestic policy as socialistic, but never foreign policy as imperialistic.

I am often accused of being anti-military, of not appreciating the sacrifices that have been made so that I can have the freedom to speak English, vote, write articles critical of the military, and express my negative opinions about U.S. foreign policy. But if the military were actually engaged in defending the United States, securing the borders, guarding the shores, patrolling the coasts, and protecting the skies then I would be as pro-military as the chairman of the joint chiefs.

What is the purpose of the military? I think it is beyond dispute that the purpose of any country having a military is defense of the country against attack or invasion, not to "rid the world of evil," as Bush proclaimed from the pulpit of the National Cathedral a few days after the 9/11 attacks.

The U.S. military should be engaged exclusively in defending the United States, not defending other countries, and certainly not attacking them. It is U.S. borders that should be secured. It is U.S. shores that should be guarded. It is U.S. coasts that should be patrolled. It is U.S. skies where no-fly zones should be enforced.

But because U.S. foreign policy is aggressive, reckless, belligerent, and meddling; because it has a history of hegemony, nation building, regime change, and jingoism; because it is the story of interventionism, imperialism, and empire; because it results in discord, strife, hatred, and terrorism toward the United States: the U.S. military—the enforcer of U.S. foreign policy—is a force for evil in the world. Because America's military heritage is not one of how our troops have repelled invaders, kept us safe from attack, or defended our freedoms, it is not honorable to serve in the military. This is a bitter pill to swallow, especially for soldiers who fought for a lie and the families of soldiers who died for a lie. America's military heritage is unfortunately one of bombs and bullets, death and destruction, intervention and invasion, and occupation and oppression. The purpose of the military has been perverted beyond all recognition. The military spreads democracy by bombs, bayonets, and bullets. The military garrisons the planet with troops and bases. The military is responsible for the network of brothels around the world to service U.S. troops who have no business being away from home. Military personnel serve simultaneously as policemen, firemen, scientists, social workers, and bullies with the world as their precinct, forest, laboratory, client, and playground.

What do providing disaster relief, dispensing humanitarian aid, supplying peacekeepers, enforcing UN resolutions, and spreading goodwill have to do with defending the country against attack? How do launching preemptive strikes, changing regimes, enforcing no-fly zones, stationing troops in other countries, and garrisoning the planet with bases have anything to do with defending the country against invasion? Here is the new role envisioned for the army by Defense Secretary Robert Gates: "Army soldiers can expect to be tasked with reviving public services, rebuilding infrastructure and promoting good governance. All these so-called nontraditional capabilities have moved into the mainstream of military thinking, planning, and strategy—where they must stay." Combat veterans, regardless of how they feel about the war in Iraq and U.S. foreign policy, should be outraged at this new vision for the Army. Is the Army explaining its new vision to young people who walk into Army recruiting centers? And with the tremendous financial incentives being offered to enlist in the military today, do young people even care what the vision of the military is or are they blinded by the dollar signs in their eyes?

But regardless of how the purpose of the military has been perverted beyond all recognition, the troops are still responsible for their actions. After all, it is the troops that are doing the actual fighting in Iraq right now—not Bush, not Cheney, not Gates, not Rice. As much as I have nothing but contempt for the architects of the war, the president who instigated the war, the neocons who welcomed the war, the Congressmen who funded the war, and the conservatives who supported the war, it is U.S. soldiers who are dropping the bombs, firing the mortars, throwing the grenades, launching the missiles, and shooting the bullets. It is U.S. soldiers who have paved the way for the rampant sectarian violence. It is U.S. soldiers who have unleashed brutality, murder, genocide, death, and destruction in Iraq. I was told by one of my critics that he agreed with me on the point of not fighting illegal and unjust wars, but that doing so was not the fault of the soldiers. Well then, whose fault is it? No one is doing the fighting except the soldiers. It doesn't matter who told them to bomb, maim, and kill or what the reason is that they were told to do these things. If the troops stop fighting, the war will grind to a halt.

I don't support the troops. I didn't support them in the last war, I don't support them in this war, and I won't support them in the next war. It is the troops that are ultimately responsible for prosecuting this senseless and immoral war. Yet, U.S. forces are generally not held responsible for any of their actions by their superiors, the government, or the general public unless they do something particularly evil that becomes an embarrassment. Most people say the troops are not responsible because they're just following orders. No soldier is responsible for the death and destruction he inflicts as long as it is state-sanctioned death and destruction. Many evangelical Christians agree, and join in this chorus of statolatry with their "obey the powers that be" mantra. Even many of those who maintain that Bush and Cheney are war criminals are hesitant to condemn the individual soldier. I am not.

First of all, the last time I looked in my Bible, I got the strong impression that it was only God who should be obeyed 100 percent of the time without question. Second, what would the attitude toward the soldier be if he were ordered to attack in some way American citizens under the guise of maintaining order? Is that an order we want U.S. soldiers to obey? Third, why would we want U.S. soldiers to follow orders to bomb, maim, kill and otherwise attack foreigners around the world that have never lifted a finger against the United States? Fourth, soldiers in other countries are not accorded this luxury. Unlike the soldiers of any other country, U.S. soldiers are always viewed by Americans as liberators and peacekeepers, never invaders and occupiers. We would we get extremely upset at foreign soldiers if they killed Americans even if they were just following orders. No supporter of the war in Iraq who uses the "obeying orders" defense would allow a German officer at the Nuremberg Trials to get away with saying that he was just obeying Hitler's orders. And fifth, if the U.S. government told someone to kill his mother, any American would be outraged if he under any circumstances went and did it. But then if the government tells someone to put on a uniform and go kill some Iraqi's mother, the typical American puts a yellow ribbon on his car and says that we should support the troops. But why should the response be any different? Why should morality be put *off* just because a uniform is put *on*? Being told to clean or paint a piece of equipment is one thing; being told to bomb or shoot a person is another.

But, it is objected, even if some commands are questionable, U.S. military effectiveness would be greatly diminished if the troops didn't obey orders. Let's hope so. How many Vietnamese and Laotians and Cambodians would be alive today if the U.S. military had been rendered impotent? We have heard a lot lately about how the United States may need to confront Iran militarily. First it was that the Iranian president was the reincarnation of Hitler, then it was Iran's ambition to build a nuclear bomb, and now it is Iran's arming of Iraqi insurgents. These are all bogus threats, of course, but when has that ever prevented the United States from going to war? Listen, every act of American military intervention in some other country was made possible because the troops blindly followed the orders of their superiors. If they had refused to do anything that was not related to actually defending the country, then there would not have been any overseas deployments, preemptive strikes, land mines buried, bombs dropped, missiles launched, torture under the guise of interrogation, and no meddling in other countries. The result of this would have been not only less anti-American sentiment, but fewer terrorists, fewer dollars wasted, fewer dead foreigners, and fewer dead American soldiers.

Now, if the purpose of the U.S. military has been perverted beyond all recognition; if the military spends more time securing the borders, guarding the shores, patrolling the coasts, and protecting the skies of other countries than it does in defense of the United States; if the military is engaged in sending its soldiers thousands of miles away to kill people and destroy their property after "liberating" them from their ruler; if U.S. foreign policy results in our military being the greatest force for evil in the world; then why in God's name would a Christian join the military and help the state carry out its evil deeds? Why would a pastor implore his congregation to pray for the troops? Why would a church display a yellow ribbon that says "we support our troops"?

There were 181,000 people who joined the military last year. Certainly, the majority of them would designate their religion as Christianity. Many Christians will not allow their children to set foot in a public school, but then encourage them, or at least not discourage them, to join the U.S. military and not only face government propaganda and immorality on a much greater scale, but participate in bringing death and destruction to the latest enemy, not of the American people, but of the U.S. government. There is universal agreement among Christians that no Christian could in good conscience work as a pimp, a prostitute, an abortionist, a drug dealer, or an exotic dancer. Adherents of other religions and atheists would also generally select more wholesome occupations. For a Christian to sell himself to the highest bidder as a contract killer would be considered a very immoral thing to do, but if the same Christian serves as a killer for hire for the U.S. government he is held in high esteem. I know I have been rather blunt, but the Russian novelist Leo Tolstoy was even more direct: "Armies will first diminish, and then disappear, only when public opinion brands with contempt those who, whether from fear, or for advantage, sell their liberty and enter the ranks of those murderers, called soldiers." Because the war in Iraq is immoral and unjust, and because there is no draft, Christians who join the military are willing accomplices to murder. Since when is murder sanctified if it is carried out by state order, in a state uniform, and with a state-issued weapon?

Christians not in the military are some of the greatest supporters of the military. Many Christians have exchanged biblical Christianity for imperial Christianity. Now, I realize that few Christians subscribe to the deviant Christianity espoused by conservative columnist Ann Coulter, who maintained after the 9/11 attacks that "we should invade their countries, kill their leaders and convert them to Christianity." But some of the same Christians who never hesitate to criticize the Catholic Church still view the war in Iraq as a modern-day crusade against Muslims. I've got some bad news for them: The Lord never sanctioned any crusade of Christians against any religion. The God of the Bible never called, commanded, or encouraged any Christian to kill, make apologies for the killing of, or excuse the killing of any adherent to a false religion. Dispensationalists who are quick to point out the distinctions between Israel and the Church often invoke the Jewish wars of the Old Testament against the heathen as a justification for the actions of the U.S. military. Although God sponsored these wars, and used the Jewish nation to conduct them, it does not follow that God sponsors American wars or that America is God's chosen nation. The last time I checked, George Bush was not God, America was not the nation of Israel, and the U.S. Army was not the Lord's army. It is not just military chaplains asking God to bless troops on their missions of death and destruction who are taking God's name in vain. Anyone using God's holy name to justify the state's wars and military interventions is taking his name in vain. Indeed, as the aforementioned Lee Griffith has said: "The claim of divine sanction for violence is among the crudest forms of blasphemy."

This love affair that Christians have with the military is an illicit affair. The unholy alliance between Christianity and the military must be broken. Christians should renounce the militarism of society. They should stop regarding the state's acts of aggression as benevolent. They should stop calling evil good and good evil. They should stop presuming divine support for U.S. military interventions. They should vigorously dissent the next time some politician says there is some great evil in the world that must be stamped out by the U.S. military. Because just war theory merely allows Christians to make peace with war, they should reject it just as they would any theory of just piracy or just terrorism or just murder. Above all, they should stay out of the military.

But what should a Christian soldier do? Resign, be a conscientious objector, or at the least follow John the Baptist's rules for soldiers, as given in the Gospel of Luke: "Do violence to no man, neither accuse any falsely; and be content with your wages." There is only one path to take when a Christian in the military is faced with an order to kill, bomb, or destroy someone or something halfway around the world that he has never met or seen, and is no real threat to him, his family, or his country: "We ought to obey God rather than men" (Acts 5:29).

Christian colleges should discontinue all ROTC programs, ban military recruiters from all their campuses, and discourage their students from enlisting in the military. Likewise, Christian pastors and youth ministers should do everything in their power to keep their young people out of the military.

Churches should treat members of the military no different than they treat employees of Wal-Mart or McDonalds. They should stop this nonsense of asking God to bless the troops. Should we pray that God blesses the troops while they drop their bombs, throw their grenades, launch their missiles, fire their mortars, and shoot their bullets? Is beseeching God to protect the troops as they shoot, bomb, maim, mine, destroy, "interrogate," and kill to carry out an evil foreign policy consistent with the Christianity in the New Testament? Yes, we should pray for the troops. We should pray that the troops come home. We should pray that no more of their blood is shed on foreign soil in some senseless war. But we should also pray that they stop bringing death and destruction to foreigners. And while we're at it, we should pray that young, impressionable students are not ensnared by military recruiters. We should likewise pray that churches stop supplying cannon fodder to the military.

The problem with the U.S. military is, of course, U.S. foreign policy. U.S. foreign policy is not only aggressive, reckless, belligerent, and meddling, it is also extremely arrogant. The United States would never tolerate another country engaging in an American-style foreign policy. Now, I think I loathe President Bush as much as any man in this room, and perhaps even more so because, as a Bible-believing Christian, I oppose his faith-based socialism, his misuse of Scripture and religion, and his doctrinal deviations from orthodox Christianity, but what if another country said that the U.S. government was corrupt and oppressive and needed a regime change and then came over here and overthrew our government? I would be outraged, as would every American. The United States has troops in about 150 countries. Would it be okay if each of these countries sent troops to the United States? If not, then why not? Would it be okay if each of the countries the United States has a military base in decided to build a base in the United States? Why not? Why the double standard? It is the height of arrogance to insist that the United States alone has the right to garrison the planet with bases, station troops wherever it wants, police the world, and intervene in the affairs of other countries.

It is high time for Christians who still defend the state, its leaders, its military, and its wars to wake up and open their eyes and recognize some cold, hard facts:

- The United States has become a rogue state, a pariah nation, an evil empire.
- The United States' military is the greatest force for evil in the world.
- The United States is the arms dealer to the world.
- The United States is not the world's policeman.

- The United States cannot redeem the world through violence.
- The United States is not the God-anointed protector of Israel that enjoys a special relationship with God.
- The United States government is the greatest threat to American life, liberty, and property—not the leaders or the military or the people of Iraq, Iran, Syria, China, Russia, or Venezuela.

Our republic is crumbling. It is imperative that we return to the noninterventionist foreign policy of the Founders. Christians, of all people, should be leading the way.

* * * * *

DOUBLE-MINDED WARMONGERS

"A double minded man is unstable in all his ways." ~ James 1:8

John McCain, like all politicians, is a double-minded man. Although some of his supporters believe one thing, and some of his supporters believe something else; McCain stands firmly with his supporters. But even worse than this duplicity is the fact that McCain is also a double-minded warmonger.

Back in October of 2001, McCain wrote an article for the *Wall Street Journal* in which he defended President Bush's planned perpetual war against terrorism:

> War is a miserable business. The lives of a nation's finest patriots are sacrificed. Innocent people suffer and die. Commerce is disrupted, economies are damaged. Strategic interests shielded by years of patient statecraft are endangered as the exigencies of war and diplomacy conflict. However heady the appeal of a call to arms, however just the cause, we should still shed a tear for all that will be lost when war claims its wages from us. Shed a tear, and then get on with the business of killing our enemies as quickly as we can, and as ruthlessly as we must.

Apparently, no one liked his article more than he did, for in a speech on March 26 of this year at the World Affairs Council in Los Angeles, McCain recycled some lines from his article of seven years ago:

> I detest war. It might not be the worst thing to befall human beings, but it is wretched beyond all description. When nations

> seek to resolve their differences by force of arms, a million tragedies ensue. *The lives of a nation's finest patriots are sacrificed. Innocent people suffer and die. Commerce is disrupted; economies are damaged; strategic interests shielded by years of patient statecraft are endangered as the exigencies of war and diplomacy conflict.* Not the valor with which it is fought nor the nobility of the cause it serves, can glorify war. Whatever gains are secured, it is loss the veteran remembers most keenly. Only a fool or a fraud sentimentalizes the merciless reality of war. *However heady the appeal of a call to arms, however just the cause, we should still shed a tear for all that is lost when war claims its wages from us.*

McCain is a double-minded warmonger.

According to McCain's article, war is a miserable business with horrific consequences for U.S. soldiers, innocents, commerce, and U.S. interests, but we should nevertheless quickly and ruthlessly be about the business of killing the latest enemy manufactured, provoked, or exaggerated by the U.S. government.

But McCain's speech is likewise a double-minded one. For someone who detests war and its million tragedies, McCain is one of the most radical warmongers of the Republican warmongers in Congress who continue to defend Bush's failed policy in Iraq and seek to escalate the war on terror. In fact, I can't imagine how McCain could be much more of a warmonger if he didn't detest war and its million tragedies.

Although McCain recently claimed that if elected, he will have won the war in Iraq and brought home most of the troops by 2013, he has also said that it would be fine with him if U.S. troops stayed in Iraq for a 100 years, that U.S. troops "could be in Iraq for 'a thousand years' or 'a million years,' as far as he was concerned," and that he "will never set a date for withdrawal." No wonder McCain recently remarked that it's "not too important" when U.S. forces leave Iraq.

McCain is a double-minded warmonger.

But even worse than this is the fact that some Christians—too many Christians—are also double-minded warmongers. The paradoxes are legion.

Although Christians are told to "follow peace with all men" (Hebrews 12:14), the Christian warmonger also thinks that Muslims or anyone labeled as an enemy by the U.S. government is not included.

Although Christians are told "Thou shalt not kill" (Romans 13:9), the Christian warmonger also thinks that the prohibition doesn't apply if one is wearing a uniform of the U.S. armed forces.

Although Christians are told to "recompense to no man evil for evil" (Romans 12:17), the Christian warmonger also thinks that the United States should perpetually retaliate for 9/11 against any individual that it labels a terrorist or any country that is accused of supporting terrorists or doesn't support U.S. efforts in the war on terror.

Although Christians are told to "obey God rather than men" (Acts 5:29), the Christian warmonger also thinks that killing for the state in any foreign country that the U.S. government sends its troops to is a patriotic duty.

Although Christians are told to "ever follow that which is good" (1 Thessalonians 5:15), the Christian warmonger also thinks that the evil being perpetrated upon Iraq by U.S. troops should be supported since it is better to fight them "over there" instead of "over here."

Although Christians are told "Whatsoever a man soweth, that shall he also reap" (Galatians 6:7), the Christian warmonger also thinks that the United States is in no way culpable for the blowback it experienced when the Twin Towers were taken out.

Although Christians are told to not be a partaker of "evil deeds" (2 John 11), the Christian warmonger also thinks that serving in the U.S. military is a noble thing for a Christian young person.

Although these things are bad enough, perhaps the most double-minded thing that Christians will ever do will occur this November when multitudes of Christians will hold their noses and vote for a bloodthirsty warmonger like John McCain because he is a Republican and not one of those evil Democrats. But if Christians would take off their Republican glasses for just a moment they would see that McCain and Obama are but peas in the same pod as Clinton. May God deliver us from warmongers—and especially double-minded, Christian, Republican warmongers.

* * * * *

J. GRESHAM MACHEN ON IMPERIALISM, MILITARISM, AND CONSCRIPTION

Who is J. Gresham Machen and why should we care what he said about imperialism, militarism, and conscription?

John Gresham Machen (1881–1937) was a conservative Presbyterian New Testament scholar who taught at Princeton Theological Seminary from 1906–1929. Because he believed that the seminary had left its historic theological position, Machen left Princeton in 1929 and founded Westminster Theological Seminary in Philadelphia, teaching there until his untimely death in 1937.

Machen was widely recognized in his day as one of the most scholarly and zealous defenders of conservative Protestantism. His most enduring works are *The Origin of Paul's Religion* (1921), *The Virgin Birth of Christ* (1930), *Christianity and Liberalism* (1923), and *New Testament Greek for Beginners* (1923), all of which are still in print today.

Machen was not a pacifist, and neither was he connected in any way with one of the historic peace churches. He was the epitome of an orthodox, conservative Christian. And that is why we should care about what he said about imperialism, militarism, and conscription. Too many Christians today believe that a conservative Christian should identify politically with the conservative movement, which today generally supports war, militarism, and an aggressive U.S. foreign policy—at least when a Republican president is in charge.

The latest poll by The Pew Research Center for the People & the Press found that voters are almost evenly divided between Barack Obama and John McCain. Among white evangelical Protestant voters, however, McCain leads Obama 68 to 24 percent. This is disturbing. And not because I think Christians should support Obama (they shouldn't) or the Democratic Party (they shouldn't). Like under George Bush, there will be no restraint on the abuse of the military under a commander in chief like John McCain. But a vote for McCain is not just a vote for four more years of George Bush. McCain is even worse on foreign policy than Bush. And unlike Bush, who merely gave the order for mass murder, McCain actually helped carry out mass murder, from the safety of his cockpit, of course.

But aside from being a flaming neoconservative interventionist with a foreign policy that often sounds more bellicose and more reckless than Bush, CFR member McCain has taken positions for abortion, gun control, the UN, amnesty for illegals, the North American Union, and global warming legislation and against free speech, tax cuts, and limited government and liberty in general. And we are supposed to believe that he is the lesser of two evils?

Some conservative Christians are already starting to hold their nose to block out the stench of McCain's "conservatism" as they prepare to vote for him in the November election because he is a Republican and not one of those evil Democrats. It's just too bad that they are not holding their nose because of McCain's dangerous view of what U.S. foreign policy should be. Even James "Focus on the Family" Dobson, who once said that he would never support McCain, is now entertaining the thought of doing so.

Given McCain's views on the military and foreign policy, and without even taking into account his positions on other issues, if Machen were alive today, would he be even a reluctant McCain supporter? I think not.

After the United States entered World War I, Machen went to France with the YMCA in early 1918 to perform relief work, occasionally having to shelter during bombardments. He was not, however, a partisan for the Allied Powers.

In reviewing a book in 1915 by a noted pro-English author, Machen remarked that the book was "a glorification of imperialism." The author "glorified war" and ridiculed "efforts at the production of mutual respect and confidence among equal nations."

Machen was not interested in the world being "made safe for democracy":

> The alliance of Great Britain with Russia and Japan seems to me still an unholy thing—an unscrupulous effort to crush the life out of a progressive commercial rival. Gradually a coalition had to be gotten together against Germany, and the purpose of it was only too plain. An alleged war in the interest of democracy the chief result of which will be to place a splendid people at the mercy of Russia does not appeal to me.

> This talk about British democracy arouses my ire as much as anything. Great Britain seems to me the least democratic of all the civilized nations of the world—with a land-system that makes great masses of the people practically serfs, and a miserable social system that is more tyrannical in the really important, emotional side of life than all the political oppression that ever was practiced. And then if there is such a thing as British democracy it has no place for any rival on the face of the earth. The British attitude towards Germany's just effort at a place in ocean trade seems to me one of the great underlying causes of the war.

He reserved his harshest words for imperialism:

> Imperialism, to my mind, is satanic, whether it is German or English.

> I am opposed to *all imperial ambitions*, wherever they may be cherished and with whatever veneer of benevolent assimilation they may be disguised.

A few months after the war began, Machen wrote that "the enormous lists of casualties" impressed him, "as nothing else has, with the destructiveness of the war."

There have been renewed calls of late for young people to perform some kind of national service. I have even heard pastors who ought to know better say that every young man should serve for two years in the military after high school. The most egregious form of national service is involuntary servitude, *prohibited* by the Thirteenth Amendment, but *permitted* if called conscription. Machen was a strong opponent of conscription:

> Even temporary conscription goes against the grain with me, unless it is resorted to to repel actual invasion, but my fundamental objection is directed against compulsory service in time of peace.
>
> The country seems to be rushing into two things to which I am more strongly opposed than anything else in the world—a permanent alliance with Great Britain, which will inevitably mean a continuance of the present vassalage, and a permanent policy of compulsory military service with all the brutal interference of the state in individual and family life which that entails, and which has caused the misery of Germany and France.

On April 2, 1917, Machen wrote about conscription to the members of Congress that represented his home state of New Jersey:

> After a residence in Europe I came to cherish America all the more as a refuge from the servitude of conscription. That servitude prevails whether the enforced service be required by a vote of the majority or by an absolute government. Compulsory military service does not merely bring a danger of militarism; it is militarism. To adopt it in this country would mean that no matter how this war results we are conquered already; the hope of peace and a better day would no longer be present to sustain us in the present struggle, but there would be only the miserable prospect of the continuance of the evils of war even into peace times.
>
> In short Americanism is in danger—American liberty and the whole American ideal of life. Is it to be abandoned without consideration, under the unnatural stress of an emergency with which the proposed change in policy has absolutely noting to do? Just when other nations are hoping that the present war will result in the diminution of armaments and the broadening of liberty, is America to be the first to take a radical step in exactly the opposite

> direction? I am not arguing against preparedness. I believe, in particular, that we should have a much more adequate navy. What I am arguing against is compulsion, which I believe to be brutal and un-American in itself, and productive of a host of subsidiary evils.

If Machen were alive today, he would be accused of being un-American or anti-American for statements like these:

> The gospel of Christ is a blessed relief from that sinful state of affairs commonly known as hundred per-cent Americanism. And fortunately some of us were able to learn of the gospel in a freer, more spiritual time, before the state had begun to lay its grip upon the education of the young.

> Princeton is a hot-bed of patriotic enthusiasm and military ardor, which makes me feel like a man without a country.

On the Sunday before the Fourth of July this year, many churches held patriotic services. I saw the following on a church sign near my house: "The American soldier and Jesus Christ. One gives his life for your freedom. The other for your soul." I can't think of anything more blasphemous than mentioning Jesus Christ—the Lord, the Son of God, the Prince of Peace—in the same breath as a U.S. soldier who bombs, maims, kills, and then dies for a lie. I think Machen would agree.

In an address delivered in 1919 that was published in *The Presbyterian* called "The Church in the War," Machen lamented that men are perfectly ready to admit Jesus

> into the noble company of those who have sacrificed themselves in a righteous cause. But such condescension is as far removed as possible from the Christian attitude. People used to say, "There was no other good enough to pay the price of sin." They say so no longer. On the contrary, any man, if only he goes bravely over the top, is now regarded as plenty good enough to pay the price of sin. Obviously this modern attitude is possible only because men have lost sight of the majesty of Jesus' person. It is because they regard him as a being altogether like themselves that they can compare their sacrifice with his. It never seems to dawn upon them that this was no sinful man, but the Lord of glory who died on Calvary. If it did dawn upon them, they would gladly confess, as men used to confess, that one drop of the precious blood of Jesus is worth more, as a ground for the hope of the world, than all the rivers of blood which have flowed upon the battlefields of France.

Conservative Christians have no business supporting, defending, or excusing the current military adventures of the United States. J. Gresham Machen is a shining example that even the most conservative of Christians can look to.

All quotations from J. Gresham Machen are taken from Ned B. Stonehouse, J. Gresham Machen: A Biographical Memoir *(3rd ed., The Banner of Truth Trust, 1987).*

* * * * *

FAITH OF OUR FATHERS

There has prevailed in some circles since the beginning of the war in Iraq the idea that a conservative should support war and militarism. To dissent is to not be a true conservative, or even worse, to be one of those nasty liberals, or worse still, to be un-American or anti-American.

The idea is bogus, of course. When a Democrat like Bill Clinton was president, 80 percent of House Republicans voted against the Clinton-ordered bombings in the former Yugoslavia. If the "liberal" Al Gore had been elected president instead of the "conservative" George Bush, and if the "liberal" President Gore had ordered the invasion of Iraq, is there any doubt that most of the "conservatives" in Congress would have opposed him?

With the exception of Ron Paul (and perhaps a handful of others who are not as consistent), the members of Congress of both parties have no principles other than supporting their party, expanding their power, glorying in their position, and getting reelected. This lack of moral principles is true of the typical self-proclaimed conservative layman. If Bush announced today on the Limbaugh and Hannity radio shows that the invasion of Iraq was a terrible mistake, and that he was ordering all U.S. forces to cease fighting and begin withdrawing, the same "conservatives" who supported the war in Iraq for five years in order to defend our freedoms and keep us safe from terrorism would suddenly turn into opponents of the war. Any "liberals" who wanted to continue the war effort would be denounced as un-American for wanting U.S. soldiers to remain in harm's way.

This idea that a conservative should support war and militarism is, unfortunately, held by a good number of conservative Christians as well. And perhaps even more strongly because of the religious element. When the typical conservative Christian sees liberal Christians deny the authority of Scripture and the bodily resurrection of Christ while expressing support for abortion and the ordaining of homosexuals, *but also oppose war and militarism*, he draws the false conclusion that it is liberal (bad) to oppose war and militarism but conservative (good) to support them.

As a conservative Christian who considers aggression, violence, and bloodshed to be contrary to the nature of Christianity, I draw a different conclusion: A broken clock is right twice a day. So what if a liberal theologian or a left-wing Hollywood actor or a leftist university professor or a Democratic congressman opposes war and militarism. Why does that make it wrong? So what if they oppose these things for different reasons than I do. At least they oppose them. So what if their opposition to war and militarism is inconsistent. At least they oppose them some of the time. I have more respect for these individuals than I do for a conservative, Christian, Republican warmonger who makes a god out of the state and its military.

The defense of war and militarism by many Evangelicals and other conservative Christians is a recent aberration. Christian history is filled with many individuals from a variety of denominations who denounced war and militarism.

According to John Cadoux, the author of the definitive investigation of the early Christian attitude toward war and military service:

> The early Christians took Jesus at his word, and understood his inculcations of gentleness and non-resistance in their literal sense. They closely identified their religion with peace; they strongly condemned war for the bloodshed which it involved; they appropriated to themselves the Old Testament prophecy which foretold the transformation of the weapons of war into the implements of agriculture; they declared that it was their policy to return good for evil and to conquer evil with good.

Perhaps the most celebrated advocate of peace was the Dutch humanist Erasmus (1466–1536). He believed that the only just and necessary war was a "purely defensive" one to "repel the violence of invaders." And because he believed that war is by "nature such a plague to man that even if it is undertaken by a just prince in a totally just cause, the wickedness of captains and soldiers results in almost more evil than good," Erasmus insisted that "all other expedients must be tried before war is begun; no matter how serious nor how just the cause." He chastised Christians for reproaches vomited out against Christ by nations of unbelievers "when they see his professed followers" warring "with more destructive instruments of mutual murder than pagans could ever find in their hearts to use." "War would be understandable among the beasts," said Erasmus, "for they lack natural reason; it is an aberration among men because the evil of war can be easily understood through the use of reason alone. War, however, is inconceivable among Christians because it is not only rationally objectionable but, even more important, ethically inadmissible."

Hugo Grotius (1583–1645), the famed Dutch jurist, Christian apologist, theorist of natural rights, and father of international law, lamented:

> Throughout the Christian world I observed a lack of restraint in relation to war, such as even barbarous races should be ashamed of; I observed that men rush to arms for slight causes, or no cause at all, and that when arms have once been taken up there is no longer any respect for law, divine or human; it is as if, in accordance with a general decree, frenzy had openly been let loose for the committing of all crimes.

His masterful three-volume work of 1625, *De jure belli ac pacis* (On the Law of War and Peace; recently reprinted by Liberty Fund as *The Rights of War and Peace*), is one of the most significant writings in the just war tradition.

In his *Philosophical Letters* (1734), the French philosopher Voltaire (1694–1778) wrote about an encounter he had in England with a Quaker named Andrew Pitt. Said Pitt:

> If we never go to war it is not because we fear death—on the contrary, we bless the moment that unites us with the Being of Beings—but it's that we are not wolves or tigers or watchdogs, but men and Christians. Our Lord, who has commanded us to love our enemies and to endure without complaining, certainly does not wish us to cross the sea and cut the throats of our brothers because some murderers dressed in red, and wearing hats two feet high, are enlisting citizens by making a noise with two little sticks beating on the tightly stretched skin of an ass. And when, after battles won, all London glitters with lights, when the sky blazes with fireworks, and the air resounds with the noise of thanksgiving, of bells, of organs, and of cannon, we mourn in silence over these murders, the cause of public gaiety.

What the British Quaker Jonathan Dymond (1796–1828) wrote against war in his *Essay on War* is still relevant today:

> But perhaps the most operative cause of the popularity of war, and of the facility with which we engage in it, consists in this; that an idea of glory is attached to military exploits, and of honor to the military profession. The glories of battle, and of those who perish in it, or who return in triumph to their country, are favorite topics of declamation with the historian, the biographers, and the poet. They have told us a thousands times of dying heroes, who "resign their lives amidst the joys of conquest, and, filled with their country's glory, smile in death;" and thus every excitement that eloquence and genius can command, is employed to arouse that ambition of fame which can be gratified only at the expense of blood.
>
> Some writers who have perceived the monstrousness of this system, have told us that a soldier should assure himself, before he engages in a war, that it is a lawful and just one; and they acknowledge that, if he does not feel this assurance, he is a "murderer." But how is he to know that the war is just? It is frequently difficult for the people distinctly to discover what the objects of a war are. And if the soldier knew that it was just in its commencement, how is he to know that it will continue to be just in its prosecution? Every war is, in some parts of its course, wicked and unjust; and who can tell what the course will be? You say—When he discovers any injustice or wickedness, let him withdraw: we answer, he cannot; and the truth is, that there is no way of avoiding the evil, but by avoiding the army.

The British preacher Vicesimus Knox (1752–1821) was a true minister of peace. In his preface to a work of Erasmus which he translated into English, Knox said of war:

> To eradicate from the bosom of man principles which argue not only obduracy, but malignity, is certainly the main scope of the Christian religion; and the clergy are never better employed in their grand work, the melioration of human nature, the improvement of general happiness, than when they are reprobating all propensities whatever, which tend, in any degree, to produce, to continue, or to aggravate the calamities of war; those calamities which, as his majesty graciously expressed it, in one of his speeches from the throne, are inseparable from a state of war.
>
> There is nothing so heterodox, I speak under the correction of the reverend prelacy, as war, and the passions that lead to it, such as pride, avarice, and ambition. The greatest heresy I know, is to shed

> the blood of an innocent man, to rob by authority of a Christian government, to lay waste by law, to destroy by privilege, that which constitutes the health, the wealth, the comfort, the happiness, the sustenance of a fellow-creature, and a fellow Christian. This is heresy and schism with a vengeance!
>
> I hope the world has profited too much by experience, to encourage any offensive war, under the name and pretext of a holy war.
>
> Let Mahomet mark the progress of the faith by blood. Such modes of erecting the Cross are an abomination to Jesus Christ. Is it, after all, certain, that the slaughter of the unbelievers will convert the survivors to the religion of the slaughterers? Is the burning of a town, the sinking of a ship, the wounding and killing hundreds of thousands in the field, a proof of the lovely and beneficent spirit of that Christianity to which the enemy is to be converted, by the philanthropic warriors?

Another British minister of peace was the acclaimed "prince of preachers," Charles Spurgeon (1834–1892). Throughout his sermons, one can find numerous references to Christianity and war:

> The Church of Christ is continually represented under the figure of an army; yet its Captain is the Prince of Peace; its object is the establishment of peace, and its soldiers are men of a peaceful disposition. The spirit of war is at the extremely opposite point to the spirit of the gospel.
>
> War is to our minds the most difficult thing to sanctify to God. The genius of the Christian religion is altogether contrary to everything like strife of any kind, much more to the deadly clash of arms
>
> If there be anything which this book denounces and counts the hugest of all crimes, it is the crime of war. Put up thy sword into thy sheath, for hath not he said, "Thou shalt not kill," and he meant not that it was a sin to kill one but a glory to kill a million, but he meant that bloodshed on the smallest or largest scale was sinful.

The American Peace Society was organized in New York in 1828 "to illustrate the inconsistency of war with Christianity, to show its baleful influence on all the great interests of mankind, and to devise means for insuring universal and permanent peace." In 1845, this peace society published *The Book of Peace: A Collection of Essays on War and Peace*, a 600-page book containing sixty-four essays on war and peace. Here are some excerpts:

> War is the grand impoverisher of the world. In estimating its havoc of property, we must inquire not only how much its costs, and how much it destroys, but how far it prevents the acquisition of wealth; and a full answer to these three questions would exhibit an amount of waste beyond the power of any imagination adequately to conceive.
>
> Christianity saves men; war destroys them. Christianity elevates men; war debased and degrades them. Christianity purifies men; war corrupts and defiles them. Christianity blesses men; war curses them. God says, thou shalt not kill; war says, thou shalt kill. God says, blessed are the peace-makers; war says, blessed are the war-makers. God says, love your enemies; war says, hate them. God says, forgive men their trespasses; war says, forgive them not. God enjoins forgiveness, and forbids revenge; while war scorns the former, and commands the latter. God says, if any man smite thee on the cheek, turn to him the other also; war says, turn not the other check, but knock the smiter down. God says, bless those who curse you; bless, and curse not: war says, curse those who curse you; curse, and bless not. God says, pray for those who despitefully use you; war says, pray against them, and seek their destruction. God says, see that none render evil for evil unto any man; war says, be sure to render evil for evil unto all that injure you. God says, if thine enemy hunger, feed him; if he thirst, give him drink: war says, if you do supply your enemies with food and clothing, you shall be shot as a traitor. God says, do good unto all men; war says, do as much evil as you can to your enemies. God says to all men, love one another; war says, hate and kill one another. God says, they that take the sword, shall perish by the sword; war says, they that take the sword, shall be saved by the sword. God says, blessed is he that trusteth in the Lord; war says, cursed is such a man, and blessed is he who trusteth in swords and guns.
>
> The evils arising from military preparations are greater in the whole than those that would be incurred by submission to any probably foreign demand they are designed to resist. War is more frequently caused by military preparations than it is supposed to be averted by them, both by encouraging in any nation supporting them, an arrogant bearing towards foreign nations, and by provoking the pride of those nations, by their defying appearance.

> Military preparations for defence are always liable to be used for purposes of aggression.

Writing in the *Christian Review* back in 1838, a Baptist minister explained how war contradicts the genius and intention of Christianity, sets at nought the example of Jesus, and violates all the express precepts of the New Testament:

> Christianity requires us to seek to amend the condition of man. But war cannot do this. The world is no better for all the wars of five thousand years. Christianity, if it prevailed, would make the earth a paradise. War, where it prevails, makes it a slaughter-house, a den of thieves, a brothel, a hell. Christianity cancels the laws of retaliation. War is based upon that very principle. Christianity is the remedy for all human woes. War produces every woe known to man.
>
> The causes of war, as well as war itself, are contrary to the gospel. It originates in the worst passions and the worst aims. We may always trace it to the thirst of revenge, the acquisition of territory, the monopoly of commerce, the quarrels of kings, the intrigues of ministers, the coercion of religious opinion, the acquisition of disputed crowns, or some other source, equally culpable; but never has any war, devised by man, been founded on holy tempers and Christian principles.
>
> There is no rank or position in an army compatible with the character of Christ. It is most certain, that we gather no army lessons from him who "came to bind up the broken-hearted, to proclaim liberty to the captives, and to comfort all that mourn." It is most certain, that no man, who makes fighting his *profession*, can find authority in the example of our Lord.
>
> It should be remembered, that in no case, even under the Old Testament, was war appointed to decide doubtful questions, or to settle quarrels, but to inflict national punishment. They were intended, as are pestilence and famine, to chastise nations guilty of provoking God. Such is never the pretext of modern war; and if it were, it would require divine authority, which, as has just been said, would induce even members of the Peace Society to fight.

Writing in the same publication just a few years later, the Baptist minister who called himself Veritatis Amans stated:

> War has ever been the scourge of the human race. The history of the past is little else than a chronicle of deadly feuds, irreconcilable hate, and exterminating warfare. The extension of empire, the love of glory, and thirst for fame, have been more fatal to men than famine or pestilence, or the fiercest elements of nature. The trappings and tinsel of war, martial prowess, and military heroism, have, in all ages, been venerated and lauded to the skies. And what is more sad and painful, many of the wars whose desolating surges have deluged the earth, have been carried on in the name and under the sanction of those who profess the name of Christ.
>
> In all cases where war has ever existed, the principles of the gospel have been violated by one or both parties. Such must always be the case in every war. Hence it must follow that if the gospel were fully obeyed, all war must cease.

The Baptist minister, economist, and educator Francis Wayland (1796–1865) considered all wars to be "contrary to the will of God," he believed that "the individual has no right to commit to society, nor society to government, the power to declare war." He further maintained that no one was obligated to support his government in an aggressive war. He depicted the Mexican War as "wicked, infamous, unconstitutional in design, and stupid and shockingly depraved in its management"—sentiments one might hear today about the war in Iraq.

Gerrit Smith (1797–1874) was a Christian philanthropist, publicist, orator, abolitionist, temperance advocate, and social reformer. He also briefly served as a member of Congress. Here is part of his speech against a bill making appropriation for the support of the Military Academy:

> The spirit of war is the spirit of barbarism; and, notwithstanding the general impression to the contrary, war is the mightiest of all the hinderances to the progresses of civilization. But the spirit of this bill is the dark, barbarous, baleful spirit of war; and, therefore, would I use all honorable means to defeat the bill.
>
> It is strange—it is sad—that, in a nation, professing faith in the Prince of Peace, the war spirit should be so rampant. That, in such a nation, there should be any manifestation whatever of this spirit, is grossly inconsistent.
>
> "My voice is still for war," are the words ascribed to a celebrated Roman. But, as he was a pagan, and lived more than two thousand years ago, it is not strange, that he was for war. But, that we, who have a more than two thousand years longer retrospect of the

> horrors of war than he had—that we, who, instead of but a pagan sense of right and wrong, have, or, at least, have the means of having, a Christian sense of right and wrong—that we should be for war, is, indeed, passing strange.

The revivalist, abolitionist, and educator Charles Finney (1792–1875) stated of war:

> But in no case is war anything else than a most horrible crime, unless it is plainly the will of God that it should exist, and unless it be actually undertaken in obedience to his will. This is true of all, both of rulers and subjects, who engage in war. Selfish war is wholesale murder. For a nation to declare war, or for persons to enlist, or in any way designedly to aid or abet, in the declaration or prosecution of war, upon any other conditions than those just specified, involves the guilt of murder.
>
> There can scarcely be conceived a more abominable and fiendish maxim than "my country right or wrong." To adopt the maxim, "Our Country right or wrong," and to sympathize with the government, in the prosecution of a war unrighteously waged, must involve the guilt of murder.

Southern Presbyterian theologian Robert Louis Dabney (1820–1898), who served as a Confederate Army chaplain and chief of staff to Stonewall Jackson, believed that "war should be only defensive. As soon as the invader is disarmed, his life should be spared; especially as individual invaders are usually private subjects of the invading sovereign, who have little option about their own acts as private soldiers." He considered defensive war to be "righteous, and only defensive war." Aggressive war "is wholesale robbery and murder."

David Lipscomb (1831–1917), the namesake of Lipscomb University, was a Church of Christ minister and magazine editor who believed that violence and warfare were incompatible with Christianity:

> Christ disavows the earthly character of his kingdom; declares that it is of a nature so different from all worldly kingdoms, that his servants could not fight for his kingdom; if they could not fight for his kingdom, they could not fight for any kingdom, hence in this respect could not be members and supporters of the earthly kingdoms.
>
> [Christ] had plainly declared that his children could not fight with

> carnal weapons even for the establishment of his own Kingdom. Much less could they slay and destroy one another in the contentions and strivings of the kingdoms of this world. It took but little thought to see that Christians cannot fight, cannot slay one another or their fellowmen, at the behest of any earthly ruler, or to establish or maintain any human government.

Although many Christians became apologists for the state during World War I, there were a few Elijahs who refused to do the state's bidding.

Before the United States entered the war, Frank Crane, a minister turned newspaper columnist, claimed that "an intelligent, twentieth-century democratic Christian should refuse to go to war." He remarked that the commandment "Thou shalt not kill" not only restrained the Christian from harming his neighbors, it also prevented him from violence against his country's neighbors. He considered war "the greatest conceivable crime." Participating in war constituted "the deepest possible offense toward Almighty God."

Episcopal bishop Paul Jones was another voice for peace:

> As I love my country, I must protest against her doing what I would not do myself because it is contrary to our Lord's teaching. To prosecute war means to kill men, bring sorrow and suffering upon women and children. . . . No matter what principles may appear to be at stake, to deliberately engage in such a course of action that evidently is unchristian is repugnant to the whole spirit of the gospel.

Jones was forced to resign.

Paul Harris Drake, minister of Christ Church in Dorchester, Massachusetts, was scheduled to preach on "The Conscientious Objector" at the Sunday morning service on June 3, 1917. His church board barred him from the pulpit. His prepared statement to the board was the following:

> "War is hell," and hell has no place in the human order of things than in the Divine order. If I, as a minister of God, am unable to believe in a hell hereafter, I certainly cannot bring myself to believe in the wisdom or righteousness of a hell here and now. . . . War orators may sing the praises of America with her hands red with the blood of my fellow-men—but I shall not!

He was also forced to resign.

Charles Fletcher Dole, a retired minister, was part of the Association for the Abolition of War. He believed that killing Germans was wrong—"just as wrong if we kill millions of them in war as if we murdered them one by one with pistols and knives. Furthermore it can accomplish no possible good for France, or Britain, or ourselves, or the world; but only evil, evil, evil to everybody."

Henry Winn Pinkham, a Unitarian minister, replying to George Gordon of the Old South Church of Boston in 1917, asked the question: "Did Jesus kill anybody in order to redeem the world?" He further stated:

> Somehow, it does not seem easy to conceive the Savior as the inspirer, helper and friend of the soldier as he rushes to stick his bayonet into the guts of a brother man. Somehow the Christian heart shudders—mine does at any rate, if not Dr. Gordon's—at the thought of Jesus clad in khaki, with a bomb in his hand, or turning the crank of a machine-gun to spatter wounds and death among his fellow men.

Harry Emerson Fosdick (1878–1969), the pastor of Riverside Church in New York City, lamented the initial Christian support of World War I:

> When the Great War broke the churches were unprepared to take a well-considered *Christian* attitude. We too were hypnotized by nationalism. We had made ourselves part and parcel of social attitudes from whose inevitable consequence we felt it immoral to withdraw. For my part, I never will be caught that way again. I hope the churches never will be caught that way. If, however, when the next crisis comes, we are going to protest effectively against war, we must win the right to make that protest, and we must win it now. Today we must make unmistakably clear our position against war.
>
> War is utterly and irremediable unchristian. It is a more blatant denial of every Christian doctrine about God and man than all the theoretical atheists on earth could devise. What I do see is that the quarrels between fundamentalists and liberals, high churchmen, broad churchmen, and low churchmen are tithing, mint, anise and cumin if the Church does not deal with this supreme moral issue of our time: Christ against war.

Although Fosdick was a modernist on the wrong side of the liberal/fundamentalist debate of his day, there was one of his theological opponents who stood with him on the subject of war.

Writing before and during World War I, the conservative Presbyterian New Testament scholar J. Gresham Machen (1881–1937) opposed imperialism, militarism, and conscription:

> Imperialism, to my mind, is satanic, whether it is German or English.
>
> Princeton is a hot-bed of patriotic enthusiasm and military ardor, which makes me feel like a man without a country.
>
> The enormous lists of casualties impresses me, as nothing else has, with the destructiveness of the war.
>
> Compulsory military service does not merely bring a danger of militarism; it is militarism. To adopt it in this country would mean that no matter how this war results we are conquered already; the hope of peace and a better day would no longer be present to sustain us in the present struggle, but there would be only the miserable prospect of the continuance of the evils of war even into peace times.

After the Great War, G. J. Heering, a theology professor in Holland and president of the International Union of Anti-Militarist Ministers and Clergymen, pulled no punches in his book *The Fall of Christianity: A Study of Christianity the State and War* (Dutch, 1928; English, 1930):

> Primitive Christianity felt instinctively that war is in complete conflict with the living values of the Gospel, with the spirit of Christ; in short, with Christian principle. After long centuries which have not been without their heroic attempts to bring to light this ancient opposition, after much mischief and especially after much shame, the Christianity of our own days, alarmed by the development of war technique, begins to notice that its alliance with the State—an alliance necessary but too close—and its consequent compromise with war have led Christianity itself, and State and people, along the highroad to destruction. Christianity begins to realize that war lets loose all the demons that Christ came to fight, that there can be no greater hindrance to the coming of God's Kingdom than war, and that the man who takes part in war is brought into a condition in which he cannot possibly pray, "Our Father." The Christianity of our day is beginning to realize (still very weakly, but at least in it is beginning) that it is called to take up its stand with all the power of its faith and with absolute

> condemnation of the whole practice and preparation of war.
>
> Those for whom war is a crime against humanity and sin against God are sometimes asked to moderate themselves, and not use such "strong words" as "crime" and "sin." But if these words express exactly what the speaker means, and what is laid upon him irresistibly by his moral and spiritual judgment, whose is the right to reproach him?
>
> First and foremost, organized Christianity must make downright protest against all war and all preparations therefore, as completely opposed to Christian principle.
>
> What moral right has the Church to exist, if it allows preparation for that war to go on, even in its own land, without the most obstinate protest and opposition? What right is left to her to go on calling herself "the Church of Christ," if she yet again makes common cause with the forces of war and tacitly gives them her sanction?

He concludes that "war causes the State to fail in the fulfillment of its duties; that it has become intolerable to the moral sense of many Christians, and that the attempts to justify war cannot stand their ground in the face of moral and rational judgment." Indeed, war and its preparation is "the greatest of all blasphemies, one which desecrates the Names of God and Christ a thousand times more than all breaches of the Sabbath."

Back before they sold out to the Republican Party, the Southern Baptists issued a number of official statements expressing their opposition to war and militarism:

> We oppose the continued large expenditure by the Government for military and naval equipment; that we oppose military training in the schools and colleges, whether denominational or state; and that we favor full and complete disarmament as rapidly as it can possibly be accomplished, except such armament as may be absolutely necessary for police duty within our own territory and on our borders. Moreover, we reaffirm our hearty approval of the international agreement to renounce war as a national policy and our gratitude at the growing conviction among Christians of the incompatibility of war with the ethical principles of our Lord Jesus Christ.
>
> We reaffirm also our utter opposition to and hatred of war as the most inexcusable and insane policy that could be pursued by the

> nations of the earth in their dealings with one another, destructive not only of human life and treasure but of all that is high and worthy in human ideals and objectives.
>
> We pledge ourselves as citizens and Christians that we will not support our government in any war except such as might be necessary to repel invasion of our land or to preserve fundamental human rights and liberties.

There is nothing "liberal" about opposition to war. There is nothing "anti-American" about opposition to militarism. And what could be more Christian than standing firmly against aggression, violence, and bloodshed?

There are today a growing number of conservative Christians who vehemently repudiate Bush's wars in Iraq and Afghanistan, the warfare state, the militarization of society, the U.S. empire of troops and bases that encircles the globe, and the imperialistic foreign policy that put them there. Are you one of them or are you a Christian warmonger?

For a collection of anti-war writings from a primarily secular point of view, see the new book by Thomas Woods and Murray Polner, We Who Dared to Say No to War *(Basic Books, 2008).*

* * * * *

THE TRIUMPH OF IMPERIAL CHRISTIANITY

> "If Christ were here now there is one thing he would not be—a Christian." ~ Mark Twain

John McCain may have lost the election, but some of his core beliefs are alive and well among the majority of conservative Christians. True, some of these Christians had their doubts about the genuineness of McCain's pro-life position, his devotion to real conservative values, his faithfulness to the Constitution, and his commitment to reducing wasteful government spending, but there was one principle that they were sure of: McCain is a war hero who served his country in the military, supported the war in Iraq, and would make an ideal choice for a commander in chief to lead the U.S. military in the perpetual war against Islamofascism.

It is bad enough that McCain is an unrepentant war criminal, but it is even worse that he is an incorrigible militarist, imperialist, interventionist, and all-around warmonger who thinks that there is no job in the world too small for the U.S. military. This is the man who jokes about killing Persians with bombs and cigarettes. This is the man who told a reporter that U.S. troops "could be in Iraq for 'a thousand years' or 'a million years,' as far as he was concerned." This is the man who wants to start another cold war with Russia. Yet, instead of rejecting McCain outright, many conservative Christians supported him until the bitter end.

But it is not just Christian support for McCain that signals the triumph of imperial Christianity. Every Republican presidential candidate, with the exception of Ron Paul, supported Bush's wars and the aggressive, reckless, meddling, militaristic, and imperialistic evil that is U.S. foreign policy. Conservative Christians would have gotten behind any Republican who received the nomination now matter how much he supported war and militarism.

The election was certainly a repudiation of George Bush and the Republican Party. However, it was generally not conservative Christians who did the repudiating. McCain, after all, still received 46 percent of the vote. Many of the 58 million people who voted for McCain had to be conservative Christians. They certainly didn't vote for Obama. A small percentage probably voted for Baldwin. A smaller percentage probably voted for Barr. An even smaller percentage probably voted for no one since voting is generally considered a "sacred duty" and it was such a "historic" election.

But instead of rejecting war, empire, militarism, imperialism, an aggressive foreign policy, and the warfare state with its suppression of civil liberties and destruction of the economy, many Christians openly embraced these things in the person of John McCain. Now, not every Christian who voted for McCain openly embraces these things, and especially those who fought back a gag reflex and cast their vote for McCain because they thought, sincerely but sincerely wrong, that he was the lesser of two evils. The problem with this latter group, however, is that the war was not even an issue, even among those who voted for McCain for the sole reason that he was more pro-life than Obama.

The terrible truth is that the vast majority of conservative Christians who voted in the recent election were not the least bit concerned about just war theory, U.S. foreign policy, the morality of the war in Iraq, the conduct of American soldiers in Iraq, the wedding parties in Afghanistan destroyed by the U.S. Air Force, the CIA's extraordinary rendition program, the hundreds of thousands of dead Iraqis, the dead, maimed, homeless, and orphaned Iraqi children, the thousands of American troops that died for a lie, the number of devastated American military families, a trillion-dollar-a-year defense budget, the proper role of the U.S. military, domestic spying programs in the name of fighting terrorism, the loss of civil liberties in the name of national security, or the open-ended perpetual war on terror.

The election is historic all right. Even though McCain lost, the election still marks the triumph of imperial Christianity over biblical Christianity.

Imperial Christians have a warped view of what it means to be pro-life. I have had Christians tell me that they despise everything about McCain, including his warmongering, but that they voted for him anyway because he was more pro-life than Obama. But don't adults and foreigners have the same right to life as unborn American babies? There should be no difference between being for abortion and for war. Both result in the death of innocents. Both are unnecessary. Both cause psychological harm to the one who signs a consent form or fires a weapon. Why is it that an American doctor in a white coat is considered a murderer if he kills an unborn baby, but an American soldier in a uniform is considered a hero if he kills an adult?

Imperial Christians have a warped view of the military. Although many of these Christians may criticize the government, they have nothing but praise for the military. They equate U.S. soldiers killing for the state in some foreign war that has nothing to do with defending the United States as defending our freedoms. They publicly honor veterans who bombed, maimed, and killed Vietnamese, Cambodians, Afghans, and Iraqis that were no threat to them, their families, or Americans (until the United States invaded their country), as war heroes, not only on every national holiday, but on special "military appreciation" days as well. Yet, aside from the ministry, they think there is no higher calling for a Christian young person than military service—even though the military spends more time securing the borders, guarding the shores, patrolling the coasts, and protecting the skies of other countries than it does in defense of the United States. Christian soldiers are expected to blindly follow their leaders when it comes to the latest country to bomb or invade. To question the morality of their orders is to question God.

Imperial Christians have a warped view of patriotism. McCain appealed to the militaristic, nationalistic impulses of the Republican base. This, to the everlasting shame of Christians, is the home of the Religious Right. To imperial Christians, patriotism is supporting militarism, imperialism, xenophobism, and especially, nationalism. Patriotism is love of country; nationalism is love of state. Patriotism results in love for the people of one's country; nationalism results in unconditional allegiance to the government of one's country. The patriot knows his country isn't always right and seeks to change its policies; the nationalist thinks his country is always right and that those who seek a change in policy are traitors. Government tools of propaganda used to get young men to fight have always been the same: nationalism and religion. And what a deadly combination they are.

Imperial Christians have a warped view of Christianity. Aggression, violence, and bloodshed are contrary to the very nature of Christianity. And so is defending, making excuses for, condoning, encouraging, and supporting evil—even if it is committed by one's government. Although God commanded the nation of Israel in the Old Testament to fight against heathen nations (Judges 6:16), the president of the United States is not God, America is not the nation of Israel, the U.S. military is not the Lord's army, the Christian's sword is the word of God, and the only warfare the New Testament encourages the Christian to wage is against the world, the flesh, and the devil. The Gospel of Luke alone records an exchange between our Lord and his disciples that is relevant to the conduct of some conservative Christians today:

> And it came to pass, when the time was come that he should be received up, he stedfastly set his face to go to Jerusalem,
> And sent messengers before his face: and they went, and entered into a village of the Samaritans, to make ready for him.
> And they did not receive him, because his face was as though he would go to Jerusalem.
> And when his disciples James and John saw this, they said, Lord, wilt thou that we command fire to come down from heaven, and consume them, even as Elias did?
> But he turned, and rebuked them, and said, Ye know not what manner of spirit ye are of.
> For the Son of man is not come to destroy men's lives, but to save them. And they went to another village. (Luke 9:51–56)

Christians who call for U.S. air strikes on some uncooperative Iraqi or Afghan village know not what spirit they are of. It is certainly not the Holy Spirit. Christian pulpits all across this land are dripping with blood, and it is not the blood of Christ. We hear more from pulpits today justifying American military intervention in the Middle East than we do about the need for American missionaries to go there. Our churches have supplied more soldiers to the Middle East than missionaries. Can you imagine the Roman army in the days of the early church recruiting from Christian churches? It is sad that the unregenerate soldier kills on behalf of the state; it is tragic when one who professes the name of Christ does likewise.

I am not optimistic about reversing the triumph of imperial Christianity. Not when blind acceptance of government propaganda, willful ignorance of U.S. foreign policy, and childish devotion to the military is the norm among conservative Christians instead of the exception.

For further reading on the subject of imperial Christianity, see G. J. Heering, The Fall of Christianity: A Study of Christianity, the State, and War *(Fellowship Publications, 1943); Anne C. Loveland,* American Evangelicals and the U.S. Military 1942–1993 *(Louisiana State University Press, 1996); and Andrew J. Bacevich,* The New American Militarism: How Americans Are Seduced by War *(Oxford, 2005).*

* * * * *

CAN A CHRISTIAN KILL FOR HIS GOVERNMENT?

This is a serious and controversial question to ask anytime, but especially in the midst of a war. But that is exactly what Bennie Lee Fudge did—in 1943.

I only know two things about Mr. Fudge: he was from Alabama and he wrote a book in 1943 called *Can a Christian Kill for His Government?* I suspect that he was a Church of Christ minister, but I don't know for certain.

Fudge doesn't claim to be adding anything new to the subject of the Christian's relationship to civil government and his participation in government wars, but says that his work "is an effort to collect in logical, systematic form, the principal arguments that have been presented by those who affirm the right of the Christian to participate in these activities, and to study these arguments in the light of the Scriptures." Following each of these arguments, Fudge presents his "reasons for holding to the opposite view."

There are no gray areas in Fudge's thinking. He considers the question of Christians killing for the government in combat to be a black or white issue:

> Either I am wrong in advising Christian boys against accepting combatant service, and will be held responsible before God for encouraging them to shirk their duty, not only to their country, but to God; or those are wrong who teach these young men to go willingly into combatant service, and will be held responsible in

> the judgment for encouraging them to violate one of the most sacred commands of God in shedding the blood of their fellow man.

Fudge condemns preachers who, under the pressure of public opinion, encourage their young men to enlist in the business of bloodshed and then later, when cooler heads prevail, change their position when some of the young men who enlisted with their blessing will never come back alive and have a chance to change their position. He astutely recognizes that wars must be sold to the public with a tremendous national propaganda campaign. He has no use for those who try to cloak wars under the banner of defense:

> It is impossible for a man to judge between offensive and defensive wars while the war is in progress and he is involved in it. Napoleon declared in his last days that he had never waged an offensive war. The people of Germany believed in World War I and also in this present war that they were defending their fatherland. It is axiomatic in war that the best defense is a good offensive.

The plan of book is straightforward. Fudge presents two propositions:

> The Bible authorizes the Christian's acting as a punitive agent of the civil government, either as a law enforcement officer or as a soldier in the army.
>
> The Bible forbids the Christian's acting as a punitive agent of the civil government, either as a law enforcement officer or as a soldier in the army.

He spends the first part of the book refuting the first proposition and the second part of the book affirming the second.

In the first part of the book, Fudge introduces a subject (15 in all), presents supporting evidence, and provides a summary in the form of three statements. This is all followed by his reply. The subjects covered are: Spiritual and Material Realms, Jewish and Roman Practice, The Instinct of Self-Preservation, Innocence and Guilt, Servants of the Kingdoms of This World, They That Take the Sword Perish with the Sword, Moral and Penal Law, Cleansing the Temple, Civil Government Ordained of God, Paul's Use of Armed Defense, Cornelius the Soldier, The Philippian Jailor, Combatant and Non-Combatant Service, The Hebrew Words for "Kill," and Historical Evidence.

Here is his section on Romans 13.

IX. CIVIL GOVERNMENT ORDAINED OF GOD

Read Romans 13:1–7. The civil government is ordained of God. Christians must be subject to it and support it for conscience' sake, which places civil government as an institution in the realm of that which is morally right. Conscience has to do with matters morally right and wrong. The God-ordained purpose of the divinely approved institution of civil government is to bear the sword, punish evil-doers, and praise the righteous. But civil government works through its citizens and subjects.

1. It is right for a citizen of the civil government, acting as an agent of the government, to bear the sword in punishment of evildoers.

2. Christians are citizens of the civil government, and Christians may do anything that is right.

3. Therefore Christians, as citizens of the civil government and acting as agents of the government, may bear the sword in punishment of evil-doers.

REPLY

The first premise is defective. Logically to draw the above conclusion, the first premise must be construed to mean, "It is right for *any* citizen of the civil government, acting as an agent of the government, to bear the sword and punish evil-doers." It is assumed that "the powers that be" of Romans 13:1 includes the civil government with all its citizens and subjects. Since this assumption would include Christians, the first premise is in reality begging the question.

A study of Romans 13 will show that Paul considers the Christian as entirely separate from "the powers that be." "Let *every soul* be in subjection to the higher powers." Paul is considering the government as one party, the Christian as another, the Christian subject to the government. This applied to *every soul* among the Christians. "He (the power, the administrator of civil government) is a minister of God to thee for good." Not that the Christian is the minister of God in this capacity, but that another party—he, third person, automatically excluding the Christian who is addressed in the second person—is such a minister. Notice the same distinction in the following verses, "But if *thou* do that which is evil, be afraid; for *he* (not thou) beareth not the sword in vain: for *he* (not thou) is a minister of God, an avenger for wrath to him that doeth evil."

Now comes the Christian's part in this order of things—"Wherefore *ye* must needs be in subjection, not only because of the wrath, but also for conscience' sake. For for this cause *ye* pay tribute also; For *they* (not ye, now) are ministers of God's service, attending continually upon this very thing. Render to all their dues: tribute to whom tribute is due; custom to whom custom; fear to whom fear; honor to whom honor." It is strikingly noticeable that in listing the services "due" the devil government by the Christian, Paul did not include "defense to whom defense is due" or "vengeance to whom vengeance is due." Those two duties have always been expected of their subjects by the civil governments, yet inspiration nowhere names them as due by the Christian. It is similarly outstanding that while he mentions that *ye* (Christians) should pay tribute, custom, honor, fear, be subject, it is always *he* or *they* when bearing the sword is mentioned. So far as Romans 13 goes, the Christian's relationship to political government is wholly passive. This is the teaching of the entire New Testament on the matter. There is not one example, command, or necessary inference of the Christian by divine sanction taking an active part in civil or military government.

Since it is clear that in Romans 13 Paul considers the sword-bearer and the Christian as separate and distinct individuals, our premise, to represent correctly the teaching of the passage, would read, "It is right for some citizens of the civil government, acting as agents of the government, to bear the sword and punish evil-doers." In this case it remains to be proved that Christians fall in that class qualified to bear the sword and punish evildoers. This is the point to be proved in the beginning, so this argument is begging the question, and there no logical argument at all.

In the second part of the book, Fudge follows basically the same format as the first. He introduces a subject (6 in all), presents supporting evidence, and provides a summary in the form of three statements. There is no reply here because Fudge is affirming his proposition that "The Bible forbids the Christian's acting as a punitive agent of the civil government, either as a law enforcement officer or as a soldier in the army." The topics in this part of the book are: God's Penal Law, International Nature of the Church, God's Use of a Prepared People, For What

May a Christian Fight?, Is It a Good Work?, and Historical Evidence.

In this last section, Fudge relies heavily on the Church Father Tertullian, such as this quote from his work *De Corona*:

> Shall it be held lawful to make an occupation of the sword, when the Lord proclaims that he who uses the sword shall perish by the sword? And shall the son of peace take part in the battle when it does not become him even to sue at law? And shall he apply the chain, and the prison, and the torture, and the punishment, who is not the avenger even of his own wrongs? Shall he, forsooth, either keep watch-service for others more than for Christ, or shall he do it on the Lord's day, when he does not even do it for Christ Himself? And shall he keep guard before the temples which he has renounced?

He also refers to modern historians who name aversion to the imperial military service, disregard for politics, and lack of patriotism as reasons the Romans persecuted the early Christians.

Fudge concludes:

> I can do anything for the government that I can do for an individual or a corporation: and, outside the things due the government by God's decree, I can do nothing for the government that I cannot do for an individual or a corporation.

Can a Christian Kill for His Government? appears to have been privately printed and distributed by the author in limited quantities. It has no doubt been out of print for decades. I only recently discovered this valuable 64-page book and reprinted it as part of my Classic Reprints series. Fudge's book is an important addition to the genre of anti-war literature from a biblical perspective.

If you are aware of any other long-forgotten anti-war books or articles that you feel are worthy of being reprinted, please contact me about including them in my Classic Reprints series.

* * * * *

PRO-LIFERS FOR MASS MURDER

> "Out of the same mouth proceedeth blessing and cursing. My brethren, these things ought not so to be. Doth a fountain send forth at the same place sweet water and bitter? Can the fig tree, my

> brethren, bear olive berries? either a vine, figs? so can no fountain both yield salt water and fresh." (James 3:10–12)

Pro-lifers are dedicated to the idea that God values all human life, they are committed to educating women about the dangers to their physical and emotional health if they undergo abortions, they are relentless in pointing out the horrors of abortion—and they are some of the most bloodthirsty warmongers on the planet.

Beginning in 1984, the Sunday in January closest to January 22 has been designed by many pro-life and religious organizations as Sanctity of Human Life Sunday. This is designed to coincide with the anniversary of the infamous *Roe v. Wade* Supreme Court decision in 1973 that overrode most state abortion statutes and effectively made abortion a fundamental constitutional right.

Every year on Sanctity of Human Life Sunday churches of all denominations observe this day with special sermons, prayers, and presentations, testimonies from former abortionists, recognition of pro-life organizations, denunciations of pro-choice politicians, Planned Parenthood, and the *Roe v. Wade* decision, calls for legislation to restrict abortion, and distribution of anti-abortion literature.

As both a Christian and a steadfast opponent of abortion (see my articles "For Whom Would Jesus Vote?" and "Is Ron Paul Wrong on Abortion?" and "The Pro-Life Assault on Ron Paul and the Constitution"), I sympathize with the pro-life cause. But I go much further than the typical pro-lifer. I don't think abortion is okay after the third trimester; that is, I believe in the right to life for everyone—including adults and foreigners.

How many churches on the recent Sanctity of Human Life Sunday mentioned the right to life of countless numbers of Iraqis and Afghans who have been killed by American bombs and bullets in unjust wars instigated by the United States? How many churches mentioned the right to life of U.S. soldiers who have died in vain and for a lie in senseless foreign wars? If the pro-lifers in churches that observed Sanctity of Human Life Sunday care about innocent children then surely they mentioned children in Iraq and Afghanistan who have lost their parents because of the U.S. waging war on their countries, children born with birth defects due to the U.S. military using depleted uranium, and children in Iraq killed by brutal U.S. sanctions? Surely they mentioned the orphaned and emotionally scarred children of dead and injured U.S. soldiers?

Although some churches may have mentioned these things, I

suspect that the number is rather small or, in the case of most evangelical churches, very insignificant. And if it be argued that the churches that observed Sanctity of Human Life Sunday should be excused because the day is just about abortion then what about the rest of the year? Do not adults have the same right to life as unborn children? Do not foreigners who are not a threat to this country have the same right to life as American babies? Do not U.S. soldiers have the same right to life that other Americans have?

But in some churches it is even worse. Not only is no mention ever made of these things, the U.S. wars in Iraq and Afghanistan are defended and celebrated. Although they may call themselves evangelical churches, they are warvangelical churches. They are churches that worship God *and* venerate the institution of the military; they are churches that preach Christ and promote warmongering Republican politicians. They are pro-lifers for mass murder.

It is only natural that most pro-lifers love Republican politicians. At the Family Research Council's Values Voter Summit held in Washington DC this past September, Rep. Mike Pence (R-IN) was the top choice of conservative activists. This same group named abortion as the top issue they were concerned about. Pence was also the top pick for vice president.

The German Nazis fought for the fatherland. The Soviet Red Army fought for the motherland. Mike Pence wants Americans to fight for the homeland. He "supported creation of the new Department of Homeland Security, the largest reorganization of the government since the beginning of the Cold War." Because of the Department of Homeland Security, "our ability to defend the homeland is more effective, efficient and organized." Pence is a committed supporter of the bogus war on terror. He even repeats the ridiculous canard that "we must take the fight to the terrorists overseas so we don't have to face them here at home."

The runner up to Pence in the Values Voters straw poll was the former preacher Mike Huckabee, who won the top spot last year. Huckabee not only supported the sending of more troops to their death in Iraq, he actually maintained that we should not withdraw from Iraq because "we are winning." This advocate of perpetual war in the Middle East had only one criticism for Bush regarding his handling of the war in Iraq: he was too timid and not sufficiently bloodthirsty.

Pence and Huckabee are no different from DeMint, Romney, Gingrich, Giuliani, McCain, Graham, Palin, and Santourm—they are all ardent supporters of war, empire, and police statism. Yet, any one of these individuals would get the support of most evangelicals as long as they played the pro-life card. Once a Republican candidate passes a pro-life litmus test (applied to just American babies), nothing else about them seems to matter. They could call for bombing Iran, Pakistan, or Yemen back to the Stone Age and it wouldn't change anything.

Why are pro-lifers so indifferent to, and in some cases so defensive of, war, militarism, and nationalism? I think the main reason is ignorance. Ignorance of the Republican Party. Ignorance of U.S. foreign policy. Ignorance of history. Ignorance of the military. Ignorance of the Bible they profess to believe. This is especially true if all one does is listen to SRN News on radio, watch Fox News on television, and read news by the American Family Association on the Internet. The importance of LewRockwell.com must here be mentioned. I have lost count of the number of Christians that have written me about how LRC has been instrumental in changing their thinking.

Pro-lifers should be just as concerned about their government sanctioning the killing of foreigners on the battlefield in an unjust war as they are about their government sanctioning the killing of babies in the womb in an abortion.

It is hypocrisy in the highest degree to talk about the sanctity of life and the evils of abortion and then turn around and show contempt for, or indifference to, the lives of adults and foreigners.

Out of the same mouth proceedeth blessing and cursing. Pro-lifers, these things ought not so to be.

* * * * *

THE GREATEST CHRISTIAN WARMONGER OF ALL TIME

I had never heard of Ellis Washington until I saw his recent *WorldNetDaily* article titled "Nation-building? No, Christian-building" and did some digging. Besides being a weekend commentator for *WorldNetDaily*, Washington is a black conservative, a graduate of the John Marshall Law School, former editor of the *Michigan Law Review*, host of an Atlanta radio program, and a lecturer and freelance writer on constitutional law, legal history, and critical race theory. He is also a devotee of radio talk show host Michael Savage (read his sickening tribute to Savage here) and, above all, the greatest Christian warmonger of all time.

I know, you think I'm grossly exaggerating. You have seen some of my articles with provocative titles like "Christian Killers?" "Pro-Lifers for Mass Murder," "Cursed Be the Christian Coalition," and "The Christian Axis of Evil" and you think I'm just trying to stimulate your interest by using hyperbole in the extreme.

I assure you that I am not exaggerating, grossly or otherwise. I assure you that I am not using hyperbole, in the extreme or otherwise. And I also assure you that Ellis Washington is the greatest Christian warmonger of all time. Yes, I know that time hasn't ended yet, and that there might remain a great deal of time for more Christian warmongers to make themselves known. But you have got to read this statement from Ellis Washington for yourself:

> If America is really serious about combating worldwide Islamic terrorism and the increasing reports of Christian genocide among the 44 Muslim nations, then let us take up the battle cry of Ann Coulter and the Muslim author who converted to Christianity and train our military not only to kill and destroy our enemies but to convert them to Christianity.

The first part of the "battle cry" Washington is referring to is this 2001 quote by Ann Coulter: "We should invade their countries, kill their leaders and convert them to Christianity. We weren't punctilious about locating and punishing only Hitler and his top officers. We carpet-bombed German cities; we killed civilians. That's war. And this is war."

The second part of Washington's "battle cry" is from a Christian convert from Islam he heard on the radio expressing this sentiment: "America must use its military to go to every Muslim nation in the world and convert them to Christianity; it is the only way to end the Muslim jihad against the West, against Christianity and against civilization."

Washington also wants to combine "Coulter's battle cry together with the Newtonian principle that to every action there is always an equal and opposite reaction" and send the U.S. military on "an international comprehensive Christian conversion campaign." "A conversion policy will obviate the need for perpetual nation building," he says.

But Washington does Coulter one better: "My one revision of Coulter is not that we *should* invade their countries: 'We *must* invade their countries, kill their leaders and convert them to Christianity.'" He wants the U.S. military to "join Christ's battle cry" and honor the Marine Corps hymn.

Washington's comments are so ludicrous and so contrary to sound Christian doctrine that every armchair Christian warrior, Christian Coalition moralist, Religious Right warvangelical, Reich-wing Christian nationalist, theocon Values Voter, Red-State Christian fascist, and God and country Christian bumpkin that I have ever criticized for supporting the wars in Iraq and Afghanistan should be ashamed and embarrassed at his comments.

Washington's mention of America's conflict with the Barbary Pirates over two hundred years ago—as if it has anything to do with the current "war on terror"—is ludicrous. But because other apologists for the "war on terror" have also brought it up, I will address that subject in a future article.

It's not often that I am rendered speechless. I have but seven brief comments to make.

One, how can *WorldNetDaily* continue to publish Washington?

Two, the attacks of 9/11 were political acts that were not undertaken because of our freedoms, way of life, culture, or religion. The reason why any Muslims hate us or are trying to kill us is because of our wretched foreign policy and occupation of their countries.

Three, the aberrant Christianity advocated by Washington will turn away multitudes of unbelievers from real Christianity.

Four, the U.S. military is not God's army. The Lord never sanctioned any crusade of Christians against any religion. The God of the Bible never called, commanded, or encouraged any Christian to kill, make apologies for the killing of, or excuse the killing of any adherent to a false religion.

Five, what kind of genuine conversion to Christianity can be obtained at the point of a gun?

Six, what Washington proposes—forced conversion—is something Muslims have been criticized for. How can he advocate that U.S. soldiers—many of whom are not even Christians—"convert" our "enemies" to Christianity?

And seven, Washington is a coward. If he believes that Christ died for our sins and rose from the dead while Muhammad was a sinner who died and stayed buried, then why doesn't he go to Pakistan, Yemen, or Saudi Arabia and stand on the street corner and preach it and see how many conversions he gets? Why doesn't he go to these countries and kill with his own hands those who reject Christianity? Why doesn't he enlist in the military himself? I know the military has relaxed its standards. Perhaps he will be allowed in. But no, Washington wants instead to send your sons, your fathers, your brothers, and your friends to do what he doesn't have the courage to do.

Ellis Washington is the greatest Christian warmonger of all time, bar none. What else needs to be said?

* * * * *

A CHRISTIAN WARMONGER ON STEROIDS

Unfazed by the disastrous wars in Iraq and Afghanistan, there can still be found Christian warmongers who defend these fiascos. But Bryan Fischer, who blogs for the American Family Association, is not your typical Christian warmonger. He is a Christian warmonger on steroids.

Fischer is the director of Issue Analysis for Government and Public Policy at the American Family Association and host of the daily "Focal Point" radio talk program on American Family Radio. But he should also be a member of the Christian axis of evil.

I first discovered Mr. Fischer when a reader alerted me to a recent column of his ("The Feminization of the Medal of Honor") about the awarding of the Medal of Honor to a soldier for heroism in Afghanistan. Army Staff Sgt. Salvatore Giunta took a bullet, pulled a soldier to safety, rescued another one from Taliban, and lived to receive his medal in person—the only one of the eight Medal of Honor winners during the wars in Iraq and Afghanistan to do so.

Fischer maintains that "we have feminized the Medal of Honor." This is a "disturbing trend" that he has noticed, but "which few others seem to have recognized." He laments that "every Medal of Honor awarded during these two conflicts has been awarded for saving life." He is upset that "not one has been awarded for inflicting casualties on the enemy." Fischer wants U.S. soldiers to do one thing—kill:

> So the question is this: when are we going to start awarding the Medal of Honor once again for soldiers who kill people and break things so our families can sleep safely at night?
>
> I would suggest our culture has become so feminized that we have become squeamish at the thought of the valor that is expressed in killing enemy soldiers through acts of braver
>
> We rightly honor those who give up their lives to save their comrades. It's about time we started also honoring those who kill bad guys.

The reaction to Fischer's column was fierce. The comments posted were overwhelmingly negative. I made the mistake of printing out the article without checking to see how long the comment section was. The comments actually took up fifty-one pages versus the one page taken up by the article. The reaction was so fierce that two days later Fischer wrote about the subject again in another column ("The Feminization of the

Medal of Honor—Part II") in which he complained that the comments about his first piece were "angry, vituperative, hate-filled, and laced with both profanity and blasphemy." (I read them all and saw very little profanity and blasphemy). Fischer deludes himself by accusing "readers who have reacted so viscerally to what I wrote" of not reading all of his 600-word piece or not reading it at all and just relying on "what others said about the column."

In his second column, Fischer begins by clarifying that "it is altogether right that we honor heroism and bravery when it is expressed in self sacrifice" and emphasizing that he believes in honoring soldiers for "exceptional bravery in defense of our own troops." But then he brings up his passion again—killing:

> What I am saying is that I am observing a trend in which we single out bravery in self-defense and yet seem hesitant to single out bravery in launching aggressive attacks that result in the deaths of enemy soldiers.
>
> It is striking that a certain amount of the criticism I have received actually verifies my thesis. In response to my call to also honor those who have killed bad guys in defense of our country, I have been called everything from savage to brute to bloodthirsty to anti-American to un-American to traitor to "expletives deleted" to the antichrist himself.
>
> Surely some of this supports my contention that we have become too squeamish to honor such valor. It's almost as if it embarrasses us, as if we feel there is something inappropriate about awarding our highest honor to those who kill the enemy in battle.
>
> It apparently is easier for us to honor valor when exhibited in self-defense, but we find ourselves reluctant to honor killing the enemy when we are the aggressor in a military setting.

I guess Fischer's ideal candidate for the Medal of Honor would be Lt. William Caley or a worker on the Manhattan Project.

After trying to justify his unholy desire with Scripture, which arguments I will examine in due course, Fischer closes his second column thusly:

> War is certainly a terrible thing, and should only be waged for the highest and most just of causes. But if the cause is just, then there is great honor in achieving military success, success which should

> be celebrated and rewarded.
>
> The bottom line here is that the God of the Bible clearly honors those who show valor and gallantry in waging aggressive war in a just cause against the enemies of freedom, even while inflicting massive casualties in the process. What I'm saying is that it's time we started imitating God's example again.

There are two issues here that need to be addressed. One, Fischer's support for U.S. soldiers killing in Iraq and Afghanistan. And two, Fischer's attempt to justify, with Scripture, his passion for killing.

Fischer just takes it as a given that the current wars the United States is embroiled in are just wars. The truth, of course, is that they are two of the most unjust wars the United States has ever fought. See, for example, five hundred random articles on the Internet, many of them mine. And, to rephrase Fischer: If the cause is unjust, then there is great dishonor in achieving military success and such success should be condemned and punished. A war that is not justifiable is nothing short of mass murder.

The mentality of Fischer and other Christian warmongers is that the enemies of the United States are enemies of freedom and if the U.S. military is doing the killing then the cause is just. But why are Iraq and Afghanistan even considered to be bad guys that are our enemies? Did Iraq and Afghanistan attack the United States on 9/11? Did any of the men that are claimed to be the 9/11 hijackers even come from Iraq and Afghanistan? Oh, but we didn't go to war just because of 9/11. Right, the Bush administration, congressional war hawks, and their willing accomplices in the media gave twenty-seven different rationales for the Iraq war alone. No Iraqi or Afghan was ever or is presently a threat to any American in the United States. And no Iraqi or Afghan was ever a threat to any American solder until the United States invaded their countries and started unleashing the full force of its military. And neither can soldiers be said to be acting in self-defense because the war itself was not for self-defense. It was an act of naked aggression that was supposed to be a cakewalk, but it backfired with disastrous results for the United States.

My greatest problem with Fischer is his misuse of Scripture. As Wilma Ann Bailey remarks in her book *You Shall Not Kill or You Shall Not Murder? The Assault on a Biblical Text* (Collegeville: Liturgical Press, 2005): "People want to kill people, and they want biblical permission to do so."

Regarding Fischer's contention that "we have become too squeamish to honor such valor" as killing our enemies, he says that "the

Scriptures certainly know nothing of such squeamishness." He then gives the example of King David, a man who had slain "his ten thousands" (1 Samuel 18:7), "fought with the Philistines, and brought away their cattle, and smote them with a great slaughter" (1 Samuel 23:5), smote the Amalekites "from the twilight even unto the evening of the next day: and there escaped not a man of them, save four hundred young men, which rode upon camels, and fled" (1 Samuel 30:17), "smote the Philistines from Geba until thou come to Gazer" (2 Samuel 5:25), and warred against the Philistines, Moab, Zobah, Syria, and Edom (2 Samuel 8:1, 2, 3, 5, 6, 13, 14). And remember, says Fischer, that David was a man after God's own heart (1 Samuel 13:14).

But as I have pointed out many times, it is wrong to invoke the Jewish wars of the Old Testament against the heathen as a justification for the actions of the U.S. military. Although God sponsored these wars, and used the Jewish nation to conduct them, it does not follow that God sponsors American wars or that America is God's chosen nation. The U.S. president is not King David, America is not the nation of Israel, the U.S. military is not the Lord's army, and God never commanded any Christian to war on his behalf. The fact that King David did what he did under divine sanction has absolutely no bearing on anything the U.S. military does.

And Fischer is not giving us the whole story of King David:

> Then David the king stood up upon his feet, and said, Hear me, my brethren, and my people: As for me, I had in mine heart to build an house of rest for the ark of the covenant of the LORD, and for the footstool of our God, and had made ready for the building: But God said unto me, Thou shalt not build an house for my name, because thou hast been a man of war, and hast shed blood. (1 Chronicles 28:2–3)

I guess King David is not a good example after all.

Fischer also invokes John the Baptist's conversation with Roman soldiers: "Christianity is not a religion of pacifism. Remember that John the Baptist did not tell the soldiers who came to him to lay down their arms, even when they asked him directly, 'what shall we do?' (Luke 3:14)." True, but neither is Christianity a religion of murder. I have discussed John the Baptist's rules for soldiers here.

Fischer's desire for "massive casualties" to be inflicted while being honored by one's god is reminiscent of a Muslim suicide bomber that Fischer would label a bad guy and our enemy.

Aside from theological differences, it is because of warmongering chickenhawk Christians like Fischer that non-Christians, nominal Christians, Catholic Christians, Orthodox Christians, and mainline Protestant Christians often have an unfavorable opinion of evangelical Christians. Fischer has also further damaged the image of the American Family Association.

Bryan Fischer is not the greatest Christian warmonger of all time, but he is without doubt a Christian warmonger on steroids.

* * * * *

THE CRIMINALITY OF WAR

Even without the WikiLeaks revelations that U.S. helicopter pilots gunned down twelve Iraqi civilians, that U.S. soldiers ignored brutal torture carried out by Iraqi security forces, that the U.S. military withheld from the public information about 15,000 Iraqi civilian deaths, that U.S. special forces have been secretly embedded with Pakistani military, that the U.S. government massacred children and was complicit in the Yemeni government taking the blame for the deed, and that U.S. troops carelessly killed civilians and then covered it up, there were numerous criminal acts perpetrated by the United States military under the guise of the war on terror.

Here are just a few representative examples:

- Members of Stryker Combat Brigade in Afghanistan Accused of Killing Civilians for Sport

According to charging documents, the unprovoked, fatal attack on Jan. 15 was the start of a months-long shooting spree against Afghan civilians that resulted in some of the grisliest allegations against American soldiers since the U.S. invasion in 2001. Members of the platoon have been charged with dismembering and photographing corpses, as well as hoarding a skull and other human bones.

- Afghanistan Wedding Party Hit by Massive Bomb

At least 21 people were killed last night and 83 wounded after a massive bomb ripped through a wedding party in a village in Kandahar where US special forces have pioneered a controversial militia programme to encourage people to defend themselves in return for development projects.

• US Troops "Murdered Afghan Civilians and Kept Body Parts"

A group of US soldiers murdered a number of Afghan civilians and took body parts as trophies, documents released by military officials allege.

• U.S. Soldiers Charged with Murdering Civilians in Afghanistan War

A dozen US soldiers have been charged with a series of crimes committed in Afghanistan, including the murder of three Afghan civilians and the subsequent cover-up, according to documents the US Army released Wednesday. CNN reports that the soldiers from the 5th Brigade, 2nd Infantry Division out of Washington state have been charged in connection with the attempted cover-up of the murder and assault of Afghan civilians, as well as the mutilation of dead Afghans, and drug use.

• Troops Carrying Out "Battlefield Executions" in Afghanistan, Seymour Hersh Says

What they've done in the field now is, they tell the troops, you have to make a determination within a day or two or so whether or not the prisoners you have, the detainees, are Taliban. You must extract whatever tactical intelligence you can get, as opposed to strategic, long-range intelligence, immediately. And if you cannot conclude they're Taliban, you must turn them free. What it means is, and I've been told this anecdotally by five or six different people, battlefield executions are taking place. Well, if they can't prove they're Taliban, bam. If we don't do it ourselves, we turn them over to the nearby Afghan troops and by the time we walk three feet the bullets are flying. And that's going on now.

• US Special Forces "Tried to Cover-up" Botched Khataba Raid in Afghanistan

US special forces soldiers dug bullets out of their victims' bodies in the bloody aftermath of a botched night raid, then washed the wounds with alcohol before lying to their superiors about what happened.

- Cluster Bombs, Decapitation Bombing Killed Hundreds

Hundreds of civilians were killed by Coalition cluster bombs and air strikes designed to decapitate the Iraqi leadership, according to a new report by New York-based Human Rights Watch (HRW), which said the high cost in civilian casualties caused by the two tactics may have violated the laws of war.

- US Army "Kill Team" in Afghanistan Posed for Photos of Murdered Civilians

Commanders in Afghanistan are bracing themselves for possible riots and public fury triggered by the publication of "trophy" photographs of US soldiers posing with the dead bodies of defenceless Afghan civilians they killed.

According to American and Pakistani sources, U.S. drone attacks in Pakistan kill ten civilians for every "militant" killed. And according to U.S. General Stanley McChrystal, of the more than thirty people who have been killed and the eighty who have been wounded in convoy and checkpoint shootings in Afghanistan since the summer of 2009, not one was found to have been a threat: "We have shot an amazing number of people, but to my knowledge, none has ever proven to be a threat," said the general.

But as bad as these war crimes are, it should never be forgotten that the wars in Iraq and Afghanistan are themselves criminal. It doesn't matter if these crimes were carried out by a few bad apples or rogue outfits, or if they are merely isolated instances or if a majority of U.S. soldiers did not participate. The danger in focusing on the above war crimes—and even terming them crimes—masks the real crime that has been perpetrated against Iraq and Afghanistan.

The invasion and occupation of Iraq and Afghanistan, the destruction of infrastructure in countries that were not a threat to the United States, and the killing and wounding of hundreds of thousands of Iraqis and Afghans who hadn't lifted a finger against any Americans until their countries were targeted by the United States is the real crime.

These wars are crimes against not only the Iraq and Afghan peoples, but against the thousands of U.S. soldiers who died in vain and for a lie, against the thousands of U.S. soldiers who needlessly suffered horrific injuries that were not worth it, against the thousands of family members of U.S. soldiers who must unnecessarily endure mental anguish over lost loved ones, and against the American taxpayers who are on the hook for trillions of dollars.

And yet, conservatives gave one of the chief war criminals, Donald Rumsfeld, the "Defender of the Constitution Award" at their annual CPAC. Fittingly, the award was presented by another one of the chief war criminals, Dick Cheney. I stand by what I have said several times about conservatives: The very heart and soul of conservatism is war. Patriotism, Americanism, and being a real conservative are now equated with support for war, torture, and militarism.

It is unfortunate that many conservative Christians are also conservative warmongers. To them I offer, and to all other conservative warmongers, the compelling insight of Howard Malcom (1799–1879), former president of Georgetown College, Kentucky. What it especially important about Malcom's treatise on the "Criminality of War" is that it was reprinted in *The Book of Peace: A Collection of Essays on War and Peace*—published by the American Peace Society in 1845, long before the horrors of twentieth-century wars were chronicled, and even before images of war were captured on photographs.

CRIMINALITY OF WAR

By Howard Malcom, D. D.
President of Georgetown College, KY

That man is a fallen and depraved creature, is every where apparent in the ferocious dispositions of his nature. Hence, to speak of him as in "a state of nature," has been to speak of him as "a savage." A savage finds in war and bloodshed his only means of honor and fame, and he becomes, both in the chase and the camp, *a beast of prey*.

In proportion as war prevails among civilized nations, it banishes whatever tends to refine and elevate, suspends the pursuits of industry, destroys the works of art, and sets them back towards barbarism. Wherever it comes, cities smoke in ruins, and fields are trodden under foot. The husband is torn from his wife, the father from his children, the aged lose their prop, and woman is consigned to unwonted toils and perpetual alarms. As it passes, the halls of science grow lonely, improvements pause, benevolence is fettered, violence supersedes law, and even the sanctuary of God is deserted, or becomes a manger, a hospital, or a fortress. In its actual encounters, every movement is immeasurably horrid, with wounds, anguish, and death; while amid the din of wrath and strife, a stream of immortal souls is hurried, unprepared, to their final audit.

That tyrants should lead men into wars of pride and conquest, is not strange. But that *the people*, in governments comparatively free, should so readily lend themselves to a business in which they bear all the sufferings, can gain nothing, and may lose all, is matter of astonishment indeed.

But the chief wonder is that CHRISTIANS, followers of the Prince of Peace, should have concurred in this mad idolatry of strife, and thus been inconsistent not only with themselves, but with the very genius of their system. Behold a man going from the Lord's Supper, fantastically robed and plumed, drilling himself into skilful modes of butchery, and studying the tactics of death! Behold him murdering his fellow Christians, and praying to his Divine Master for success in the endeavor! Behold processions marching to the house of God to celebrate bloody victories, and give thanks for having been able to send thousands and tens of thousands to their last account with all their sins upon their heads! Stupendous inconsistency!

Surely this matter should remain no longer unexamined. It *cannot*. In this age of light, when every form of vice and error is discussed and resisted, this great evil, the prolific parent of unnumbered abominations, must be attacked also. Christians are waking up to see and do their duty to one another, to their neighbors, and to the distant heathen. They cannot continue to overlook *war*. I persuade myself that there are few, even now, who object to its being discussed.

I propose not to discuss the whole subject of war;—a vast theme. I shall abstain from presenting it in the light of philosophy, politics, or patriotism; in each of which points of light I have studied it, and feel that it demands most serious attention. In the following observations, war will be discussed only as it concerns a Christian.

Happily, there are few who would oppose the prevalence and perpetuity of peace. The need of discussion lies not in the bloodthirsty character of our countrymen, nor in the existence of active efforts to propagate and prolong the miseries of war; but in the *apathy* that prevails on this subject, and the almost total want of reflection in regard to it. A military spirit is so wrought into the habits of national thinking, and into all our patriotic pomps and festivals, that the occasional occurrence of war is deemed a matter of course. Even the fervent friends of man's highest welfare seem to regard a general pacification of the world, and the disuse of fleets and armies, as a mere Utopian scheme, and chose to give their money and prayers to objects which seem of more probable attainment. This apathy and incredulity are to be overcome only by discussion.

The following observations will be confined to two points.

I. *War is criminal because inconsistent with Christianity.*
II. *This criminality is enormous.*

I. ITS INCONSISTENCY WITH CHRISTIANITY.

1. It contradicts the entire genius and intention of Christianity.

Christianity requires us to seek to amend the condition of man. War always deteriorates and destroys. The world is at this moment not one whit better, in any respect, for all the wars of five thousand years. If here and there some good may be traced to war, the amount of evil, on the whole, is immeasurably greater. Christianity, if it prevailed, would make earth once more a paradise. War makes it a slaughter house, a desert, a den of thieves and murderers, a hell. Christianity cancels and condemns the law of retaliation. War is based upon that very principle. Christianity remedies all human woes. War makes them.

The *causes* of war are as inconsistent with Christianity as its effects. It originates in the worst passions, and the worst crimes, James iv., 1, 2. We may *always* trace it to the thirst of revenge, the acquisition of territory, the monopoly of commerce, the quarrels of kings, the coercion of religious opinions, or some such unholy source. There *never* was a war, devised by man, founded on holy tempers, and Christian principles.

All the features, all the concomitants, all the results of war, are opposed to the features, the concomitants, the results of Christianity. The two systems conflict in every point, irreconcilably and forever.

2. War sets at naught the entire example of Jesus.

"Learn of me," says the Divine Examplar. And can we learn fighting from him? His conduct was always pacific. He became invisible when the Nazarites sought to cast him from their precipice. The troops that came to arrest him in the garden, he struck down, but not dead. His constant declaration was, that he "came not to destroy men's lives, but to save."

True, he once instructed his disciples to buy swords, telling them that they were going forth as sheep among wolves. But the whole passage shows he was speaking by parable, as he generally did. The disciples answered, "here are two swords." He instantly replies, "it is enough." If he had spoken literally, how could two swords suffice for twelve Apostles? Nay, when Peter used one of these, it was too much. Christ reproved him, and healed the wound. He meant to teach them their danger, not their refuge. His metaphor was misunderstood, just as it was when he said, "beware of the leaven of the Pharisees," and they thought he meant bread.

Once he drove men from the temple. But it was with "a whip of small cords." *Moral* influence drove them. A crowd of such fellows was not to be overcome by one man with a whip. He expressly declared that his servants *should not* fight, for his kingdom was not of this world. His whole life was the sublime personification of benevolence. He was the PRINCE OF PEACE.

Do we forget that Christ is our example? Whatever is right for us to do, would in general have been right for him to do. Imagine the Savior robed in the trappings of a man of blood, leading columns to slaughter, setting fire to cities, laying waste the country, storming fortresses, and consigning thousands to wounds, anguish and death, just to define a boundary, settle a point of policy, or decide some kingly quarrel. Could "meekness and lowliness of heart" be learned from him thus engaged?

There is no rank or station in an army that would become the character of Christ. Nor can any man who makes arms a profession find a pattern in Christ our Lord. But he *ought* to be every man's pattern.

I need not enlarge on this point. It is conceded; for no warrior thinks of making Christ his pattern. How then can a genuine imitator of Christ, consistently be a warrior?

3. War is inconsistent not only with the NATURE of Christianity, and the EXAMPLE OF JESUS, but it violates all the EXPRESS PRECEPTS of Scripture.

Even the Old Testament does not sanction war *as a Custom*. In each case, there mentioned, of lawful war, it was entered upon by the express command of God. If *such* authority were now given, we might worthily resort to arms. But without such authority, how dare we violate the genius of Christianity, and set at naught the example of Christ? The wars mentioned in olden times were not appointed to decide doubtful questions, or to settle quarrels. They were to inflict national punishment, and were intended, as are pestilence and famine, to chastise guilty nations.

As to the New Testament, a multitude of its precepts might be quoted, expressly against all fighting. "Ye have heard, &c., an eye for an eye, but I say unto you *resist not evil.*" "Follow peace with all men." "Love one another." "Do justice, love mercy." "Love your enemies." "Follow righteousness, faith, charity, peace." "Return good for evil." "Let all bitterness, and wrath, and anger, and clamor, and evil speaking, be put away from you, and ye kind one to another, tender-hearted, forgiving one another as God for Christ's sake hath forgiven you." "If my kingdom were of this world, then would my servants fight," etc. "If ye forgive not men their trespasses, neither," &c. "Be ye not overcome of evil, but overcome evil with good." "If thine enemy hunger, feed him, if he thirst, give him drink." "Render not evil for evil, but contrariwise blessing." Such passages might be indefinitely multiplied. They abound in the New Testament. How shall they be disposed of? No interpretation can nullify their force, or change their application. Take *any* sense the words will bear, and they forbid war. They especially forbid *retaliation*, which is always advanced as the best pretext for war.

Such texts as have been just quoted, relate to the single matter of retaliation and fighting. But belligerent nations violate *every* precept of the gospel. It enjoins every man to be meek, lowly, peaceable, easy to be entreated, gentle, thinking no evil, merciful, slow to anger, quiet, studious, patient, temperate, &c. Let a man rehearse, one by one, the whole catalogue of Christian graces, and he will see that war repudiates them all.

Examine that superlative epitome of Christianity, our Lord's sermon on the mount. Its nine benedictions are upon so many classes of persons; the poor in spirit, mourners, the meek, the merciful, the peace-makers, the persecuted, the reviled, those who hunger after righteousness, and the pure in heart. In which of these classes can the professed warrior place himself? Alas, he shuts himself out from all the benedictions of heaven.

The discourse proceeds to teach, not only killing, but anger is murder. It expressly rebukes the law of retaliation; and exploding the traditionary rule of loving our neighbor, and hating our enemy, it requires us to love our enemies, and do good to those that despitefully use us. Afterward, in presenting a form of prayer, it not only teaches us to say, "Forgive our trespasses as we forgive those that trespass against us," but adds, "If ye forgive not men their trespasses, neither will your Heavenly Father forgive you." What a peace sermon is here! What modern peace society goes further, or could be more explicit?

But let us take a few of the Christian graces more in detail. The Christian is required to cherish a sense of direct and supreme responsibility to God. The *irresponsible* feelings of a soldier are a necessary part of his profession, as Lord Wellington said recently, 'A man who has a nice sense of religion, should not be a soldier.' The soldier makes war a *profession*, and must be ready to fight any nation, or any part of his own nation, as he is ordered. He must have no mind of his own. He must march, wheel, load, fire, charge, or retreat, as he is bidden, and because he is bidden. In the language of THOMAS JEFFERSON, "The breaking of men to military discipline, is breaking their spirits to principles of passive obedience." The nearer a soldier comes to a mere machine, the better soldier he makes. Is this right for a Christian? Is it compatible with his duty to "examine all things, and hold fast that which is good?"

The *contempt of life* which is so necessary in a soldier, is a sin. He must walk up to the deadly breach, and maintain ground before the cannon's mouth. But life is inestimable, and belongs to God. He who masters the fear of death, does it either by religious influence, or quenching the fear of God, and all concern about a future state. There is not a gospel precept, which he who makes arms a profession, is not at times compelled to violate.

Nor is there a Christian grace which does not tend to diminish the value of a professed soldier. Some graces are, it is true, useful in camp; where a man may be called to act as a servant, or laborer. It is then desirable that he be honest, meek, faithful, that he may properly attend to a horse, or a wardrobe. But such qualities spoil him for the field. He must there cast away meekness, and fight; he must cast away honesty, and forage; he must cast away forgiveness, and revenge his country; he must not return good for evil, but two blows for one.

Survey an army prepared for battle; see a throng, busy with cannons, muskets, mortars, swords, drums, trumpets, and banners. Do these men look like Christians? Do they talk like followers of the meek and lowly Jesus? Do they act like friends and benefactors of the whole human race? Are the lessons they learn in daily drill, such as will help them in a life of faith?

Mark this army in the hour of battle. See attacks and retreats, battalions annihilated, commanders falling, shouts of onset, groans of death, horses trampling the fallen, limbs flying in the air, suffocating smoke, and thousands smarting in the agony of death, without a cup of water to quench their intolerable thirst! Do the principles of Christianity authorize such a scene? Are such horrors its fruits?

Inspect the field when all is over. The fair harvest trampled and destroyed, houses and batteries smoking in ruin, the mangled and suffering strewed among dead comrades, and dead horses, and broken gun-carriages. Prowlers strip the booty even from the warm bodies of the dying, jackals howl around, and disgusting birds are wheeling in the air;

while the miserable wife seeks her loved one among the general carnage. Does all this look as if Christians had been there, serving the God of mercy? Could such works grow out of the system, heralded as bringing "*Peace on earth*"?

Turn your eyes to the ocean. A huge ship, bristling with implements of death, glides quietly along. Presently "a sail!" is called from sentinel to sentinel. All on board catch the sound, and gaze on the dim and distant outline. At length she is discovered to be a ship of war, and all strain their eyes to see her flag. On that little token hangs the important issue; for no feud, no jealousy exists between the crews. They do not even know each other. At length the signal is discerned to be that of a foe. Immediately what a scene ensues! Decks cleared and sanded, ports opened, guns run out, matches lighted, and every preparation made for bloody work. While waiting for the moment to engage, the worst passions of the men are appealed to to make them fight with fury; and they are inspired with all possible pride, hatred, revenge or ambition.

The fight begins! Death flies with every shot. Blood and carnage cover the decks. The rigging is cut to pieces; the hull bored with hot shot. The smoke, the confusion, the orders of officers, the yells of the wounded, the crash of timbers, the horrors of the cockpit, make a scene at which infernal fiends feel their malignity sated. At length one party strikes, and the strife is stayed. The conquered ship, ere her wounded can be removed, sinks into the deep. The victor, herself almost a wreck, throws overboard the slain, washes her decks, and turns toward her port, carrying the crippled, the agonized, and the dying of both ships! What anguish is there in that ship! What empty berths, late filled with the gay-hearted and the profane! What tidings does she carry, to spread lamentation and misery over hundreds of families!

Yet in all this, there was no personal feud or malice, no private wrong or offence. All was the mere result of some cabinet council, some kingly caprice. Could any enormity be more cold blooded and diabolical?

But no where does war wear such horrors as in a siege. The inhabitants are shut up; business, pleasure, education, intercourse are all checked; sorrow, terror, and distress prevail. Bombs fall and explode in the streets; citizens are killed in their houses, and soldiers on the ramparts. Women and children retreat to the cellars, and live there cold, dark, comfortless, terrified. Day after day, and month after month, roll tediously on, while the gloom constantly thickens, and the only news is of houses crushed, acquaintances killed, prices raised, and scarcity increased. Gladly would the citizens surrender, but the governor is inexorable. At length, to all the horrors *famine* is added. The poor man, out of employ, cannot purchase customary comforts at the increased prices. His poverty becomes deeper, his sacrifices greater. But the siege continues. The middle classes sink to beggary, the poorer class to starvation. Anon, breaches are made in the wall; and all must work amid galling fire to repair them. Mines are sprung, blowing houses and occupants into the air. Still no relief comes. Dead animals, offal, skins, the very carcass of the slain, are eaten. The lone widow, the bereft mother, the disappointed bride, the despairing father, and the tender babe, mourn continually. Then comes *pestilence*, the necessary consequence of unburied dead, and unwonted hardships, and intolerable wo. At length, the city yields; or is taken by storm, and scenes even more horrid ensue. A brutal soldiery give loose to lust, and rapine, and destruction; and the indescribable scene closes with deserted streets, general ruin, and lasting lamentation.

This picture is far from being overwrought. The history of sieges furnish realities of deeper horror. Take for instance the second siege of Saragossa in 1814, or almost any other.

Now is this Christianity? Is it *like* it? Christianity cannot alter. If it will necessarily abolish all war, when the millennium shall give it *universal* influence, then it will abolish war now, *so far as it has influence*; and every man who receives it *fully* will be a man of peace. If religious persons may make fighting a trade on earth, they may fight in heaven. If we may lawfully cherish a war spirit here, we may cherish it there!

I close by quoting the words of the great Jeremy Taylor. "As contrary as cruelty is to mercy, and tyranny to charity, so contrary is war to the meekness and gentleness of the Christian religion."

II. WAR IS ONE OF THE MOST AWFUL AND COMPREHENSIVE FORMS OF WICKEDNESS.

What has been said, has gone to show how inconsistent, *in principle*, are war and Christianity. A few considerations will now be offered, illustrative of the *practices* of war. We shall be thus led to see, not only that it contradicts the genius, and violates the precepts of Christianity, but that it does so in the most gross and gigantic manner.

1. It is the worst form of robbery.

Common robberies are induced by want: but war commits them by choice, and often robs only to ravage. A man who rushes to the highway to rob, maddened by the sight of a famished family, may plead powerful temptation. But armies rob, burn, and destroy, in the coolest malice. See a file of men, well fed and well clothed by a great and powerful nation, proceed on a foraging party. They enter a retired vale, where a peaceful old man by hard handed toil supports his humble family. The officer points with his sword to the few stacks of hay and grain, laid up for winter. Remonstrances are vain—tears are vain. They bear off his only supply, take his cow, his pet lamb; add insult to oppression, and leave the ruined family to an almshouse or starvation. Aye, but the poor old man was an *enemy*, as the war phrase is, and the haughty soldiery claim merit for forbearance, because they did not conclude with burning down his house.

The seizure or destruction of public stores, is not less robbery. A nation has no more right to steal from a nation, than an individual has to steal from an individual. In principle, the act is the same; in magnitude, the sin is greater. All the private robberies in a thousand years, are not a tithe of the robberies of one war. Next to killing, it is the very object of each party to burn and destroy by sea, and ravage and lay waste on land. It is a malign and inexcusable barbarity, and constitutes a stupendous mass of theft.

In one of the Punic wars, Carthage, with 100,000 houses, was burnt and destroyed, so that not a house remained. The plunder carried away by the Romans, in precious metals and jewels alone, is reported to have been equal to *five millions of pounds of silver*. Who can compute the number of similar events, from the destruction of Jerusalem to that of Moscow? Arson, that is, the setting fire to an inhabited dwelling, is, in most countries, punishable by death. But more of this has been done in some single wars, than has been committed privately, since the world began. When some villain sets fire to a house and consumes it, what public indignation! What zeal to bring to justice! If, for a succession of nights, buildings are fired, what general panic! Yet how small the distress, compared to that which follows the burning of an entire city. In one case, the houseless still find shelter, the laborer obtains work, the children have food. But oh, the horrors of a general ruin! Earthquake is no worse.

It should not be overlooked, that a great part of the private robberies in Christendom, may be traced to the deterioration of morals, caused by war. Thousands of pirates, received their infamous education in national ships. Thousands of thieves, were disbanded soldiers. War taught these men to disregard the rights of property, to trample upon justice, and refuse mercy. Even if disposed to honest labor, which a military life always tends to render unpalatable, the disbanded soldier often finds himself unable to obtain employment. The industry of his country has been paralysed by the war; and the demand for labor slowly recurs. The discharged veteran therefore is often compelled to steal or starve. Thus war, by its own operations, involves continual and stupendous thefts, and by its unavoidable tendencies, multiplies offenders, who in time of peace prey upon community.

2. It involves the most enormous Sabbath breaking.

The Sabbath *cannot* be observed by armies. Common camp duty forbids it. Extra duties are assigned to Sunday—such as parades, drill, inspections, and reviews. Seldom is any effort made to avoid marches, or even battles, on Sunday. I have been able to find, in all history, but one battle postponed on account of the Sabbath. In thousands of instances, as in the case of Waterloo, it has been the chosen day for conflict.

War tends to abolish the Sabbath, even when the army is not present. The heavy trains of the commissary must move on. The arsenal and the ship yard must maintain their activity. Innumerable mechanics, watermen, and laborers, must be kept busy. During our late war with England, who did not witness on all our frontiers, even in the States of New England, the general desecration of the holy day? Men swarmed like ants on a mole hill, to throw up entrenchments; the wharves resounded with din of business; and idlers forsook the house of God to gaze upon the scenes of preparation.

Do Christians consider these unavoidable results, when they give their voice for war? No. The calm consideration of such concomitants, would make it impossible for them to advise or sanction the profane and abominable thing.

3. War produces a wicked waste of national wealth.

The disbursements of a belligerent government, drawn of course by taxation from the laboring community, form an incalculable amount. Our last war with England cost us more than a hundred millions of dollars per annum. During the last 175 years, ENGLAND has had *twenty-four* wars with France, *twelve* with Scotland, *eight* with Spain, and *two* with America, besides all her other wars in India and elsewhere. These have cost her government, according to official returns, *three thousand millions* of pounds sterling, or FIFTEEN THOUSAND MILLIONS OF DOLLARS! The war which ended at Waterloo, cost France £700,000,000, and Austria £300,000,000, or five thousand millions of dollars! How much it cost Spain, Sweden, Holland, Germany, Prussia and Russia, I have no means of knowing, but at least an equal sum. Thus one long war cost Europe at least forty thousand millions! The annual interest of this sum, at five per cent., is two thousand millions of dollars,—enough almost to banish suffering poverty from Europe! For all this, NOTHING has been gained. Nay, the spending of it thus has produced an aggregate of vice and poverty, pain and bereavement, more than, without war, would have come upon the whole human family since the flood! Who then can begin to compute the cost of *all* the wars even in Europe alone?

We often hear much railing against useless expenditure, and proposals for economy in dress, furniture, &c., and it is well. But those who insist on these modes of frugality should be consistent. Let them remember that all the retrenchments they recommend are but as the dust of the balance compared to the expenditures of a war. But vast as are the expenses of belligerent governments, they do not constitute a tenth of the true expenses of war! We must reckon the destruction of property, private and public—the ruin of trade and commerce—the suspension of manufactories—the loss of the productive labor of soldiers and camp followers. But who can reckon such amounts?

Further, let it be considered that all these items must be doubled and trebled in cases of *civil* wars, and that such form a large part of the catalogue.

Further still, war causes the great bulk of taxation even in time of peace! Witness the annual appropriations for fleets and standing armies, forts, arsenal, weapons, pensions, &c. Even since our last war with England, we have been paying *annually*, for the above objects, about *ten* times us much as for the support of our civil government!! "The war spirit" is taxing our people to the amount of unnumbered millions, *now* in time of profound peace. A single 74 gun ship, beside all her cost of construction and equipment, costs in time of peace, while afloat, $200,000 per annum—eight times the salary of the President of the United States. *Nearly all the taxes paid by civilized nations, go in some form or other to the support of war!* All the British debt which is grinding her people into the dust, was created by war. The cost of the wars of Europe alone, in only the last century, would have built all the canals, railroads, and churches, and established all the schools, colleges, and hospitals, wanted on the whole globe!

4. War is the grossest form of murder.

Private murders are atrocious—those of war far more so. But the contrary opinion prevails; and we adduce proofs. War enhances the crime of murder on the following accounts:

(1.) It is more cold-blooded and cruel.

Malice prompts private murder, and the proof of it is necessary to conviction by a jury; and the more cool and calculating, the more guilt. But murder in war is more cool and calculating, than even in a duel. The question of war or peace is calmly debated, deliberately resolved upon, and proclaimed in form. Armies are raised, and drilled, and marched, and engaged, with all coolness and calculation. The contending hosts know not each other, cherish no personal hate, and seldom know the true grounds of the contest. All is done with whatever of aggravation attends deliberate homicide.

(2.) It is more vast in amount.

Computation falters when we estimate the numbers slain in war or by reason of it. Three hundred thousand men fell in one battle, when Attila, king of the Huns, was defeated at Chalons. Nearly the entire army of Xerxes, consisting of four millions of persons, perished. Julius Caesar, in one campaign in Germany, destroyed half a million. More than half a million perished in one campaign of Napoleon, averaging 3000 men a day. Paying no attention to the innumerable wars among Pagans before and since the birth of Christ, nor to all the wasting wars of the past seventeen centuries, it is matter of distinct calculation that about five millions of nominal Christians have been butchered by nominal Christians, *within the last half century!* What then has been the total of war-murders since creation?

Nor is the number of the *slain* the real total. Multitudes of "the wounded and missing" die; multitudes perish out of armies and fleets without battle, by hardships, exposure, vice, contagion, and climate. We ought, therefore, at least to double the number slain in engagements, to arrive at true sum; and make *ten millions of men* destroyed within half a century by Christian nations' quarrels!

(3.) Deaths caused by war, arc accompanied by horrid aggravations of suffering.

The wretches die, not on beds of down, surrounded by all that can relieve or palliate suffering. No soft hand smooths the couch, or wipes the brow. No skilful physician stands watching every symptom. The silence, the quiet, the cleanliness, the sympathy, the love, the skill, that divest the chamber of death of all its horror, and half its anguish, are not for the poor soldier. Private murder is always done in haste, and the sufferer is often dismissed from life in a moment. Not so in war. Few are killed outright. The victim dies slowly of unmedicated wounds. Prostrate amid the trampling of columns and of horses which have lost their riders, or in a trench, amid heaps of killed and wounded, he dies a hundred deaths. If, mangled and miserable, he finds himself still alive, when the tide of battle has passed, how forlorn his condition! Unable to drag himself from the ghastly scene, his gory limbs chilled with the damps of night, tortured with thirst, and quivering with pain, his heart sickened with the remembrance of home, and his soul dismayed at the approach of eternal retributions, he meets death with all that can make it terrific.

(4.) The multitudes murdered in war, are generally sent to hell.

The thought is too horrible for steady contemplation; but we are bound to consider it. "No murderer hath eternal life." Soldiers are murderers in intent and profession, and die in the act of killing others, and with implements of murder in their hands. Without space for repentance, they are hurried to the bar of God. On what grounds may we affirm their salvation? O that those that know the worth of souls, would dwell on this feature of the dreadful custom!

(5.) War first corrupts those whom it destroys, and thus aggravates damnation itself.

Bad as are most men who enlist in standing armies, war makes them worse. They might at any rate be lost, but their vocation sends them to a more dreadful doom. The recruit begins his degradation, even in the rendezvous, ere he has lodged a week within its walls. He grows still worse in camp.

In the army, vice becomes his occupation. His worst passions are fostered. His Sabbaths are necessarily profaned. He becomes ashamed of tender feelings, and conscientious scruples. Thus an old soldier is generally a hardened offender; and the shot that terminates his life, consigns him to a death rendered more terrible by his profession. Had the money and time, which has been lavished to equip and drill and support him as a soldier, been spent for his intellectual and moral improvement, he might have been an ornament to society, and a pillar in the church.

Mark his grim corpse as men bear it to the gaping pit into which whole cart-loads of bodies are thrown. The property, nay the liberty of a whole nation is not a price for his soul! How then can Christians with one hand give to the support of missions, and with the other uphold a custom which counteracts every good enterprise?

CONCLUDING REMARKS.

How strange, how awful, that to such a trade as war, mankind has, in all ages, lifted up its admiration! Poetry lends its fascinations, and philosophy its inventions. Eloquence, in forum and field, has wrought up the war spirit to fanaticism and frenzy. Even the pulpit, whose legitimate and glorious theme is "PEACE ON EARTH," has not withheld its solemn sanctions. The tender sex, with strange infatuation, have admired the tinselled trappings of him whose trade is to make widows and orphans. Their hands have been withdrawn from the distaff, to embroider warrior's ensigns. The young mother has arrayed her proud boy with cap and feather, toyed him with drum and sword, and trained him, unconsciously, to love and admire the profession of a man-killer.

The universal maxim has been, "in peace prepare for war;" and men are all their days contributing and taxing themselves to defray the expenses of killing each other. Scarcely has a voice been lifted up to spread the principles of peace. Every other principle of Christianity has had its apostles. Howard reformed prisons; Sharp, and Clarkson, and Wilberforce arrested the slave-trade. Carey carried the gospel to India. Every form of vice has its antagonists, and every class of sufferers find philanthropists. But who stands forth to urge the law of love? Who attacks this monster WAR? We have not waited for the millennium to abolish intemperance, or Sabbath breaking; but we wait for it to abolish war. It is certain that the millennium cannot come, till war expires.

Shall it so remain? Shall this gorgon of pride, corruption, destructiveness, misery and murder, be still admired and fed, while it is turning men's hearts to stone, and the garden of the Lord into the desolation of death? Let every heart say *no.* Let Christians shine before men as sons of peace, not less than as sons of justice and truth. If wars and rumors of wars continue, let the church stand aloof. It is time she was purged of this stain. Her brotherhood embraces all nations. Earthly rulers may tell us we have enemies; but our heavenly King commands us to return them good for evil; if they hunger, to feed them; if they thirst, to give them drink.

Rise then, Christians, to noble resolution and vigorous endeavors! Retire from military trainings, and spurn the thought of being hired by the month to rob and kill. Refuse to study the tactics, or practice the handicraft of death; and with "a hope that maketh not ashamed," proclaim the principles of *universal peace*, as part and parcel of eternal truth.

A portion of our missionary spirit should be expended in this department. Shall we pour out our money and our prayers, when we hear of a widow burnt on her husband's funeral pile, or deluded wretches crushed beneath the wheels of Juggernaut, but do nothing to dethrone this *Moloch* to whom hundreds of millions of Christians have been sacrificed? Among the fifty millions of the Presidency of Bengal, the average number of suttees (widows burned, &c.) has for twenty years been less than 500, or in the proportion of one death in a year for such a population as

Philadelphia. What is this to war? Every *day* of some campaigns has cost more lives!

We must not abstain from effort, because of apparent obstacles. What great reform does not meet obstructions? The overthrow of Papal supremacy by Luther, the temperance movement, and a host of similar historic facts, show that truth is mighty, and when fairly and perseveringly exhibited, will prevail. It can be shown, that in attempting to abolish all war, we encounter fewer impediments than have attended various other great changes. Even if it were not so, we have a duty to discharge whether we prevail or not. Moral obligation does not rest on the chance of success.

Our obstacle are neither numerous nor formidable. No classes of men *love* war for its own sake. If it were abolished, those who now make it a profession, could all find profitable and pleasanter employment in peaceful pursuits. Men's *interests* are not against us; but the contrary. The people are not *blood-thirsty*. What serious impediment is there to obstruct the diffusion of peace principles? None more than beset even the most popular enterprise of literature or benevolence. Our only obstruction is apathy, and the unfortunate sentiment that the millennium is to do it away, we know not how. But we might as well do nothing against intemperance, or Sabbath-breaking, or heresy; and wait for the millennium to do them away. Nothing will be done in this world without means, even when the millennium shall have come.

Do you ask what *you* can do? Much, very much, whoever you are. Cherish in yourself the true peace-spirit. Try to diffuse it. Assist in enlightening your neighbors. Talk of the horrors of war, its impolicy, its cost, its depravity, its utter uselessness in adjusting national disputes. Teach children correctly on this point, and show them the true character of war, stripped of its music and mock splendor. Banish drums and swords from among their toys. Proclaim aloud the Divine government, and teach men how vain it is, even in a righteous cause, to trust an arm of flesh. Insist that patriotism, in its common acceptation, is not a virtue; for it limits us to love *our country*, and allows us to hate and injure other nations. Thus if Canada *were* annexed to our Union, we must, *on that account*, love Canadians. But if South Carolina should secede, we must withdraw part of our love, or perhaps go to war and kill as many as possible. O how absurd to act thus, as though God's immutable law of love was to be obeyed or not as our boundaries may be.

> "Lands intersected by a narrow sea,
> Abhor each other. Mountains interposed,
> Make enemies of nations who had else,
> Like kindred drops, been mingled into one."

Let us feel and disseminate the sentiment that true patriotism is shown only by *the good*. A man may claim to be a patriot, and love "his country," whose feelings are so vague and worthless that he loves no one in it! He loves a mere name! or rather, his patriotism is a mere name. Whole classes of his fellow-citizens may remain in vice, ignorance, slavery, poverty, and yet he feels no sympathy, offers no aid. Sodom would have been saved, had there been in it ten righteous. These then would have been patriots. These would have saved their country. We have in our land many righteous. These are our security. These save the land from a curse. These therefore are the only true patriots.

Let us unite in "showing up" military glory. What is it? Grant that it is all that it has ever passed for, and it still seems superlatively worthless. The wreaths of conquerors fade daily. We give their names to dogs and slaves. The smallest useful volume guides its author a better and more lasting name. And how absurd, too, is it to talk to common soldiers and under officers about military glory! Among the many millions who have toiled and died for love of glory, scarcely a score are remembered among men! Who of our revolutionary heroes but Washington and Lafayette are known in the opposite hemisphere? Who of our own citizens can tell over a half dozen distinguished soldiers in our struggle for independence? Yet that war is of late date. Of the men of former wars we know almost nothing. Essentially stupid then is the love of military renown in petty officers and the common private. They stake their lives in a lottery where there is hardly a prize in five hundred years!

Let us print and propagate peace principles. Public opinion has been changed on many points by a few resolute men. Let us keep the subject before the people till every man forms a deliberate opinion, whether Christianity allows or forbids war. Let us at least do so much that if ever our country engages in another war, we shall feel no share of the guilt. Let us each do so much that if we should ever walk over a battle-field, stunned with the groans and curses of the wounded, and horror-struck at the infernal spectacle, we can feel that we aid *all we could* to avert such an evil. Let us clear *ourselves* of blame. No one of us can put a stop to war. But we can *help* stop it—and combined and persevering effort *will* stop it.

* * * * *

KILLING IS YOUR LIFE WORK

I don't know who first said it, but the aphorism "Join the Army, travel the world, meet interesting people, and kill them" has been around as long as I can remember.

The primary job of the soldier is to kill people and destroy property, not to clean and paint equipment, refurbish aircraft, march in formation, attend technical schools, play war games, take rank tests, go on maneuvers, practice on the firing range, restore basic services, rebuild infrastructure, spread goodwill, promote good governance, or provide disaster relief.

At issue is not the question as to whether the U.S. military should be defending the country, but whether the U.S. military should be killing people and destroying property overseas. This is the question now, in regard to Iraq and Afghanistan, and it was also the question before, during, and after World War I.

Long before the "What Would Jesus Do?" (WWJD) fad, Congregational minister Charles Sheldon (1857–1946), in 1896, wrote *In His Steps: What Would Jesus Do?* Based on a series of sermons, *In His Steps*, which became one of the best-selling books of all time, is the story of a minister who challenged his church members to not do anything without first asking "What Would Jesus Do?"

Although most Christians in America have probably heard of In His Steps, few have probably heard of a similar book by Sheldon in 1931 called *He Is Here*. Like his first book, in *He Is Here* Sheldon presents in story form the things that he thinks Jesus would say and do if he were now here among us.

What caught my eye about this latter book is Sheldon's story of an admiral in the U.S. Navy who was told by a mysterious visitor to stop grieving about the loss of a few lives since his whole life had been devoted to the trade of killing.

From *He Is Here*, here is chapter 3, "Killing Is Your Life Work":

> The Admiral had just returned from the great naval demonstration at Panama. As he recalled his own part in the stately review, and saw again the great war machines maneuvering in the battle formation—heard the roar of the mighty guns of which he was so proud—listened to the "zoom" of the air fleet as it circled over the canal—his hear swelled. These were the nation's defenses; and the fact that he had played no small part in influencing Congress, and the public, to provide those mighty instruments of naval power, filled him with satisfaction.
>
> He felt, in fact, very well pleased with himself. Life had been good to him. He had been born of a wealthy and socially prominent

family—there was nothing of the commonplace about him. Promotion in his chosen profession had come to him, not sensationally, but in dignified order, from one rank to another—no vulgar scramble, but a gentlemanly climb up the heights of seniority, until at last he had arrived at his present rank. Now, with official commendation still ringing in his ears, he could look forward with complacent pride to honorable retirement, and easy years during which he would live over again, in memory, the vents of his distinguished career.

The servant announced a visitor. His Bishop—ah, yes, he would be glad to see the Bishop. They were old friends, classmates in the University. The Admiral was a staunch churchman, when his duties would permit. And the Bishop was jolly, and good company. Together they talked for a while—the small talk of friends who have known each other since school days. Then the Bishop congratulated him upon the way he had handled the fleet.

"Wonderful—really a marvelous demonstration of your skill as commander. The Secretary of the Navy personally told me that your handling of the flagship Oneonta was masterly."

"That is indeed gratifying," replied the Admiral, glowing with pride at the compliment. Then a note of hesitation came into his voice. "But—we cannot afford to fall behind the other powers. We must have a larger air force, and more submarines—particularly submarines; in those important department we lag behind more than one of the other great powers. I have devoted a great deal of thought to the matter of maintaining our forces at the proper strength. And I will tell you, confidentially, that one of the things in which I feel the greatest pride is the new combined gas bomb and torpedo which our navy has developed from ideas and plans suggested by me. It was tried out for the first time at Panama. Its destructive power is greater, far greater, than any bomb yet devised. I may claim that I invented it; and I consider it one of the most important achievements of my— "

The telephone interrupted him, with that insistent note which portended news of importance. The Admiral picked up the receiver—an excited voice came to his ears.

"Admiral—? This is Ensign Howard—I have to report, sir, that the flagship Oneonta—"

"My God!" exclaimed the Admiral, his face like ashes.

“There has been an explosion—” the Ensign sign’s shaking voice gave the terrible details. “The ship? Badly damaged, we fear. The men? There has been loss of life—Captain Blake says at least fifty are dead or badly injured—” and then the Admiral groaned, and his face was drawn and gray—”a man accidentally dropped one of the new gas bombs—it fell among the others—set them off—”

The new gas bombs!

The stricken Admiral staggered to his chair, dropped his face into his hands.

“My ship—my men—my life work—”

”*Killing* is your life work—why are you not pleased with your success?”

The Admiral’s head came up in sudden amazement. That was not the Bishop’s voice—and that was not the Bishop, but a stranger in the chair his friend had just been occupying. Something in the stranger’s manner was so authoritative, so accusing, that for a moment it drove even the terrible news from the Admiral’s mind. But the next words the man uttered struck him with the force of a blow.

“Your whole life has been devoted to the trade of killing. Why are you do grieved at the loss of a few more lives?”

And then—for one of the few times in his life—the Admiral felt fear. Already shaken by the terrible disaster, he was totally unable to rebuke this stranger.

“But—these were—my own men,” he tried to say, brokenly. “The men our country has trained for its protection—”

”So are those of all the other countries—those whom you would be rejoiced to kill if you were at war; they, too, are trained for their countries’ protection.”

The stranger stood, with blazing eyes fixed upon the Admiral, and said in a voice that stabbed like a sword:

“*You* perfected that terrible instrument of destruction—the blood of those young men is upon your head—*you* are their murderer!”

The Admiral cowered, unable to speak.

"What else than murderers are men trained as you have been? The great War, in which you took part, killed ten million young men, crippled and tortured and mangled ten million more, broke the hearts of fathers and mothers all over the world, wasted unknown billions of God's money, and left a legacy of suspicion and hate among the nations. But some of my disciples—"

He paused, and the Admiral caught himself whispering the word, "disciples!" *Who* could speak that word—?

"My disciples," repeated the stranger, "have created a new force in the world—the force which will be stronger than brute force. And there are treaties, and solemn oaths and pacts, signed by the nations to do away with war. Why, then, do you and men like you exclaim in horror at this disaster which is caused by the devices which you yourself made—yet you remain unmoved after all that great horror of killing during that War—killing for which you are not only in part responsible, but which causes you pride for the part you took in it?"

The Admiral attempted to assert himself, to speak as he was wont to speak; but his voice would not obey his will. His visitor went on:

"The millions your country spends upon war devices, if put to better use, would be enough to feed all the hungry, and give work to all the unemployed. During the naval display from which you have just returned, you wasted other millions in entertainment, in evolutions, in gun fire, in and under water and in God's sky. And all this was for the purpose of training young men to kill. Is it the work of men made in God's image to practice killing on a scientific and stupendous scale? Is it the purpose of humanity to make killing the main business of a liftetime?"

At this, the Admiral's rage suddenly broke through the spell that had held him. He stepped forward with clenched hand raised as if to strike. But the look on the visitor's calm face again halted him, and he stood still. The voice was saying:

"Oh man, made for other uses, will you step out from your place, and spend the rest of your life entreating the world to stop this madness of brute force, this wicked and stupid waste of men's lives, this appeal to the lowest in man? Will you, Brother man?"

> The Admiral was stunned by the words—why they were a demand, more than a question! He stared at this figure seated where the Bishop had been. What! Step out of his honored and dignified place as a servant and citizen of the republic, abandon his dream of retirement for life's comfortable memories, join the ranks of the traitor pacifists whom he had always held in scornful contempt—do this unthinkable thing simply because—this unknown—but *was* he?
>
> In an impulse of the moment the Admiral turned his head to gaze at the etching of the battle ship formation at which the Bishop was looking when he had last seen him. And when he turned back, there sat the Bishop as he had been when he first entered.
>
> "You—*heard*?"
>
> "I heard all—" the Bishop's head, too, was bowed, his proud look had vanished.
>
> "It—it was *he*!"
>
> They stared at each other, humbled, humiliated.
>
> "He actually asked you to resign from the navy, and go out into the world to work for international amity and peace?"
>
> "He not only asked me to do so, he demanded it."
>
> There was a long moment of silence between the two old friends.
>
> "And will you do a thing like that?" asked the Bishop.
>
> There was a still longer silence.
>
> "I do not know," said the Admiral at last; and the silence deepened in the Admiral's room.

The year after Sheldon's *He Is Here* was published, Albertus Pieters (1869–1955), a minister, former missionary in Nagasaki, Japan (1891–1898, 1904–1910), and professor in the Western Theological Seminary of the Reformed Church in America at Holland Michigan (1926–1939), penned a reply to "Killing Is Your Life Work" because his "heart was stirred with indignation" when he read it. In his book *The Christian Attitude Towards War* (Eerdmans, 1932), Pieters states that "for a man to utter against the American Navy such words as those of Dr. Sheldon, is to be guilty of a foul insult against the people and the government of the United States."

Pieters lays down two propositions:

Proposition A—War is always wrong.
Proposition B—War is sometimes right.

He maintains that these propositions are universal, "intended to cover all possible cases, past, present, and future," and contradictory, "one must be false, and the other must be true."

Now, unless one ignores the fact that God in the Old Testament commanded the nation of Israel to war against heathen nations, and unless one is such an ardent pacifist that he would be opposed to fighting a war in genuine self-defense (not in Bushspeak self-defense, which makes even the U.S. invasion of Iraq self-defense), proposition B seems to be the right choice. Pieters even says that "any man who holds that war is always wrong is to me theologically a heretic and politically a potential traitor."

But when we see what Pieters' definition of war is, it is apparent that he is presenting a false dichotomy:

> The word "war" is used here in its ordinary meaning, for armed conflict between two forces, one of which, at least, represents a legitimate government. It involves the deliberate killing of men not individually convicted of any crime, because by such homicide the government to which they belong can be coerced: the object being to attain some end desired by the government under whose orders the military force operates.

He later adds that this "deliberate slaughter" is not only sometimes right, but "in accordance with the spirit of Jesus, and in harmony with holy love."

That Pieters speaks of honoring U.S. presidents such as Abraham Lincoln and Woodrow Wilson, "by whose authority war was waged," shows what kind of wars he deems acceptable: any war fought by the U.S. government.

Pieters' problem is that he places too much trust in the government:

> To sum up the entire discussion from the Christian standpoint, war is sometimes,—perhaps seldom, but certainly sometimes,—right, and when waged by governments conscious of their responsibility to God, and desirous only of establishing righteousness in the

> earth, is an activity in which Christian men may take part without violating either the divine law of homicide or the law of love.
>
> In the time of war, it is the duty of the individual Christian citizen, and of the Church as an organized body, to accept the decision of the State to make war, as a just and right decision, unless the contrary appears with extraordinary and unmistakable clearness.
>
> The decision of the constituted authorities must be usually accepted as a right decision, without further question.
>
> That being the case, and the decision of the government to wage war being accepted as a right decision, the duties of the Christian citizen and of the Church become plain. The former must obey the orders of his government, even to the extent of bearing arms if called upon to do so. The latter must teach with insistence the Christian duties that must be in the foreground in time of war. They are, first of all, the duty of obedience.

Now, I know that Charles Sheldon was more of a social reformer than a minister of the New Testament (2 Corinthians 3:6), and that he preached more of a social gospel than the gospel of the grace of God (Acts 20:24), but that doesn't negate the truth of his anti-war position.

I have pointed out before that when conservative Christians see liberal Christians deny the authority of Scripture and the bodily resurrection of Christ while expressing support for abortion and the ordaining of homosexuals, *but also oppose war and militarism*, they draw the false conclusion that it is liberal (bad) to oppose war and militarism but conservative (good) to support them.

It also bears repeating that there is nothing "liberal" about opposition to war. Just like there is nothing "anti-American" about opposition to militarism. And what could be more Christian than standing firmly against aggression, violence, and bloodshed?

I think that Murray Rothbard, in *The Ethics of Liberty*, makes a profound statement about the libertarian attitude toward war that bears repeating:

> In condemning all wars, regardless of motive, the libertarian knows that there may well be varying degrees of guilt among States for any specific war. But his overriding consideration is the condemnation of any State participation in war. Hence, his policy is that of exerting pressure on all States not to start or engage in a war, to stop one that has begun, and to reduce the scope of any

persisting war in injuring civilians of either side or no side.

Needless to say, instead of Professor Pieters' *The Christian Attitude Towards War*, I recommend C. John Cadoux's *The Early Christian Attitude to War* (London: Headley Bros. Publishers, 1919).

* * * * *

A CHRISTIAN KILLER PAR EXCELLENCE

As I wrote in "Christian Killers" way back in 2004, the phrase ought to be just as perplexing as Christian adulterers, Christian drug addicts, Christian prostitutes, Christian pimps, Christian gangsta rappers, or Christian acid rockers.

A Christian fighting the bogus war on terror in Iraq and Afghanistan while in the "service" of the U.S. military is a Christian killer. He is not a hero. He is not defending our freedoms. He is not protecting the United States. He is not fighting "over there" so we won't have to fight "over here." He is not avenging the 9/11 attacks. He is not keeping American safe from terrorists. He is not ensuring that we continue to speak English. He is not guaranteeing our First Amendment rights. He is not fighting for truth, justice, and the American way.

And he is certainly not defending the United States, guarding U.S. shores, securing U.S. borders, patrolling U.S. coasts, and enforcing no-fly zones over U.S. skies.

We can dismiss a buffoon and opportunist like Rudy Giuliani for equating Osama bin Laden with Hitler and saying that he "wanted to be the one" to kill him since he is better known as a drag queen than a Christian.

But what are we to make of Doug Giles, a conservative Christian columnist for TownHall.com and the "senior pastor" of Clash Church, meeting inside the Residence Inn in Aventura, Florida?

Giles is a Christian killer par excellence. He is not a Christian warmonger on steroids and he is not the greatest Christian warmonger of all time, but he is a Christian killer par excellence.

Giles is the author of the article "Why Christians Should Rejoice That UBL Is Dead and in Hell." I am reproducing his entire article, not only because it is short, but because it has to be read in its entirety to be believed:

> Let me go on the record stating that as a Christian I am completely

cool with our Navy SEAL Team Six killing Usama. Or is it Osama? Does anyone know? I heard he liked it both ways. Anyway, the only thing that makes me sad about bin Laden's death, as an orthodox Christian, is that a). It didn't happen on Christmas or Easter, and b). The rude SEAL Team Six didn't include me along to pull the trigger.

Apparently, the SEALs require those who go on their missions to be physically and psychologically fit to the nth degree and stuff—y'know, like being able to swim like Esther Williams during a hurricane with a wildebeest strapped to one's back. When they told me that, I was like, "Whatever." And the SEALs were like, "Pfff." And thus they chose someone else to whack that wacky bastard. So, I guess I'll have to settle for seconds and wait to play the forthcoming Xbox video game based on the Abbottabad raid entitled, SEAL Team Six: Who's Yo' Mama, Usama? But I digress.

So, why do I bring up my Christianity in conjunction with my satisfaction with Usama getting capped? Well, it's principally because of the rank anti-biblical bollocks coming from pastors and priests who believe that Christians should not be happy that bin Laden has now been eaten by groupers at the bottom of the Indian Ocean (or wherever the heck they tossed his damnable corpse).

For instance, Bill O'Reilly had a Catholic priest, Father Beck, on his show this past week who not only said we should dial down on our biblical joy that this evil SOB was shot but that we should've "loved him," "forgiven him," and "not judged him" because "we don't know what was in Usama's wittle heart that caused him to kill tens of thousands of people worldwide."

To hear this cat talk, it sounds like all UBL simply needed was some Xanax, a new coloring book and a little face time with Dr. Drew because his daddy didn't love him enough or something.

Well, Father Crock—I mean Beck—call me a heretic because I believe those commands to "love, forgive and not judge" don't extend to a sick, twisted, violent, God-hating, woman abusing, implacable, wicked dog like bin Laden but rather to personal verbal detractors of one's faith (y'know, people who don't pose a grave global security threat. Duh).

It's like I wrote in my best selling book, *Raising Righteous & Rowdy Girls*, about how I raised my girls: If you're made fun of,

> ridiculed, or maligned for your beliefs, don't sweat it; love and pray for your enemies and learn what I've learned over many years: Other people's animosity can actually sell a lot of books.
>
> However, should someone want to physically harm you in some form or fashion (say, a rapist or a terrorist) then it's okay for you to defend yourself and hurt him or, if need be, kill him. Call me the devil. In my world the good person should live and the evil person should die.
>
> Hey, Christian Love Machine: Usama wasn't some angry blogger who merely said mean crap about Christians and western culture; he was a malevolent, murderous Saladin wannabe who was part and parcel of the massive, heartless slaughter of men, women and children both here and abroad. Remember? If not, here's UBL's résumé of death.
>
> Christians should rejoice because bin Laden was decidedly evil; his body is currently the main course for coconut crabs at 300 feet; and his soul is browning on Dante's BBQ. Providence, via our ministers of death, the bad ass SEAL Team Six, plucked a foul weed from this planet and officially ended his reign of terror. I guarantee that when the SEALs' 5.56mm round exited Usama's brain at 3,000 feet per second the Father, Son and Holy Spirit stood up and said to each other, "High five!" and then after that congratulatory moment simultaneously said like preternatural triplets, "Who's next?" And you know what? We should feel the same way.

Giles is a Christian killer par excellence because he doesn't even think it necessary to put on a military uniform before he blows someone away, in the name of the Lord, of course.

Now, I make no apologies for Osama bin Laden. I deplore any acts of terrorism he may have planned, instigated, attempted, inspired, or carried out. I repudiate his religion, his invective, and any evil he may have thought, spoken, or performed. I even abhor his unkempt beard.

(The preceding paragraph is for those who planned on e-mailing me about how I am a defender of bin Laden, pro-Muslim, insensitive to the families who lost loved ones on 9/11, and/or an America-hating liberal scumbag.)

Although I believe that bin Laden was evil, I am not stupid enough to think, like Rudy Giuliani, that bin Laden should be equated with Hitler or Stalin. I also believe that Bush, Obama, the vast majority of the members of Congress, and the leadership of both major political parties are evil, but I would never make the mistake of likening any of them to Hitler or Stalin.

Giles charges bin Laden with killing tens of thousands of people worldwide. I think he is confusing him with George W. Bush.

It is sad to see that nothing has brought out patriotism in Americans like the murder of someone they don't like. Yet, most Americans that cheered the Seal Team Death Squad for assassinating Osama bin Laden in the same breath mentioned the terrorist attacks of 9/11. But when has the U.S. government ever actually laid out the evidence that bin Laden was connected with 9/11? On the FBI's Ten Most Wanted list, there is no connection given between bin Laden and 9/11:

> Usama Bin Laden is wanted in connection with the August 7, 1998, bombings of the United States Embassies in Dar es Salaam, Tanzania, and Nairobi, Kenya. These attacks killed over 200 people. In addition, Bin Laden is a suspect in other terrorist attacks throughout the world.

Bin Laden also appears on the FBI's Most Wanted Terrorists list. Again, there is no mention of his connection with the attacks of 9/11.

When asked about this curious omission, FBI spokesman Rex Tomb said: "The reason why 9/11 is not mentioned on Osama bin Laden's Most Wanted page is because the FBI has no hard evidence connecting bin Laden to 9/11."

President Bush rejected an offer in 2001 by the Taliban to turn over bin Laden to a neutral country for trial if the United States presented evidence that he was responsible for the 9/11 attacks. Bush refused and said: "There's no need to discuss innocence or guilt. We know he's guilty."

In an interview with bin Laden first published on September 28, 2001, he denied any involvement in the 9/11 attacks:

> I have already said that I am not involved in the 11 September attacks in the United States. As a Muslim, I try my best to avoid telling a lie. I had no knowledge of these attacks, nor do I consider the killing of innocent women, children, and other humans as an appreciable act. Islam strictly forbids causing harm to innocent women, children, and other people.
>
> Whoever committed the act of 11 September are not the friends of the American people. I have already said that we are against the American system, not against its people, whereas in these attacks, the common American people have been killed.

Was bin Laden lying? Perhaps. But he is certainly more believable than the lying George WMD Bush.

But even if bin Laden planned every detail of the 9/11 attacks himself, the perpetrators of those attacks died with their victims. Is there any evidence that bin Laden directly killed anyone? He may have killed Soviet soldiers when they invaded Afghanistan while supplied with weapons by the CIA, but he was applauded as a freedom fighter back then.

Rick Giles also maintains that bin Laden posed a grave global security threat. This was a threat of our making. For years U.S. foreign policy has been aggressive, reckless, belligerent, interventionist, and meddling. U.S. foreign policy sows discord among nations, stirs up strife where none existed, intensifies the hatred that many foreigners around the world have for Americans and each other, and creates terrorists faster than we can kill them.

And perhaps someone should tell Christian killer par excellence "Pastor" Giles that rejoicing in the damnation of another soul is not a Christian attitude, though I suspect that his grasp of Christianity isn't any better than his knowledge of U.S. foreign policy.

* * * * *

THE WARMONGER'S FRUIT OF THE SPIRIT

It seems sensible and logical that followers of someone called the Prince of Peace would not act like they are following Mars, the Roman god of war.

As I have maintained whenever I speak about Christianity and war, if there is any group of people that should be opposed to war, empire, militarism, the warfare state, an imperial presidency, blind nationalism, government war propaganda, and an aggressive foreign policy it is Christians, and especially conservative, evangelical, and fundamentalist Christians who claim to strictly follow the dictates of Scripture and worship the Prince of Peace.

I have also maintained throughout these wars in Iraq and Afghanistan that, even though it is Christianity above all religions that should be opposed to the evils of war and militarism, in the Church will be found some of the greatest supporters of the military and the current wars.

The "criminality of war," as Howard Malcom, president of Georgetown College, wrote in 1845, is not "that tyrants should lead men into wars of pride and conquest," but that "the people, in governments comparatively free, should so readily lend themselves to a business in which they bear all the sufferings, can gain nothing, and may lose all." That people would act this way, Malcom says, is an "astonishment indeed." "But," he continues, "the chief wonder is that Christians, followers of the Prince of Peace, should have concurred in this mad idolatry of strife, and thus been inconsistent not only with themselves, but with the very genius of their system."

I have heard and read many Christians criticize Obama—and rightly so—for his horrendous policies, but I have heard and read little or nothing from Christians of how Obama has continued the war in Iraq, escalated the war in Afghanistan, and expanded the bogus war on terror to other countries.

The above sign from a church in Maryland can unfortunately be seen almost anywhere in the United States. Although some Christians have begun to criticize Obama and the Democrats for the things that only a short time ago they were silent about when perpetrated by Bush and the Republicans, support for the military among Christians—no matter where it goes, why it goes, what it does, how much it costs, how long it stays, and how many foreigners it kills—is so entrenched, so sacrosanct, that I am at the same time bewildered and embarrassed, angered and ashamed.

The result of this mindset is a perversion of the very Scriptures that Christians claim to believe and follow. So, just as Christian warmongers would, if they were honest, recite The Warmonger's Psalm (Psalm 23), assent to The Warmonger's Beatitudes (Matthew 5:3–12), and pray The President's Prayer (Matthew 6:9–13), so they would acknowledge that they manifest The Warmonger's Fruit of the Spirit (Galatians 5:22–23).

In contrast to the works of the flesh (adultery, fornication, uncleanness, lasciviousness, idolatry, witchcraft, hatred, variance, emulations, wrath, strife, seditions, heresies, envyings, murders, drunkenness, and revellings), the Apostle Paul in the Book of Galatians mentions the fruit of the Spirit: love, joy, peace, longsuffering, gentleness, goodness, faith, meekness, and temperance.

But in place of these virtues, warmongers have substituted pride, indifference, vengeance, ignorance, malice, arrogance, lust, foolishness, and blasphemy.

Christian warmongers have pride in the U.S. military—the greatest cause of terrorism and instability in the world. They are indifferent to the tremendous suffering of foreigners who get in the way of the U.S. military. They want vengeance for 9/11 now matter how many innocent Muslims have to die. They have a tremendous and willful ignorance of the true nature of U.S. foreign policy. They have malice toward foreigners who never harmed Americans until the U.S. military starting bombing them. They have an arrogant "USA, USA" patriotism that supports an interventionist and militaristic foreign policy. They lust for the blood of foreigners by supporting bombing, drone attacks, torture, and indiscriminate killing. They make foolish statements like the military is defending our freedoms by fighting in Iraq and Afghanistan. They blaspheme God by asking him to bless and protect U.S. soldiers.

I realize that I am making some serious accusations, but the truth is simply that most Christian warmongers don't care whether there are Predator drone attacks against Afghan and Pakistani peasants as long as a Republican-controlled government gets to conduct the attacks.

* * * * *

NUKE 'EM AND GOD WILL BLESS YOU

> "My God, what have we done?" ~ Robert Lewis, co-pilot of the Enola Gay

Americans love anniversaries, and especially of horrific events. Every year at this time we are reminded that the atomic bombs the United States dropped on Hiroshima on Monday, August 6, 1945 ("Little Boy"), and on Nagasaki on Thursday, August 9 ("Fat Man") ended World War II (or began the Cold War, depending on how you look at it).

Since the 9/11 attacks, we have heard a lot of talk about Iraq, Iran, or some terrorist group having weapons of mass destruction; that is, nuclear weapons. Yet, when it is pointed out that the United States is the only country that has actually used these weapons of mass destruction—against civilians no less—we are told that it was necessary to incinerate 200,000 people—civilians—to save the lives of "thousands and thousands" (Harry Truman's original number) or "millions" (George H. W. Bush's figure) of American soldiers who might die invading Japan.

So, according to the American myth that is trotted out every year, the atomic bombing of Japan was not only justified and necessary, but sane and moral. After all, the U.S. Army Air Force had already killed 100,000 Japanese civilians when it firebombed Tokyo on the night of March 9, 1945, with seventeen hundred tons of bombs. "War is hell." "All's fair in love and war." "Remember Pearl Harbor."

I write now, not about Truman's decision to drop the bomb or to rethink World War II, but about the United States using nuclear weapons again in another "good war."

It was recently brought to light that U.S. Air Force chaplains at Vandenberg Air Force Base in California were appealing to the Bible and just war theory in a mandatory Nuclear Ethics and Nuclear Warfare session for missile officers in order to morally and ethically justify the launching of nuclear weapons.

In other words, nuke 'em and God will bless you.

A watchdog group, Military Religious Freedom Foundation, filed a complaint on behalf of thirty-one instructor and student missile launch officers.

The program has since "been taken out of the curriculum and is being reviewed," said David Smith, chief of public affairs of Air Education and Training Command at Randolph Air Force Base in Texas. It turns out that the Air Force has been citing Christian teachings in its missile officer training materials for twenty years.

A forty-three-page PowerPoint presentation given in the Nuclear Ethics and Nuclear Warfare session by Chaplain Captain Shin Soh can be viewed here.

Many armchair Christian warriors, Christian Coalition moralists, Religious Right warvangelicals, Reich-wing Christian nationalists, theocon Values Voters, imperial Christians, Red-State Christian fascists, and God and country Christian bumpkins might object, not to the existence of a Nuclear Ethics and Nuclear Warfare session that appeals to Scripture to soothe the consciences of religious people, but to the cancellation of such a program because it "takes God out of government" and other nonsense. David French, senior counsel at the American Center for Law and Justice, dismissed complaints about the program as what he called "another attempt to cleanse American history of its religious realities." "It's about cleansing religion from the public square and building a completely secular society and military," added French.

I am not one of those Christians and I think French should go to France.

I wish I could say that the only things wrong with the PowerPoint presentation are that page sixteen is duplicated and page forty-three is blank.

I find the presentation to be a blasphemous misuse and perversion of Scripture to justify the idea that Christians can launch nuclear weapons with the blessing of God.

I want to focus on the examples given in the presentation from the Old Testament, the Intertestamental Period, and the New Testament. I reproduce the text of the presentation exactly as it appears.

On page eighteen we are told that there are "many examples of believers engaged in wars in the Old Testament." Here are the four examples we are given:

- Abraham organized an army to rescue Lot (Gen 14)
- Judges (Samson, Deborah, Barak)—God is motivating judges to fight and deliver Israel from foreign oppressors
- David is a warrior who is also a man after God's own heart
- Hebrews 11:32–34 uses as examples of true faith those OT believers who engaged in war in a righteous way

Chaplain Shin Soh should have just said what he meant: Abraham organized an army to rescue Lot, so nuke 'em and God will bless you. God motivated judges to fight and deliver Israel from foreign oppressors, so nuke 'em and God will bless you. David was a warrior and a man after God's own heart, so nuke 'em and God will bless you. Hebrews 11:32–34 uses as examples of true faith those OT believers who engaged in war in a righteous way, so nuke 'em and God will bless you.

What does Abraham, "the friend of God" (James 2:23), rescuing his nephew Lot have to do with launching nuclear weapons? Absolutely nothing, of course, unless you are deluded enough to think that the United States is the "friend of God" and other nations are God's enemies.

So, God motivated judges to fight and deliver Israel from foreign oppressors. Does this also mean that God motivates U.S. soldiers to fight and oppress foreigners? I didn't think so.

True, David was a warrior (Psalm 144:1) and a man after God's own heart (1 Samuel 13:14), but he was also an adulterer (2 Samuel 11:2–4) and a murderer (2 Samuel 12:9). And besides, because David was a man of war, the Lord said to him: "Thou shalt not build an house for my name, because thou hast been a man of war, and hast shed blood" (1 Chronicles 28:3).

The "OT believers" mentioned in Hebrews 11:32–34 include four judges (already discussed), King David (already discussed), and Samuel and the prophets. What they did is irrelevant since, as the presentation says, they did it "in a righteous way." There is nothing righteous about nuking cities. And especially nuking civilians after their military strikes a military target like the Pearl Harbor Naval Base. And besides, the Bible in Hebrews actually says that these people in the Old Testament "wrought righteousness" (Hebrews 11:33), not that they did something in a righteous way. At least get your Scripture straight before you pervert it.

There is one PowerPoint slide on the "Inter-testimental [sic] Period":

- Maccabees—Jewish revolt against their Syrian oppressors
- No pacifistic sentiment in mainstream Jewish history

What Chaplain Shin Soh means to say is that since the Jews revolted against the Syrians and there is no pacifistic sentiment in mainstream Jewish history then go ahead and nuke 'em and God will bless you.

Although it is true that God commanded the nation of Israel in the Old Testament to fight against heathen nations (Judges 6:16), the president of the United States is not God, America is not the nation of Israel, the U.S. military is not the Lord's army, the Christian's sword is the word of God, and the only warfare the New Testament encourages the Christian to wage is against the world, the flesh, and the devil.

On pages twenty-one through twenty-three we are given six examples from the New Testament:

- Luke 3:14—John the Baptist doesn't tell the Roman soldiers to leave the army before being baptized
- Luke 7:10—Jesus uses the Roman centurion as a positive illustration of faith
- Acts 10:2, 22, 35 Paul interacts with Cornelius, a Roman army officer—known as "devout and God fearing"
- Romans 13:4 In spite of personal blemishes, God calls the emperor to be an instrument of justice
- II Timothy 2:3 Paul chooses three illustrations to show what it means to be a good disciple of Christ
    - Farmer—work hard and be patient
    - Athlete—be self disciplined, train
    - Soldier—be willing to put up with hardship
- Revelation 19:11 Jesus Christ is the mighty warrior

Again, Chaplain Shin Soh should have just said what he meant: John the Baptist doesn't tell the Roman soldiers to leave the army before being baptized, so nuke 'em and God will bless you. Jesus uses the Roman centurion as a positive illustration of faith, so nuke 'em and God will bless you. Peter (the chaplain wrongly says Paul) interacts with Cornelius, a Roman army officer, so nuke 'em and God will bless you. In spite of personal blemishes, God calls the emperor to be an instrument of justice, so nuke 'em and God will bless you. Paul uses the illustrations of a farmer, an athlete, and a soldier to show what it means to be a good disciple of Christ, so nuke 'em and God will bless you. Jesus Christ is the mighty warrior, so nuke 'em and God will bless you.

Regarding Roman soldiers, centurions, and army officers, it's funny how apologists for the U.S. military never refer to the ones that beat and crucified Jesus Christ, an innocent man (Matthew 27:4). They would be more akin to U.S. soldiers that kill foreigners in unjust wars or train to launch nuclear missiles at civilians. On John the Baptist, I have written a whole article here.

The emperor was "an instrument of justice" in his empire; he was not the policeman of the world. Unless Chaplain Shin Soh wants to acknowledge the U.S. empire of troops and bases that encircles the globe, he might want to rethink his example. He can't have it both ways.

The Bible does liken a Christian to a soldier (2 Timothy 2:3, Philemon 2, Philippians 2:25). But as soldiers, Christians are admonished to "put on the whole armor of God" (Ephesians 6:11), "the breastplate of righteousness" (Ephesians 6:14), and "the helmet of salvation" (Ephesians 6:17). The weapons of the Christian soldier are not carnal (2 Corinthians 10:4); his shield is "the shield of faith" (Ephesians 6:16) and his sword is "the word of God" (Ephesians 6:17). Not exactly a description of a soldier in the U.S. military.

It is blasphemous to even remotely imply that since Jesus Christ is pictured as a mighty warrior, so nuke 'em and God will bless you.

The New Testament section of the presentation closes with this statement: "If war in the natural order is inherently unethical, it cannot be a good illustration in the spiritual order." Sorry chaplain, wrong again. First, it depends on what kind of war. War that is *truly* defensive (not just said to be defensive like Bush declaring the Iraq war to be defensive) or war that is divinely sanctioned (limited to Jews in the Old Testament, not U.S. wars) is not inherently unethical. Anything else is not just unethical; it is wholesale murder. And second, the Bible records Jesus as saying: "Behold, I come as a thief" (Revelation 16:15). Although stealing is inherently unethical, it is a good illustration in the spiritual order because the Lord Jesus made the illustration.

On page thirty-two of the presentation, under "Nuclear Ethics," the question is asked: "Can we exercise enough faith in our decision makers, political and military, to follow through with the orders that are given to us?" This is a good question, and one that all current and potential U.S. military personnel should consider. I would say that our decision makers, political and military, are the last people that anyone should put faith in.

The presentation concludes with a statement by a Captain Charles H. Nicholls that I wholeheartedly agree with: "Those of us on missile or bomber crews must also make the decision now. Before taking the oath of office or donning the uniform, we must commit ourselves to duty. We must decide now that our mission is compatible with our morality, or else we must resign our commissions." This is a great statement. I would say—nuclear mission or no nuclear mission—that since so much of what the military does is immoral (like, for instance, bombing, invading, and occupying other countries that were no threat to the United States), those young people that can't find a good job or are looking for money for college should not even consider the military in any capacity. And to those entrusted with nuclear weapons, we can only hope and pray that they resign their commissions. God will not bless them for launching nukes just because they were following the orders of political and military decision makers.

* * * * *

ARE YOU AN IMPERIAL CHRISTIAN?

The tenets of imperial Christianity include things like blind nationalism, belief in American exceptionalism, willful ignorance of U.S. foreign policy, childish devotion to the military, cheerleading for the Republican Party, acceptance of the U.S. empire, and support for a perpetual war on terror—all, of course, with a Christian twist for effect. In other words, the views of Mike Huckabee, Sarah Palin, Michele Bachmann or Rick Perry.

I have some simple yet pointed questions for Christians who subscribe to, or can be characterized by, the above things:

- Is the president of the United States God?
- Is America the nation of Israel?
- Is the United States the client state of God?
- Is the U.S. military the Lord's army?
- Does the United States enjoy a special relationship with God that other nations don't have?
- Is the Christian's sword anything but the word of God?
- Does the Bible command any Christian to kill any adherent of a false religion?
- Does the Bible command any Christian to go on a crusade against Muslims?
- Does "obeying the powers that be" mean that Christians should always do anything and everything the government says?
- Does the Bible say that anyone other than God should receive unconditional obedience?

- Is it okay for Christians to participate in U.S. government wars just because God commanded the Jews in the Old Testament to go to war?
- Does the Lord approve of everything the U.S. government does?
- Does the Lord approve of everything the government of Israel does?
- Is being patriotic more important than being biblical?
- Is the Republican Party the party of God?
- Is it more scriptural for a Christian to be in the military than in the ministry?
- Does God need America's help to protect Israel?
- Does God need the U.S. military to maintain order throughout the world?
- Is the U.S. military a godly institution?
- Is the CIA a godly institution?
- Did God command the United States to build over 1,000 foreign military bases?
- Did God command the United States to station troops in over 150 countries?
- Does God always approve of U.S. foreign policy?
- Is it biblical that churches send more soldiers to the Middle East than missionaries?
- Did God appoint the United States to be the world's policeman?
- Does the New Testament command churches to hold special military appreciation days?
- Does the New Testament command churches to glorify the military on the Sunday before national holidays?
- Have U.S. wars always been just, right, and good?
- Are all Muslims terrorists?
- Was every Iraqi and Afghan killed by the U.S. military a terrorist?
- Does the New Testament encourage Christians to wage war against anyone or anything but the world, the flesh, and the devil?

If you are a Christian and answered in the affirmative to one or more of these questions, then I understand why you are an imperial Christian. Repent.

But if you are a Christian and answered in the negative to all of these questions, then why are you an imperial Christian? Why do you make apologies for the state, its leaders, its military, its wars, its imperialism, and its interventionism? Why are you so devoted to the Republican Party? Why do you sing songs to the state in church on the Sunday before national holidays? Why do you encourage Christian young people to join the military? Why do you recite meaningless prayers for God to bless U.S. troops engaged in unjust wars?

Think about these things. Pray about them. Meditate on them. Just don't be an imperial Christian.

* * * * *

THEOLOGICAL SCHIZOPHRENIA

It is bad enough that Republican warmongers like Mitt Romney, John McCain, Lindsey Graham, and Allen West are whining about the supposed cuts to the defense budget that are due to take place because of the failure of the congressional "supercommittee," but it is disgusting and shameful that a professor of practical theology and seminary chancellor would do likewise.

The defense "cuts," of course, are not really cuts at all, just reductions in the rate of spending increases of the bloated defense budget.

So, who is this Christian warmonger that is so upset about defense budget "cuts" that he thinks they are a deeply disturbing, draconian, recklessly dangerous, self-destructive absurdity.

He is not a member, with Jerry Falwell, Pat Robertson, James Dobson, Hal Lindsey, Cal Thomas, and Pat Boone, of the Christian axis of evil, although he should be. He is not a Christian killer par excellence, like Doug Giles. He is not a Christian warmonger on steroids, like Bryan Fischer. And neither is he the greatest Christian warmonger of all time. That designation goes to Ellis Washington.

He is Michael Milton, the newly elected chancellor/CEO of Reformed Theological Seminary in Charlotte, North Carolina. Milton holds a B.A. from Mid-America Nazarene University, an M.Div. from Knox Theological Seminary, and a Ph.D. from the University of Wales, Lampeter. He is the former pastor of the First Presbyterian Church of Chattanooga, Tennessee, in addition to founding two other churches and a Christian school. Milton is the host and speaker on Faith for Living, which can be seen on television and heard on radio. He has also released three music CDs and is the author of several books.

But perhaps I should also note that Dr. Milton has a diploma from the Defense Language Institute, holds a commission in the U.S. Army Reserves as a chaplain, and was elected in 2010 by the Chief of Chaplains to the College of Military Preachers and appointed an instructor at the Armed Forces Chaplain School. He is also the founding director of the Chaplain Ministries Institute in Charlotte. I also note that on October 14, 2001, it was announced that Reformed Theological Seminary had "been approved by the NC SAA Program to receive the GI Bill under the provisions of Title 38 and 10, United States Code!"

Milton is a theological schizophrenic. Schizophrenia has been described as a mental disorder characterized by a disintegration of thought processes and of emotional responsiveness that most commonly manifests itself as auditory hallucinations, paranoid or bizarre delusions, or disorganized speech and thinking.

I know of no other way to describe Milton after reading his latest post on the Faith for Living blog hosted by his seminary:

> The failure of the bipartisan super committee to take decisive action to reverse the 15 trillion-dollar debt crisis this country needs from becoming another Greece has, predictably, failed. Now the Washington blame game begins. However, the greatest losers are the American people and, specifically, those Americans who courageously and proudly wear the uniform of the armed services.
>
> As threats of cuts are made to their very mission, our brave troops are on the ground, in the air, and on the seas fighting, defending, and protecting this nation from the continuing threats to our very existence as a people. The absurd decision to tie massive cuts to the US military as an "incentive" to force action by the super committee was one of the biggest mistakes ever made by Washington DC, and they have made a few recently. Of all the things that the government does, providing a military to "defend the Constitution of the United States against all enemies, foreign and domestic" just happens to be one of the clearest.
>
> Scripture teaches that God has ordained government for the good of man. Civil authority, according to St. Paul, has been granted the power of the sword to punish evil, thereby protecting the innocent: "For he is the minister of God to thee for good. But if thou do that which is evil, be afraid; for he beareth not the sword in vain: for he is the minister of God, a revenger to execute wrath upon him that doeth evil" (The Epistle to the Romans 13:4 KJV). The present talk of defense cuts flies in the face of our nation's duty and our proud heritage.
>
> We have had draw downs before—after WWII, after Vietnam, and after the Gulf War, but we have never had to think about draco-

> nian reductions while we were in the middle of a war! It is this very point that is deeply disturbing, and recklessly dangerous. The consequences of even the talk of such tinkering with our defenders, even if reasonable heads prevail to stop this absurdity, will have their consequences.
>
> Have we not learned our lesson? Reagan's military build-up in the 1980s reversed the ill-advised draw downs after Vietnam (just one front in a larger, trans-generational Cold War) and, according to scholars like Paul Kengor of Grove City College and the American Center for Vision and Values, "All of these ventures [the strengthening of defense] had the effect of demonstrating a stronger, resurgent America, not only economically but also militarily. Suddenly, the country that had left Vietnam no longer appeared to lack resolve" (The Crusader: Ronald Reagan and the Fall of Communism by Dr. Paul Kengor, HarperCollins, 2007, 82).
>
> Kengor went on to demonstrate that President Reagan understood that America was still at war. According to this preeminent Reagan scholar, his action in strengthening the military greatly contributed to bringing down the Soviet Union. Why now, when our sacred military members are risking their lives to fight "over there" so we don't fight "over here," would the president and other congressional leaders think that it is any different? To reduce military strength or even to talk about it as an option is to demoralize our troops while they are literally in the midst of a battle for our way of life.
>
> Some may call it treason. I would call it self-destructive. As a minister of the gospel I would also call it irresponsible and immoral, given that God has called our civil authorities to protect our people against evil. May God have mercy and bless the troops who bravely carry on their mission to defend this nation, even while others who have taken the same oath are allegedly using the military as pawns in a Washington election year. There are times when the Church should speak up. Because our life and liberty is at stake, I think that time is now.

Milton holds to every armchair warrior, red-state fascist, reich-wing nationalist, imperial Christian fallacy known to man.

As I mentioned above, cutting the bloated defense budget is to Milton a deeply disturbing, draconian, recklessly dangerous, self-destructive absurdity. The "cuts" fly "in the face of our nation's duty and our proud heritage." Never mind that the real defense budget is $1 trillion, that the United States spends more than the rest of the world combined, and that most defense spending is really spending on offense.

Milton idolizes members of the military. They are our "brave troops." They "courageously and proudly wear the uniform of the armed services." God should "bless the troops." U.S. soldiers are never Christian killers, murders, accomplices to murder, criminals, dupes, mercenaries, or part of the president's personal attack force willing to obey his latest command to bomb, invade, occupy, and otherwise bring death and destruction to any country he deems necessary. They are "our sacred military members."

Milton is likewise deceived about the real mission of the military. He thinks they are "our defenders" who "defend this nation" and protect "this nation from the continuing threats to our very existence as a people." The government provides a military to "defend the Constitution of the United States against all enemies, foreign and domestic." U.S. troops "fight 'over there' so we don't fight 'over here.'" They are "in the midst of a battle for our way of life." But is this what the U.S. military actually does? Unfortunately, most of what the military does is more offense than defense, more foreign than domestic, and more civilian than martial. I think Milton needs a course in DOD 101.

Milton says that we are "in the middle of a war." The United States is actually in the middle of several wars. But rather than saying we should not cut defense because we are fighting wars, why not examine the wars we are fighting to see if they are just, right, and necessary? Since the undeclared, unconstitutional wars in Iraq and Afghanistan, and Yemen, Pakistan, and everywhere else, are clearly—except to Christian warmongers and imperial Christians—unjust, immoral, and unnecessary, the only sensible solution is to end the wars, not increase the defense budget.

Like other Christian apologists for the state, its military, and its wars that I have written about who appeal to Romans 13 to justify their blind nationalism, their cheerleading for the Republican Party, their childish devotion to the military, their acceptance of national-security state, and their support for perpetual war, Milton seeks to justify a large defense budget by doing the same thing. This, of course, is ludicrous, since the passage has nothing to do with the government providing national defense. But let's assume for a moment that it does. Fine. How does that justify bloated military budgets, foreign wars, militarism, imperialism, and policing the world? When it comes to the military budget, conservatives adopt the same fallacy as liberals do when it comes to education. To liberals more spending on education means better education; to conservatives more spending on defense means better defense.

And finally, why do conservatives always invoke the name of the criminal, warmongering, budget-busting, deficit-increasing, liberty-destroying, government-expanding, economic and foreign interventionist St. Reagan? Anyone remotely familiar with the Reagan record would not be impressed with Milton's name-dropping. For the complete and utter evisceration of Reagan, see Murray Rothbard's "The Reagan Phenomenon," "Ronald Reagan, Warmonger," and "Ronald Reagan: An Autopsy."

What is so bad about theological schizophrenics like Michael Milton is that they have a position of influence over many young people. We can only hope and pray that this is one college administrator that students never get to know.

* * * * *

A WAR PRAYER FOR THE TWENTY-FIRST CENTURY

Since the bombs began to fall on Baghdad in March of 2003, churches, Christian leaders, religious organizations, and individual Christians have been telling us to pray for U.S. soldiers fighting in Iraq. We have been told to pray for the safety of U.S. troops while they defend our freedoms, protect us from another terrorist attack, rid the world of weapons of mass destruction, bring to justice the perpetrators of the 9/11 attacks, fight the global war on terrorism, liberate the Iraqi people, spread democracy, fight "over there" so we don't have to fight "over here," protect American interests in the Middle East, ensure the security of Israel, and make the world a better place.

There are several problems with these war prayers.

First, our "enemies" are praying the same war prayers. The citizens of other countries likewise ask God to bless and protect their troops. How is the Lord going to take care of both sides in the same way? American Christians just assume that God will not bless and protect the troops on the other side. American troops alone are dear to the heart of God.

Second, why is it that war prayers never seek to limit war? In his "Prayer before Battle" from "Some New Prayers" (CWE, 69:137), Erasmus gives us a model:

> Almighty king of Sabaoth, that is, of armies, you determine both war and peace for the regions of the earth by means of your angels appointed for the task. You gave new heart and strength to the boy David, so that although he was small, without weapons, and

> unskilled in war he attacked and overthrew the giant Goliath with a sling. If we are fighting for a just cause, if we are forced to fight, I pray you, first, to turn the hearts of our enemies to the desire for peace, so that no Christian blood may be spilt upon the earth; or to spread the fear that men call panic; or to let victory be gained with the least shedding of blood and the smallest loss by those whose cause is more pleasing to you, so that the war may be quickly concluded and we may sing songs of triumph with one accord to you, who reign in all and above all. Amen.

Third, why are we only asked to pray war prayers? Why is it that we are never enjoined to pray prayers for peace and non-intervention? It is never suggested that we pray for impressionable young men and women to not be ensnared by military recruiters. It is never suggested that we pray that American troops are never sent to fight on foreign soil. It is never suggested that we pray for the safety of innocent civilians in the country the U.S. military is bombing. It is never suggested that we pray for the safety of foreign soldiers defending their homeland against attack. It is never suggested that we pray that the U.S. military only be used for genuinely defensive purposes. It is never suggested that we pray that the United States return to a noninterventionist foreign policy. It is never suggested that we pray for Congress to limit the president's ability to wage war. Instead of all these things, we are told *ad nauseam* to "pray for the troops."

Fourth, war prayers are vague and presumptuous. What exactly does it mean when we are told to pray for the troops? Is it their safety and protection we are supposed to pray for? Should we pray that God keep them safe while they fly their helicopter gunships, pilot their bombers, and drive their tanks? This sounds like a strange thing to request since U.S. troops are the ones that did the invading of a sovereign country. Should we pray that God protect them while they drop bombs, throw grenades, launch missiles, fire mortars, and shoot bullets? This too sounds a bit odd since U.S. troops are the ones fighting an unnecessary, senseless, and immoral war. Would we ask God to keep someone safe while he was committing a crime? Then why should we ask God to protect U.S. soldiers who are committing a crime against the Iraqi people?

Fifth, and most significantly, war prayers are dishonest. Although not usually vocalized, implicit in every war prayer is a request for victory. It doesn't matter what country U.S. troops are fighting in or the reason they are fighting. A war prayer for God to protect the troops is not just a prayer for the troops to be kept safe for some indefinite period; it is a prayer for the troops to be kept safe while they are vanquishing whatever group of people the U.S. government claims is the enemy. If war prayers were honest prayers they would openly and boldly call upon God to help U.S. forces crush the enemies of the United States.

Mark Twain (1835–1910) recognized the true nature of war prayers a hundred years ago. In his brief story called "The War Prayer," Twain tells of a church service held on the Sunday before "the battalions would leave for the front." A "war chapter" was read from the Old Testament, followed by a long prayer from the pastor that God would protect the "noble young soldiers," encourage them "in their patriotic work," and "bear them in His mighty hand." At the end of the prayer a mysterious stranger appears and addresses the congregation. He claims to be from the throne of God. After explaining that he was "commissioned of God" to put into words the other part of the pastor's prayer that he and the congregation prayed in their hearts, the stranger uttered a real war prayer:

> O Lord our Father, our young patriots, idols of our hearts, go forth to battle—be Thou near them! With them—in spirit—we also go forth from the sweet peace of our beloved firesides to smite the foe. O Lord our God, help us to tear their soldiers to bloody shreds with our shells; help us to cover their smiling fields with the pale forms of their patriot dead; help us to drown the thunder of the guns with the shrieks of their wounded, writhing in pain; help us to lay waste their humble homes with a hurricane of fire; help us to wring the hearts of their unoffending widows with unavailing grief; help us to turn them out roofless with their little children to wander unfriended the wastes of their desolated land in rags and hunger and thirst, sports of the sun flames of summer and the icy winds of winter, broken in spirit, worn with travail, imploring Thee for the refuge of the grave and denied it—for our sakes who adore Thee, Lord, blast their hopes, blight their lives, protract their bitter pilgrimage, make heavy their steps, water their way with their tears, stain the white snow with the blood of their wounded feet! We ask it, in the spirit of love, of Him Who is the Source of Love, and Who is ever-faithful refuge and friend of all that are sore beset and seek His aid with humble and contrite hearts. Amen.

Although Twain dictated "The War Prayer" around 1904–1905, it was not published until 1923 in Albert Bigelow's anthology of Paine's writings called *Europe and Elsewhere* (Harper & Brothers, pp. 394–398). Twain is supposed to have remarked to a friend that only the dead were permitted to tell the truth.

But Mark Twain was not the only one to shed light on the true nature of war prayers. Back in 1845, the American Peace Society assembled a collection of sixty-four essays by a variety of authors and from a wide range of viewpoints on the subjects of war and peace. It is titled *The Book of Peace: A Collection of Essays on War and Peace*. Essay No. XLI is called "War-Prayers." After pointing out that pagans have their war prayers, and explaining how "our prayers, if made in accordance with the pacific principles of the gospel, would oppose war, and be discarded by all war-makers as hostile to their designs," the author puts forth a war prayer that honest chaplains should pray on the eve of battle:

> O Lord of hosts, smile upon thy servants now marshaled before thee for the work of death. Breathe into them, O God of war, the spirit of their profession. Let them for the time forget thy prohibition of old, *thou shalt not kill*, and also those commands of thy gospel which bid them do good unto *all* men, to love even their enemies and turn the other cheek to the smiter. Thou knowest, Omniscient Father of all, this is no time for the application of such principles; and we pray thee to animate them with sentiments more appropriate to the awful duties of this hour, and thus prepare them for a signal and glorious triumph over their enemies. Fill them with the spirit of war, and enable them, in humble reliance on thee, to shoot, and stab, and trample down their foes. Nerve every arm, direct every blow; guide every sword, every bayonet, every bullet to the seat of life, that we may soon reap a glorious harvest of death. Thou knowest, O God most holy, that our enemies, murderers in heart, if not in deed, all deserve the damnation of hell; and we beseech thee to aid us in sending as many of them as possible to the place "where the worn dieth not, and the fire is not quenched." Fight thou for us, and give thy servants a great victory, for which all the people shall praise thee.

And back in 1793, Anna Barbauld expressed her opposition to war in *Sins of Government, Sins of Nations*. She includes in her work this brutally honest caustic prayer:

> God of Love, father of all families of the earth, we are going to tear in pieces our brethren of mankind, but our strength is not equal to our fury, we beseech thee to assist us in the work of slaughter. Whatever mischief we do, we shall do it in thy name; we hope, therefore, thou wilt protect us in it.

Well, since 9/11 "changed everything," what we need is a war prayer for the twenty-first century. Just as honest Christian warmongers should recite the Warmonger's Psalm, assent to the Warmonger's Beatitudes, manifest the Warmonger's Fruit of the Spirit, and pray the President's Prayer, so they should pray a war prayer like this:

> O Lord God of war, we beseech thee to bless our troops in their latest military adventure. Go with U.S. soldiers as they travel around the globe to intervene in the affairs of other countries. Use the U.S. military to smite the enemies of the United States just like thou used the children of Israel in the Old Testament to smite the heathen nations. We ask for thy special protection on the U.S. soldiers who have invaded Iraq and Afghanistan and now occupy those countries. Guide every bomb to its target, and every bullet to the heart of its victim. We pray that thou would send these Muslims to hell who dare to plant roadside bombs to harm U.S. soldiers. We know that thou will look after widows and orphans—so please help our soldiers, thy soldiers, to create as many widows and orphans as possible. Destroy the young Iraqi and Afghan children with bullets, malnutrition, or disease before they grow up and become suicide bombers. We beseech thee to guide all Predator drones to their targets in Pakistan and all the other countries where terrorists and their families need to be killed. Fill U.S. soldiers, thy servants, with the spirit of indifference to the death and destruction that they are causing. Avenge the United States, thy country, for the 9/11 terrorist attacks. We also humbly request that thou move upon Congress to not only increase funding for this war, but the overall military budget as well so thy people can fight another just war against the Muslim infidel. All these things we ask in the name of the Prince of Peace.

We know, of course, that no war prayers like this will ever be prayed in public. No matter where or why U.S. troops are fighting, we will still simply be told to pray for the troops. But has anyone ever stopped to consider what the Lord thinks about these war prayers?

* * * * *

AND YOUR POINT IS?

From a biblical perspective, the worst thing about Christian apologists for war, the military, and the warfare state is not their willful ignorance of U.S. foreign policy, their blind nationalism, their childish devotion to the military, their cheerleading for the Republican Party, their acceptance of the national-security state, or their support for perpetual war, but their misuse of Scripture.

What follows are examples of some of the Old Testament Scripture verses often quoted or referred to before or after some Christian warmonger seeks to defend U.S. wars, the U.S. empire, or the U.S. military as a divine institution.

Abraham, "the friend of God" (James 2:23)," "armed his trained servants" to rescue his nephew Lot (Genesis 14:14).

The LORD brought the Jews "out of the land of Egypt by their armies" (Exodus 12:2).

"The LORD is a man of war" (Exodus 15:3).

The LORD told the children of Israel that he would "destroy all the people to whom" they came, and make their enemies "turn their backs" unto them (Exodus 23:27).

The LORD commanded the children of Israel to "destroy" the altars of the Amorites, the Canaanites, the Hittites, the Perizzites, the Hivites, and the Jebusites, "to break their images, and cut down their groves" (Exodus 34:11–13).

After "Israel vowed a vow unto the LORD, and said, If thou wilt indeed deliver this people into my hand, then I will utterly destroy their cities," "the LORD hearkened to the voice of Israel, and delivered up the Canaanites; and they utterly destroyed them and their cities" (Numbers 21:2–3).

Moses told the children of Israel to arm themselves "unto the war" and war against the Midianites. So Israel slew all the males and "took all the women of Midian captives, and their little ones, and took the spoil of all their cattle, and all their flocks, and all their goods." Then they "burnt all their cities wherein they dwelt, and all their goodly castles, with fire." And "took all the spoil, and all the prey, both of men and of beasts." But "Moses was wroth with the officers of the host, with the captains over thousands, and captains over hundreds, which came from the battle" because they "saved all the women alive," which had caused the children of Israel to "commit trespass against the LORD." So Moses commanded Israel to "kill every male among the little ones, and kill every woman that hath known man by lying with him" and to "keep alive" for themselves "all the women children, that have not known a man by lying with him" (Numbers 31:1–18).

When the children of Israel went out to battle, they were accompanied by priests (Deuteronomy 20:2).

Joshua and "about forty thousand prepared for war passed over before the LORD unto battle, to the plains of Jericho" (Joshua 4:13). The Jews blockaded the city and "utterly destroyed all that was in the city, both man and woman, young and old, and ox, and sheep, and ass, with the edge of the sword" (Joshua 6:21).

Joshua "utterly destroyed all the inhabitants of Ai" and burnt the city, with Israel taking "the cattle and the spoil" for themselves "according to the word of the LORD which he commanded Joshua" (Joshua 8:26–28).

The LORD sent Gideon to save Israel from the Midianites by smiting them (Judges 6:13–16).

The LORD commanded Saul to "smite Amalek, and utterly destroy all that they have, and spare them not; but slay both man and woman, infant and suckling, ox and sheep, camel and ass" (1 Samuel 15:3).

King David, a man after God's own heart (1 Samuel 13:14), was "a man of war" (1 Samuel 16:18) who had slain "his ten thousands" (1 Samuel 18:7), and said: "Blessed be the LORD my strength, which teacheth my hand to war and my fingers to fight" (Psalm 144:1).

The LORD commanded David to go and fight against the Philistines and he would deliver them into his hand. David then smote the Philistines with "a great slaughter," thereby saving the inhabitants of Keilah (1 Samuel 23:4–5).

David smote the Amalekites "from the twilight even unto the evening of the next day: and there escaped not a man of them, save four hundred young men, which rode upon camels, and fled" (1 Samuel 30:17).

David warred against the Philistines, Moab, Zobah, Syria, and Edom (2 Samuel 8:1, 2, 3, 5, 6, 13, 14), and "the LORD preserved David whithersoever he went" (2 Samuel 8:14).

Israelites from the tribes of Reuben, Gad, and Manasseh, "men able to bear buckler and sword, and to shoot with bow, and skilful in war," made war with the Hagarites. Many of the enemy were slain "because the war was of God" (1 Chronicles 5:18–23).

When the Jews rebuilt the wall of Jerusalem, half of the people worked and "the other half of them held both the spears, the shields, and the bows, and the habergeons" (Nehemiah 4:16–18, 21).

My reply to all of the above is simply this: And your point is?

Really, that is all I have to say.

What these imperial Christians are trying to say is that because the Jews in the Old Testament did X, Christians under the New Testament should support the U.S. government and its military doing Y.

But as I have pointed out numerous times, both in lectures and in articles, it is wrong to invoke the Jewish wars of the Old Testament against the heathen as a justification for the actions of the U.S. government and its military. Although God sponsored these wars, and used the

Jewish nation to conduct them, it does not follow that God sponsors American wars or that America is God's chosen nation. The U.S. president is not Moses, Joshua, King David, or God Almighty, America is neither the nation of Israel nor God's chosen nation, the U.S. military is not the Lord's army, and the Lord never sanctioned any Christian to go on a crusade, commanded him to war on his behalf, or encouraged any Christian to kill, make apologies for the killing of, or excuse the killing of any adherent to a false religion.

And as Philip Kapusta writes in *Blood Guilt: Christian Responses to America's War on Terror* (New Covenant Press, 2011):

> In fighting against these nations, the armies of Israel acted as God's agents of wrath and were used to execute His judgments. The wars of Israel were always to be at God's command, subject to His laws, and for the occupation and the defense of the Land of Promise. The children of Israel could only kill when killing in the name of God—that is, when killing in obedience to a direct mandate from God.
>
> Unlike the children of Israel, who were brought out of Egypt and given a land of their own and provided with a set of laws to govern them within God's divine kingdom, Christians have not been given a similar tract of land to defend or fight for. Neither have Christians been given a king upon earth who enforces *God's laws* when violated.

Some armchair Christian warriors, evangelical warvangelicals, Catholic just war theorists, reich-wing Christian nationalists, Red-State Christian fascists, pro-life hypocrites, theocon Values Voters, Christian Coalition moralists, and Religious Right warmongers are a little more savvy.

To sound a little more scriptural, they will also quote or refer to some verses in the New Testament before or after they seek to defend U.S. wars, the U.S. empire, or the U.S. military as a divine institution.

Jesus told a centurion he had "great faith" and healed his servant (Matthew 8:5–13).

Jesus "went into the temple of God, and cast out all them that sold and bought in the temple, and overthrew the tables of the moneychangers, and the seats of them that sold doves" (Matthew 21:12).

John the Baptist told soldiers: "Do violence to no man, neither accuse any falsely; and be content with your wages," but did not tell them to leave the military (Luke 3:14).

Jesus delivered a parable about a king going to war (Luke 14:31).

Jesus told his disciples: "He that hath no sword, let him sell his garment, and buy one" (Luke 22:36).

Jesus "made a scourge of small cords" and drove the moneychangers out of the temple (John 2:14–15).

Cornelius the Roman centurion was a just man that feared God, gave much alms, and prayed always (Acts 10:1–2).

The Apostle Paul said: "The powers that be are ordained of God" (Romans 13:1).

The Christian is commanded to "endure hardness, as a good soldier of Jesus Christ" (2 Timothy 2:3).

The "armies of heaven" will follow Christ when he returns (Revelation 19:14).

Jesus Christ is depicted as bearing a "sharp sword" and using it to "smite the nations" as he rules them with "a rod of iron" (Revelation 19:15).

Again, my reply is simply: And your point is?

American military officers are not surrogates for Jesus Christ. Whatever Jesus Christ did or will do has absolutely no relevance to what the U. S. military does in Afghanistan. And if a Christian warmonger wants to do what Jesus did, then why not start with doing "no sin" and not having "guile found in his mouth" (1 Peter 2:22)?

Although the New Testament does liken a Christian to a soldier (Philemon 2, Philippians 2:25), as soldiers Christians are admonished to "put on the whole armor of God" (Ephesians 6:11), not Marine body armor, have on "the breastplate of righteousness" (Ephesians 6:14), not a Navy uniform, shod their feet "with the preparation of the gospel of peace" (Ephesians 6:15), not Army boots, and wear "the helmet of salvation" (Ephesians 6:17), not an Air Force pilot helmet. The weapons of the Christian soldier are not carnal (2 Corinthians 10:4). His shield is "the shield of faith" (Ephesians 6:16), not an M1 Abrams tank, and his sword is "the word of God" (Ephesians 6:17), not an M-16. The only warfare the New Testament encourages the Christian to wage is against the world, the flesh, and the devil.

Regarding Roman soldiers and centurions, isn't it strange how that apologists for the U.S. military never refer to the ones scourged, stripped, crowned with thorns, mocked, smote, spit on, and crucified Jesus Christ?

And besides, there is a big problem with justifying the activities of the U.S. military because soldiers are not condemned in the New Testament; slave owners are not condemned either (Ephesians 6:9; Colossians 3:22, 4:1; 1 Timothy 6:1; 1 Peter 2:18).

On John the Baptist and soldiers, I have written a whole article here. Is not war the highest form of violence? On Romans 13, I have written articles here and here.

When all else fails, the Bible does say there is "a time of war" (Ecclesiastes 3:8). But of course, that doesn't justify the war in Iraq, even though Jerry Falwell implied it did.

To hear some Christians talk about war and the military just like Republican politicians, one gets the impression they think the GOP is God's Own Party instead of a pack of rabid war-crazed defenders of militarism and empire.

Which is worse, "deceived" Muslims using the Koran to justify jihad, suicide bombers, and IED attacks or "enlightened" Christians using the Bible to justify war, torture, and drone strikes? The answer should be quite obvious.

* * * * *

LEGITIMATE MURDER?

Is killing another human being ever justifiable? Is committing acts of violence ever permissible? Is murder ever legitimate?

In an otherwise good article on self-defense, "The Use of Deadly Force in Self-Defense," a Christian writer in the *Berean Searchlight* loses his way when he brings up the subject of killing in war. Here are the relevant paragraphs:

> War is another area where the taking of human life is legitimate in the eyes of God. When the soldiers asked John the Baptist, "And what shall we do?" it is true that John advised them to "do violence to no man" (Luke 3:14). However, these instructions must be considered in light of the fact that he did not insist that these soldiers quit being soldiers. This means that the *violence* in which he forbad them to engage must have had to do with some sort of *illegal* violence. The Greek word for *violence* here has the idea of *shaking*, and just might be the idea behind our modern word *shakedown*, the illegal use of power or authority to extort money from people. The rest of John's words here would suggest that this is what he had in mind, as he went on to tell them to "be content with your wages."
>
> We know from Ezekiel 45:9 that the orderly execution of judgment and justice by soldiers in the line of duty is not considered violence, for here God says to "*remove* violence" *by engaging in*

> *the execution of judgment and justice.* In addition, David said, "Blessed be the Lord my strength, *which teacheth my hands to war, and my fingers to fight*" (Psa. 144:1). Clearly, the taking of human life in times of war cannot be a sin if God Himself taught David how to be good at it.

The writer's opening and closing statements are not only irresponsible and careless; they are also evil and dangerous.

On John the Baptist and soldiers, since I have written an entire article on the subject here. I will just say:

1. Is not killing in an unjust war the highest form of violence?

2. Too much should not be read into John the Baptist not telling soldiers to quit since the Apostle Paul likewise never told slave owners to free their slaves (Ephesians 6:9; Colossians 4:1).

3. Nothing said or not said by John the Baptist or done or not done by Roman soldiers can justify the actions of the U.S. military in Iraq or Afghanistan.

The context of the passage the writer refers to in the book of Ezekiel speaks of a future time when the princes of Israel shall no more oppress the people of Israel (Ezekiel 45:8). It has nothing whatsoever to do with soldiers, then or now. Just read it: "Thus saith the Lord GOD; Let it suffice you, O princes of Israel: remove violence and spoil, and execute judgment and justice, take away your exactions from my people, saith the Lord GOD" (Ezekiel 45:9). It also doesn't say anything about how anyone is to "remove violence," although it seems clear that stopping the committing of violence is what is meant. One thing is for sure, it certainly doesn't say to "remove violence" by engaging in the execution of judgment and justice."

It does not follow that because the Lord taught David to fight and war for him as the leader of the Old Testament Israelites that the taking of human life in times of war cannot be a sin.

It is wrong to invoke the Jewish wars of the Old Testament against their enemies as a justification for the actions of any government and its military. Although God sponsored these wars, and used the Jewish nation to conduct them, it does not follow that God sponsors other wars, any country is God's chosen nation, any country has a divine mandate to wage war, any leader is like King David, or that any army is the Lord's army.

The LORD commanded the children of Israel to "destroy" the altars of the Amorites, the Canaanites, the Hittites, the Perizzites, the Hivites, and the Jebusites, "to break their images, and cut down their groves" (Exodus 34:11–13). Does this mean that the U.S. military should invade Muslim countries and destroy their mosques? Only to imperial Christians.

And besides, David obviously abused his skill set because the Lord said to him: "Thou shalt not build an house for my name, because thou hast been a man of war, and hast shed blood" (1 Chronicles 28:3). King David also had multiple wives. Does this mean that Christians can do the same?

I said that the writer's opening and closing statements were evil and dangerous. Take a look at them again:

> War is another area where the taking of human life is legitimate in the eyes of God.
>
> Clearly, the taking of human life in times of war cannot be a sin if God Himself taught David how to be good at it.

Notice that the writer did not offer any caveats; killing in war is legitimate and is not sinful.

This means that not only are U.S. troops off the hook for killing tens of thousands of people in Iraq and Afghanistan (and millions in Germany, Japan, Korea, and Vietnam), but that German soldiers who killed Polish, Russian, British, French, and American soldiers in World War II did nothing illegitimate. It also means that Japanese soldiers in World War II did not sin when they killed Chinese or American soldiers. The writer's blanket and careless statements mean that no soldier who ever has taken the life of "the enemy" while engaged in war has ever done anything illegitimate or sinful. This is ludicrous.

Killing in a war that is unjust or not a war of genuine self-defense is wholesale murder. And yes, that goes for the wars in Iraq and Afghanistan. Wearing a government uniform doesn't make it legitimate. Using a government weapon doesn't make it legitimate. Getting a government paycheck for doing it doesn't make it legitimate. Flying a government plane or helicopter doesn't make it legitimate. Sailing on a government ship doesn't make it legitimate. Killing government-declared enemies doesn't make it legitimate. Killing government-demonized foreigners doesn't make it legitimate. Following a government order doesn't make it legitimate. Fighting under a government flag doesn't make it legitimate.

Murder can never be legitimate.

* * * * *

IS GOD AGAINST DRONES?

He is not, according to former CIA analyst and current Christian axis of evil candidate Mark D. Tooley, as long as it is just the United States that is using them.

I first wrote about Christian "leaders" moonlighting as apologists for Bush and the Iraq war—the Christian axis of evil—back in 2006. The original group of inductees included Jerry Falwell, Pat Robertson, James Dobson, Hal Lindsey, Cal Thomas, and Pat Boone, with *WorldNetDaily* publisher Joseph Farah getting an honorable mention.

Since then I have written about other candidates like Tod Kennedy, a pastor; Craig Parshall, a lawyer; Doug Giles, a Christian killer par excellence; Bryan Fischer, a Christian warmonger on steroids; Michael Milton, a seminary chancellor and theological schizophrenic; Joe Carter, a conservative Christian warmonger; and Ellis Washington, the greatest Christian warmonger of all time.

Now we have Mark Tooley asking the question: "Is God against Drones?" He might as well have asked if he could join the Christian axis of evil. Tooley is the president of The Institute on Religion and Democracy (IRD), "a faith-based alliance of Christians who monitor, comment, and report on issues affecting the Church." "We are Christians working to reaffirm the church's biblical and historical teachings, strengthen and reform its role in public life, protect religious freedom, and renew democracy at home and abroad," says the group's mission statement. Founded in 1981, the IRD is headquartered in Washington D.C.

To get a sense of where Tooley might be headed in his article on drones, we can look at the IRD's issue statement on "War & Peace":

> Christian citizens in a great democracy like the United States, living in a world with all too many oppressive and aggressive regimes, regularly confront questions of war and peace: When is it right to use force to keep or restore international peace? When is it necessary to intervene militarily to stop a tyrant from killing his people?
>
> These are not easy questions. The IRD helps U.S. Christians to wrestle with such questions, without giving easy answers. We believe that the Christian tradition offers valuable resources to guide our thinking. The Scriptures direct us to seek peace, but warn that there are evildoers from whom the citizens must be protected. This is why, according to the apostle Paul, the state "bears the sword" (Romans 13:4).

> The IRD works within the "just war tradition" that has been the Christian mainstream. That tradition offers criteria to help discern when and how the state should resort to military force.
>
> The IRD has examined how those criteria might apply in situations ranging from the Cold War to the first Persian Gulf War, the U.S. response after September 11, 2001, and the current Iraq War. We have not offered firm answers to these questions of political judgment; we try to help Christian citizens draw their own conclusions.
>
> At the same time, the IRD has challenged church leaders who categorically oppose every U.S. military action since the 1960s. We respect a genuine pacifism that is willing to pay the price of not resisting evil. But we dispute the dishonest quasi-pacifism that pretends that all dangers could be averted by disarming our nation and appeasing its enemies. Within denominations that affirm the just war tradition, the IRD has contested the pacifist and quasi-pacifist minority that has tried to monopolize the church's social witness.

The two questions in the first paragraph are not difficult questions to answer at all. It is never right "to use force to keep or restore international peace" or "intervene militarily to stop a tyrant from killing his people," unless, of course, you are the world's self-appointed policeman hell bent on carrying out an interventionist and evil foreign policy.

The state bearing the sword in Romans 13 has nothing whatsoever to do with national defense, as I wrote about here.

The "just war tradition" is used to justify rather than to prevent war. Just war theory can be used effectively by all sides to justify all wars. As I pointed out in "The Warmonger's Lexicon," to a warmonger a just war means any war the United States engages in.

I can give a firm answer as to how the "just war tradition" relates to these situations: it doesn't.

What is wrong with categorically opposing "every U.S. military action since the 1960s"? And doing so has nothing to do with disarmament or appeasement or being a "pacifist" or "quasi-pacifist." Is there any good reason not to oppose the Vietnam War—a war in which over 58,000 Americans died so they could get their names on a wall? Is there any good reason not to oppose the War in Iraq—a war in which 4,448 Americans died for a lie? Is there any good reason not to oppose the War in Afghanistan—a war in which 2,169 Americans died in vain?

The proliferation of the use of drone aircraft overseas with ordnance capable of killing an individual person or destroying an entire village has made the president alone the judge, jury, and executioner. And if that weren't bad enough, drone strikes more often than not have killed more innocent civilians than "terrorists" or "insurgents." Now the president claims the power to target for death via drone anyone anywhere in the world—including American citizens—on the suspicion that they *might* threaten U.S. national security. So much for due process of law.

So, then, according to Mark Tooley, why is God not against drones? There are several reasons.

One, "Religious Leftists" are against them. Tooley mentions David Gushee, a liberal Baptist ethicist at Mercer University; Susan Brooks Thistlethwaite, former president of Chicago Theological Seminary, and now a fellow at the Center for American Progress; and Jonathan Merritt, a liberal Baptist columnist. Tooley doesn't like Gushee's stating that drones exemplify a "disturbing combination of American arrogance and self-righteousness" and "that America would never accept China or Russia launching drone attacks inside the U.S." Tooley takes issue with Thistlethwaite for complaining "that some drone targets do not actually present an 'imminent' threat" and others kill civilians. Tooley is upset with Merritt for liking "Gushee's comparison of U.S. drone attacks to China or Russia launching strikes in the U.S." The Religious Left is "reliably opposed to whatever tools are currently deployed in defending America."

Two, America is the "exceptional" nation. Why, because "the United States is the most powerful nation." With this power "flows responsibility not just for the security of our own people but also a wider duty for upholding a global peace." American power helps to keep wars largely contained to "places like Afghanistan, Somalia and Sudan" and "provides an approximate peace for most of the world." In other words, the U.S. military fights "over there" so we won't have to fight "over here." The Religious Left can't comprehend the distinction between the United States and China employing drones due to their "seething anti-Americanism."

Three, the United States is the policeman of the world. Says Tooley: "Absent a global police force, the United States is the final arbiter of an approximate global stability. That stability requires America to deter, contain and sometimes deploy lethal force against renegade states and terror groups." Since Afghanistan and Pakistan "are unable to police their own nations," U.S. drone strikes are justified and necessary.

And four, "homicidal terrorists" are dedicated to killing Americans. The U.S. is locked in an "ongoing conflict" with terror groups.

So, is God against drones?

Tooley is asking the wrong question. Asking if God is against drones is like asking if God is against guns or knives. The question is very ambiguous. It all comes down to how drones are used. Drones can actually serve some useful purposes like tracking the spread of wildfires or helping to find missing hikers. Just like a gun can be used for self-defense and a knife can be used to cut a steak. What Tooley is asking about, and what he supports, is the use of drones by the U.S. military and CIA to kill people around the world that are *perceived* as threats to U.S. military personnel, American interests, and national security.

It is easy to pick on "Religious Leftists." Just like a broken clock is right twice a day, they may oppose drone strikes one day, and then support humanitarian military crusades the next; they may oppose drone strikes one day, and then support "good wars" the next.

But it is not just religious leftists that oppose the use of drones for targeted killings. I am anything but a religious leftist, and I oppose not only the use of drones for targeted killings, but the wars in Iraq and Afghanistan, the U.S. Navy as a global force for good, American exceptionalism as a pretense for imperialism, the United States as the world's policeman, the U.S. empire of troops and bases that encircles the globe, a reckless, belligerent, and interventionist U.S. foreign policy, and the whole bogus, liberty-destroying war on terror.

There is certainly nothing wrong with using drones for defense, but the U.S. military wouldn't know a defensive war if it saw one. With over a thousand foreign military bases and troops in over 150 countries and territories, the U.S. military is engaged in offense, not defense.

No wonder "homicidal terrorists" are dedicated to killing Americans. Could U.S. foreign policy have anything to do with it or do they just hate us for our freedom and values?

Drones used to wage unnecessary and unjust wars are evil, just like tanks, planes, bombs, bullets, and grenades that are used to wage unnecessary and unjust wars. It all depends on how they are used.

* * * * *

JANUS CHRISTIANS

> "Were it not for the support offered by several tens of millions of evangelicals, militarism in this deeply and genuinely religious country becomes inconceivable." ~ Andrew Bacevich (Colonel, U.S. Army, Ret.).

This is one of the most sobering statements in Dr. Bacevich's important book *The New American Militarism: How Americans Are Seduced by War* (Oxford, 2005). Whether you agree or disagree with evangelical support for militarism, the fact remains that the largest group of Americans that the government can count on to support the institution of the military, the empire of troops and bases that encircles the globe, large defense budgets, overseas military interventions, the perpetual war on terror, and now torture is evangelical Christians—and the more conservative the more bloodthirsty.

Why?

If there is any group that should oppose these things, it is conservative Christians who profess to be in subjection to the Bible. There is something gravely wrong with evangelical Christianity when socialists like Chris Hedges and Noam Chomsky get it right and conservative Christians get it wrong.

Christian warmongers are looking in the Bible, but they are looking in the wrong place. Everything in the Bible is written for us, but not to us. Although there are some exceptions, most Christian warmongers are Janus Christians.

Janus was the two-headed Roman god of gates and doors. With faces that looked in two different directions, he could see forward and backward at the same time. Because he was considered the god of beginnings, our first month, January, was named after him.

So, what do many evangelicals have in common with the Roman god Janus?

Plenty.

Janus Christians are always looking backward to the Old Testament or forward to the Book of Revelation to justify Christian participation in U.S. government wars and military interventions.

We are continually told by every Christian apologist for war and the military that because God sponsored wars in the Old Testament against heathen nations (Judges 6:16), and used his chosen nation of Israel (Deuteronomy 7:11–12) to conduct them, that this justifies Christian killing for the state in some foreign war.

But since the president of the United States is not God, America is not his chosen nation, the U.S. military is not the Lord's army, the Christian's sword is the word of God, and the only warfare the New Testament encourages the Christian to wage is against the world, the flesh, and the devil, Christians who look backward to the Old Testament to justify their warmongering are looking in the wrong place. The Lord has made no promise since Old Testament times to any nations or individuals that he would fight and kill their enemies or help them to do so.

Savvy Christian warmongers not only appeal to the past, they also look to the future. Here is an example from, of all places, a theological journal:

> That Christ Himself will engage in actual, blood-shedding, life-taking warfare when He returns to set up His kingdom is significant. He cannot be the Righteous One, the Holy One, if war is inherently evil and the combatant's role satanic. When He comes, the Lord will instruct His people to engage in that future warfare (cf. Obad 15–21). Would He demand His people to commit sin? Of course not! Therefore, warfare cannot be inherently sinful. Rev 19:11–21.

Christ establishing his future kingdom by force is certainly significant, but completely irrelevant to men engaging in aggressive warfare today. It does not follow that because the Lord will instruct people to war on his behalf in the future that it is okay for people to war on their own behalf now. Just as Christ ruling all nations with a rod of iron (Revelation 20:15) does not mean that it is permissible for a world dictator to do the same now. Warfare without the express command of Christ is certainly inherently evil and sinful. Offensive war is nothing but wholesale murder; defending one's country from attack is not waging war at all, it is self-defense—but only when it is truly defensive, which, of course, it rarely is. God is holy; men are sinners. No one is innocent in relation to God. The Lord could wipe out the bulk of mankind like he did with Noah's flood (Genesis 7:21–23) and still be just as holy. No man has any right to kill his fellow man—on any scale—just because God has the right to do so himself or by the means of his choosing. It can't be emphasized too much that Christ judges and makes war "in righteousness" (Revelation 19:11); man never does.

Oh, Janus Christians do appeal to the New Testament to try and justify Christian participation in U.S. government wars and military interventions, but when they do their arguments are worse than pathetic. For example, in the aforementioned theological journal, the following arguments are given "supporting the believer's participation in the military":

- Jesus' approval of a king who waged war against a wicked people (Matt 21:33–41).
- After Peter cut off the ear of the servant of the high priest (John 18:11), Jesus did not tell him to rid himself of his sword, merely to resheath it—for future use?

- In John 18:36 Jesus stated that it would have been proper for His disciples to defend His kingdom with swords if it had been an earthly kingdom.

In the first Scripture cited, there is neither a king nor warfare mentioned in the biblical passage cited. Strike one. In the second Scripture cited, the Lord told Peter to put away his weapon because he had to fulfill Scripture and be taken and crucified. Strike two. In the third Scripture cited, the author is exactly correct—it would have been proper if Christ's kingdom were an earthly kingdom—but defending Christ's kingdom is about as far removed as waging war for the U.S. military as one can possibly get. Strike three.

If there has there ever been a case of the word of God being "blasphemed" (Titus 2:5) or handled "deceitfully" (2 Corinthians 4:2) and more than this I have never seen it.

Janus Christians, because they are so blinded by the state and the military, have failed to notice the ethical instructions for Christians found throughout the New Testament.

Christians are admonished to "be patient toward all men" (1 Thessalonians 5:14), to not "render evil for evil unto any man" (1 Thessalonians 5:15), to "abstain from all appearance of evil" (1 Thessalonians 5:22), to "abhor that which is evil" (Romans 12:9), to "bless them" that persecute them (Romans 12:14), to "live peaceably with all men" (Romans 12:18), to "avenge not" themselves (Romans 12:19), to "overcome evil with good" (Romans 12:21), to "follow after the things which make for peace" (Romans 14:19), to be "slow to wrath" (James 1:19), and to "seek peace, and ensue it" (1 Peter 3:11).

Christians should be marked by their love (John 13:35; 1 Thessalonians 3:12), quietness (1 Thessalonians 4:11; 2 Thessalonians 3:12), holiness (1 Thessalonians 4:7; 1 Peter 1:15), hospitality (Romans 12:13; Titus 1:8), meekness (Ephesians 4:2; Titus 3:2), longsuffering (Galatians 5:22; Colossians 1:11), forbearance (Ephesians 4:2; Colossians 3:13), subjection (Titus 3:1; 1 Peter 5:5), temperance (Galatians 5:23; 2 Peter 1:6), godliness (1 Timothy 2:2; 2 Peter 1:16), humility (James 4:10; 1 Peter 5:5), and good works (Ephesians 2:10; Titus 3:8).

Christians should be more willing to accept suffering than to inflict it (2 Timothy 2:3, 4:5; James 5:10; 1 Peter 2:20–21, 3:17, 4:1, 16).

Christians should pray that they "may be delivered from unreasonable and wicked men" (2 Thessalonians 3:2) instead of calling for U.S. military action against them.

The New Testament ethic for the Christian is one of peace,

endurance, acceptance, non-violence, non-aggression, and non-retaliation. Does this mean that we invite foreign armies to bomb our cities and land on our shores? No, but it at least means that Christians have no business being part of the U.S. military and supporting or participating in the invasion, subjugation, and occupation of other countries, the bombing, maiming, and killing of foreigners on their soil, the doing of things that provoke hatred toward the United States and create terrorists, like nation building, intervening in the affairs of other countries, and policing the world.

It doesn't matter how many people the Jews killed in the Old Testament or how many times the Lord ordered them into battle; likewise, it doesn't matter how many people will die at some future Battle of Armageddon. What matters is right now under the New Testament in the Church Age. For a Christian to not know that is to manifest a tremendous ignorance of the Bible he professes to believe. Christians should be New Testament Christians, not Janus Christians.

* * * * *

A NINETEENTH-CENTURY ANTI-WAR TRIUMVIRATE

A shorter version of this essay was presented at the 2013 Austrian Economics Research Conference at the Mises Institute.

Alexander Campbell, Tolbert Fanning, and David Lipscomb had three things in common. They all lived during the nineteenth century. They were all ministers in the Church of Christ denomination. And they were all vehemently anti-war.

To the historic Peace Churches must be added, at least for the nineteenth and early twentieth centuries, the Church of Christ, the Disciples of Christ, and the Christian Churches that came out of the "Restoration Movement" of the early nineteenth century. One of the largest groups of religious conscientious objectors during World War I was from the Church of Christ.

Campbell, Fanning, and Lipscomb were three outstanding nineteenth-century opponents of war and proponents of peace. All wrote well before the horrors of World War I, with Campbell and Fanning writing their anti-war works even before the carnage of the so-called Civil War. My paper explores the connection between the anti-war views of Campbell, Fanning, and Lipscomb and modern libertarians and examines to what extent their overall political, economic, and religious philosophy paralleled their libertarian anti-war views.

Alexander Campbell (1788–1866) was born in Ireland, attended the University of Glasgow, and immigrated to America in 1809 with his family to join his father, Thomas Campbell, a Presbyterian minister who had immigrated to Pennsylvania two years previously. The elder Campbell soon left the Presbyterians, forming a Christian society in 1809 and a church in 1811. Alexander began preaching in 1810, and was ordained in 1812. He was soon acknowledged as the leader of what became known as the Restoration Movement. Campbell embarked on preaching tours, engaged in religious debates, and, in 1840, founded Bethany College in what is now Bethany, West Virginia, where he lived until his death. He also edited and published two journals, the *Christian Baptist*, from 1823–1830, and the *Millennial Harbinger*, from 1830 until his death in 1866. At the outbreak of the Civil War in 1861, Campbell expressed grief and disgust at the willingness of Christians to slaughter and destroy. He wrote in the *Millennial Harbinger* to not only dissuade Christians from participating in the Civil War, but to condemn the war as a monstrosity that "caps the climax of human folly and gratuitous wickedness." Campbell reminded his readers that "no Christian man who fears God and desires to be loyal to the Messiah, the Prince of Peace, shall be found in the ranks of so unholy a warfare."

I shall present Campbell's anti-war views from his famous "Address on War" that was originally delivered in May, 1848, in Wheeling, Virginia, published in the *Millennial Harbinger* in July the same year, and printed in the *Congressional Record* in 1937 at the request of Rep. Joseph B. Shannon (D-MO).

Tolbert Fanning (1810–1874) was born in Tennessee, and raised in Tennessee and Alabama. He began preaching at age 19, and made several preaching tours with Alexander Campbell. He graduated from Nashville University in 1835, established a school for girls in Franklin, Tennessee, in 1837, and then founded and served as the first president of Franklin College. He began the *Christian Review* magazine in 1844 and, with William Lipscomb, the brother of David, the *Gospel Advocate* in 1855. Like Campbell, Fanning opposed Christian participation in the Civil War at its outbreak.

I shall present Fanning's anti-war views from his March 1847 article in the *Christian Review* titled simply "War."

David Lipscomb (1831–1917) was born in Tennessee, lived briefly in Illinois and Georgia, and then spent the rest of his life in Tennessee. His family was active in the Restoration Movement before he was born. Lipscomb was baptized by Tolbert Fanning in 1845. He graduated from

Franklin College in 1849, and, with James Harding (the namesake of Harding University), founded the Nashville Bible School in 1891. The school was named in his honor as Lipscomb University after his death. Lipscomb began preaching in 1856, and made numerous preaching tours throughout the South. In 1866, Lipscomb began again to publish the *Gospel Advocate*, which his brother and Fanning had edited until it was forced to suspend publication at the start of the Civil War. He served as the magazine's editor for fifty years. The magazine is still published today. Like Campbell and Fanning, he opposed Christian participation in the Civil War at its outbreak. During the war, he was to Southerners a traitor; after the war, he was to Northerners a Southern sympathizer. Although Lipscomb was Alexander Campbell's most noted disciple, and their lives overlapped, there is no evidence that the two ever met.

I shall present Lipscomb's anti-war views from his 1889 book, *Civil Government: Its Origin, Mission, and Destiny, and the Christian's Relation to It*, which was originally published as a series of articles in the Gospel Advocate from 1866 to 1867.

Campbell on War

I first turn to Alexander Campbell. Although he waited until the end of the Mexican War to speak out against it, Campbell says he often reflected with intense interest "on the desolations and horrors of war, as indicated in the sacrifice of human life, the agonies of surviving relatives, the immense expenditures of a people's wealth, and the inevitable deterioration of public morals."

Campbell builds his case against Christian participation in war slowly and punctuates it by a series of questions. He begins by asking: "Has one Christian nation a right to wage war against another Christian nation?" But after concluding that "in strict logical and grammatical truth, there is not, of all the nations of the earth, one properly called a Christian nation," he rephrases the question as: "Can Christ's kingdom or church in one nation wage war against his own kingdom or church in another nation?" Campbell answers his question with another question: "Where is the man so ignorant of the letter and spirit of Christianity as to answer this question in the affirmative?" But in reply to those who have some difficulty with the question and might hypothetically tell him that the form of his question "meets not the exact state of the case," Campbell posits another question: "What, then, says the Bible on the subject of war?" After briefly surveying the Jewish wars of the Old Testament, Campbell concludes that "what the God of Abraham did by Abraham, by Jacob, or by any of his sons, . . . is of no binding authority now" because of the "new administration of the universe" whereby "Jesus Christ is now the Lord and King of both earth and heaven." Having established this fact, Campbell shifts his focus to the participation of the Christian individual in war.

Again, he begins with a question: "Can an individual, not a public functionary, morally do that in obedience to his government which he cannot do in his own case?" He concludes that "we cannot of right, as Christian men, obey the POWERS THAT BE in any thing not in itself lawful and right according to the written law" of Jesus Christ. Campbell then advances a step further and affirms:

> A Christian man can never, of right be compelled to do that for the state, in defence of state rights, which he cannot of right do for himself in defence of his own personal rights. No Christian man is commanded to love or serve his neighbor, his king, or sovereign more than he loves or serves himself. This conceded, and, unless a Christian man can go to war for himself, he cannot for the state.

Christians have no commandment as respects the works peculiar to a soldier or the prosecution of a political war. They are to "live peaceably with all men to the full extent of their power" because "the spirit of Christianity is essentially pacific."

But it's not just war, for, says Campbell, "a Christian man cannot conscientiously enter upon any business, nor lend his energies to any cause which he does not approve; and, in order to approve, he must understand the nature and object of the undertaking." He then skillfully applies this dictum to war:

> Nothing, it is alleged, more tends to weaken the courage of a conscientious soldier, than to reflect upon the originating causes of wars and the objects for which they are prosecuted. These, indeed, are not always easily comprehended. Many wars have been long prosecuted, and some have been terminated after many and long protracted efforts, before the great majority of the soldiers themselves, on either side, distinctly understood what they were fighting for.

To Campbell, "the most convincing argument against a Christian becoming a soldier may be drawn from the fact that he fights against an innocent person." If soldiers from warring sides meet in public out of uniform "they would, most probably, have not only inquired after the welfare of each other, but would have tendered to each other their assistance if called for." But if a uniform is their only introduction to each other, it serves as "the signal that they must kill or be killed." How could a Christian man, says Campbell, "thus volunteer his services, or hire himself out for so paltry a sum, or far any sum, to kill to order his own brother man who never offended him in word or deed."

Campbell had some harsh words regarding the soldier—"the professional and licensed butcher of mankind" who, with his "vulgar profanity, brutality, and debauchery" hires himself "to lay waste a country, to pillage, burn, and destroy the peaceful hamlet, the cheerful village, or the magnificent city; and to harass, wound, and destroy his fellow-man, for no other consideration than his paltry wages, his daily rations, and the infernal pleasure of doing it."

Campbell also laments the pernicious influence of the warrior spirit on society. Women are fascinated with soldiers "whose profession it is to make widows and orphans." Young mothers dress their boys as soldiers, training them "for the admired profession of a man-killer." The glorification of military leaders in schools and colleges also echoes this false spirit. Campbell is especially troubled that this delusion is found in the pulpit. He considers war prayers as "desecrating the religion of the Prince of Peace." He mocks the idea of chaplains on both sides of a conflict offering up prayers for "the success of rival armies, as if God could hear them both, and make each triumphant over the other, guiding and commissioning swords and bullets to the heads and hearts of their respective enemies." He is aghast that there would be a thanksgiving and rejoicing that God has caused "ten or twenty thousand of our enemies" to be sent to hell and myriads of widows and orphans to be made "at the bidding of some chieftain, or of some aspirant to a throne." In some cities, St. Paul has been "driven out of the church to make room for Generals and Commodores renowned in fight."

Campbell sums up his address with eight points.

1. The guilty generally make war and the innocent suffer its consequences.
2. The right given to the Jews to wage war is not vouchsafed to any other nation.
3. Prophecies indication that the Messiah would be the Prince of Peace.
4. The Gospel is a message which results in producing "peace on earth and good will among men."
5. The precepts of Christianity positively inhibit war.

6. The beatitudes of Christ are not pronounced on patriots, heroes, and conquerors; but on peacemakers.
7. War is folly because it can never be the criterion of justice, it can never be a satisfactory end of the controversy, and because peace is always the result of negotiation.
8. War is wicked because soldiers engaged in killing their brethren have no personal cause of provocation whatsoever; soldiers seldom, or ever, comprehend the right or the wrong of the war; the innocent are punished with the guilty, wars constrain the soldier to do for the state that, which, he were to do in his own case, the state would condemn him to death; and because wars are the pioneers of all other evils to society.

Give me the money "that has been spent in wars," says Campbell, "and I will clear up every acre of land in the world that ought to be cleared— drain every marsh—subdue every desert—fertilize every mountain and hill—and convert the whole earth into a continuous series of fruitful fields, verdant meadows, beautiful villas, hamlets, towns, cities, standing along smooth and comfortable highways and canals, in the midst of luxuriant and fruitful orchards, vineyards, and gardens." "I would found, furnish, and endow, he continues, "many schools, academies, and colleges, as would educate the whole human race—build meeting-houses, public halls, lyceums, and furnish them with libraries adequate to the wants of a thousand millions of human beings."

Campbell's anti-war views were grounded in logic and Scripture. Based on Christ's declaration that his kingdom was not of this world, Campbell reasoned that if the cause of Christ should not be defended militarily, then surely no lesser cause would be sufficient for Christians to take up arms. If Christ would not have his servants take up the sword in defense of his life, for whose life ought it to be taken up?

Campbell concludes his "Address on War" with wonder and shame that he has not spoken out or written out his views. He laments that he might have "saved some lives" if he had published something two or three years previously.

Fanning on War

Tolbert Fanning begins by marveling that nations and individuals still settled their difficulties "by mortal combat—not questioning at all, the divine right of slaying their fellows." He says he writes not for savages or infidels, "but for the civilized nations of the earth, and for such professed

Christians as feel authorized of God and their country, to take the life of their brother man." He then offers nine arguments against war, with the sixth argument itself containing nine reasons, based on the New Testament, why there is no such thing as "christian war."

Fanning doubts whether distinctions can be made among "just" wars, "offensive" wars, and "defensive" wars. No one has ever read in history of a people who acknowledge themselves the offending party—"all plead justification, on the ground of aggressions from the enemy." Indeed, "there is scarcely, in the annals of Time, an account of an important war, in which both parties did not operate, both offensively and defensively." As soon as war is declared, the technicalities of offensive and defensive war are forgotten.

Fanning considered the causes of war to be love of conquest, territory, lust, and plunder. He lamented the "fame of military chieftains" that "exerts a vast influence" on the mind of youth. Because "all the causes of war are fleshly," the idea of "holy wars" is "utterly inadmissible."

In answer to the question of whether the Christian institution permits its subjects to engage in war, Fanning pointedly says: "Christians, as a nation, church, or individuals, have no divine authority for engaging in war, offensive or defensive, for fame, plunder, revenge, or for the benefit of themselves or their enemies."

The silence of Christ as to the particulars of worldly governments is to show "that his religion could exist, regardless of particular forms of civil governments." Christianity was "designed to flourish under every form of human government, and even without the form of human legislation."

Fanning offers nine reasons "for believing that Christians have no right to engage in war."

> 1. If the spirit of war had existed in the government of Christ, we might reasonably suppose he would have appealed to arms to establish it.
> 2. The command "Resist not evil" cannot be reconciled with the spirit or practice of war.
> 3. No people have engaged in bloody deeds without transgressing the precept of loving our enemies.
> 4. The idea of revenge is wholly incompatible with the spirit and genius of Christianity.
> 5. We are commanded to follow peace with all men.
> 6. The spirit that Christians are commanded to cultivate forever

precludes the spirit and practice of war.
7. Christ's declaration that his kingdom was not of this world is demonstrable evidence that Christian war had no countenance from the Savior.
8. The early Christians did not feel themselves at liberty to fight and destroy the Almighty's creatures.
9. The early Christians did not even take part in civil government.

Because he believed that "the whole teaching of the New Testament, is to impress the spirit of long suffering and forbearance; and to sacrifice property and life itself, rather than deny the Savior," Fanning even eschewed Christian participation in wars of self-defense.

Fanning did not specifically mention soldiers or the institution of the military. But with all that he said in condemnation of Christians engaging in war, it is hard to believe that Fanning could ever be in favor of Christians "serving" in the military. The only thing he said that could be taken as a reference to this is simple yet profound: "We read no place in scripture, or in history, of General Peter, Col. Paul, Capt. John, or even Ensign Luke."

Lipscomb on War

Last, but not least, there is David Lipscomb. Because he is writing on the Christian's relation to government, he focuses on the state as the instigator of war. Just listen to these three statements:

> The chief occupation of human governments from the beginning has been war. Nine-tenths of the taxes paid by the human family, have gone to preparing for, carrying on, or paying the expenses of war.

> All the wars and conflicts of earth, all the desolation, ruin and blood-shed, between separated nations, or distinct peoples, are the fruits of human government.

> The people of Maine and Texas, of England and India, could never become enemies or be involved in strife and war, save through the intervention of human government to spread enmity and excite to war. Individuals in contact might, through conflict of interest, or personal antipathy, become embittered, and engage in war with each other, but distinct nations or peoples could have no strife save as they should be excited and carried on by these human governments.

Lipscomb also brings the religious element into this: "All the wars and strifes between tribes, races, nations, from the beginning until now, have been the result of man's effort to govern himself and the world, rather than to submit to the government of God."

He lamented the then-recent Civil War and the spectacle "of disciples of the Prince of Peace, with murderous weapons seeking the lives of their fellowmen." He considered it "abhorrent to the principles of the religion of the Savior, who died that even his enemies might live," that "brethren for whom Christ died" were found "imbruing their hands in the blood of their own brethren in Christ, making their sisters widows and their sisters' children orphans."

Lipscomb thought it immoral to kill on behalf of government: "Christians cannot fight, cannot slay one another or their fellowmen, at the behest of any earthly ruler, or to establish or maintain any human government." And neither can they vote to make others fight: "A man who votes to bring about a war, or that votes for that which logically and necessarily brings about war is responsible for that war and for all the necessary and usual attendants and results of that war."

Echoing Alexander Campbell, Lipscomb concludes that "Christ disavows the earthly character of his kingdom," declaring "that it is of a nature so different from all worldly kingdoms, that his servants could not fight for his kingdom." And "if they could not fight for his kingdom, they could not fight for any kingdom." And unlike Christian warmongers of today, for Lipscomb that included the kingdom of the United States.

Politics, War, and the State

My conclusion will focus on politics, war, and the state. It is impossible to be a libertarian and not be anti-war. War is not only nothing but state-sponsored terrorism, violence, and aggression; it is also the health of the state. The connection between the anti-war views of Campbell, Fanning, and Lipscomb and modern libertarians is a strong one. In fact, because they don't sanitize soldiers or call killing for the state serving the country, they are more consistent than some modern libertarians. Their shared religious philosophy certainly guided their anti-war views, but cannot be said to be solely responsible for such views

There remains to be seen the economic and political views of the members of this anti-war triumvirate and to what extent their overall philosophy paralleled their libertarian anti-war views.

Campbell received his early education from his father, an education steeped in the tradition of John Locke. He spoke favorably of Adam Smith and other classical liberals. He admired Thomas Jefferson. He was a fierce defender of the separation of church and state. He wrote in the *Christian Baptist* that "the clergy have ever been the greatest tyrants in every state, and at the present they are, in every country in Europe, on the side of the oppressors of the people who tramp on the rights of men." He defended the importance of private property. He used at Bethany College the works of Francis Wayland, the great Baptist champion of liberty, property, and peace that Campbell frequently references in the *Millennial Harbinger*. He opposed Christian participation in politics, considering it "a moral pestilence." "The spirit of politicians and the spirit of God," said Campbell, "are as antagonistic as flesh and spirit, as hatred and love, as heaven and hell; and he that would faithfully and truly serve the one, must abjure all allegiance to the other." Campbell considered patriotism to be a "pagan virtue" that had "no special place in the Christian religion." Although he believed that the state existed to punish crimes against men, he did not believe in using state power to punish sins against God. He was very critical of moral societies looking to the state to help stamp out sin. He considered the Church to be God's answer to the world's evils. Were it not for the prevalence of injustice and violence in the world, thought Campbell, "civil government would be wholly unnecessary." With these views on the nature and role of government, I don't see how we can describe Campbell as anything but a libertarian.

I have only a little information about Fanning's economic and political views. From his article on war we can see that he spoke favorably of the early Christians not taking part in civil government. Lipscomb wrote in a book on Franklin College in 1906 that Fanning "never voted or took part in the political and civil contests of the country." And in Libscomb's book, *Civil Government*, he quotes from this statement of Fanning:

> All the powers of the world are created by violence, and must necessarily be upheld by force; but the Lord established his kingdom by peaceable means—by love and kindness. Worldly governments are all under the prince of this world, and the government of Christians is administered by the Prince of Peace. These two characters of government are antipodal to each other. Spiritual government is to "break in pieces and consume" all of Satan's principalities; but the great work is not to be accomplished by violence but by love. Christ was not of the world neither were his disciples, and Christians in the nineteenth century should not be instruments in the hands of the devil to carry out his purposes.

Based on what little information we have, and because he did not condemn government merely because of its war making, Fanning can certainly be classified as at least a classical liberal.

Lipscomb was as fervently anti-state as he was anti-war. He distinguished human government from the government of God. He believed that the "essential elements" of human government were "evil." Human government, said Lipscomb, "bears the same relation to hell that the church bears to heaven." Echoing Murray Rothbard and Hans Hoppe, Lipscomb described civil government as resting "on force as its foundation." Civil power is "founded on force, lives by it and it is its only weapon of offence or defence." Government is not benevolent. Its rulers oppress their subjects "for their own benefit." Christians should submit to human government when doing so does not directly violate Scripture, but should also work "to seek its destruction." This should be accomplished, not by violence and the sword, but by "spreading the religion of Christ and so converting men from service to the earthly government to service to the heavenly one." Christians should neither participate in government nor vote. They should not use the civil powers "to promote righteousness, morality, or good to humanity." Even more so than Campbell, we can't describe Lipscomb as anything but a libertarian.

With examples like these, why is it that the greatest supporters of war and the military continue to be conservative Christians? I have given many reasons for this in my many articles and lectures on Christianity and war. But now we must add two more: ignorance or rejection of the nineteenth-century anti-war triumvirate of Alexander Campbell, Tolbert Fanning, and David Lipscomb.

* * * * *

CHAPTER 2
CHRISTIANITY AND THE MILITARY

SHOULD A CHRISTIAN JOIN THE MILITARY?

Christian enthusiasm for war is at an all-time high.

Gullible Christians have not just tolerated the state's nebulous crusade against "evil," they have actively promoted both it and the overgrown U.S. Military establishment. Because the Republican Party is in control of the federal government instead of the "ungodly" Democrats, because President Bush is the commander in chief instead of the "immoral" Bill Clinton, and because the "enemy" is the easily-vilifiable Muslim infidel, many Christians, who certainly ought to know better given the history of state-sponsored persecution of Christians, "heretics," and other religious groups over the past two thousand years, have come to view the state, and in particular its coercive arm, the military, as sacrosanct.

For far too long Christians have turned a blind eye to the U.S. Global Empire of troops and bases that encircles the world. Many Christians have willingly served as cannon fodder for the state and its wars and military interventions. Christians who haven't died (wasted their life) for their country in some overseas desert or jungle increasingly perpetuate the myth that being a soldier in the U.S. Military is a noble occupation that one can wholeheartedly perform as a Christian.

The Question

The question of whether a Christian should join the military is a controversial one in some Christian circles. By a Christian I don't just mean someone who accepts the title by default because he was born in "Christian" America or "Christian" Europe. In this respect, everyone but Jews and atheists could be classified as Christians. The mention of a Christian in this article should be taken in the narrower sense of someone who professes to believe that Jesus Christ is the Saviour (Luke 2:11) and that the Bible is some kind of an authority (Acts 17:11). It is true that this may be too broad a definition for some Christians, and it is also true that many who profess to be Christians hold defective views on the person of Christ and the nature of the Atonement. But for the purposes of this article, the "broadness" of this definition and the permitting of these "defects" do not in any way affect the question: Should a Christian join the military? In fact, the narrower one's definition of what constitutes a real Christian, the stronger the case can be made against a Christian joining the military.

The idea that there are certain things Christians should not do is not only scriptural (1 Corinthians 6:9–11; Galatians 5:19–21), it is readily acknowledged by Christians and non-Christians alike. Christians have historically applied this idea to occupations as well. But it is not just unlawful occupations like pimp, prostitute, drug dealer, and hit man that Christians have shied away from. Most Americans—whether they be atheist or theist—would have a problem with those occupations as well. Everyone knows that there are also certain lawful occupations that Christians frown upon: bartender, exotic dancer, casino card dealer, etc. This prohibition is also usually extended to benign occupations in not so benign environments. Therefore, a clerk in a drug store or grocery store is acceptable, but a clerk in liquor store or an x-rated video store is not. Likewise, most Christians would not work for an abortion clinic, for any amount of money, whether in the capacity of a doctor or a secretary. In other places of employment, however, a Christian might have no problem with being employed, only with working in a certain capacity. This explains why some Christians might not wait tables in restaurants that forced them to serve alcohol, but would feel perfectly comfortable working for the same restaurant in some other capacity, like a bookkeeper or janitor.

The larger question of whether a Christian (or anyone opposed to the federal leviathan) should work for the state is not at issue. Someone employed by the state as a teacher, a mailman, a security guard, or a park ranger is providing a lawful, moral, non-aggressive, non-intrusive service that is in the same manner also provided by the free market. Thus, it might be argued that working for the BATF, the CIA, the FBI, or as a regulation-enforcing federal bureaucrat is off limits, whereas these other occupations are not. The question then is which of these two groups the U.S. Military belongs in. Given the actions of the U.S. Military since Sherman's state-sponsored "total war" against Southerners and Indians, the host of twentieth-century interventions, subjugations, and "liberations," and the current debacle in Iraq, it should be obvious.

The question before us then is whether a Christian should join the military. Although my remarks are primarily directed at the idea of a Christian being a professional soldier (a hired assassin in some cases) for the state, they are also applicable to serving in the military in any capacity.

To save some people the trouble of e-mailing me to ask if I have ever been in the military, I will say now that, no, I have never been in the military. For some strange reason, many Americans think that if you have not "served" your country in the military then you have no right to criticize it. There are three problems with this attitude.

First of all, this is like saying that if you have not "served" in the Mafia then you have no right to criticize John Gotti. It reminds me of fellow travelers in the 1950s, 1960s, and 1970s saying that if you have not lived in the Soviet Union then you have no right to criticize it. So no, I am not a veteran, but I have family members who were in the military and have lived near military bases and been intimately associated with military personnel since I was ten years old. No, I am not a veteran, but I am a student of history ("Those who cannot learn from history are doomed to repeat it"—George Santayana), and was born with enough common sense to know government propaganda when I see it. I can also read above a tenth-grade level, which is about all it takes to compare the wisdom of the Founding Fathers with the drivel from Bush, Cheney, Wolfowitz, Powell, and Rumsfeld.

Secondly, some of the most vocal critics of the military have been in the military, like USMC Major General Smedley Butler. So it is not just non-veterans who are critics of the military.

The third problem with the knee-jerk reaction to this article and me because I have never been in the military is that it is misplaced indignation. I am only examining the question of whether a Christian should join the military. Criticism of the military is not my direct purpose.

Another objection to an article of this nature is that if it were not for the U.S. Military then no one would have the freedom right now to write anything. But if the military exists to defend our freedoms, and does not just function as the force behind an aggressive, interventionist U.S. foreign policy, then why are our troops scattered across 150 different regions of the world? Why doesn't the military control our borders? Why do we need a Department of Homeland Security if we already have a Department of Defense? Why, with the biggest military budget ever do we have less freedom in America now than at any time in history? The U.S. Military could not even defend the Pentagon. The case could even be argued that U.S. Military intervention is the cause for much of the anti-American sentiment in the world. So, like Brad Edmonds, I don't owe and still do not owe the military anything. I trust in God Almighty to keep me safe from a nuclear attack, not the U.S. Military.

The Commandments

Using the Ten Commandments (Exodus 20:3–17) as a guide, it is my contention that the military is no place for a Christian. As a Christian under the authority of the New Testament, I am perfectly aware that the Ten Commandments are in the Old Testament and were originally given to the nation of Israel. But I am also cognizant that the Apostle Paul said: "Whatsoever things were written aforetime were written for our learning" (Romans 15:4) after he had just recited many of the Ten Commandments (Romans 13:8–9).

1. Thou shalt have no other gods before me (Exodus 20:3).

The state has historically been the greatest enemy of Christianity. Yet, many Christians in the military have made the state their god. Members of the military are totally dependent on the state for their food, clothing, shelter, recreation, and medical care. They are conditioned to look to the state for their every need. But the state demands unconditional obedience. Shoot this person, bomb this city, blow up this building—don't ask why, just do it because the state tells you to. The soldier is conditioned to believe that whatever he does is right because it is done in the name of the state. The state's acts of aggression are regarded as acts of benevolence. Then, once the benevolent state is viewed as never doing anything wrong, it in essence becomes the all-seeing, all-knowing, omniscient state, since it would take absolute knowledge to know for certain that the person shot, the city bombed, or the building blown up "deserved" it.

2. Thou shalt not make unto thee any graven image (Exodus 20:4).

The state has an image that it expects its citizens to reverence and pledge allegiance to. This is especially true of people serving in the military. Perhaps the most famous picture of the flag is the raising of the flag by U.S. troops at Iwo Jima on February 23, 1945. But there is another picture of the flag that has occurred thousands of times that the state does its best to suppress: the picture of the flag-draped coffin of a life wasted in the service of one of the state's needless wars. Foreigners who object to our intervention in their country and our military presence across the globe burn American flags in protest. But they are not protesting because we are capitalists who believe in liberty, freedom, and democracy and they do not share our values. Christians in the military must reverence what has often justly come to be viewed by most of the world as a symbol of oppression. They must also pledge their allegiance to it. Christians blindly recite the Pledge of Allegiance without even bothering to find out where it came from, what its author intended, and how the state uses it to instill loyalty to the state in the minds of its youth. Never mind that the author was a socialist Baptist minister, Francis Bellamy (1855–1932), who was forced to resign from his church in Boston because of his socialist ideas (like preaching on "Jesus the Socialist"). Never mind that the idea for Bellamy's pledge of allegiance was taken from Lincoln's oath of allegiance imposed on Southerners after the successful Northern invasion of the Southern states. Never mind that "republic for which" the flag "stands" was, in Bellamy's eyes, "the One Nation which the Civil War was fought to prove." The Pledge is an allegiance oath to the omnipotent, omniscient state. There is nothing inherently wrong with the United States having a flag, but it has been made into a graven image that no Christian, in the military or otherwise, should bow down to.

3. Thou shalt not take the name of the LORD thy God in vain (Exodus 20:7).

The state will tolerate God and religion as long as He and it can be used to legitimize the state. God's name is taken in vain when it is used to justify the state's wars and military interventions. Some Christians in the military envision themselves as modern-day crusaders warring against the Muslim infidel. Indeed, the president even termed his war on terrorism "this crusade." Others, all the way up to the commander in chief, invoke the name of God or His words in Scripture to give authority to their unconstitutional, unscriptural, and immoral military adventures. When a young Christian man (or woman, unfortunately) leaves home and joins the military he often learns to take God's name in vain in ways that he never could have imagined. There is a reason the old expression is "cuss like a sailor," not cuss like a mechanic, an accountant, or a fireman. Singing "God Bless America" while cognizant of the abortions, promiscuity, and pornography that curse America is taking God's name in vain. Likewise, military chaplains asking God to bless troops on their missions of death and destruction are taking God's name in vain. Many Christians were upset a few years ago when the 9th U.S. Circuit Court of Appeals (which covers Alaska, Arizona, California, Hawaii, Idaho, Montana, Nevada, Oregon, and Washington) tried to strike out the phrase "under God" from the Pledge of Allegiance (which was only added in 1954). They should have cheered instead, for even though the two federal judges (the decision was 2–1) who made the ridiculous ruling that the inclusion of the phrase "under God" was an unconstitutional "endorsement of religion" ought to have their head examined, America is not a nation "under God," and to say that it is (as when one recites the Pledge of Allegiance), is the epitome of using God's name in vain.

4. Remember the sabbath day, to keep it holy (Exodus 20:8).

Although the sabbath day is technically the Jewish seventh day (Saturday) and not the Christian first day (Sunday), the basic principle is still the same. Christians the world over set aside the first day of the week to attend church services. Christians in the military are often deployed to some strange city or remote country for months at a time and are therefore forced to violate the precept of "not forsaking the assembling of ourselves together" (Hebrews 10:25). Defense consultant Josh Pollack, in his "Saudi Arabia and the United States, 1931–2002," has documented that during the early decades of the American troop presence in Saudi Arabia, Air Force chaplains were forbidden to wear Christian insignia or hold formal services. During the First Gulf War of Bush the Elder, the importation of Bibles for Christian troops was discouraged, and no alcohol was permitted to U.S. troops in accordance with Islamic Law.

5. Honour thy father and thy mother (Exodus 20:12).

It used to be thought that following one's father into the military was a noble thing that honored him. Thankfully, this is not so much the case anymore. Is it honoring to one's father and mother for a Christian to accept the state's amoral values that are taught in the military and reject the values learned from a Christian upbringing? The temptations in the military for a Christian young person away from home for the first time are very great. Joining the military is one of the surest ways for a Christian to dishonor his parents by associating with bad company and picking up bad habits. This is not to deny that some Christians who are well grounded in the Scriptures live an exemplary life while in the military and are a positive force for good. But see the next point.

6. Thou shalt not kill (Exodus 20:13).

This is perhaps the greatest reason for a Christian not to join the military. But there is a difference between killing and murdering. Under certain conditions, a Christian would be entirely justified in taking up arms to defend himself, his family, and his property against an aggressor.

If America was attacked, Christians could in good conscience kill and maim enemy invaders. However, when was the United States ever in danger from Guatemala, Vietnam, Indonesia, Grenada, Panama, Kosovo, Cuba, Haiti, Afghanistan, Iraq, North Korea, or any of the other places where the United States has intervened militarily? How then can a Christian justify killing any of them on their own soil? The old adage, "Join the army, meet interesting people, kill them," is now just "join the army and kill them" since you can't meet anyone at 10,000 feet before you release your load of bombs. The U.S. Military turns men into callous killers. The D.C. sniper, Lee Harvey Oswald, and Timothy McVey all learned how to kill in the military. When a Christian in the military is faced with an order to kill, bomb, or destroy someone or something halfway around the world that he has never met or seen, and is no real threat to him, his family, or his country, there is really only one option: "We ought to obey God rather than men" (Acts 5:29).

7. Thou shalt not commit adultery (Exodus 20:14).

Human nature being what it is, the forcing of men and women together, especially for extended periods on Navy ships, has been the source of many broken marriages and unwanted pregnancies. Christians in the military also face incredible temptations when they are deployed overseas. In his seminal work *Blowback: The Costs and Consequences of American Empire*, Chalmers Johnson has described the network of bars, strip clubs, whorehouses, and VD clinics that surround U.S. bases overseas. The former U.S. naval base at Subic Bay in the Philippines "had no industry nearby except for the 'entertainment' business, which supported approximately 55,000 prostitutes and a total of 2,182 registered establishments offering 'rest and recreation' to American servicemen." At the annual Cobra Gold joint military exercise in Thailand: "Some three thousand prostitutes wait for sailors and marines at the South Pattaya waterfront, close to Utapao air base." The prohibition in this commandment applies equally as well to men who are not married, for "whosoever looketh on a woman to lust after her hath committed adultery with her already in his heart" (Matthew 5:28).

8. Thou shalt not steal (Exodus 20:15).

Through its system of forced revenue collection (the income tax), the state is guilty of stealing untold trillions of dollars from working Americans. Very little of that money is spent for constitutionally authorized purposes. One of the largest expenditures of the state is its bloated military budget. Training, feeding, housing, transporting, paying, and arming thousands of troops all over the planet is a very expensive undertaking. Robert Higgs has estimated the true military budget in fiscal year 2004 to be about $695 billion. Besides being the recipient of stolen money, a Christian in the military may have to steal the lives of the sons and daughters of parents he has never met. He may have to steal land in foreign countries to build bases on. He certainly steals the resources of the countries he bombs. Christians in the military should heed the words of the Apostle Paul: "Let him that stole steal no more: but rather let him labour, working with his hands the thing which is good, that he may have to give to him that needeth" (Ephesians 4:28).

9. Thou shalt not bear false witness against thy neighbour (Exodus 20:16).

The state is the greatest bearer of false witness that there has ever been. The latest round of lies concerns the war in Iraq. Continual government lies about Iraq's supposed weapons of mass destruction, aluminum tubes, chemical and biological weapons, threat to the United States, tie to al Qaeda, and link to the September 11th attacks are the rule rather than the exception. The Christian in the military is supporting a lie and living a lie when he devotes his time and energy to supporting a U.S. war machine based on deception, disinformation, falsehood, and lies.

10. Thou shalt not covet (Exodus 20:17).

Young people generally join the military for the wrong motive. Bored, indecisive, in trouble, unemployed, seeking to get away from home—these are some of the reasons why young men and women join the military. But perhaps the greatest reason young people join the military today is because of covetousness. Recruitment slogans all emphasize how much money an enlistee can earn towards his college education. Then there are enlistment bonuses, free medical care, commissary and exchange shopping privileges, the lucrative retirement program, and the future "veterans preference" to help get that government job after retirement. But aside from money, some people covet an increase in prestige ("The few, the proud, the Marines"). Others covet the power that powerful weapons bring. Some Christian young people join the military because they are patriotic, loyal Americans who have been conditioned to think that they owe the state something ("Ask not what your country can do for you, but what you can do for your country"). Their patriotism is noble, but misdirected.

The Conclusion

Should a Christian join the military? Should anyone join the military? The U.S. Military, although officially called the Department of Defense, is the state's arm of aggression. If it limited itself to controlling our borders, patrolling our coasts, and protecting our citizens instead of intervening around the globe and leaving death and destruction in its wake then perhaps it might be a noble occupation for a Christian. But as it is now, the military is no place for a Christian.

The argument that you have to become one of them to win them is fallacious. No one would think of becoming a pimp or a prostitute in order to convert them to Christianity. The fact that a Christian is compared to a soldier (2 Timothy 2:3) is no more a scriptural endorsement of Christians in the military than God being compared to "a mighty man that shouteth by reason of wine" (Psalm 78:65) is an endorsement of drunkenness.

When the nation of Israel rejected the LORD and desired a king "like all the nations" (1 Samuel 8:5), God described "the manner of the king that shall reign over them" (1 Samuel 8:9):

> And he said, This will be the manner of the king that shall reign over you: He will take your sons, and appoint them for himself, for his chariots, and to be his horsemen; and some shall run before his chariots.
> And he will appoint him captains over thousands, and captains over fifties; and will set them to ear his ground, and to reap his harvest, and to make his instruments of war, and instruments of his chariots.
> And he will take your daughters to be confectionaries, and to be cooks, and to be bakers.
> And he will take your fields, and your vineyards, and your oliveyards, even the best of them, and give them to his servants.
> And he will take the tenth of your seed, and of your vineyards, and give to his officers, and to his servants.
> And he will take your menservants, and your maidservants, and your goodliest young men, and your asses, and put them to his work.
> He will take the tenth of your sheep: and ye shall be his servants.
> And ye shall cry out in that day because of your king which ye shall have chosen you; and the LORD will not hear you in that

> day.
> Nevertheless the people refused to obey the voice of Samuel; and they said, Nay; but we will have a king over us;
> That we also may be like all the nations; and that our king may judge us, and go out before us, and fight our battles (1 Samuel 8:11–20).

Christians should remember that "the weapons of our warfare are not carnal" (2 Corinthians 10:4), and that we wield "the sword of the spirit, which is the word of God" (Ephesians 6:17).

That criticizing the military or recommending that Christians don't join it is seen as being un-American or traitorous shows just how effective the state has been with its propaganda. The United States is the greatest country on earth for a Christian to live in, but in spite of its military, not because of it.

* * * * *

CHRISTIAN KILLERS?

There is no doubt that many of the soldiers responsible for the recent death and destruction in Fallujah are Christians. And there is no doubt that many Americans who call for more death and destruction in Iraq and elsewhere are Christians as well.

Christian Killers.

The phrase should be a contradiction in terms. If someone referred to Christian adulterers, Christian drug addicts, Christian prostitutes, Christian pimps, Christian gangsta rappers, or Christian acid rockers, most Christians would get an extremely perplexed look on their face. But when Christians in the military continue killing for the state, and Christians not in the military call for more killing in the name of the state, many Christians don't even raise an eyebrow.

In some respects, this is the fault of religious "leaders." Christians in the pew are in many cases just blindly following their pastors, priests, elders, and ministers who, instead of preaching the gospel, are preaching the same pro-war politics their congregation hears on the Sean Hannity radio show or else they are not denouncing the debacle in Iraq for what it is: unscriptural, immoral, and unconstitutional. Conservative religious leaders are in some cases nothing more than cheerleaders for George Bush and the Republican Party.

But even if a Christian hears nothing but pro-war propaganda from the pulpit, it is still no excuse, for Christians have access to the truth if they will just put forth the effort to look for it. They have a Bible they can read for themselves. They have the example of some principled Christian leaders who have opposed the debacle in Iraq from the beginning. They have an abundance of alternative news sources to receive information from besides the pro-war propaganda they get from the Fox War Channel and the *War Street Journal*. It is unfortunate that some Christians won't read anything unless it was written by some other Christian they know and usually agree with. God forbid that they should read something by someone outside of their denomination, circle, or "camp"—or even worse, someone they consider to be a nominal Christian or not a Christian at all.

To justify their consent or silence, and to keep their congregations in line, Christian leaders repeat to their parishioners the mantra of "obey the powers that be," a loose paraphrase of Romans 13:1, as if that somehow means that they should blindly follow whatever the president or the government says, and even worse, that it overturns the commandment "Thou shalt not kill" (Exodus 20:13; Deuteronomy 5:17), which is repeated in the New Testament (Matthew 19:18; Romans 13:9). The way some Christians repeat the "obey the powers that be" mantra, one would think that they would slit their own mothers' throats if the state told them to do so.

Under what circumstances, then, is a Christian justified in or excused from killing another human being? Is it ever all right for a Christian to be a "killer"? As I see it, there are four circumstances under which a Christian could justifiably kill or be excused from killing: capital punishment, self-defense, accidents, and "just" wars.

A Christian who *lawfully* carried out capital punishment would not be committing murder. Although the subject of capital punishment is sometimes hotly debated, the Bible sanctions it before the law (Genesis 9:6), under the law (Numbers 35:16–21, 30–31), and under the New Testament (Acts 25:11; Romans 13:4). For more on the death penalty see Walter Block.

No one, Christian or otherwise, would fault a man for killing another man in self-defense. Only the most diehard pacifist would refuse to act in self-defense if he was attacked. This would have to include the protection of one's family as well, for if the Bible condemns a Christian for not providing for his own house (1 Timothy 5:8), how could a Christian not ensure by whatever means necessary the protection of his family's life?

Accidents happen. And sometimes someone is tragically killed. This does not make the perpetrator a murderer. The Jews were commanded in the Old Testament to establish cities of refuge (Numbers 35:6,

11–15) to which someone might flee that killed his neighbor unawares or ignorantly (Numbers 35:11; Deuteronomy 19:4–5).

Most Christians would wholeheartedly agree with these first three propositions. The problem is with war; specifically, the fact that all wars are not created equal. The vast majority of wars in the world's history have been destructive, unjust, and immoral. What constitutes a just war is a question I have answered in the essay "Christianity and War." Obviously, an aggressive, preemptive war against a country with no navy or air force, an economy in ruins after a decade of sanctions, and that was no threat to the United States is not a just war.

A Christian fighting for the U.S. Government in Iraq doesn't fall under any of these circumstances.

After Bush launched his nebulous "war on terrorism" by having Afghanistan bombed back to the Stone Age to supposedly rid the world of Osama bin Laden, al-Qaeda, and the Taliban, he announced to the world his "axis of evil" and went to war against Iraq to, depending on what day it was, rid the world of the evil Saddam Hussein or because Iraq violated U.N. resolutions or to destroy Iraq's supposed stockpiles of weapons of mass destruction or because of the perceived connection between al-Qaeda and Iraq or to liberate the Iraqi people or to bring democracy to Iraq.

Christians who support or remain silent about Bush's "war against terrorism" are terribly inconsistent. If the state were to say: "Here Christian, put on this uniform, take this gun, go to your hometown, and kill your father," Christians would recoil in horror and refuse to obey the state. But if the state were to say: "Here Christian, put on this uniform, take this gun, go to Iraq, and kill someone else's father," I am afraid that many Christians would reply, "When does my plane leave?"

Why is it that the same Christian who would not do the former has no qualms about doing the latter?

Christians who voted for George W. Bush (even if it is true that he was in fact the lesser of two evils—a dubious proposition), or make excuses for his invasion of Iraq, are supporting a man with blood on his hands (Iraqi blood and American blood). The fact that the president himself never killed anyone is irrelevant—Adolf Hitler never gassed a single Jew.

What, then, is a Christian to do? What should any citizen do? Even though it is no longer posted in the public schools, most people know the answer: "Thou shalt not kill" (Exodus 20:13). Stop killing or supporting or making excuses for those who do. Quit ignoring the fact that the United States has a global empire of troops and bases that inevitably leads to more killing. Realize that it is the interventionist foreign policy of the United States that is the main reason why the world hates us. Acknowledge that the reason more countries don't hate us is because we bribe them with foreign aid (after the money is first confiscated from U.S. taxpayers).

It is true that the Bible commands the Christian: "Submit yourselves to every ordinance of man for the Lord's sake" (1 Peter 2:13). And it is true that it also says: "Let every soul be subject unto the higher powers" (Romans 13:1). But it doesn't take a seminary education to see that this doesn't trump the commandment: "Thou shalt not kill." To know when to submit and when to be in subjection, we have some relevant biblical examples to go by—two in the Old Testament book of Daniel and two in the New Testament book of Acts.

In Daniel chapter 3, we read that King Nebuchadnezzar "made an image of gold, whose height was threescore cubits, and the breadth thereof six cubits: he set it up in the plain of Dura, in the province of Babylon" (Daniel 3:1). It was then decreed that when the music started, everyone was to "fall down and worship the golden image that Nebuchadnezzar the king hath set up" (Daniel 3:5). The penalty for noncompliance was to be "cast into the midst of a burning fiery furnace" (Daniel 3:6). It was then charged that Shadrach, Meshach, and Abed-nego would not worship the golden image (Daniel 3:12). When brought before the king and threatened with being cast into the furnace, Shadrach, Meshach, and Abednego answered the king: "If it be so, our God whom we serve is able to deliver us from the burning fiery furnace, and he will deliver us out of thine hand, O king. But if not, be it known unto thee, O king, that we will not serve thy gods, nor worship the golden image which thou hast set up" (Daniel 3:17–18). Although Nebuchadnezzar did cast them into the furnace, and God did deliver them, the point is that these three Hebrews did not submit and were not subject to King Nebuchadnezzar.

In Daniel chapter 6, we read that King Darius made a decree that "whosoever shall ask a petition of any God or man for thirty days," except from the king, "shall be cast into the den of lions" (Daniel 6:7). But "when Daniel knew that the writing was signed, he went into his house; and his windows being open in his chamber toward Jerusalem, he kneeled upon his knees three times a day, and prayed, and gave thanks before his God, as he did aforetime" (Daniel 6:10). For his disobedience, Daniel was cast into the den of lions, but God delivered him. The point, however, is that Daniel did not submit and was not subject to King Darius.

In Acts chapter 4, the Apostles Peter and John were imprisoned by the leaders of the Jews and then brought before them and commanded "not to speak at all nor teach in the name of Jesus" (Acts 4:18). But instead of submitting and being in subjection, they replied: "Whether it be right in the sight of God to hearken unto you more than unto God, judge ye. For we cannot but speak the things which we have seen and heard" (Acts 4:19-20). They even prayed for boldness to continue speaking (Acts 4:29).

In Acts chapter 5, some apostles were put in prison by order of the high priest (Acts 5:17–18). They were freed by an angel and ordered to "stand and speak in the temple to the people all the words of this life" (Acts 5:20). These apostles were then brought before the leaders of the Jews and asked: "Did not we straitly command you that ye should not teach in this name? And, behold, ye have filled Jerusalem with your doctrine, and intend to bring this man's blood upon us" (Acts 5:28). But rather than apologizing and submitting and being subject to them, the apostles replied: "We ought to obey God rather than men" (Acts 5:29).

To say, as some Christians do, that because "The LORD is a man of war" (Exodus 15:3), and God allows wars between nations, that it is honorable for Christians to enthusiastically participate in U.S. wars of aggression is about the most profound demonstration of biblical ignorance that one could manifest.

Perhaps I should close by saying that I have never advocated, nor am I now advocating, nor do I intend to advocate in the future, any armed resistance to the government or any aggression against the government in any way. The pen is mightier than the sword. "The weapons of our warfare are not carnal" (2 Corinthians 10:4). However, as Thomas Jefferson said in the Declaration of Independence:

> We hold these truths to be self-evident, that all men are created equal, that they are endowed by their Creator with certain unalienable rights, that among these are life, liberty and the pursuit of happiness. That to secure these rights, governments are instituted among men, deriving their just powers from the consent of the governed. That whenever any form of government becomes destructive to these ends, it is the right of the people to alter or to abolish it, and to institute new government, laying its foundation on such principles and organizing its powers in such form, as to them shall seem most likely to effect their safety and happiness. Prudence, indeed, will dictate that governments long established should not be changed for light and transient causes; and accordingly all experience hath shown that mankind are more disposed to suffer, while evils are sufferable, than to right themselves by abolishing the forms to which they are accustomed. But when a long train of abuses and usurpations, pursuing invariably the same object evinces a design to reduce them under absolute despotism,

> it is their right, it is their duty, to throw off such government, and to provide new guards for their future security.

And, as even Abraham Lincoln said (long before his invasion of the Southern states):

> Any people anywhere, being inclined and having the power, have the right to rise up and shake off the existing government, and form a new one that suits them better. This is a most valuable, a most sacred right—a right which we hope and believe is to liberate the world.

What is a Christian (or anyone) going to do when he faces God at the Judgment and has to give an account of his actions? Suppose he is asked a simple question: "Why did you kill those people defending their homes in Iraq?" And suppose he replied: "Because the U.S. government told me to." What do you suppose would be the Lord's reaction to such a reply? But what else could a man say? He could not say that the United States was under attack. He could not say that Iraq was a threat to the United States. He could not say that he was protecting his family. He could not say that he was protecting his property. He could not even legitimately say that he was protecting himself, since he was in fact a trespasser on someone else's property intending to do the owner great bodily harm.

"Cursed be he that taketh reward to slay an innocent person. And all the people shall say, Amen" (Deuteronomy 27:25).

* * * * *

THE HEBREW MIDWIVES VS. THE CHRISTIAN SOLDIER

> "Onward, Christian soldiers, marching as to war,
> With the cross of Jesus going on before.
> Christ, the royal Master, leads against the foe;
> Forward into battle see His banners go!"

There is no denying the fact that the Bible likens a Christian to a soldier:

> Thou therefore endure hardness, as a good soldier of Jesus Christ (2 Timothy 2:3).

> And to our beloved Apphia, and Archippus our fellowsoldier, and to the church in thy house (Philemon 2).

> Yet I supposed it necessary to send to you Epaphroditus, my brother, and companion in labor, and fellowsoldier, but your messenger, and he that ministered to my wants (Philippians 2:25).

As soldiers, Christians are admonished to "put on the whole armor of God" (Ephesians 6:11). The Apostle Paul, who himself said: "I have fought a good fight" (2 Timothy 4:7), told a young minister to "war a good warfare" (1 Timothy 1:18).

But this is not the Christian soldier I am referring to. The Christian soldier I am referring to is the Christian solider in the U.S. military. As I have pointed out again and again, the fact that the Bible likens a Christian to a soldier does not in any way justify American Christians bombing and killing foreigners for the U.S. military.

If the U.S. military was engaged in guarding our borders, patrolling our coasts, and genuinely defending the country instead of establishing and guarding a U.S. global empire, then perhaps a soldier would be a noble occupation that one could wholeheartedly perform as a Christian.

The Department of Defense is a euphemism. Its 700,000 civilian employees, its 2.3 million military personnel, and its $419.3 billion FY 2006 budget (up 41% since FY 2001) have very little to do with defense. The real defenders of the country are those who serve in the U.S. Border Patrol and the Coast Guard, neither of which is part of the Department of Defense.

The Christian soldier in the Bible fights against sin, the world, the flesh, and the devil. He wears "the breastplate of righteousness" (Ephesians 6:14) and "the helmet of salvation" (Ephesians 6:17). The weapons of the Christian are not carnal (2 Corinthians 10:4); his shield is "the shield of faith" (Ephesians 6:16) and his sword is "the word of God" (Ephesians 6:17).

But now more than ever, the Christian in the military faces the possibility of having to kill (in the name of freedom and democracy, of course) for the state in some foreign country that we are not at war with (there has been no declaration of war in the United States since World War II) and many Americans can't even locate on a map.

Although I don't agree with some of his theological tenets, the theologian Karl Barth (1886–1968) made a profound observation during his discussion of the sixth commandment:

> Killing in war . . . calls in question, not merely for individuals but

> for millions of men, the whole of morality, or better, obedience to the command of God in all its dimensions. Does not war demand that almost everything that God has forbidden be done on a broad front? To kill effectively, and in connexion therewith, must not those who wage war steal, rob, commit arson, lie, deceive, slander, and unfortunately to a large extent fornicate, not to speak of the almost inevitable repression of all the finer and weightier forms of obedience? And can they believe and pray when at the climax of this whole world of dubious action it is a brutal matter of killing? It may be true that even in war many a man may save many things, and indeed that an inner strength may become for him a more strong and genuine because a more tested possession. But it is certainly not true that people become better in war. The fact is that war is for most people a trial for which they are no match, and from the consequences of which they can never recover. Since all this is incontestable, can it and should it nevertheless be defended and ventured? (*Church Dogmatics*, vol. III, pt. 4, p. 454).

The Christian in the military can't hide behind the state as if he is not responsible for his actions, as Barth again says:

> The state wages war in the person of the individual. In war it is he, the individual man or woman, who must prepare for, further, support and in the last analysis execute the work of killing. It is part of the responsibility that in so doing he must risk his own life. But the decisive point is that he must be active in the destruction of the lives of others. The question whether this is permissible and even obligatory is not merely addressed to the state; it is also addressed specifically and in full seriousness to the individual (*Church Dogmatics*, vol. III, pt. 4, p. 464).

Blind obedience to the state is not a tenet of New Testament Christianity.

Fortunately, Christians faced with killing in the name of the state have an example in the Bible to guide them—the Hebrew midwives:

> And the king of Egypt spake to the Hebrew midwives, of which the name of the one was Shiphrah, and the name of the other Puah;
> And he said, When ye do the office of a midwife to the Hebrew women, and see them upon the stools, if it be a son, then ye shall kill him; but if it be a daughter, then she shall live.
> But the midwives feared God, and did not as the king of Egypt commanded them, but saved the men children alive.
> And the king of Egypt called for the midwives, and said unto them, Why have ye done this thing, and have saved the men

> children alive?
> And the midwives said unto Pharaoh, Because the Hebrew women are not as the Egyptian women; for they are lively, and are delivered ere the midwives come in unto them.
> Therefore God dealt well with the midwives: and the people multiplied, and waxed very mighty.
> And it came to pass, because the midwives feared God, that he made them houses (Exodus 1:15–21).

The state said "kill"; the Hebrew midwives said "no." The midwives did not repeat the "obey the powers that be" mantra that warmongering, Bush-worshipping, state-apologizing Christians incessantly repeat to justify their idolatry.

God give us more Hebrew midwives.

* * * * *

THE WARMONGER'S PSALM

The love affair that many conservative, evangelical, and fundamentalist Christians have with the military is an illicit affair. It is contrary to the tenor of the New Testament. It is an affront to the Savior. It is a cancer on Christianity.

Because the war in Iraq is going so badly, and because of the pseudo-Christianity and socialist agenda of George WMD Bush, many Christians have begun to denounce Bush and his war. Some have even criticized both from the beginning. Yet, these same Christians see no problem with Christians joining the military knowing that they might have to bomb, maim, and kill for the state in some foreign war that has nothing to do with defending the United States.

The well-known Twenty-third Psalm has encouraged and comforted the people of God for centuries. Many Christians can recite it from memory. It is a disgrace that many of these same Christians encourage young people to join the military where they will have the opportunity to do such comforting things as bomb, maim, and kill. Because these Christians think so highly of the military, perhaps they should rewrite the Twenty-third Psalm to make it more in line with their theology.

Since no one has done so yet, like the Beatitudes, I have taken the liberty to revise the Twenty-third Psalm as the Warmonger's Psalm:

> The military is my god; I shall not want.
> The army maketh me to lie down in green pastures: the navy

> leadeth me beside the still waters.
> The air force restoreth my soul: The marines leadeth me in the paths of war for the state's sake.
> Yea, though I walk through the deserts of Iraq, I will fear no evil: for the military is with me; thy bombs and thy bullets they comfort me.
> The joint chiefs preparest a table before me in the presence of mine enemies: the secretary of defense anointest my head with oil; my tank runneth over.
> Surely death and destruction shall follow the military all the days of my life: and I will dwell on the bases of the military for ever.

This love affair that many conservative, evangelical, and fundamentalist Christians have with the military is grounded in their blind obedience to the government, based on an unrestricted, absolute interpretation of Romans 13:1, from which they have derived the "obey the powers that be" mantra. Of course, this obedience to the state is very selective, which shows what hypocrites these people are. None of these Christians would kill their mother if the government told them to do so, but they would see nothing wrong with killing someone else's mother if the state gave them a uniform and a gun. But as Joseph Sobran has so eloquently said: "Government, as we know it, is the real enemy. It produces nothing except distortions of social life, through war, taxation, regulation, and the general redistribution of wealth and resources."

I am not anti-American and anti-military; I am anti-American empire and anti-militarism.

There are plenty of veterans who have written critically about the U.S. military. If I am dismissed because I have never "served," then there are Michael Gaddy, James Glaser, and the courageous Kevin Benderman. "Who hath ears to hear, let him hear" (Matthew 13:43).

* * * * *

STATE SANCTIFIED MURDER

I was recently told that the commandment, "Thou shalt not kill" (Exodus 20:13), does not apply to killing in war. I was not told that it did not apply to killing in a just war. And neither was I told that it did not apply to killing in a defensive war. There were no qualifications on the nature of the war. Confirmation that this is indeed the case soon followed: although the war in Iraq is stupid, unnecessary, and unconstitutional, Christians can in good conscience join the military, not only knowing that they might have to go to Iraq and bomb, maim, and kill for the state, but can actually do these things without any fear of negative consequences by God at the judgment because they "obeyed orders" and "obeyed the powers that be."

Christians who volunteer for the military and their pastors who encourage them are basically saying that killing someone you don't know and may never have seen, in his own territory, is not murder (and therefore is not prohibited by the sixth commandment) if the U.S. government says that he should be killed.

State sanctified murder.

As a Bible-believing Christian, I reject this ghastly statolatry, and for two reasons:

> Thou shalt have no other gods before me (Exodus 20:3).
>
> We ought to obey God rather than men (Acts 5:29).

It doesn't take a Ph.D. in theology or even a Bible-college education to see that killing someone for the state in an aggressive, unconstitutional, non-defensive, foreign war is immoral. Killing someone for the state can be murder for the simple reason that the state can sanctify nothing. It is the state itself that needs sanctification. The state is the greatest killing machine in history. The twentieth century was the bloodiest century in human history precisely because of state aggression.

It is incredible that Christians would even think of using the "obeying orders" defense. Rudolf Hoess, Hermann Goering, and Alfred Jodl used it at the Nuremberg Trials:

- I thought I was doing the right thing. I was obeying orders.
- We had orders to obey the head of state.
- I don't see how they can fail to recognize a soldier's obligation to obey orders. That's the code I've live by all my life.

It didn't work. Jodl was hanged in Nuremberg in 1946 and Hoess was hanged in Poland in 1947. Goering committed suicide by taking a cyanide pill on the day before his scheduled hanging.

Lieutenant William Calley used it after the My Lai Massacre on March 16, 1968: "I felt then and I still do that I acted as I was directed, and I carried out the orders that I was given, and I do not feel wrong in doing so."

Lawyers for some of the defendants in the Abu Ghraib Prison abuse scandal also say "their clients were only following orders when they took part in alleged abusive acts at the prison."

If no one in the military obeyed orders, then, it is argued, the military would not function very well. Good. That is exactly what we need, and for two reasons. One, if our soldiers are given orders to bomb, torture, maim, kill, and destroy people (and property) half way around the world that have never lifted a finger against the United States then those are the types of orders that we don't want soldiers in any country obeying. And second, since the military has very little to do with actually defending the country, the fact that it was not able to function very well doesn't seem like such a bad thing. Just think, if the military was dysfunctional enough then there would be no more bases built overseas, there would be no more U.S. troops stationed on foreign soil, there would be no more bombs dropped, there would be no more land mines buried, there would be no more torture disguised as interrogation, there would be no more "regime changes," there would be no more invasions, there would be no more creating terrorists because of our reckless foreign policy, there would be no wasting of billions of dollars of the taxpayers' money, and finally, the root would be destroyed—the insidious policy of interventionism.

Maybe, just maybe, the military could actually patrol our coasts and guard our borders. In that case a Christian could in good conscience "join up."

It is a sad day when conservative Christian pastors preach that Christians in the military should not commit treason by refusing to drop a nuclear bomb on a city when ordered by the state to do so instead of preaching that it would be immoral to incinerate tens of thousands of people by using such a weapon.

What are these pastors going to say when U.S. troops are directed to attack American citizens in the name of fighting terrorism? Will they still encourage their young men to join the military? Is it going to take an assault by the military on their own family before they preach the Scripture that "we ought to obey God rather than men" (Acts 5:29) instead of repeating the mantra "obey the powers that be"?

If the commandment, "Thou shalt not kill" (Exodus 20:13) never applies in wartime then what about the prohibition against adultery? What about the commandments against stealing, lying, swearing, and coveting? If killing in war is never murder then is torture permitted? It is certainly better to just torture someone for a few days than to kill him.

The great mystery here is why the subjects of war and the military turn some Christians into apologists for the state. This includes many Christians who otherwise denounce Bush and the U.S. global empire.

State sanctified murder—will it abide the judgment? I am not taking my chances.

* * * * *

KILLING HEARTILY IN THE NAME OF THE LORD

> "Whether therefore ye eat, or drink, or whatsoever ye do, do all to the glory of God" (1 Corinthians 10:31).
>
> "And whatsoever ye do in word or deed, do all in the name of the Lord Jesus, giving thanks to God and the Father by him" (Colossians 3:17).
>
> "And whatsoever ye do, do it heartily, as to the Lord, and not unto men" (Colossians 3:23).

When the Apostle Paul says "ye" in the above verses, he is writing to Christians. Depending on their particular ethical or religious beliefs, Muslims, atheists, Jews, and other non-Christians may have an option, but Christians have no choice in the matter. "Whatsoever" means "whatsoever." No part of life can be excluded from the above commands —including military service. "Whatsoever" is all-inclusive; that is, it includes eating a meal, taking a walk, reading a book—and killing for the state.

The Christian solider in today's military is not exempt; he must perform his assigned duties with these commands in mind. But can he? There exists the strong possibility that men (and sometimes women) in the military will be required to do things other than cleaning, painting, refurbishing, drilling, marching, attending schools, taking tests, playing war games, going on maneuvers, practicing on the firing range, reading pornography, and frequenting prostitutes.

Can a Christian soldier plant land mines "to the glory of God"? What about dropping bombs? What about firebombing cities like Dresden and Tokyo as the United States did to Germany and Japan during World War II? What about atomic weapons? Can a Christian soldier pilot an Enola Gay "to the glory of God" knowing that its cargo will incinerate thousands of women and children?

Can a Christian soldier obtain information from a prisoner "in the name of the Lord Jesus"? The Secretary of Defense, Donald Rumsfeld, who is currently being sued in federal court for the torture scandal in Iraq and Afghanistan, was named in a report by Amnesty International as authorizing prisoner abuses like stress positions, sensory deprivation, hooding, stripping, isolation, the use of dogs in interrogations, and, if a "military necessary," exposure to cold weather or water, inducing the perception of suffocation, and death threats. Whether one terms these things torture, cruelty, abuse, or, as one caller to the Michael Savage radio show recently said, "embarrassment," is irrelevant—can a Christian soldier be an inquisitor "in the name of the Lord Jesus, giving thanks to God and the Father by him"?

Can a Christian soldier kill "heartily, as to the Lord"? Knowing that "God shall bring every work into judgment, with every secret thing, whether it be good, or whether it be evil" (Ecclesiastes 12:14), knowing that "we must all appear before the judgment seat of Christ" (2 Corinthians 5:10), and knowing that "every one of us shall give account of himself to God" (Romans 14:12)—can a Christian kill heartily in the name of the Lord?

Some people who don't profess to be Christians have no trouble with killing. Lt. Gen. James N. Mattis, who commanded the 1st Marine Division in the 2003 invasion of Iraq, was recently criticized and admonished to choose his words "more carefully" after he publicly said that it was "a hell of a lot of fun" to shoot people. *National Review*'s Jonah Goldberg has written that "one of the most important and vital things the United States could do after 9/11 was to kill people." But Christians who claim that they can kill heartily in the name of the Lord are saying something much worse than Mattis and Goldberg.

The war in Iraq in particular causes Christian soldiers to fail the "killing heartily" test. By no stretch of the imagination can the war in Iraq be considered a "just war." This means that the Christian soldier cannot go to Iraq to the glory of God in the name of the Lord Jesus to kill heartily as to the Lord. But it goes much deeper than just the war in Iraq. Can a Christian soldier bomb, interrogate, and kill for the state in Afghanistan, Vietnam, Nicaragua, Honduras, Panama, Haiti, the Dominican Republic, the Philippines, Cuba, Nicaragua, Yugoslavia, Kuwait, or any of the other countries the United States has intervened in since 1890?

Yet, in spite of all the lies about the Iraq–al Qaeda connection and weapons of mass destruction, Christian soldiers in Iraq are still cheered on by Christian preachers in the pulpit and Christian laymen in the pew. Some of the same Christians who never hesitate to criticize the Catholic Church view the war in Iraq as a modern-day crusade against Muslims.

All Christians are certainly not calling for more bloodshed in Iraq, but why do so many continue to defend the necessity of the war, make excuses for the United States still being in Iraq, incessantly repeat the mantras of "God bless our troops" and "obey the powers that be," support the president because "he is a Christian," or remain silent about the evils of this war?

It is a shame that the *unorthodox* theologian, Karl Barth (1886–1968), had more sense than *orthodox* Christians:

> The Church can and should raise its voice against the institution of standing armies in which the officers constitute *per se* a permanent danger to peace. It can and should resist all kinds of hysterical or premature war scares. It exists in this aeon. Hence it is not commissioned to proclaim that war is absolutely avoidable. But it is certainly commissioned to oppose the satanic doctrine that war is inevitable and therefore justified, that it is unavoidable and therefore right when it occurs, so that Christians have to participate in it. (*Church Dogmatics*, vol. III, pt. 4, p. 460).

Why, then, do Christians—even Christians who don't agree with President Bush's Christianity—defend, promote, apologize for, excuse, tolerate, or ignore Bush's unjust, immoral, and unscriptural war.

First, September 11th: Many Christians continue to believe that Iraq was behind the September 11th attacks even though the president himself now says otherwise: "We have no evidence that Saddam Hussein was involved with the September 11th attacks." And if Hussein was the mastermind behind the attacks, who is to say that invading and destroying Iraq was the appropriate response? If Hussein was an evil dictator who was hated by his people (as we are continually told), then how does that justify making war on an entire country of people who were Saddam Hussein's enemies? But, of course, those of us who can read know that the September 2000 publication, *Rebuilding America's Defenses: Strategies, Forces and Resources For A New Century* [see a summary and analysis of this 90 page document here], by the Project for the New American Century (PNAC), shows that the attack on September 11th was merely the "new Pearl Harbor" that could be used to justify the United States taking military control of the Persian Gulf region regardless of whether Saddam Hussein was in power. There is also no evidence that Hussein was connected with al Qaeda, although there is plenty of evidence from mainstream sources that he was connected with our CIA until the first Persian Gulf War. There is no doubt that Saddam Hussein was a corrupt, evil ruler. But the world is full of corrupt, evil rulers. It always has been and always will be. In fact, many would say that the Bush administration is corrupt and evil.

Second, Israel: Evangelical Christians are typically supporters of

Israel. But how this translates into supporting the war in Iraq defies comprehension. The arguments justifying the war are usually some variation of either: "God has America in Iraq to protect Israel" or "God has America in Iraq to ensure or bring about the fulfillment of biblical prophecies related to Israel." To the first argument I would say: nonsense. Iraq was no threat to Israel. And if Israel thought Iraq was a threat then it would take action like it did on June 7, 1981, when it bombed a nuclear power plant near Baghdad that was believed (apparently falsely) to be designed to make nuclear weapons to attack Israel. Rather than protecting Israel, the opposite has occurred. The presence of the United States military in Iraq (and throughout the Middle East) increases Muslim hatred of both America and Israel and therefore increases terrorism. To the second argument I would say: more nonsense. God doesn't need America to do anything. He could wipe out America tomorrow and it wouldn't change a thing as far as His purposes are concerned: "Behold, the nations are as a drop of a bucket, and are counted as the small dust of the balance" (Isaiah 40:15). That includes the United States of America. Gullible Evangelical Christians are being used by neoconservatives. Neoconservatives who defend everything done by the government of Israel and smear as anti-Semitic the slightest criticism of that government (which is propped up by billions of dollars of U.S. foreign aid) are not doing so because of their love of Bible prophecy. Evangelical Christians need to realize that the government of Israel is not the people of Israel. And I say this as a premillennialist and a dispensationalist.

Third, Islam: Although Bush thinks that Muslims and Christians worship the same God, Orthodox Christians consider Islam to be false religion. Although I don't think that any pro-war Christian actually believes that it is okay for Christians to kill adherents of false religions, the thousands of Iraqi civilian deaths are regularly dismissed as collateral damage because they are Muslims. A variation of this is that it is okay to kill Muslims in Iraq because they are Muslims who are trying to kill Jews. Have Christians forgotten that "the weapons of our warfare are not carnal" (2 Corinthians 10:4), and that we wield "the sword of the spirit, which is the word of God" (Ephesians 6:17)? The references in the Bible to Christian soldiers (Philippians 2:25, 2 Timothy 2:3, Philemon 2) and Christian warfare (Ephesians 6:11, 1 Timothy 1:18, 2 Timothy 4:7) are references to spiritual warfare—The God of the Bible never called, commanded, or encouraged any Christian to kill, make apologies for the killing of, or excuse the killing of anyone that adheres to a false religion.

Fourth, "the Lord is a man of war" (Exodus 15:3): That this is a true statement there is no question, but how this phrase justifies the United

States becoming a country of war shows how warped the Christianity of some people is.

Fifth, the war on terrorism: Some Christians, who are supposed to be non-aggressive (I didn't say cowardly or pacifistic), argue that aggressive warfare is justified because we must do something to fight against terrorism; a pre-emptive war is acceptable because we must get them before they declare a jihad against us. But this ignores two things that have been eloquently pointed out before. First, as Tom Fleming has said: "We cannot defend Americans at home by killing Iraqis in the Middle East." And second, as Pat Buchanan has said: "Before we invaded Iraq, not one American had been killed by an Iraqi in a dozen years. Since we invaded, 1,500 Americans have died and the number of insurgents has multiplied from 5,000 to 20,000. By Don Rumsfeld's own metric, our intervention is creating more terrorists than we are killing. We are fighting a guerrilla army that our own invasion called into being." To which I would add: the past interventions of the United States around the world are the root of terrorist acts against us. Wouldn't it be easier, cheaper, and safer for American troops if the United States quit making terrorists instead of trying to war against them? Turning off the bath water always yields better results than bailing out the tub. Like the war on poverty, the war on drugs, the war on tobacco, and the new war on fat, the war on terrorism is a tragic joke.

Sixth, conservatism: Since most conservative Republicans support the war and most of the "evil" liberal Democrats are opposed to it, many Christians, who are by nature conservative people, are in bed with the conservative wing of the Republican Party because they view the Republican Party as honest, trustworthy, anti-Communist, limited government, anti-abortion, pro-family, pro-religion, or some other defining characteristic. Yet, conservatives have historically been known "for their blind nationalism, their readiness to engage in military adventure throughout the world, their envious Puritanism." And the Republican Party has always been the party of big government, plunder, and sellouts. Christians have been deceived.

Seventh, the military: as I have previously and recently pointed out, and intend to explore in more detail in the future, the military, which *in its present form* does little to actually defend the country, is held in great esteem by too many Christians.

Eighth, the state: As a class, Christians are law-abiding people. Yet, many of them are under the impression that Christians should support the war in Iraq because Christians should always do what the government says. But Christians who hold to that opinion are not thinking. No

Christian in the United States has been commanded to fight in Iraq or to support the war. The government would like everyone to "support the troops," but no one has been put in jail (not yet) for refusing to support the war or for denouncing the war. So actually, Christians can repeat the "obey the powers that be" mantra every minute of the day and still oppose the war. So why don't they? What many pro-war Christians are really subscribing to is the false notion that they should never oppose anything that the government says or does. Yet, even Christians who regularly ignore the dictates of the state (seatbelt laws, speed limits) lose their mind when it comes to war. They still think that the only problem with the war in Vietnam was that we didn't win. Why is something so destructive as war the great exception? Why is it alright in the minds of some Christians for someone to put on a uniform and kill someone half way around the world when it would be murder here in the United States? Christian warmongers are idolaters, as Ludwig von Mises wrote in *Omnipotent Government*:

> Modern war is not a war of royal armies. It is a war of the peoples, a total war. It is a war of states which do not leave to their subjects any private sphere; they consider the whole population a part of the armed forces. Whoever does not fight must work for the support and equipment of the army. Army and people are one and the same. The citizens passionately participate in the war. For it is their state, their God, who fights.

The great mystery to me is why any Christian would be concerned about the state in the first place, for as FEE president Richard Ebeling explains:

> There has been no greater threat to life, liberty, and property throughout the ages than government. Even the most violent and brutal private individuals have been able to inflict only a mere fraction of the harm and destruction that have been caused by the use of power by political authorities.

Can a Christian kill heartily (or defend those that do) in the name of the Lord? If it is acceptable then go ahead and bomb, destroy, interrogate, maim, and kill (or defend those that do)—as long as you do it heartily to the glory of God in the name of the Lord Jesus as you give thanks to God and the Father by him. Just be ready to give an account of yourself at the judgment. If it is not acceptable to kill heartily or defend those that do, then don't do it—regardless of the consequences. It will spare you from having blood on your hands at the judgment.

* * * * *

GOD BLESS OUR TROOPS?

> "If soldiers were to begin to think, not one of them would remain in the army." ~ Frederick the Great

You see it on bumper stickers, church signs, and the ubiquitous yellow ribbons—God Bless Our Troops. You hear it prayed from the pulpit and the pew—God Bless Our Troops. You hear it uttered by Evangelicals, Catholics, and nominal Christians—God Bless Our Troops.

Why should He?

Because they are in harm's way? Because they are brave? Because they are protecting our freedoms? Because they are fighting for democracy? Because they are fighting terrorism? Because they are righteous and the enemy is evil? Because "God is love"? Because some of my relatives are in the military? Because a soldier is an honorable profession? Because "the Lord is a man of war"?

American Christians are either naïve or just plain stupid. Don't they realize that the citizens of other countries incorporate the same slogan into their signs, prayers, and speeches? How is God supposed to bless the troops on both sides? Oh, that is simple, says the typical American Christian: God is not supposed to bless the troops on the other side. In fact, he will not bless them, not as long as they are fighting against American troops.

So the real answer to the "why should he" question is because they are American troops. American troops must be especially dear to the heart of God. They are made up for the most part of professing Christians (except for the Buddhists in the military who now have their own chaplain, Lt. j.g. Jeanette Gracie Shin), and supported by professing Christians. They defend this great "Christian" nation, they perform humanitarian acts, they help spread democracy and American values, they fight against terrorism and evil, they protect our freedoms, they keep us safe.

So what could possibly be wrong with asking God to bless our troops?

Christians will generally agree with you if you denounce some of the more outrageous abuses of the government; most will concur if you condemn the welfare state; many will go along with you if you disparage one of the presidents (excepting, of course, Abraham Lincoln, Ronald Reagan, and George WMD Bush); some will put up with you if you criticize the U.S. global empire; a few will even tolerate you if you denigrate the warfare state; but once you question the military in any way—its size, its budget, its contractors, its bureaucracy, its efficiency, its purpose, and especially its acts of death and destruction as the coercive arm of the state—many Christians will brand you as a pacifist, a liberal, a communist, an anti-war weenie, a traitor, a coward, an appeaser, or an America-hater.

How about a sane, rational, individual?

Conservative Christians that consider Bush to be a stupid biblical illiterate and a sorry excuse for a Christian, that don't support the United States engaging in foreign wars, that rail against American troops being in Iraq, and acknowledge that we are in an unconstitutional, undeclared war nevertheless win the prize for being the most insane and irrational when they maintain that there is nothing wrong with a Christian joining the military and going to Iraq to kill people as long as the government says that is where he should go. What makes this so nonsensical is that it is not a question of a Christian being drafted or in some way forced to go into the military and then being told by his pastor that he should "obey the powers that be," it is purely voluntary.

The Christian in the military is not exempt either. Christian soldiers who bomb, interrogate, and kill for the state cannot hide behind the lame excuse that they are just following orders. The Christian soldier in the U.S. military is there by choice. He was not drafted. He was not forced to enlist at the point of a gun. If he can read then he has no excuse for being ignorant of the folly of the hundred-plus years of U.S. wars and interventions abroad. If he can see then he has no excuse for joining a military that does everything but actually defend the country.

Why do conservative Christians have such a love affair with the U.S. military? Andrew Bacevich, in his fascinating new work, *The New American Militarism: How Americans Are Seduced by War* (Oxford, 2005), has a whole chapter on the subject. This is a book that all conservative Christian apologists for the military ought to read. Yet, most of them will never read it even though the author is a conservative, religious, a West Point graduate, a Vietnam veteran, and a former professional soldier. And sadly, many of them will never even know the book existed, including the very people who claim to be so well-read. How many Christian critics of my book, *Christianity and War and Other Essays Against the Warfare State*, have ever bothered to read any of the books listed at the end under "For Further Reading"? Some pastors who claim to be bookworms that are so well-read are in actuality way behind the times.

Bacevich wastes no time in his preface, but gets right down to business: "This is a book about the new American militarism—the misleading and dangerous conceptions of war, soldiers, and military institutions that have come to pervade the American consciousness and that have perverted present-day U.S. national security policy." Chapter 5, "Onward," specifically addresses why the military is held in such high esteem by too many Christians. In a word: Vietnam:

> For conservative Christians after Vietnam, the prerequisite for fulfilling America's mandate as divine agent was the immediate reconstitution of U.S. military power.
>
> In the aftermath of Vietnam, evangelicals came to see the military as an enclave of virtue, a place of refuge where the sacred remnant of patriotic Americans gathered and preserved American principles from extinction.

Because of the cultural upheaval and moral crisis that was triggered by and coincided with the war in Vietnam, "Militant evangelicals imparted religious sanction to the militarization of U.S. policy and helped imbue the resulting military activism with an aura of moral legitimacy." "Moreover," says Bacevich,

> Some evangelicals looked to the armed services to play a pivotal role in saving America from internal collapse. In a decadent and morally confused time, they came to celebrate the military itself as a bastion of the values required to stem the nation's slide toward perdition: respect for tradition, an appreciation for order and discipline, and a willingness to sacrifice self for the common good. In short, evangelicals looked to soldiers to model the personal qualities that citizens at large needed to rediscover if America were to reverse the tide of godlessness and social decay to which the 1960s had given impetus.

Evangelical Christians could not have made a bigger mistake.

Bacevich faults Billy Graham and other evangelical leaders for "courting politicians and being romanced in return." Graham supported U.S. policy in Vietnam, saying that "Americans should back their President in his decision to make a stand in Viet Nam." At the same time, Jerry Falwell, one of the most loyal supporters of Bush's war in Iraq, touted the U.S. soldier in Vietnam as "a champion for Christ."

There soon developed an unholy alliance between evangelical Christians and the military. Bacevich dates the ratification of this "entente" as May 1, 1972, when Billy Graham was given the Sylvanus

Thayer Award by the Association of Graduates of the U.S. Military Academy. This is awarded annually at West Point to a citizen "whose outstanding character, accomplishments, and stature in the civilian community draw wholesome comparison to the qualities for which West Point strives, in keeping with its motto: 'Duty, Honor, Country.'"

So, should an American Christian pray for God to bless our troops? Not when blessing our troops means allowing them to injure, maim, kill, and destroy property while they themselves come out unscathed. American Christians should pray for an end to this foolish war. They should pray for the troops to be brought home. They should pray for Congress to end funding for this war. They should pray for Bush to leave office in disgrace for being a lying, bloody warmonger. They should pray for Congress to follow the Constitution and rein in presidential war-making ability. They should pray for the healing of the thousands of U.S. soldiers who have been injured in this senseless war. They should pray for the end of military recruiters preying on young, impressionable students. They should pray for the dissolution of the alliance between the Religious Right and the Republican Party. They should pray for the resignation of Christian "leaders" who defended this immoral war. They should pray for pastors to have the guts to stand before their congregation and denounce Bush and the war, specifically, not just in generalities. They should pray for pastors to stop recommending military service to their young men. They should pray for Christians to stop blindly following the state. They should pray for Christian families to stop supplying cannon fodder to the military. Yes, there are many things Christians can pray for, but certainly not "God Bless Our Troops."

Let there be no mistake about the extent of my criticisms of Christian soldiers and the U.S. military. I don't want to see any American soldiers killed in Iraq or anywhere else. And yes, if someone is going to die, I would rather see an Iraqi soldier die than an American soldier die, but only for the same reason that I would rather see a person die in someone else's family than in my own family. I don't want to see any American soldiers die in Iraq for the same reason that I don't want to see anyone die in a car accident or because they slipped in the bathtub.

It is bad enough when Christian pastors moonlight as cheerleaders for Bush and his war, but those pastors who oppose Bush's pseudo-Christianity, his socialist domestic policies, and his interventionist foreign policies are woefully inconsistent when they encourage (or do nothing to discourage) the young men in their church to join the military and then "obey the powers that be" when it comes to bombing, interrogating, and killing for the state.

* * * * *

THINK, CHRISTIAN

> "And so to every sailor, soldier, airman, and marine who is involved in this mission, let me say you're doing God's work." ~ George H. W. Bush, December 1992

> "And to those watching tonight who are considering a military career, there is no higher calling than service in our Armed Forces." ~ George W. Bush, June 2005

Even though the war in Iraq is a miserable reality, even though the number of dead American soldiers is approaching the 1,800 mark, even though more prisoner abuse scandals are unfolding, even though the number of insurgents is growing, and even though the war on terrorism is creating more terrorists, still Christians are defending Bush, the war, and the military.

No matter how anti-Christian Bush's actions are, some Christians continue to defend him because he professes to be a Christian. It doesn't matter how often the lies that got us into the war in Iraq are exposed, many Christians still support this war—they are just upset about the manner in which it has been fought. But the worst thing is that no matter what their opinion of Bush (or any president) or his war (or any war), most Christians persist in their holy sacrosanct reverence for the military.

In fact, it appears that support for the military among Christians is actually growing. The troops are now the object of pity. Isn't it terrible that they don't get to see their families for weeks and months on end? Isn't it disgraceful that they lack the armor they need for protection. Isn't it tragic that they might suffer from psychological health issues after they return from Iraq? And, horror of horrors, they are facing injury or death every day as they fight for our freedoms.

Never mind that every soldier in Iraq joined the military voluntarily. Never mind that every member of the Guard and Reserve knew that he might be called to active duty. Never mind that no American soldier has any business in Iraq. Never mind that every soldier who harbors doubts about the wisdom of the U.S. military being in Iraq had a hundred years of American foreign interventions to learn from. Never mind that every soldier who participates in U.S. wars and interventions is ignoring the wisdom of the Founding Fathers. Never mind that the military does very little to actually defend the United States.

Just never mind. Support the troops, defend the troops, pray for the troops, write to the troops, send things to the troops, applaud the troops, make apologies for the troops, worship the troops—just never mind where they are, how they were sent there, what they are doing there, and when they are leaving.

Many Christians have practically elevated military "service" to the level of the Christian ministry. Both presidents named George Bush have done so, as the above quotations show. Christian defenders of the military ought to pay more attention to the words of those who have been in the military instead of disqualifying me from criticizing the military because I have never "served."

The following comments about life in the military are from some of my readers. Although the Bible says that "in the mouth of two or three witnesses shall every word be established" (2 Corinthians 13:1), I present here four "witnesses."

My first witness is R. M., an Army veteran from Massachusetts:

> I remember my Vietnam "era" service. Pornography (in the PX) and Prostitution (downtown Leesville) were readily available at Fort Polk. Sometimes the drugs were so pervasive in the billets that I thought we might draw anti-aircraft fire, the place got so high. Alcohol abuse? No comment necessary. Kipling said it best: "Men who live in barracks are never plaster saints."

My second witness is J. O., a Marine Corps veteran from Colorado:

> I just finished reading "God Bless our Troops?" and I agree 100%. I served from 89–93 USMC infantry along with growing up a military dependent and I know many of those Christians who are just as you described. It boggles my mind to hear their comments regarding the military especially since most admit that they have not served nor been a dependent at any point in their lives. They make the military especially the Marines and Army infantry MOS's specifically out to be, well, almost like King Arthur's Knights in shining armor or something. I am left scratching my head after hearing their descriptions and saying: "But that's not how it is." The unit I was in along with men from other units we mainly went out drinking, looking for sex, and the occasional fight at each liberty call we got. That was just fun for us.
>
> I try to tell these Christians some of my past experiences but they don't want to hear it. I even went so far as to show some uncut raw Reuters footage of Marines in action in Iraq that I found, cussing and all. They either didn't want to see it or were offended by the cussing or something. As they are walking away I say, "Why are you offended? Its just the way they talk is all. Its like

that in peacetime as well." On another occasion I'll sit there laughing at one marine's joke on a video (crude and sexual) and the Christians get really offended. Once again I say that's just the sense of humor besides its funny as hell!

I just don't understand Christians like Jerry Falwell for example. I am still left scratching my head because I have never in my life experienced the type of "military" that they describe or envision.

My third witness is L. G., an Army veteran from South Dakota:

I just read your piece from today's Lew Rockwell. Well put. I find it hard to believe that so many nominal 'Christians' think that the military is some kind of enclave of virtue. I was in the Army for 4 years ('84–'88). Let us forget, for a moment, that the purpose of the military is to kill and destroy property—as if that is not bad enough. How does the military hold up when it comes to instilling what Christians call "values"? Well, I was shocked at the pervasiveness of drunkenness and sexual immorality among my fellow soldiers. A half-hearted review of the divorce and unwed pregnancy statistics of military personnel would give one an outline for a book on military culture. Go to a VA hospital and see which department is the busiest—it will be the alcohol and drug treatment program. Military culture is rotten to the core (despite the clean-shaven, spit-shined façade), and it corrupts those who enter therein.

My fourth witness is T. S., a Navy veteran from Florida:

As a Christian, I made a foolish decision to enlist in the United States Navy. I served from 1990 to 1994. At the age of 18 I entered boot camp. I was placed in a company of 80 men. Never did I meet one professing Christian. It was either mold to the ways of the others or be a cast out. The military has very few standards when it comes to sexual perversion, filthy communication, or alcohol abuse. The military does have some strict standards when it comes to drug abuse, but that did not stop two Marines and I from obtaining a large sum of hashish in Spain. Many other Marines and Sailors purchased drugs that were brought and used upon the ship. Pornography and sexual perversion is out of control within the United States Military. Many a young man was first introduced to pornography within the military. God only knows the number of innocent minds that have been perverted. I can remember walking into a break room full of sailors on my ship and

> there on the television I saw hard-core pornography. I still suffer from some of the things these eyes saw in the Navy. I also recall the military sponsoring strippers at the club on base.
>
> I also became a drinker of alcohol within the military. It was easy to obtain alcohol on the Little Creek Amphibious Base, either from the club or from beer vending machines. The sale and drinking of alcohol is not discouraged but encouraged by many within the ranks of the United States Military. I can remember coming back from the Persian Gulf in 1991. Our ship had not seen a port of call in months. Our only stop before crossing back over the Atlantic was in Rota, Spain. Now, what do you think was on the mind of every sailor that day? I can tell you for I was there. Every sailor was either drunk, stoned, or seeking sex through one of the numerous prostitutes available at a very cheap price.

My conclusion is this: If Christians desire their son or daughter to live by Christian values, they should not allow them to join the United States Military. Many Christians will not allow their children to attend public schools, but then allow them to join an evil, wicked, and murderous United States Military.

Think, Christian. The presence or absence of the Christian values of these witnesses is irrelevant. This is eyewitness testimony. So aside from all that is wrong with U.S. foreign policy, wars, and interventions, why would a Christian even think of joining the military or reenlisting if he had the misfortune of already being in it?

Because of September 11th? Not even Bush uses that excuse anymore. Because of money for college? "The love of money is the root of all evil" (1 Timothy 6:10). Because of family tradition? Some families have a tradition of gluttony and drunkenness. Because of the war on terrorism? Our actions are making more terrorists. Because the military is fighting for our freedoms? Our freedoms are fast disappearing. Because you have to go where they are to "win them to Christ"? "It is never right to do wrong in order to get a chance to do right" (Bob Jones Sr., Chapel Sayings). Because of foreign tyrants? John Quincy Adams said that America "goes not abroad seeking monsters to destroy." Because the military is defending the country? The military is defending a lot of countries, but certainly not the United States. Because there is no higher calling than military service? Don't be deceived.

What, then, is a Christian, or anyone else for that matter, to do? How about mowing lawns, trimming trees, or making hamburgers? A needy service is performed, it doesn't cost the taxpayers a dime, and no one gets killed. Think, Christian.

* * * * *

JUST SAY NO

The recent court-martial of Sgt. Kevin Benderman that resulted in a prison sentence, a reduction in rank, and a dishonorable discharge—all because he refused to continue killing for the state—is an example to all Christians in the military. It doesn't matter whether Sgt. Benderman is Protestant or Catholic, evangelical or liturgical, conservative or liberal, dedicated or backslidden, or even whether he is a Christian at all. He is a rebuke to all Christians in the military.

Christians in the military who have no trouble killing for the state in Iraq because they think they are in a modern-day crusade against Islam are sadly mistaken. The Lord never sanctioned any crusade of Christians against any religion. Likewise, Christians in the military who have no trouble killing for the state in Iraq because they think they are doing their patriotic duty in a just cause are sorely deceived. Patriotism has nothing to do with killing foreigners on command in what is one of the most unjust wars in history. It is generally these types of Christians who wrongly consider Sgt. Benderman to be a coward and a traitor. They are both without hope since they would probably make apologies for any of the state's foreign interventions and fight for the state in any war, especially if it was started by a Republican president and approved by a Republican Congress.

But there is another group of Christians in the military that there is hope for. This group recognizes that the Iraq war is not a good idea. Some of them would go further and say that it is unconstitutional. Others would even say that the war is unjust. But still, they choose to fight. Why? There are, of course, a variety of reasons for this behavior.

To some, it is their job. After all, they are in the military, and isn't the military supposed to kill people? They would never kill anyone in civilian life unless it was in self-defense, but since they "joined up," they feel obligated to continue participating in the state's wars.

To some, the reason is fear. Fear of being court-martialed or going to prison like Sgt. Benderman. Fear of being called a coward or a traitor. Fear of a dishonorable discharge. Fear of being ridiculed back home. Fear of reprisals from others in the military. Fear of being labeled as un-American or anti-American. Fear of being called an anti-war weenie by some washed-up, has-been, pompous ass.

To some, it is because they have a superstitious reverence for the military. Even though they have doubts about the wisdom of the military being in Iraq, even though the military does very little to actually defend the country, and even though it has committed grave injustices, still they fight on because they think the military "defends our freedoms" or "keeps us free."

To some, it is because they have heard the "obey the powers that be" mantra from their pastor so many times that they think it is a sin *not* to kill people if ordered to do so by the state.

To some, the attitude is: it will all be over soon. They know that they will shortly be out of the military or that their tour in Iraq will soon come to an end. They are just enduring to the end and hoping that they will not be killed or have to kill. But if they have to kill, they will do so because of one of the above reasons.

In order for any of these excuses to soothe the conscience of the Christian soldier, he must subscribe to what I have expressed elsewhere as state-sanctified murder. This is the ghastly belief that the commandment "Thou shalt not kill" (Exodus 20:13) does not apply to killing anyone in any war as long as the U.S. government says that he should be killed. With his conscience thus assuaged, the Christian soldier thinks that he will not have to answer to God at the judgment as to why he killed some nameless raghead who did not want him occupying his country.

The Christian soldier is in effect modifying the Sixth Commandment. There is a parallel to this editing of the commandments in George Orwell's *Animal Farm*.

After the animals rebelled against Mr. Jones and changed the name of his Manor Farm to Animal Farm, they reduced the principles of Animalism to seven commandments:

1. Whatever goes upon two legs is an enemy.
2. What ever goes upon four legs, or has wings, is a friend.
3. No animal shall wear clothes.
4. No animal shall sleep in a bed.
5. No animal shall drink alcohol.
6. No animal shall kill any other animal.
7. All animals are equal.

These were inscribed on the wall of the barn "in great white letters that could be read thirty yards away." After the commandments were read aloud, Orwell says that "all the animals nodded in complete agreement, and the cleverer ones at once began to learn the Commandments by heart."

After the pigs moved into Mr. Jones' farmhouse and began sleeping in the beds, Clover ("a stout motherly mare") "thought she remembered a definite ruling against beds." Unable to read the Seven Commandments inscribed on the barn, she summoned Muriel ("the white goat"), who claimed she was able to read them: "'No animal shall sleep in a bed *with sheets*,' she announced finally." Orwell then says: "Curiously enough, Clover had not remembered that the Fourth Commandment mentioned sheets; but as it was there on the wall, it must have done so."

Later, after the pigs had found some whiskey in the farmhouse cellar and began to drink alcohol, "there occurred a strange incident which hardly anyone was able to understand." Squealer ("a small fat pig") was found one night sprawled beside a broken ladder underneath the place on the barn where the Seven Commandments were written. Nearby were a paint brush and an overturned container of white paint. Squealer was helped back to the farmhouse but "none of the animals could form any idea as to what this meant, except old Benjamin" ("the donkey"), until a few days later when Muriel read the Seven Commandments written on the barn. As Orwell says: "They had thought the Fifth Commandment was 'No animal shall drink alcohol,' but there were two words that they had forgotten. Actually the Commandment read: 'No animal shall drink alcohol *to excess*.'"

In between these two events, there was another incident when one of the Seven Commandments was edited—the one commandment that is the same in the Judeo-Christian Ten Commandments—an incident that relates specifically to the Christian soldier killing for the state. Four pigs, three hens, a goose, and three sheep were executed on order of Napoleon ("a large, rather fierce-looking Berkshire boar"). But, as Orwell says:

> A few days later, when the terror caused by the executions had died down, some of the animals remembered—or thought they remembered—that the Sixth Commandment decreed "No animal shall kill another animal." And though no one cared to mention it in the hearing of the pigs or the dogs, it was felt that the killings which had taken place did not square with this. Clover asked Benjamin to read her the Sixth Commandment, and when Benjamin, as usual, said that he refused to meddle in such matters, she fetched Muriel. Muriel read the Commandment for her. It ran: "No animal shall kill any other animal *without cause*." Somehow or other, the last two words had slipped out of the animals' memory. But they saw now that the Commandment had not been violated;

for clearly there was good reason for killing the traitors who had leagued themselves with Snowball.

Christian soldiers who kill for the state are, consciously or unconsciously, likewise editing the sixth commandment:

- Thou shalt not kill *unless it is a Muslim infidel.*
- Thou shalt not kill *unless you are invading another country.*
- Thou shalt not kill *unless you are occupying another country.*
- Thou shalt not kill *unless you are in the military.*
- Thou shalt not kill *unless the state says it is okay to kill.*
- Thou shalt not kill *unless a Republican president starts a war.*
- Thou shalt not kill *unless it is a conservative-supported war.*
- Thou shalt not kill *unless you are protecting Halliburton employees.*

In addition to the Hebrew midwives (Exodus 1:15–21), Christians have another example in the Bible to guide them in this matter of killing for the state: Saul's footmen.

After David killed Goliath, it was said of him: "Saul hath slain his thousands, and David his ten thousands" (1 Samuel 18:7). Naturally, this did not please King Saul. In fact, "Saul was very wroth, and the saying displeased him; and he said, They have ascribed unto David ten thousands, and to me they have ascribed but thousands: and what can he have more but the kingdom? And Saul eyed David from that day and forward" (1 Samuel 18:8–9). Three times in 1 Samuel 18 it is said that Saul feared David (1 Samuel 18:12, 15, 29) "because the LORD was with him, and was departed from Saul" (1 Samuel 18:12). Left unchecked, envy can turn into hatred, and hatred into harm. Thus, it is said of Saul: "And Saul spake to Jonathan his son, and to all his servants, that they should kill David" (1 Samuel 19:1). After Saul himself tried to kill David, he fled, eventually ending up in Nob, the home of Ahimelech the priest (1 Samuel 21:1). Unfortunately, one of Saul's servants, Doeg the Edomite, was there (1 Samuel 21:7). When Saul later questioned his servants about David, Doeg spoke up and revealed that David had not only gone to Ahimelech in Nob, but that Ahimelech had helped David, even giving him the sword of the dead Goliath (1 Samuel 22:9–10). Ahimelech was summoned to King Saul, who said to him: "Why have ye conspired against me, thou and the son of Jesse, in that thou hast given him bread, and a sword, and hast enquired of God for him, that he should rise against me, to lie in wait, as at this day?" (1 Samuel 22:13). Saul would not listen to Ahimelech's pleadings and said: "Thou shalt surely die, Ahimelech, thou, and all thy father's house" (1 Samuel 22:16).

But then something went wrong. Saul, as the head of state, gave the execution order—but it was refused:

> And the king said unto the footmen that stood about him, Turn, and slay the priests of the LORD; because their hand also is with David, and because they knew when he fled, and did not shew it to me. But the servants of the king would not put forth their hand to fall upon the priests of the LORD (1 Samuel 22:17).

It is true that Ahimelech and the priests died anyway at the hand of Doeg the Edomite (1 Samuel 22:18–19), but Saul's footmen, because they refused to kill for the state, are an example for, and a rebuke to, all Christians in the military.

I appeal now to all Christians in the military: Just say "no" when it comes to killing for the state. To all parents: Just say "no" when it comes to encouraging your children to join the military. To all pastors: Just say "no" to glorifying the military in your sermon illustrations. To all church youth directors: Just say "no" when your young people seek guidance regarding joining the military. To all school counselors: Just say "no" when it comes to the military option. To all young people: Just say "no" to the recruiters who entice you with cash bonuses. To all veterans: Just say "no" when it comes to recommending a career in the military. And to all voters: Just say "no" to politicians who start wars.

Just say "no"!

* * * * *

WHAT'S A CHRISTIAN SOLDIER TO DO?

As the war in Iraq drags on into almost its fourth year with no end in sight, still American soldiers continue to fight and bleed, not for the American people, but for the president, the U.S. government, and the military-industrial complex. No one is fighting and bleeding and dying to "defend our freedoms" or anyone else's freedoms. What makes this even more disturbing is that the majority of American soldiers would claim to be Christians or at least identify with Christianity.

American Christian soldiers should know better. Unless they have had their head in the sand for the past three years, and have watched nothing but Fox News, listened to no one besides Sean Hannity, and read nothing but the *Weekly Standard*, they can't help but see anywhere they look that this war is not just unconstitutional, unnecessary, immoral, unjust, and senseless, but is also unscriptural.

It is unconstitutional because only Congress has the authority to declare war. It is unnecessary because Iraq was no threat to the United States. It is immoral because it was based on lies. It is unjust because it is not defensive. It is senseless because over 2,200 Americans have died in vain. But this war is also unscriptural because it is in opposition to the practice of the early church, it is against Christian "just war" principles, it perverts the Old Testament, and it is contrary to the whole spirit of the New Testament. Participants in the war violate the express teaching of the sixth commandment: "Thou shalt not kill." Supporters of the war violate the first commandment: "Thou shalt have no other gods before me."

So what's a Christian soldier to do?

The great Reformer Martin Luther (1483–1546), who certainly could never be accused of being a pacifist, had some words of wisdom for the Christian soldier of his day that are just as applicable to the American Christian soldier today:

> "Suppose my lord were wrong in going to war." I reply: If you know for sure that he is wrong, then you should fear God rather than men, Acts 4 [5:29], and you should neither fight nor serve, for you cannot have a good conscience before God. "Oh, no," you say, "my lord would force me to do it; he would take away my fief and would not give me my money, pay, and wages. Besides, I would be despised and put to shame as a coward, even worse, as a man who did not keep his word and deserted his lord in need." I answer: You must take that risk and, with God's help, let whatever happens, happen. He can restore it to you a hundredfold, as he promises in the gospel, "Whoever leaves house, farm, wife, and property, will receive a hundredfold," etc. [Matt. 19:29]. (*War and Christian Ethics*, p. 159)

To this could be added the words of the Russian novelist Leo Tolstoy (1828–1910):

> The opinion expressed in your estimable letter, that the easiest and surest way to universal disarmament is by individuals refusing to take part in military service, is most just. I am even of opinion that this is the only way to escape from the terrible and ever increasing miseries of militarism.
>
> Armies will first diminish, and then disappear, only when public opinion brands with contempt those who, whether from fear, or for

> advantage, sell their liberty and enter the ranks of those murderers, called soldiers; and when the men now ignored and even blamed—who, in despite of all the persecution and suffering they have borne—have refused to yield the control of their actions into the hands of others, and become the tools of murder—are recognized by public opinion, to be the foremost champions and benefactors of mankind. Only then will armies first diminish and then quite disappear, and a new era in the life of mankind will commence.

Every American soldier that names the name of Christ should immediately declare himself a conscientious objector and get out of the military as soon as possible. Every Christian young person who ever thought about joining the military should banish the thought forever. The unholy alliance between evangelical Christians and the military must be broken. These things should be done, not because the war did not go as planned, but because it was a grave injustice from the very beginning.

Why, then, will many Christian soldiers continue to fight for the state no matter how unjust the war or military action? I have previously given a number of reasons, but I think the main reason is fear: fear of being court-martialed, fear of being associated with certain opponents of the war, fear of going to prison, fear of being called a coward, fear of life after the military, fear of being branded as anti-American, fear of veterans in the family, fear of being termed a quitter, fear of retaliation by others in the military, fear of being labeled as "anti-war," fear of public opinion, fear of being ostracized, fear of ridicule—everyone of them a fear of man.

"The fear of man bringeth a snare: but whoso putteth his trust in the LORD shall be safe" (Proverbs 29:25).

* * * * *

THE HYPOCRISY OF THE AMERICAN CHRISTIAN SOLDIER

Can a Christian be a soldier? Stephen Mansfield thinks he can, and tells us so in his new book, *The Faith of the American Soldier* (Tarcher/Penguin, 2005). But are the two "callings" compatible? Does the combination not rather lead to a cognitive dissonance from which there is no escape?

Mansfield is a former pastor whose "love of things military has moved him to earn a master's degree in history and public policy and a doctorate in history and literature." This love of the military runs in his family, for we are also told in "About the Author" that "members of his family have been fighting for their country since the American Revolution."

To write this book, dozens of "men and women who have heroically served in their country's wars" were interviewed. Mansfield and "his research team" visited the battlefields of Iraq, "the plain" of West Point, the 101st Airborne at Fort Campbell, Kentucky, and the headquarters of USCENTCOM at MacDill Air Force Base in Tampa, Florida.

The author has also written books about two war criminals: Britain's Winston Churchill (*Never Give In: The Extraordinary Character of Winston Churchill* [Cumberland House Publishing, 2002]) and our own George WMD Bush *(The Faith of George W. Bush* [Tarcher/Penguin, 2003]).

Mansfield introduces his book with the account of Lance Corporal James Gault cutting an Iraqi insurgent in half "almost exactly at the waist" with his .50 caliber machine gun. Gault watched in shock as "the man's torso tilted forward, left his lower half, and fell to the street." But then we are presented with a paradox: "James Gault is a Christian and a warrior." Mansfield says of Gault: "He has killed, and he will kill again. In fact, he believes 'the bad guys *have* to die.' To kill in a righteous cause is what Gault has come to Iraq to do, and he does not shrink from the charge." But then we read that "Gault is also a Christian, a man who believes that Jesus is God, that He rose from the dead, and that the Bible is the truth of God for all men."

Gault is a Christian killer.

The fact that he attended church before he deployed to Iraq and heard his pastor exhort the congregation to pray "for our young hero while he is overseas" doesn't change anything. And neither is anything different because Gault's pastor, his family, and the leaders of his church laid their hands on his shoulders and prayed that God would make his hands skillful to battle the Lord's enemies.

Gault is still a Christian killer.

Ripping a man in half perplexes our man Gault: "He knows he is a follower of Jesus, and he knows that he is called to be a Marine, but the violence he unleashed leaves him needing assurance that he has killed in a righteous cause, that his country is doing the will of God in Iraq." Gault is tormented. He wants his chaplain to tell him that "our enemies are the enemies of God." He wants someone to explain to him "how this is a war between good and evil." Gault needs to know that he is "a servant of Jesus." He needs to be sure that he is "a soldier of Christ."

Gault is not alone. There are thousands of Christians who have faced the same dilemma. Christians in the military who can bomb, maim, and kill for the state without thinking twice about it have a seriously defective form of Christianity. Christian soldiers who reason that it is not for them to judge whether a war is just or unjust are deceiving themselves. "Soldiers must know, in clear terms," says Mansfield, "not only why they fight but also if their cause is just."

Unfortunately, however, Mansfield never addresses these questions. He aims to explore and celebrate "the religious nature of America's military heritage" while cautioning us that "this is not to be confused, though, with a celebration of war. Only the immoral or the deformed of soul can exalt war itself, with all of the grinding horrors that it brings." But can "America's military heritage" and "a celebration of war" be separated? Not when the true nature of this heritage is one of invasion, imperialism, oppression, interventionism, hegemony, belligerency, bellicosity, jingoism, death, and destruction—things never associated by Mansfield with "America's military heritage."

The book fails to deliver on another point as well. According to the dust jacket: "*New York Times*-bestselling author Stephen Mansfield surveys America's wars from a religious and theological perspective in order to understand the theological framing and spiritual rationale for each, where they came from, and what effect they had on behavior on the battlefield." Since the book has no index, I have carefully gone through it searching for references to the American wars that the author is supposed to survey. The results are disappointing. Aside from the current war in Iraq and Afghanistan, there are references to fourteen conflicts (the only declared wars in U.S. history were the War of 1812, the Mexican War, the Spanish-American war, WWI, & WWII). Most of these references have nothing to do with surveying the war "from a religious and theological perspective."

Mentioned one time each, but just in passing, is the Pequot War of 1637, the War of 1812, the Mexican War, the Spanish-American War, the war "to win the American West," and the conflict in Kosovo.

The Korean War is mentioned twice. The first time is just a passing reference. The second occasion consists of one paragraph in which Mansfield says that the war had a religious dimension because "the Communist forces of North Korea took pride in publicly persecuting missionaries and desecrating churches" and "subjected captured American chaplains to horrendous torture."

The Civil War also comes up twice. The first time is likewise just a passing reference. Four and a half pages are then devoted to accounts of chaplains during the conflict.

The Gulf War is cited as the place where "the first hint on the battlefield that a new brand of warrior was seeking a vital faith in the field." It is also mentioned one more time in the context of anti-Semitism.

There are three references to the American Revolutionary War if we count the mention of someone fighting "under George Washington." The second mention is of "minutemen in the American Revolution." There are three pages about pastors and chaplains during the American Revolution—hardly a survey of one of America's wars "from a religious and theological perspective."

The conflict in Mogadishu, Somalia, merits four references; however, none of them consist of more than a bare mention of the place.

The Vietnam War comes up on five occasions. It is mentioned in passing three times. Russell's father "had been a ranger in Vietnam." Vietnam vets were spit on. POWs in Vietnam had courage. The only thing of substance is a discussion of chaplains in the Vietnam War that takes up two pages.

Mansfield brings up World War I six times. Twice we are told that a certain man's father had been a chaplain in World War I. Two other times we are told something else about chaplains. World War I is just causally mentioned the other two times. That's it.

World War II is mentioned seven times. The "ghost of a soldier" from World War II would be amazed at the technology used in modern warfare. A soldier's uncles fought in World War II. Others fought in World War II. The essential role of the chaplain was recognized "by the advent of World War II." During the war, "The chaplains' corps ballooned from a few hundred to nearly ten thousand." This leaves one reference of substance to World War II. Mansfield devotes six pages to the account of the American transport ship *Dorchester* and its four military chaplains.

Mansfield's book is a fraud. It no more "surveys America's wars from a religious and theological perspective" than the Secretary of Defense pays attention to the number of dead Iraqis.

So what is *The Faith of the American Soldier* about? What is the point the author is trying to get across? Mansfield says that the book is "the product of a search for the meaning of the American warrior code and the faith that gave it birth." Because he considers a nation's "warrior code" to be "an extension of its soul, the embodiment of its highest ideals," the "guiding dream" of the book is "to understand that code and to honor it as the distilled greatness of a people." This is gobbledygook. Each of the book's five chapters contains vignettes of soldiers in Iraq, with a religious element, interspersed with some historical references and psychobabble. The message of the book can be reduced to this: Some American soldiers have been religious, many are religious right now, and others need to be more religious.

The first chapter introduces us to the Millennials—the generation who came of age around the dawn of the new century. The Millennial is "better informed about his world than any generation that has been called upon to fight its nation's wars." He is a "new brand of warrior." Millennials serving in the military in Iraq "take hold of religion as much as any army had in the nation's history." Their "unique approach to religion" is "changing American at war." Their religion is characterized by an "unchurched faith" that rejects "the structures, doctrines, and standards of traditional faith in pursuit of spiritual experience, loving community, and stories that have power to define their lives." Mansfield explains that Millennials are

> eager for spirituality but suspicious of institutions, hungry for truth but bored by systematics, inspired by stories but repelled by standards, desperate for religious experience but put off by religious style, hoping for spiritual family but disgusted by empty conformity, longing for God but wondering if he is there.

The spirituality of the Millennials is "perfectly suited for adaptation to the battlefield." It is utilitarian, pragmatic, eclectic, and experimental.

The second chapter begins with the story of the Shield of Strength carried by many American soldiers—a "God and Country" trinket with a picture of the American flag and the words "One Nation Under God" on one side and the modified words of a Scripture verse on the other. Mansfield calls it "almost the classic Millennial military icon." He claims that it is "the emblem most often carried by members of the military in Afghanistan and Iraq." The amazing diversity of the faith of Christian soldiers is the next theme Mansfield picks up. But they have a "new brand of faith," one that is "more effective in meeting the needs of soldiers than traditional chapel services." This "new brand of faith" results in some strange "Christian" activities like a tank crew quoting aloud the Scripture they have memorized. I wonder what Scriptures they would quote while they were cutting a man in half like the Lance Corporal at the beginning of the book? Isn't it wonderful that the Christian American soldier today can listen to a sermon from his home church on his iPod or watch his favorite preacher on a mini-DVD player? A "simplistic, one-answer-fits-all kind of spirituality" is out and a "working, experience-oriented, 'real' religion" is in. But still the soldiers seek out the chaplains: "What do I want? Sir, I wanna' know that Jesus is in my Humvee." This assurance is provided by various rituals: praying, saying a blessing, reciting a confession, listening to worship music, making the sign of the cross over a Humvee, and, of course, carrying the Shield of Strength. But after all this, Mansfield ends on a sad note: The diverse faith of the Millennials "cannot be relied upon to guide the conduct of warriors in any meaningful way." The Millennials "informal faith" leads to a "variety of warrior codes" that result in "an unevenness if not an inconsistency to the conduct of warriors in the field."

The third chapter is about those "men of cloth and steel"—military chaplains. Mansfield considers them "among the noblest figures in the field." He compares them to the priests of Israel leading the Jews into battle, but also to priests in Roman armies sacrificing animals and reading their entrails. Military chaplains are said to be the successors of the colonial fighting parsons—pastors who led militias into battle. The reader is led to believe that the chaplains of today are doing a great service to the country like those who served under George Washington in the Revolutionary War. Mansfield writes as if all the wars that America has been involved in are created equal: "Chaplains continued to earn respect during the wars to win the American West and the Spanish-American War." It doesn't matter how unjust the cause, chaplains serve the Lord by ministering to the troops. Thus, Mansfield can laud "one bold chaplain" who constantly urged Marines "courage in their task by quoting scriptures and praying aloud" as he accompanied them on their mission—going door to door looking for insurgents in Fallujah. Chaplains who do have doubts about the justness of a particular war certainly aren't free to express their opinion, as Mansfield's account of a private questioning his chaplain shows:

I went to a chaplain and asked if he thought God was on our side and if we were really fighting evil by fighting the insurgents. You could see he wasn't sure, or at least that he didn't want to say. He hesitated. Then he said: "Well, the president says we are fighting for democracy and the values of freedom. So we must be doing a good thing." I thought to myself, Man, that's the answer I expected from my government professor back home, not from a spokesman for God.

The fourth chapter returns to the idea of a "warrior code." Mansfield explains:

> The warrior code takes a soldier and makes him a knight. It connects the natural life of a fighter to a supernatural understanding of the warrior calling. His duties are transformed into holy sacrifices; his sense of self is reformed into an image of the servant in pursuit of valor. He becomes part of a fellowship, a noble tradition that flows through him and carries him beyond the mediocre and the vain.

But is this something that Christians should involve themselves in? Mansfield maintains that "the foundation of any religiously influenced warrior code is a theology of war." He then brings up "the moral basis for war," and insists that Augustine's "Just War Theory" provides "the basis for any warrior code." Mansfield claims that "there was some consideration of the Just War theory" before the Bush administration invaded Iraq in March of 2003. He specifically refers to a February 10, 2003, lecture by Michael Novak on Christian Just War doctrine with specific reference to Iraq. The speech was a "brilliant exposition of the Augustinian theory of war as it has been applied through the ages, the contemporary applicability of those teachings, and the moral moorings of the Bush Doctrine." Moral moorings? Bush's war is one of the most immoral interventions in U.S. history. It is against every Christian Just War principle that has ever been thought of. Any "warrior code" that can't discern the unjust nature of this war is not a code that any Christian should follow.

The fifth chapter opens with "the basic facts of the Abu Ghraib prison scandal as they are presented in the Schlesinger Panel's report and as they have surfaced in interviews with guards at the scene." But Mansfield considers "a refusal to learn the lessons of Abu Ghraib and thus allow such scandals to reoccur" as "perhaps a greater misfortune." Men and women under "dire stress" may "descend into barbarism" if they don't have moral leadership, core values held before them, and a noble sense of mission. They need a "faith-based warrior code." Mansfield never even considers that perhaps we just shouldn't put men and women in situations like guarding the Abu Ghraib prison to begin with. But even worse, he is not averse to war at all. A "heartfelt warrior code" provides the restraint "to immoral behavior under the stress of war." How about the immoral nature of the Bush doctrine and war itself? There is nothing wrong with this war that Mansfield can't fix with his "faith-based warrior code." We are introduced to a confused, young Christian soldier named Bob Daniels who wonders

> if true Christians are on the wrong side of this thing. Maybe the terrorists are doing god's will. Maybe God wants to destroy the America that secular humanism built and restore her to be that city on a hill she is supposed to be. I came over here all fired up thinking we were fighting against evil. Now I'm wondering if we are evil.

And what is Mansfield's solution? Does he tell this young soldier that he has been deceived by the president and the U.S. government? Does he tell this young soldier about the history of U.S. wars and interventions that have helped create terrorists and enemies of the United States? No, "what Bob Daniels needs is what a faith-based warrior code would give him: an assessment of Islam that would frame his fight against terror."

It is in the Epilogue that we see in full bloom the real hypocrisy of the American Christian soldier. Mansfield describes how a band of Marines, fully dressed for battle, hold their rifles aloft "as though to say, 'Here, O Lord, receive this weapon into Your service.'" Then they recite the doxology, quote a verse of scripture together, pause in silence for each man to confess his sins, quote another verse of scripture, sing a hymn, have a responsive reading (during which time some soldiers kiss their Shield of Strength trinket), say "Amen"—and then go out and fight and kill for the U.S. government.

In the end, Mansfield is no different than the state-worshipping, Bush-idolizing, Republican Party-adoring, pious Christian warmongers who do all but call for my death as a traitor because I dare to criticize their leader and his war.

"The only defensible war is a war of defense," said G.K. Chesterton. Perhaps Mansfield ought to read him before he writes another book justifying Christian participation in U.S. wars.

* * * * *

SHOULD CHRISTIANS SUPPORT SLAVERY?

Should Christians support the government-enforced, involuntary slavery of human beings? Slavery was, of course, a great evil, and although there are many slavery myths that still linger, there is no denying that some Christians attempted to justify that "peculiar institution." A greater evil, however, is that some Christians would support—right now, in the twenty-first century—not only government-enforced slavery, but government-mandated slavery.

The government-mandated slavery I am referring to is military conscription.

During the so-called Civil War, both sides drafted conscripts, although draftees were able to hire substitutes. The U.S. government drafted soldiers during both world wars. There was also military conscription in force between 1948 and 1973 when the U.S. government faced off against the Soviet Union during the Cold War and fought the undeclared wars in Korea and Vietnam.

Now we have Congressman Charles Rangel (D–NY), the incoming

chairman of the House Ways and Means Committee, once again proposing to reinstate the military draft. He actually introduced legislation to reinstate the draft back before Bush invaded Iraq, but his bill (H.R. 163) was defeated in the House in October of 2004 by a vote of 402–2. In 2005 Rangel introduced H.R. 2723, the "Universal National Service Act of 2005." Earlier this year, he introduced H.R. 4752, the "Universal National Service Act of 2006." Each of these proposed pieces of legislation would "provide for the common defense by requiring all persons in the United States, including women, between the ages of 18 and 42 to perform a period of military service or a period of civilian service in furtherance of the national defense and homeland security."

Now wait a minute, Mr. Vance. I thought you were talking about slavery? The draft isn't slavery. The draft is all about defending and protecting the country. The draft is something all patriotic Americans should support. Didn't the evil liberal Bill Clinton dodge the draft?

But I am talking about slavery. The draft is a form of slavery or involuntary servitude. Although this practice was supposedly outlawed by the Thirteenth Amendment to the Constitution, the Supreme Court ruled in *Arver v. United States* (1918) that

> as we are unable to conceive upon what theory the exaction by government from the citizen of the performance of his supreme and noble duty of contributing to the defense of the rights and honor of the nation as the result of a war declared by the great representative body of the people can be said to be the imposition of involuntary servitude in violation of the prohibitions of the Thirteenth Amendment, we are constrained to the conclusion that the contention to that effect is refuted by its mere statement.

What else are you going to call the draft if it is not slavery or involuntary servitude? A young person is told that he must join the military. He is then told when to go to bed and when to get up. He is told when to eat and when to sleep. He is told to move here or move there. He is told what he is allowed to do and what he is not allowed to do. And worst of all, he is told that a certain group of people is the "enemy" and therefore must be bombed into submission or killed.

The draft is not at all about defending and protecting the country. It is about getting cannon fodder to fight in an immoral and unnecessary overseas war. How many young men who didn't know where Vietnam was located would think of going there to kill or be killed unless they were forced to do so? A real invasion of American soil would necessitate, not the conscription of young men to fight, but the need for Americans of all ages to wait in line in order to get a chance to shoot the invaders. Every able-bodied man (and even some women) would fight without having to be coerced or threatened.

The draft is something that all patriotic Americans should abhor because, as Congressman Ron Paul (R–TX) has said: "A government that is willing to enslave some of its people can never be trusted to protect the liberties of its own citizens."

Should we fault Clinton for dodging the draft? It has been correctly pointed out that "he craftily manipulated the system, but he had the proper and legal right to do everything he did. He was never AWOL, never guilty of failing to report, was never a criminal under public law." Although Clinton's action of sending U.S. troops to Bosnia and elsewhere was reprehensible, he should not be condemned for using whatever legal means he could to avoid being sent to Vietnam. It is too bad that more young men didn't use whatever means they could, legal or otherwise, to avoid being sent to Vietnam. Fifty-eight thousand Americans and perhaps two million Southeast Asians are dead because millions of American soldiers obeyed the dictates of the state.

Why, then, would Christians who are opposed to slavery be in support of military conscription? The answer is because they are not opposed to the state. In fact, many Christians are in love with the state. Sure, they may complain about paying their taxes or following some regulation, get upset with Supreme Court decisions about abortion, and even get outraged about government-funded pornographic art, but when it comes to the subject of war and the military they lose their mind. Bombing, maiming, interrogating, and killing are okay as long as it is done in service for the state. The military and the CIA are great employment opportunities for Christian young people. Even if they acknowledge that a war like the one in Iraq is unconstitutional and unnecessary—and even immoral and senseless—some Christians still say that the troops are not responsible and we should support them.

What are the Christians who live by the "obey the powers that be" mantra going to do when the state conscripts their young women? Congressman Rangel's bills already amend the Military Selective Service Act to authorize the military registration of females. What are these Christians going to do when U.S. troops are directed to attack American citizens in the name of fighting terrorism? Will they still encourage their children to join the military?

Christians who continue to defend Bush's war of aggression in Iraq are in a state of denial. They refuse to believe that the president lied the country into war. They refuse to believe that loving one's country has nothing to do with loving the government. They refuse to believe that being patriotic does not mean blindly following whatever the government says. They refuse to believe that the alliance between evangelical Christianity and the military is an unholy one. And they also refuse to believe that war is the health of the state.

Should Christians support slavery in the form of military conscription? Of course not. The draft, whether into the military or into some form of "national service," is about serving the state. Of all people, Christians should vehemently oppose serving what has historically been the enemy of real Christianity.

The only ones who "owe it" to the country to fight in unconstitutional, unjust, immoral, and unnecessary wars of aggression are the pathetic chickenhawks, the diehard armchair warriors, the "conservative" apologists for President Bush, the Republican Party loyalists, the writers for *National Review*, the unholy Christian warmongers, and anyone else calling for more money to be spent and more troops to be sent to fight the terrible waste of money and lives that is the war in Iraq.

* * * * *

THE HYPOCRISY OF CHRISTIAN MILITARISTS

Although I have written previously about the hypocrisy of both American Christian soldiers and Christian warmongers, there is another group of Christians that are hypocrites as well: Christian militarists.

As I have pointed out again and again, there is an unholy alliance between conservative, evangelical, and fundamentalist Christians and the military. Although some of these Christian militarists may oppose the Iraq War, the stationing of U.S. troops around the globe, and U.S. foreign policy in general, they wholeheartedly support the U.S. military as the defender of our freedoms. They see no problem with Christians joining the military and then going off to fight some foreign war that has nothing to do with defending the United States because soldiers should "obey the powers that be" and submit to their commander in chief. In this respect they are hypocrites.

One very recent event reminds us of another respect in which Christian militarists are hypocrites: the death of Kurt Waldheim on June 14.

Born in Vienna in 1918, Waldheim became an Austrian diplomat after World War II. He served as Secretary-General of the United Nations from 1972 to 1981 and as president of Austria from 1986 to 1992. The problem with Waldheim is that, not only was he a member of the German Wehrmacht during World War II, but that he was allegedly complicit in Nazi war crimes. Although it was never officially established that Waldheim had actually committed any atrocities during the war, he was the only head of a "friendly" country to be barred from the United States. In an interview before being elected president of Austria, Waldheim said about his wartime service: "What I did during the war was nothing more than what hundreds of thousands of other Austrians did, namely fulfilled my duty as a soldier."

Kurt Waldheim ought to be a role model for Christian militarists. He served his commander in chief. He obeyed the orders of his superiors.

Like President Bush, the Christian militarist believes that (outside of the ministry, I suppose) there is no higher calling than military service. But what about soldiers in other countries? Doesn't the dictum apply to them as well?

What the Christian militarist really believes is that there is nothing greater than being in the United States military. How dare "enemies" of the United States join their country's military and fight against the United States! And if they are drafted into the military to fight an obviously unjust war (since it is against the United States), they should desert or surrender rather than wage war against the United States. How dare they try to kill American soldiers!

If members of the U.S. Armed Forces should obey orders then why not the soldiers in other countries? Aren't they justified in bombing, maiming, and killing for their country if their government orders them to do it? And why should we get upset if they kill civilians? It is inevitable that there will be collateral damage in any conflict. And after all, an order is an order. There would be chaos in the ranks if soldiers stopped to question their orders.

If Christian militarists were honest they would admit that they don't think that foreign soldiers should "obey the powers that be." They should not obey orders if it means killing Americans. They should refuse to obey their superiors and suffer the consequences. American soldiers should obey orders because the U.S. military defends our freedoms and protects the free nations of the world from communists and Muslims. And after all, we were attacked on September 11th and our president is a Christian.

The bottom line is this: If foreigners should question serving in their military and obeying orders then why not Americans? Especially since the U.S. military is the greatest force for evil in the world today. Since that is something I have written about many times over the past few years, I won't revisit that subject here. But I will say this: Christians should end their illicit love affair with the U.S. military, and they should do it now, before the government enlists their support for next foreign military intervention.

All Christian warmongers are Christian militarists, but not all Christian militarists are Christian warmongers. Thank God that some Christian militarists recognize the Iraq War for what it is: an immoral, unjust, unnecessary, unscriptural war of aggression. But when it comes to the subject of the military as the coercive arm of the warfare state, they fail to think consistently. Indeed, many of them turn into full-fledged apologists for the state if you dare criticize the military in any way.

Some Christian militarists are veterans who refuse to admit that they fought for a lie, some are nationalists who adhere to the notion of "my country, right or wrong," some are super-patriots who blindly follow the U.S. government, some are idealists who refuse to see the U.S. military for what it really is, and some sincerely believe that the troops defend our freedoms, but all of them are hypocrites when it comes to people joining the military and obeying orders.

* * * * *

SHOULD A CHRISTIAN BE A MILITARY CHAPLAIN?

If the question was whether a Christian should be a pimp, a prostitute, an abortionist, a drug dealer, a contract killer, a topless dancer, or a bouncer in a strip joint, then the answer would quite obvious. Adherents of other religions and atheists would also generally select more wholesome occupations. Even Christian parents whose children selected more benign careers like blackjack dealer, swimsuit model, bartender, tobacco farmer, x-rated video store clerk, or Hooters waitress would generally want their children to aspire to something better.

But should a Christian be a military chaplain?

When I say a military chaplain I mean a chaplain paid by, and answerable to, the state. The United States has had military chaplains since the Revolutionary War. As a Christian, I am not opposed to the general idea of a chaplaincy. I would not be against any man who aspired to be a chaplain or any organization that wanted to have a chaplain.

But should a Christian be a military chaplain?

Although it is not my intent in this article, the case could be made that we should not have taxpayer-funded chaplains in the military or anywhere else. As a Protestant, I object to my tax dollars being paid to a Roman Catholic priest to conduct mass in an army barracks, a naval vessel, or a military chapel. Roman Catholics should likewise be against a Protestant minister being paid by the government to hold an evangelistic service on Sunday and teach Protestant doctrine the rest of the week. Jews, Muslims, Mormons, agnostics, and atheists—if they are really serious about their religion or non-religion—should be opposed to either scenario.

Taxpayer-supported chaplains have to serve two masters: God and the state. Compromise is inevitable. He that pays the piper calls the tune. The Southern Baptists actually recognized this back in 1918, and stated in a resolution that because

- Religious liberty cannot be absolute where any of its appointments or appropriations are by authority of the state;
- The army Chaplain appointed by state authority as the religious teacher of the country's soldiers is dependent on the state for support and is amenable to the state for regulation of duties and conduct;
- The different Christian denominations of this republic can and would send voluntarily through their agencies, religious teachers to all departments of the army and navy;

It is resolved that

> the Congress of the U4nited States be memorialized to consider the propriety and rightfulness of abolishing the Army Chaplaincies leaving the religious services to the discretion and election of the different Christian denominations, which services shall in nowise hinder in any military movement of the army or any part of it, these services seeking only for an open door and protection as American citizens in performance of said religious duties.

To become a chaplain in the U.S. military, one must obtain an ecclesiastical endorsement from an organization approved by the Pentagon as an Endorsing Ecclesiastical Organization. According to the chaplain requirements on the Army Chaplain Corps website, the endorsement should certify that one is:

- A clergy person in your denomination or faith group.
- Qualified spiritually, morally, intellectually and emotionally to serve as a Chaplain in the Army.
- Sensitive to religious pluralism and able to provide for the free exercise of religion by all military personnel, their family

> members and civilians who work for the Army.

Any conservative, evangelical, or fundamentalist Christian who thinks he can meet the third qualification without compromising his convictions is naïve.

Denominations, associations, fellowships, and other ecclesiastical groups who think that their chaplains can serve both God and country are deceived: "No man can serve two masters" (Matthew 6:24). Here are two similar statements, from two entirely different groups, about being a military chaplain:

> U.S. Army Chaplains serve both God and country by bringing their unique gifts with which they are endowed by God, to the Soldiers of our nation in the broad, challenging, diverse, and ever changing environment of the Army.

> The United States Military is an exciting place to minister. The chaplain, while serving God as a minister of the Gospel, also serves his country.

The first statement is from the U.S. Army; the second is from the Fundamental Baptist Fellowship International. Ecclesiastical groups of any stripe ought to be discouraging men to stay away from the military instead of encouraging them to become chaplains.

Back in 2005 a Navy chaplain, Gordon Klingenschmitt, got into hot water with the Navy for preaching a message in a chapel service that was "not inclusive and might offend people." He then fought an extended battle with the Navy over the right to pray in Jesus' name.

But it is not just over religion that some chaplains get into trouble. A Southern Baptist chaplain in the Air Force, Garland Robertson, suffered for daring to question a military action. After "serving" in Vietnam, Robertson attended seminary and was then reactivated as an Air Force chaplain. On the eve of the first attack on Iraq in 1991, he wrote that the vice president's statement that the American people were behind the invasion "must be clarified to indicate that the American people are not united in their decision to support a military offensive against the aggression of Saddam Hussein in Kuwait." For this he was visited by an officer from the Chief of Chaplains who "indicated that compromise was essential for becoming a successful military chaplain." Said Robertson of this meeting: "I suggested that 'cooperation' was the more suitable word, but he quickly confirmed his intentional use of 'compromise.' 'If Jesus had been an Air Force chaplain,' he told me, 'he would have been courtmartialed.' But he said that compromise is necessary in order to maintain a presence."

But supposing it were possible to serve as a military chaplain without compromising one's convictions, should a Christian be a military chaplain? Definitely not—and for two reasons. First, one would have to join the military. And second, one would have to support the activities of the military.

I have already made the case that a Christian has no business in the military—including the National Guard. I have admonished Christians to think before they decide to join the military, regardless of family tradition, patriotism, signing bonuses, or money for college. I have made it clear that God never called any Christian to be a Christian killer. I have explained why a Christian cannot kill heartily in the name of the Lord. I have also showed the hypocrisy of the American Christian soldier. A Christian should not be a military chaplain for the simple reason that it is impossible to do so without joining the military. Because I have already written so much in these and other articles against Christians joining the military, I will only reiterate here that the military has a bad effect on one's mind and morals.

U.S. Marine Corps Major General Smedley Butler (1881–1940)—a Congressional Medal of Honor winner who could never be accused of being a pacifist, an appeaser, or a traitor—not only eloquently stated that "war is a racket," he also spoke about the effect on the mind of military "service":

> Like all the members of the military profession, I never had a thought of my own until I left the service. My mental faculties remained in suspended animation while I obeyed the orders of higher-ups. This is typical with everyone in the military service.

The immoral environment of the military is no secret. Here is a note I received from M.A., an ex-Marine:

> The Marine Corps is like a frat party in between the hard work. For the most part, they are irresponsible, alcoholic, sex addicts. The married Marines that I served with didn't think twice about cheating on their spouses during deployments. And speaking of deployments, if the U.S. military ever gets disbanded, the world-wide brothel industry would shut down overnight. The behavior of my fellow Marines in Thailand I found to be utterly repulsive. What a shame it is to have de facto ambassadors of the United States—i.e., the people whom 'represent' America to for-

> eigners—behaving in such a way. Hedonists with guns. That's the Marine Corps.

I have received scores of e-mails just like this. In fact, I would say that most veterans who write me do so in agreement with what I write about the military, the war in Iraq, and U.S. foreign policy. It is the Christian chickenhawks and armchair warriors who are my most vocal critics.

One cannot "serve" in the military—and especially in an influential position like a chaplain—and not support the activities of the military. Just ask Eli Israel, the Army sniper turned war resister. Rather than guarding our borders, patrolling our coasts, and actually defending the country, the history of the U.S. military is the history of meddling, aggression, invasion, and occupation. The military is the enforcer of the reckless, imperialistic U.S. foreign policy. The purpose of the military has been perverted beyond repair by our interventionist foreign policy.

To those who are currently serving as a military chaplain or are thinking about becoming a chaplain that *support* the U.S. global empire and the current use of the military, and to those who are currently serving as a military chaplain or are thinking about becoming a chaplain that *object* to both, I would ask the same thing: Is asking God to bless and protect the troops as they shoot, bomb, maim, mine, destroy, "interrogate," and kill for a rogue state with an evil foreign policy consistent with the Christianity you find in the New Testament?

If you *don't* believe that the United States is a rogue state with an evil foreign policy, please read or reread my lecture titled "War, Foreign Policy, and the Church." If you still don't see a problem with U.S. foreign policy, then perhaps you overlooked a key statement I made in that lecture and elsewhere: blind obedience to the state is not a tenet of New Testament Christianity.

If you *do* believe that the United States is a rogue state with an evil foreign policy, then why are you in (or thinking about joining) the U.S. military? How can you recognize the harmful and often deadly effects of American foreign policy carried out by the U.S. military and yet participate, by your silence or by your feigned consent, in perpetuating the myth that U.S. troops defend our freedoms when they bomb, invade, and occupy other countries? Do you (or will you) tell concerned soldiers not be concerned about killing the "enemy" since it is "not murder" to kill someone in wartime?

George Zabelka and William Downey found all this out the hard way. They were the Catholic and Protestant Army Air Force chaplains assigned to the 509th Composite Group in charge of delivering the atomic bombs to their Japanese targets. Both later renounced their actions.

Here is the prayer Chaplain Downey offered before the Enola Gay took off from Tinian Island for Hiroshima on August 6, 1945 (you can listen here to an actual recording of the end of Downey's prayer, introduced by Edward R. Murrow):

> Almighty Father, who wilt hear the prayer of those that love thee, we pray thee to be with those who brave heights of thy heaven and who carry the battle to our enemies. Guard and protect them, we pray thee, as they fly the appointed rounds. May they, as well as we, know thy strength and power, and armed with thy might may they bring this war to a rapid end. We pray thee that the end of the war may come soon and once more we may know peace on earth. May the men who fly this night be kept safe in thy care, and may they be returned safely to us. We shall go forward trusting in thee knowing that we are in thy care now and for ever. In the name of Jesus Christ, Amen.

Contrast this prayer with what Chaplain Zabelka said later:

> For the last 1700 years the Church has not only been making war respectable: it has been inducing people to believe it is an honorable profession, an honorable Christian profession. This is not true. We have been brainwashed. This is a lie.
>
> There is no way to conduct real war in conformity with the teachings of Jesus.
>
> As an Air Force chaplain I painted a machine gun in the loving hands of the nonviolent Jesus, and then handed this perverse picture to the world as truth. I sang "Praise the Lord" and passed the ammunition. As Catholic chaplain for the 509th Composite Group, I was the final channel that communicated this fraudulent image of Christ to the crews of the Enola Gay and the Boxcar.

All of this may be true, say some Christians, but how can we reach servicemen and servicewomen with the Gospel? There are plenty of other ways without becoming a chaplain. See, for example, Armed Forces Baptist Missions.

Should a Christian be a military chaplain? Not if he opposes compromise with the state, the state's military, the state's wars, and the state's foreign policy. Where are the chaplains today who will renounce the Iraq war, U.S. foreign policy, the U.S. military, and their commander in chief and be willing to suffer the consequences? There have been some regular soldiers who have done so. Why are the chaplains so quiet? Is it because they are not the ones having to fight, and bleed, and die for a lie? Because of a severe shortage in its Chaplain Corps, the Army is looking for a few good chaplains. Let's hope that the Army doesn't find any.

* * * * *

FOR CHRIST AND FOR CAESAR

> "And he said unto them, Render therefore unto Caesar the things which be Caesar's, and unto God the things which be God's" ~ Luke 20:25

Are bombing, maiming, destroying property, killing, and genocide compatible with biblical Christianity? Patrick Henry College apparently thinks so. The war in Iraq is all of the above, yet this Christian college not only offers Army ROTC, it also offers its students as cannon fodder to the U.S. military.

Patrick Henry College is a distinctively Christian liberal arts college in Virginia known for being friendly to homeschoolers. The founder and chancellor is Michael Farris, the founder of the Home School Legal Defense Association. The college's motto is "For Christ and For Liberty." Imagine my surprise when I saw in the college's *News & Events* that "for a growing number of PHC upperclassmen and alumni, the motto 'for Christ and for liberty' has translated into service to their country through the United States military."

The mission of Patrick Henry College "is to prepare Christian men and women who will lead our nation and shape our culture with timeless biblical values and fidelity to the spirit of the American founding." The vision of Patrick Henry College "is to aid in the transformation of American society by training Christian students to serve God and mankind with a passion for righteousness, justice, and mercy, through careers of public service and cultural influence."

The college will fail on both counts as long as it remains a military-friendly college.

A culture shaped by the military is not compatible with timeless biblical values. A culture shaped by today's military does not exhibit fidelity to the spirit of the American Founding. One cannot serve God and mankind in the military. However, in the military one can certainly disobey God and kill mankind.

In the college's aforementioned *News & Events*, we are introduced to two current students who have enlisted in the military, one recent graduate who just began basic training, and two alumni serving in the U.S. Marine Corps.

Kyle, a junior, explains why he joined the Marines:

> I joined because I am willing and capable to do what is necessary to protect and preserve my country, even to the point of giving my own life.
>
> I am joining the Marine Corps for the same reason I came to PHC. I would sum it up as a debt of honor we owe to our faith and to our country for the heritage and the sacrifices from which we have benefited.

Although this young man acknowledges that "not everyone can serve in the military," he believes that "everyone who is able should at least try."

Another junior, Gabe, says: "As a Christian soldier, I will gain skills that will enable me to take a very concrete, physical stand for liberty, while simultaneously furthering my long-term ability to lead the culture and to preserve the legacy of freedom bequeathed to my generation."

The writer of the *News & Events* column remarks that Kyle and Gabe "are joining the military simply to be of use to their country."

A recent graduate, John, "joined to be Marine Corps infantry—a ground-pounder." Because he believes that "someone is going to have to make sacrifices," he maintains that he "would rather it be those who willingly undertake its defense than innocent civilians caught in the blast of a terrorist's bomb, or enemy country's attack."

Another recent graduate, Aaron, remarks that the "times of classic military frustration" have not shaken his faith in God's leading him to where he is today. He adds: "My time in the Marines has definitely been fulfilling, and I am confident that I made the right decision in joining." Like Kyle, Aaron advises everyone join try service in the military: "If a student is an able-bodied male, they should seriously consider the military for a period of time, even if they know they do not want it to be a career."

The third recent graduate, Kevin, believes that he did not in end up in the military by accident: "God is good and has directed my steps."

I don't know what kind of Christianity they follow at Patrick Henry College, but speaking as a conservative, Bible-believing Christian, I want no part of it.

Why on earth would a Christian young person even think about joining the military? Some want to join for the enlistment bonuses, others for the generous benefits, others for the tuition assistance, others for the career training, and others for the world travel. Some no doubt believe that they would be defending our freedoms and keeping us safe from terrorist attacks. Some probably think that the military will instill discipline, toughen them up, and make them a man. Some have the purely spiritual motive of sharing the love of Christ or being a Christian example to their fellow soldiers. Some would simply be following in the footsteps of their father, brother, or friend.

Although Patrick Henry College may pride itself on its challenging curriculum, its spiritual environment, its qualified instructors, its beautiful campus, and its high academic standards, there is something missing from the education each student receives.

That something is the terrible truth about the U.S. military.

The military is a force for evil in the world. The military spreads democracy by bombs, bayonets, and bullets. The military enforces a belligerent U.S. foreign policy. The military is the world's unwanted and unloved policeman. The military garrisons the planet with troops and bases. The military is responsible for the network of brothels around the world to service U.S. troops who have no business being away from home. The military accounts for one third of all federal spending. The military accounts for over one half of total world military spending. The military increases terrorism by its foreign occupations.

The military does not defend our freedoms. The military does not secure our borders. The military does not patrol our coasts. The military does not guard our shores. The military does not fight terrorists over there so we don't have to fight them over here. The military does not protect our First Amendment rights. The military does not keep us safe. The military does not ensure that we can speak English. The military is not retaliating against the perpetrators of the 9/11 attacks.

The greatest danger to American life, liberty, and property is not the leaders or the military of Iran, China, Russia, or Venezuela: It is the government of the United States.

If they really want to honor Christ and the Bible, Christian colleges should discontinue all ROTC programs, ban military recruiters from all their campuses, and discourage their young people from enlisting in the military. It is bad enough when atheists, agnostics, pagans, and the irreligious join the military, but it is an indelible blot on Christianity when Christians do the same.

Patrick Henry College: For Christ and for Caesar.

* * * * *

ACCOMPLICE TO MURDER

Is there any reason a Christian who was opposed to the war in Iraq could in good conscience still join the military? I have previously explained why Christians have no business joining the military, even to serve as a military chaplain. I have also expressed my opposition to the National Guard. But what about a Christian joining the military to be a witness for Christ or to serve his fellow soldiers? What could possibly be wrong with that? My short answer is that one would be an accomplice to murder, that's what wrong with it. My long answer follows below.

Because I often write about the incompatibility of Christianity and military service, I receive many e-mails from servicemen who wish to get out and young men who wish to get in. (For the record, I also get e-mails from super-patriots calling me a traitor or a communist because I dare question the activities of the military). For those desiring to separate from the military or become a conscientious objector, I refer them to James Glaser, a Marine Corps Vietnam veteran, or to Mike Reith, a retired Air Force major. Because they recognize that war is the health of the state, both of these veterans discourage young men from following in their footsteps. For those thinking about joining the military, I try to answer myself because of how strongly I am opposed to not just Christians, but anyone enlisting in the military.

Here is a note I received recently from a sincere young man who is thinking about joining the military. He opposes the war in Iraq, and is concerned about having to take human life. I have omitted his name from his letter, which is reprinted below in its entirety with his permission:

> Hello, I am a self professed Christian (to better define my Christianity: I am a firm believer in Christ, and my faith dictates my actions, and I strive to better myself in my walk, and live a Christ centered life). I am also looking towards the military to become a navy corpsman (a field medic attached to a marine unit). As a medic, I would not be fighting for my country (because I cannot fully agree with the reasons we are at war), but rather I would be there for my fellow soldiers who do in fact believe in the cause. I would view my job as serving the troops, and applying my skills of medical aide to help the troops. I also am very missions minded, and would view my deployment as a mission field, and a way to share the gospel with troops and/or; whoever I come in contact with as a witness of God's love. Anyway, I have not joined yet, but am seriously considering it. I am a high school grad, almost 18 years old from California, just trying to seek the opinions from intelligent and respectable people before I make my decisions. I

would appreciate a response with any information, verses, or insight you may have. Thank you so much for your time. God Bless.

P.S. I know that I would be in a defensive position as a medic, and would only shoot to defend myself or others, but what if I was given a direct order to kill (or cause death), I still am thinking about things like this. Again, thank you.

Dear ____:

I am not sure if you have read my book, *Christianity and War and Other Essays Against the Warfare State*, or any of my articles on this subject archived at LewRockwell.com. If so, then you probably have some idea of the negative things that I am going to say about Christians joining the military. Either way, I would encourage you to read the fourteen articles I have written specifically about Christianity and the Military.

You have expressed a desire to be a medic to take care of your fellow soldiers. On the surface that seems like a noble thing to do. There are, however, some things you ought to consider.

First of all, there is no guarantee that by joining the military you would be assigned to care for wounded soldiers in Iraq (or Afghanistan). Don't listen to what the recruiters tell you. You can't trust them. They have been caught lying too many times. There is no way they can guarantee that you will wind up a medic in a war zone.

Second, even if you did wind up in Iraq, there is no guarantee that you would stay there. Military personnel are constantly moved from place to place. You may be placed in a situation where you will be doing anything but helping wounded soldiers.

Third, although you have acknowledged that the troops in Iraq have no good reason for being there, there is more too it than that. The troops are not merely neutral observers caught in a crossfire. The troops in Iraq are responsible for death, destruction, and genocide against the Iraqi people. If you think that genocide is too strong a word to describe what is happening in Iraq, see Lew Rockwell's "None Dare Call It Genocide." To serve as a medic so you can help your fellow soldiers means that you would be an accomplice to murder. What would you think of a physician who was willingly employed by a criminal gang to patch up the gang members after they were injured in the course of committing crimes? What is the war in Iraq if it is not a crime against the Iraqi people? Although he was not a Christian, Mahatma Gandhi did make a scriptural statement when he said: "Non-cooperation with evil is as much a duty as cooperation with good."

Fourth, if you didn't serve as a medic in Iraq then someone else would. Over 181,000 people joined the U.S. military last year. It's not as though U.S. troops would be going without medical care just because you didn't enlist.

And fifth, if you really want to attend to people that need medical care, then you should consider helping Iraqis wounded by American bombs and bullets. After all, the United States invaded Iraq, not the other way around. Now, don't get me wrong. Even though I don't support what the troops are doing in Iraq, I don't want to see any U.S. soldier injured or killed. But I also don't want to see any Iraqis injured or killed either. It would not, of course, be wise for you to actually attempt to treat wounded Iraqis. The U.S. government would label you as an enemy combatant and ship you off to Guantanamo Bay. And right or wrong, the Iraqis would try to kill you because you are an American.

You have also expressed a desire to share the gospel. Your attitude of viewing your deployment as a mission field is one that all Christians should have. You sound like a clean young man who is committed to serving our Lord. Joining the military will corrupt you. Yes, some Christians emerge unscathed and remain faithful to Christ, but many more do not. You should not enlist because "no man can serve two masters" (Matthew 6:24). Joining the military means that you will be expected to unconditionally follow orders. You will be pressured to practically make a god out of the military. Because the purpose of the U.S. military has shifted from defending the country to intervening in other countries, the role that the U.S. military plays in the world is an evil one. To enlist would violate the admonition to "abstain from all appearance of evil" (1 Thessalonians 5:22). Remember the words of Bob Jones Sr.: "It is never right to do wrong in order to get a chance to do right."

You mentioned in closing that you would only shoot in self-defense. Joining the military means that you may be put into a position where you will have to kill or be killed. But is it really self-defense if you kill an Iraqi who is trying to kill you? How can it be considered self-defense when American soldiers travel thousands of miles from their homeland to invade a country that not only never attacked their country, but was never even a credible threat to their country? Is it self-defense if a thief kills you because you catch him with a gun in your house in the middle of the night and you fire your gun at him? You indicate that you are hesitant about following an order that might result in the death of someone. Since U.S. troops are the invaders, you should be just as cautious about justifying the shooting of someone in Iraq with the self-defense excuse. You are the one who is ultimately responsible for the people you kill, not the president and the secretary of defense. Not only will you have to live the rest of your life with the memories of the people you killed (or think you killed), you will also have to give an account of yourself to God at the judgment (Romans 14:12).

Don't enlist; don't be an accomplice to murder.

* * * * *

LETTER TO A CHRISTIAN YOUNG MAN REGARDING JOINING THE MILITARY

The following letter was sent to a Christian young man I know who was considering joining the military. He hasn't joined as of yet, and I hope and pray that he doesn't. I am posting this letter publicly in the hope that it might persuade some Christian young men I don't know from joining the military.

Dear ______:

I have been told that you are thinking about joining the military. I hope I am misinformed. I understand that you are having trouble finding a job, but think that, as a Christian young man, you are making a big mistake if you join today's military.

First of all, you were raised in a Christian home and went to Christian schools your whole life. You will be needlessly exposed to much wickedness in the military. You will unnecessarily face temptations that you have never been exposed to. Why put yourself in this position? It is a fact that there is a network of brothels around the world to service U.S. troops stationed overseas. I know that you are a clean young man and have a girlfriend, but don't deceive yourself into thinking that you can remain clean in the military. Because I write on war and military issues, I have scores of veterans, Christian and otherwise, who have written me that will back up everything I am saying.

Second, it is one thing to join the military out of a sense of patriotism, but how does joining the military for financial reasons make you any different than a mercenary? I know that sounds harsh, but would you consider joining the military if you had a good job right now?

Third, the senseless wars in Iraq and Afghanistan have no end in sight. There is no guarantee that you will not be sent to Iraq, Afghanistan, or some other God-forsaken place where you could be in danger of losing life or limb. And for what?

Fourth, you can't trust military recruiters. Like a car salesman, they are trying to make their monthly quota. They have been caught on tape lying to young men, even telling them that no troops were being sent to Iraq anymore.

Fifth, I know that you have a very low opinion of the new president, Barack Obama. I share your opinion completely. As a member of the military, Obama would be your commander in chief. You could be sent anywhere to fight for Obama. Are you willing to fight and possibly die because Obama thinks it necessary to send American troops into some other war?

Sixth, in the military, you will be expected to blindly follow the orders of your officers. Independent thought is not tolerated. Please consider the words of U.S. Marine Corps Major General Smedley Butler (1881–1940), a two-time Congressional Medal of Honor winner: "Like all the members of the military profession, I never had a thought of my own until I left the service. My mental faculties remained in suspended animation while I obeyed the orders of higher-ups. This is typical with everyone in the military service." Major General Butler became disillusioned with military service and wrote a famous book called *War Is a Racket* in which he said: "War is a racket. It always has been. It is possibly the oldest, easily the most profitable, surely the most vicious. It is the only one international in scope. It is the only one in which the profits are reckoned in dollars and the losses in lives."

Seventh, the purpose of the U.S. military is to defend America. But not only is the military not being used in defense of the country, it is being used to guard the borders, patrol the coasts, and defend the shores of other countries. The purpose of the military has been perverted by the interventionist foreign policy of the United States. There are American troops stationed in 147 countries and 10 territories. I know this for a fact because I have researched this in official Department of Defense documents and written about it on many occasions. The current use of the military is contrary to the American Founding Fathers' policy of nonintervention in the affairs of other countries.

Eighth, joining the military may have an adverse effect on your future family. I know that you have a girlfriend that you are very serious about. You should know that the breakup of marriages and relationships because of soldiers being deployed to Iraq and elsewhere is epidemic. Multiple duty tours and increased deployment terms are the death knell for stable families. What makes you think that the military will never send you away from your family for an extended period of time? You know that the possibility exists, so why gamble with your family? And then, as if being away from your family wasn't bad enough on you and them, some soldiers come home with such physical and/or mental problems that they are unable to return to civilian life. Debt, doctors, and divorce lawyers soon consume their finances.

Ninth, joining the military means that you may be put into a position where you will have to kill or be killed. What guarantee do you have that you will be in a non-combat role? Can you in good conscience pull the trigger against any "enemy" that the U.S. government sends you thousands of miles away to kill?

And finally, you would have problems even if you went into the military as a chaplain. Taxpayer-supported chaplains have to serve two masters: God and the state. Compromise is inevitable. He that pays the piper calls the tune. To become a chaplain in the U.S. military, one must obtain an ecclesiastical endorsement from an organization approved by the Pentagon as an Endorsing Ecclesiastical Organization. According to the chaplain requirements, one of the things that the endorsement should certify is that a military chaplain should be "sensitive to religious pluralism and able to provide for the free exercise of religion by all military personnel, their family members and civilians who work for the Army." I know that you are a conservative Christian and are averse to compromising your religious convictions. You will, however, be expected to do just that. As a chaplain, you would be expected to ask God to bless the actions of U.S. troops even if they were fighting in an unjust war. Can you in good conscience do this?

Please remember that if you join the military, there is no getting out until your enlistment period is up. I hope and pray that you don't make the mistake of joining.

In Christ Jesus our Savior,
Laurence Vance

If any readers are veterans, consider themselves to be Christians, agree with the sentiments expressed in this letter, and would be willing to let me append their name, branch, and rank to any future use of this letter, please contact me. The fact that you "served" and I didn't might be what is needed to help persuade some young man (or woman) to not join the military.

* * * * *

THE CHRISTIAN'S GOLDEN CALF

"Thou shalt have no other gods before me." ~ (Exodus 20:3)

Most people know the story of Aaron's golden calf.

After the Jews came out of Egypt, while Moses was up on Mount Sinai receiving from God the ten commandments on "tables of stone, written with the finger of God" (Exodus 31:18), the children of Israel complained to Aaron, Moses' brother: "Up, make us gods, which shall go before us; for as for this Moses, the man that brought us up out of the land of Egypt, we wot not what is become of him" (Exodus 32:1). So, after the people donated their gold, Aaron made a golden calf and proclaimed: "These be thy gods, O Israel, which brought thee up out of the land of Egypt" (Exodus 32:4). Then Aaron made an altar, the people offered offerings, and they all had themselves one wild party (Exodus 32:6); that is, until Moses came down from the mount (Exodus 32:19).

Some, perhaps, also know the story of Jeroboam's golden calves.

Years later in the history of Israel, when most of the tribes rebelled under Jeroboam, he "made two calves of gold" and said to the people: "Behold thy gods, O Israel, which brought thee up out of the land of Egypt" (1 Kings 12:28). After placing one calf in Bethel and the other in Dan (1 Kings 12:29), Jeroboam appointed his own priests, ordained a feast, burnt incense, and made offerings on an altar, "sacrificing unto the calves that he had made" (1 Kings 12:32). The people likewise worshipped before these golden calves (1 Kings 12:30). As a consequence, the tribes that sinned under Jeroboam were "carried away out of their own land to Assyria unto this day" (2 Kings 17:22–23).

Ever since these incidents, a golden calf has referred to some object that is undeservedly worshipped or venerated.

To their shame, American Christians, who profess to serve the Lord God and the Lord Jesus Christ, and wouldn't think of making a god out of gambling, Internet porn, or alcohol, have a god—a golden calf—they honor, reverence, and pay homage to. This god demands perpetual thanksgivings. This god demands obeisance on national holidays. This god demands special appreciation days. This god demands songs to be sung in praise to it. This god demands prayers to the Lord God on its behalf. This god demands sacrifices of young men and women. This god demands signs, buttons, shirts, bumper stickers, yellow ribbons, and lapel pins inscribed with its various names and slogans. This god tolerates no criticism of its activities.

The Christian's golden calf is the U.S. military.

Not all Christians, mind you, but a great many Christians from throughout Christendom have exchanged biblical Christianity for imperial Christianity. From Catholic just-war theorists who oppose abortion (but not the killing of people outside of the womb) to progressive Christians who oppose the war in Iraq (but not military intervention in Darfur) to the Religious Right who oppose the persecution of Christians in Muslim countries (but not the American killing of Muslims in Muslim countries)—Christians of all branches and denominations are engaged an idolatrous affair with the U.S. military.

The worst offenders are the independent, evangelical, fundamentalist, and other conservative Christians. And I say this as one of them. With them it is the majority who bow before the golden calf. Yes, the majority. That is the conclusion I reached during the Bush years and that is still my conclusion now. In spite of the waning support for the war in Iraq and the venom directed toward Barack Obama by right-wing Christians, Christian reverence for the military remains unchanged.

I don't make this golden calf accusation lightly. I say it after years of listening to conservative Christians, talking with them, reading hundreds of e-mails from them (both friend and foe), hearing scores of reports from disconsolate church members about their warmongering pastors and church leaders, reading numerous books, articles, blogs, and newsletters by Christian defenders of war and the warfare state, seeing the negative reaction to my book *Christianity and War*, and reading countless pathetic attempts to justify Christian participation in the state's wars.

I still see on church signs and church websites the "support our troops," "pray for our troops," and "God bless our troops" mantras. It doesn't matter where U.S. troops go, how many go, how long they stay, or what they do when they are there—support for the military is a fundamental of the faith, right up there with the Virgin Birth and the Deity of Christ.

And here is a resolution passed by the Wisconsin Fellowship of Baptist Churches at their annual meeting last year:

> C. Support for Soldiers: Whereas there are young men and women from our country and our churches in military service, and some in perilous situations around the world, and whereas we appreciate their sacrifices and willingness to protect our freedom, BE IT RESOLVED that we will pray for our troops, support them in tangible ways as we have opportunity, and encourage them to make their field of service a harvest field for the Kingdom of God.

These are conservative, independent Baptist churches—and they are spewing forth anti-biblical nonsense.

And it is not just Red-State Christian fascists, Reich-wing Christian nationalists, theocon Values Voters (who recently expressed their support for warmonger Mike Huckabee in a Family Research Council Values Voter Summit), Christian Coalition moralists, and "God and country" social conservatives who support federal funding of school vouchers, abstinence education, and faith-based initiatives who venerate the military. It is also Christians who don't consider themselves part of the Religious Right, Christians who don't vote, Christians who oppose an interventionist U.S. foreign policy, Christians who denounce abuses of the FBI, CIA, IRS, and BATF, Christians who oppose the Iraq War, Christians who caution against Christian service in the military, and Christians who oppose basically every other government institution.

Support for the military among Christians is pervasive, systemic, sacrosanct, and codified.

It is also an unholy alliance, an illicit affair, an affront to the Saviour whom Christians worship as the Prince of Peace, a blight on Christianity, and the worse form of statolatry. It also violates the whole tenor of the New Testament:

> Wherefore, my dearly beloved, flee from idolatry (1 Corinthians 10:14).

> And what agreement hath the temple of God with idols? for ye are the temple of the living God; as God hath said, I will dwell in them, and walk in them; and I will be their God, and they shall be my people (2 Corinthians 6:16).

> Little children, keep yourselves from idols. Amen (1 John 5:21).

I fear that things are hopeless. I see no end in sight to churches publicly honoring veterans, praising the troops for defending our freedoms, turning national holidays into military recognition days, having special military appreciation days, encouraging or not discouraging their young men (and sometimes women) to join the military, helping young men to become military chaplains, ostracizing those who disparage the military, equating admiration for the military with patriotism and criticism of the military with treason, imploring church members to pray for the troops, regarding the military's acts of aggression as benevolent, presuming divine support for U.S. military interventions, accepting the militarism of society, having a superstitious reverence for the military, and remaining in willful ignorance of U.S. foreign policy and its use of the military as a force for evil in the world.

I have spoken about these things again and again and written about them time after time after time after time. I am afraid that my words are being heard and read for the most part by the wrong group of Christians—those who already reject the warfare state and a militarized Christianity.

The day is long past (if it ever existed) when the function of the U.S. military was limited to what it should be: defending the United States, securing U.S. borders, guarding U.S. shores, patrolling U.S. coasts, and enforcing no-fly zones over U.S. skies—not defending, guarding, patrolling, attacking, invading, or occupying other countries. And not providing disaster relief, dispensing humanitarian aid, supplying peacekeepers, enforcing UN resolutions, nation building, spreading goodwill, launching preemptive strikes, changing regimes, enforcing no-fly zones, rebuilding infrastructure, reviving public services, promoting good governance, stationing troops in other countries, garrisoning the planet with bases, and killing foreigners in their countries and destroying their property.

A military not strictly for defense of U.S. borders, shores, coasts, and skies is nothing more than the president's personal attack force staffed by mercenaries willing to obey his latest command to bomb, invade, occupy, and otherwise bring death and destruction to any country he deems necessary.

Christian, it is time to slay the golden calf.

* * * * *

HOW TO DEMILITARIZE YOUR CHURCH

Veterans Day is one of those holidays, along with Memorial Day and the Fourth of July, when it isn't safe for non-imperial Christians who think the state should be separated from the church to attend church on the Sunday before one of these holidays. Especially troublesome is when one of these holidays, or Flag Day, actually falls on a Sunday.

In many churches, Sunday services on or before these holidays are unbearable because they feature, or are wholly devoted to, the glorification of the U.S. military. Because the Christian's golden calf is the military, it is necessary to demilitarize American churches.

Although the extent to which you can demilitarize your church depends on whether you are a pastor or church leader, some other person of influence, or just a typical layman, here are some suggestions.

First, recognize the need to demilitarize your church. Although I assume that most of you reading this article are opposed to the glorification of the military in church (or anywhere else), it is still crucial that you educate yourself as to the problems with the military—its unnecessary size, its bloated budget, its inefficiency, its merchants-of-death contractors, its murderous mercenaries, its weapons of mass destruction, its unconstitutional mission, its inability to protect its own headquarters, its foreign interventions, its foreign occupations, its overseas bases and troop deployments—and just how much the military has pervaded all of society. I recommend, first of all, two chapters in my book *Christianity and War and Other Essays Against the Warfare State*: "The Military" and "Christianity and the Military." All of the essays are available in my article archive on this website. Since the publication the second edition of my book in January of last year, I have written many additional articles on the military and Christianity and the military. Again, see my article archive on this website. Second, see the excellent collection of articles on this website by Tom Engelhardt. Third, read Nick Turse's *The Complex: How the Military Invades Our Everyday Lives* (Henry Holt, 2009). And last, but not least, see the Chalmers Johnson trilogy: *Blowback*, *The Sorrows of Empire*, and *Nemesis*. You must be ready for opposition, and not just from veterans. Your whole church may in fact be against you.

Second, there are some practices that you need to stop, or try to get others to stop, in order to demilitarize your church. No more turning holidays into military appreciation days. No more special military appreciation days. No more recognizing current members of the military or veterans. No more encouraging current members of the military or veterans to wear their uniforms on the above-mentioned holidays. No more treating military personnel differently from other occupations. No more references to military personnel "serving" in the military. No more unspecific and unspecified prayers for "the troops in harms way." No more military guest speakers. No more justifying service in the military because the Bible mentions soldiers. No more "God Bless Our Troops" or "Pray for Our Troops" or "Thank a Veteran" slogans on church signs, bulletins, and websites. No more equating patriotism with admiration for the military. No more calling soldiers returning from overseas heroes. No more blasphemous nonsense about the troops dying for our freedoms like Christ died for our sins.

Third, there are some things that you can do to immunize your church from something that causes more deaths than swine flu—the U.S. military. Warn young people about the evils of "serving" in the military. And that includes being a chaplain, a medic, or a National Guardsman. I would feel like a failure as a parent, a pastor, or a youth director if one of my "kids" joined today's military. Here is a letter I wrote to a Christian young man about joining the military. Instruct people about the true nature of the military. In many cases, they are simply just ignorant of the fact that the military is doing everything else but defending the United States, securing U.S. borders, guarding U.S. shores, patrolling U.S. coasts, and enforcing no-fly zones over U.S. skies. Emphasize the need for missionaries to be sent to the Middle East instead of U.S. troops. If Christians in the

United States are so concerned about the threat of Islam, then they should do everything they can to convert Muslims to Christianity instead of wanting American Christian soldiers to kill them heartily in the name of the Lord. Never cease to point out that although God in the Old Testament commanded the nation of Israel to fight against heathen nations, the president of the United States is not God, America is not the nation of Israel, the U.S. military is not the Lord's army, the Christian's sword is the word of God, and the only warfare the New Testament encourages the Christian to wage is against the world, the flesh, and the devil. Pay no attention to military advertising slogans like the new one that says the Navy is "A Global Force for Good."

Now, none of this means that churches should not reach out to those in the military and their families. Nothing I have said precludes a church from having a military ministry. Remember, demilitarizing your church means treating soldiers just like plumbers, barbers, or truckers.

Because of rampant nationalism, imperialism, and red-state fascism, demilitarizing your church won't be easy. But "whether they will hear, or whether they will forbear" (Ezekiel 2:7), it is a necessary endeavor.

* * * * *

SIGNS OF THE TIMES

The Sunday before Memorial Day is not one of my favorites. The "patriotic" things that go on in churches in celebration or acknowledgment of Memorial Day are downright sickening.

Churches encourage their veterans to wear their military uniforms. Special recognition is given to those who "served." Prayers are offered on behalf of the troops, not that they would cease fighting foreign wars, but for God to keep them out of harm's way and protect them. Mention is made of the troops defending our freedoms.

Churches decorate their grounds and the inside of their buildings with U.S. flags. Sometimes it is a few large flags hanging from the ceiling or adorning the walls. Sometimes it is many small flags stuck in the ground near the church entrance. Sometimes it is both. Some congregations are asked to recite the pledge of allegiance.

Churches sing hymns of worship to the state instead of hymns of worship about the person of Christ and his work. Songs like "My Country, 'Tis of Thee," "America the Beautiful," "We Salute You, Land of Liberty," and "This Is My Country." Some churches go even farther and sing "God Bless the U.S.A." or "God Bless America." Too many churches sing the blasphemous "Battle Hymn of the Republic."

I know these practices are widespread because of the scores of people that have e-mailed me in disgust about what occurred in their churches on the Sunday before Memorial Day.

In most cases it is not even necessary to visit a church on the Sunday preceding Memorial Day to know what goes on inside. Just look at the sign outside of the church. Instead of a verse of Scripture or an announcement of an upcoming event, you are more likely to see some patriotic slogan, often with a Christian theme.

I have personally seen two signs this year that I find particularly offensive, not only to my Christian faith, but to reality:

Pray for the Troops,
God be with them.

The American soldier and Jesus Christ,
one gives his life for your freedom,
the other for your soul.

Yes, we should pray for the troops. The Bible tells us in 1 Timothy 2:1 that "supplications, prayers, intercessions, and giving of thanks, be made for all men." But what should we pray? That God would bless the troops while they injure, maim, kill, and destroy property where they have no business being in the first place? That God would be with them while they wage unjust and immoral foreign wars? Since when does wearing a military uniform excuse killing someone you don't know in his own territory that was no threat to any American until the U.S. military invaded and occupied his country? How about instead praying that the troops come home where they belong or that Christian families stop supplying cannon fodder to the military?

That Christ gave his life for our souls is indisputable, but do American soldiers give their lives for our freedoms? You know, the freedoms we have steadily lost since the troops starting defending our freedoms after 9/11? Has there been in American history any foreign war, military action, CIA covert action, or intervention of any kind in any country that was for the purpose of defending our freedoms mentioned in the Bill of Rights? Of course not. Not one Iraqi or Afghan killed by U.S. forces was ever a threat to our freedoms. The troops don't defend our freedoms, and neither do they fight "over there" so we don't have to fight "over here." And I can't think of anything more blasphemous than mentioning Jesus Christ, the Lord, the Son of God, the Prince of Peace in the same breath as a U.S. soldier who unjustly bombs, maims, kills, and then dies in vain and for a lie.

It is time for Christians to slay the golden calf of the military. Christians should stop joining the military. They should stop encouraging their young men to enlist. They should stop being military chaplains and medics. American churches must be demilitarized.

It is a terrible blight on evangelical Christianity that our churches have sent more soldiers to the Middle East than missionaries. If Christians are so concerned about the threat of Islamofascism, then what better way to confront it than with the Gospel of Christ?

* * * * *

SUPPORT OUR TROOPS?

In the last ten years, with only a minuscule number of resistors, U.S. soldiers have put boots on the ground—and bombed, droned, maimed, and killed countless thousands of people—in Iraq, Afghanistan, Yemen, Pakistan, Somalia, and Libya. Over 1 million soldiers have "served" in Iraq. Although President Obama has announced that U.S. troops will leave Iraq by the end of the year, he has also said that some will be sent to Uganda in search of monsters to destroy. And then there are the other 140 countries being occupied by U.S. troops.

I have seen signs expressing support for the troops in front of all manner of businesses, including self-storage units, bike shops, and dog grooming. I have heard accounts of restaurants like Taco Bell and retail stores like Sears asking for donations for the military as a show of support for the troops.

It doesn't seem to matter to most Americans how many wars the troops are involved in, how senseless the war the troops are fighting, how many lies the war is based on that the troops are fighting, how many countries the United States has troops in, how many foreign bases the United States has troops on, how many billions the United States spends on the troops, how many foreign civilians are injured, maimed, or killed by U.S. troops, or even how many U.S. troops die in vain. It doesn't seem to matter what U.S. troops do, where they do it, and to whom to do it to.

None of this seems to matter to American Christians either. Nevertheless, the last place I would expect to see something about supporting the troops is in a church bulletin. I must have severely underestimated the extent of the military fetish that some Christians have because I recently came across a church bulletin from an evangelical church with a whole page devoted to supporting the troops. Thank God I did not have the misfortune of having to attend the church to get a copy of their bulletin.

Here is the page of the church bulletin in question, verbatim, atrocious formatting and all. I have only removed the names that are mentioned.

SUPPORT OUR TROOPS

We still need items to send to our adopted unit.
They are requesting the following items

Nuts - peanuts, almonds, pistachios, sunflower seeds,Chips
movies DVD, Music CDs - Country, Pop
socks for boots, footie/running socks
candy-red vines, jawbreakers, twizzlers, jellybeans, hard candy, peppermint
Dunkin Dounuts coffee, creamer,
Hand sanitizer, hand lotion
microwave popcorn
Individual packs of drink mix for water bottles
crackers, cheese, peanut butter, chocolate M&Ms
power bars,,snickers marathon energy bars
trail mix, granola bars
hot choclate
blistex chap stick,
mini flashlights
Life savers, Pretzels
Beef jerky
Cards, letters, pictures and holiday appropriate items.

We will be sending Leaves of Thanksgiving to our soldiers. Please take a minute to fill one out letting them know how thankful you are for them, their service & their sacrifice. A BIG
Thank you to ____ ____ for creating the leaves.

Also, we are collecting non-breakable Christmas ornaments to send to our troops, please bring them by next Sunday if you'd like to participate.

If you'd like to contribute to the boxes we'll be delivering for the troops , please see the list in the church foyer. We are trying to get Thanksgiving & Christmas items to them in enough time for them to enjoy them.

Thank you to Pastor ____ for mailing 12 boxes at the Post Office this week

I have only four brief things to say about this.

To begin with, the church should be ashamed of the horrible job of typing and formatting that went into their bulletin. There is absolutely no excuse for this.

Secondly, as I have typed on my keyboard until my fingers were numb, U.S. troops don't defend our freedoms, and neither do they fight "over there" so we don't have to fight "over here." U.S. soldiers died unnecessarily, duped, in vain, and for a lie—all 4,500 that died in Iraq and all 1,800 that died in Afghanistan. Every death was senseless. The blood of one American soldier was not worth any "good" or any "benefit" in Iraq or Afghanistan that has resulted from these wars. And I am the one who has been called un-American and worse. Go figure.

Thirdly, why should anyone support U.S. troops fighting in unjust, immoral wars? It is our troops that have invaded and occupied foreign countries. It is our troops that have dropped the bombs, thrown the grenades, launched the missiles, fired the mortars, and shot the bullets that have resulted in the maiming and killing of hundreds of thousands of people that were no threat to the United States. Should the politicians, the president, the secretary of defense, the Joint Chiefs of Staff, and the congressmen that fund unconstitutional wars receive a share of the blame? Of course they should. But how could any Christian write a thank-you note to soldiers he doesn't even know that are invaders and occupiers engaged in these things?

And finally, what is the cause of churches adopting a unit, sending things to soldiers, thanking the troops, and polluting their church bulletins with such nonsense? The answer is two-fold. One, colossal ignorance of the U.S. government, U.S. foreign policy, American history, and the Bible. And two, holding erroneous opinions like these:

- The Republican Party is the party of God.
- A theological conservative should be a political conservative.
- Opposition to war and militarism is an exclusively left-wing idea.
- The American state is a divine institution.
- The U.S. military defends our freedoms.

Support our troops? Why would any church even think of such a thing?

* * * * *

A CONSERVATIVE CHRISTIAN WARMONGER

Finally, the truth comes out. At long last, we now know why Joe Carter is not and can never be a Christian libertarian—because he is a conservative Christian warmonger.

According to his profile at the Acton Institute PowerBlog:

> Joe Carter is a Senior Editor at the Acton Institute. Joe also serves as an editor at the The Gospel Coalition, online editor for First Things, and as an adjunct professor of journalism at Patrick Henry College. He is the co-author of *How to Argue like Jesus: Learning Persuasion from History's Greatest Communicator* (Crossway).

Although I am familiar with the Acton Institute, and appreciate its defense of the free market, I had never heard of Joe Carter until I was directed to a series of posts he wrote attacking the idea that one can be a Christian libertarian. If you are interested in reading them, see here, here, here, and here. If you are interested in reading some responses, see here, here, here, and here.

I never bothered to respond to Carter because (1) I am much too busy writing other things, (2) I have already made the case for Christian libertarianism in a lecture I gave at the Mises Institute on "Is Libertarianism Compatible with Religion?" and (3) because I have a number of friends who are in fact Christian libertarians: David Theroux of the Independent Institute, Jacob Hornberger of the Future of Freedom Foundation, William Anderson of Frostburg State University, Doug Bandow of the Cato Institute, Andrew Napolitano of Fox News, Shawn Rittenour and Jeff Herbener of Grove City College, Guido Hulsmann of the University of Angers, Lew Rockwell and Tom Woods of the Mises Institute, Norman Horn of LibertarianChristians.com, Timothy Terrell of Wofford College, Gerard Casey of University College Dublin, Jason Jewell of Faulkner University, Robert Murphy of Free Advice, Gary North of GaryNorth.com, and Jeff Tucker of Laissez Faire Books (my apologies to any of my friends I have inadvertently forgotten).

But it's not just Christian libertarianism that Carter has a problem with.

One post of his that I do feel compelled to respond to is "How to Love Liberty More Than a Libertarian Economist." The economist in question is Brian Caplan, a Professor of Economics at George Mason University who blogs at EconLog. In his attack on libertarianism, Carter refers to a post by Caplan titled "My Beautiful Bubble." To this post of Caplan, the conservative Steve Sailer replied: "Of course, if there were a big war, it would be nice to be defended by all those dreary American you despise. And, the irony is, they'd do it, too, just because you are an American." Caplan replied to Sailer's comment in another post titled "Reciprocity and Irony: A View from My Bubble." In his post, Carter reprinted the concluding part of Caplan's reply in full:

> 1. I pay good money for these protective services. So I don't see why my American defenders deserve any more gratitude than the countless other people—American and foreign—I trade with.
>
> 2. Since my American defenders are paid by heavy taxes whether I like it or not, they deserve far less gratitude than my genuine trading partners, who scrupulously respect the sanctity of my Bubble.
>
> 3. In fact, I think my American "defenders" owe me an apology. My best guess is that, on net, the U.S. armed forces increase the probability that a big war will adversely affect me. While they deter some threats, they provoke many others. If I lived in a Bubble in Switzerland (happily neutral since 1815), at least I'd know that I was getting some value for my tax dollars.

I take no sides in any dispute between Carter and Caplan or Caplan and Sailer. I only mention all of the above to provide the necessary context for Carter's closing paragraphs:

> What Caplan misses in Sailor's criticism is that the "dreary Americans" are not protecting him because of the pittance he pays in taxes. They are protecting him because they love liberty more than he does.
>
> Caplan's libertarianism leads him (rightly, I believe) to embrace pacifism. As he says, the foreign policy that follows from libertarian principles is not isolationism, but opposition to all warfare. The [sic] is internally consistent yet self-defeating since the conclusion is that libertarianism means loving liberty only to the point that you are not required to defend it by means of warfare.
>
> In contrast, I—like many other veterans in America—served my country (fifteen years in the Marine Corps) precisely because I loved freedom. I loved it so much that I was willing to sacrifice some of my own freedom, or even my life if necessary, to secure it for myself, for my nation, and for libertarian pacifists like Caplan. He is able to afford the luxury of living in his beautiful

> bubble because other Americans have bought that liberty for him. For over two centuries, American soldiers, sailors, airmen, and Marines have paid the cost necessary to allow people like him to live freely. We have provided him with the safety and security he needs to crawl off in his elite bubble and forget that people like us exist.
>
> Caplan is free to move to Switzerland, though I suspect he'll keep his Bubble in Arlington, Virginia. As a libertarian economics professor at George Mason he's smart enough to do the calculus. He knows that his optimal choice is to stay put and keep free-riding on the benefits provided by other people—whether liberal, conservative, or libertarian—who love liberty more than he does.

I want to focus on Carter's remarks about the military in the first and third paragraphs because most of the statements he makes are typical of conservatives, and especially conservative Christian warmongers.

According to the Department of Defense, "All four active services met or exceeded their numerical accession goals for fiscal year 2011." Here are the actual numbers:

> Army—64,019 accessions, with a goal of 64,000
> Navy—33,444 accessions, with a goal of 33,400
> Marine Corps—29,773 accessions, with a goal of 29,750
> Air Force—28,518 accessions, with a goal of 28,515

This means that 155,754 Americans joined the military in fiscal year 2011 (Oct. 1, 2010–Sept. 30, 2011). Does anyone besides Joe Carter actually believe that even a majority of those who joined the military did so because they loved liberty more than Brain Caplan? Could it rather have something to do with being talked into it by lying military recruiters, the billions the military spends on advertising, the No Child Left Behind Act, the promise of free money for college, the desire to get away from home, the chance to kill foreigners for real instead of just in video games, revenge for 9/11, the adventure, the world travel, family tradition, or the generous retirement benefits? I suspect the main reason is the economy; i.e., the poverty draft.

Sorry, Joe, you—like many other veterans in America—didn't serve your country. You served the state. You helped maintain a global empire of troops and bases. You helped carry out an evil interventionist foreign policy. You didn't defend anyone's freedoms. You didn't preserve the American way of life. You didn't uphold the Constitution. You didn't protect the nation. You didn't "uphold the freedoms of life, liberty and the pursuit of happiness for future generations" like the lying Marine Corps recruiting postcard says that was sent to high school students. Your death wouldn't have secured anything. Your death would have been in vain.

And as for American soldiers, sailors, airmen, and Marines paying the cost for over two centuries to allow libertarians to live freely—instead of defending our freedoms, they have jeopardized our freedoms. But don't take my word for it; take it from VMI grad and Army reservist Jacob Hornberger: "The Troops Don't Defend Our Freedoms" and "An Open Letter to the Troops: You're Not Defending Our Freedoms."

Oh, U.S. troops have been busy for over two centuries, but they have been busy doing more intervening in foreign countries than defending Americans' freedoms. Things like disaster relief, humanitarian aid, nation building, regime change, assassinations, forcibly opening markets, bombing, invading, occupying, maiming, torturing, killing, peacekeeping, enforcing UN resolutions, preemptive strikes, spreading democracy at the point of a gun, garrisoning the planet with troops and bases, training foreign armies, rebuilding infrastructure, reviving public services, unleashing civil unrest, policing the world, intervening in other countries, and fighting foreign wars.

Americans today face the triple threat of the warfare/national security/police state, largely due to conservatives in Congress (fully supported by conservative Christians outside of Congress) during the Bush years not overturning all the evils of the federal government that were already in place and adding much more evil of their own

One reason why conservative Christians like Joe Carter are so different from, and so puzzled by, Christian libertarians is because they are conservative Christian warmongers who worship the golden calf of the military.

* * * * *

SHOULD WE ASK GOD TO BLESS THE TROOPS?

If you go to church at all you've probably heard the prayer requests: "Protect our troops in harm's way," "Shield our men and women overseas from the enemy," "Keep our brave soldiers safe," "Defend our soldiers as they defend our freedoms." And even if you don't attend church, you've seen the signs outside of business and on bumper stickers: "God bless our troops."

But does anyone ever stop and consider whether we should ask God to bless the troops?

The war Afghanistan, like the war in Iraq, is a monstrous evil. U.S. troops are not defending our freedoms, protecting America, upholding the Constitution, keeping us safe from terrorists, preserving our way of life, fighting them "over there" so we don't have to fight them "over here," or any of the other blather that passes for reality now a days. To those on the receiving end of American bombs, missiles, and bullets in Afghanistan (and Pakistan, Yemen, etc.), U.S. troops are attackers, invaders, trespassers, occupiers, aggressors, and killers. I conclude with Jacob Hornberger of the Future of Freedom Foundation that

> after 10 years of invasion, occupation, torture, killings, incarcerations, renditions, assassinations, death, destruction, anger, hatred, and the constant threat of terrorist retaliation, it's time to admit that the military invasion of Afghanistan, like that of Iraq, was horribly wrong.

And as much as Americans also don't want to admit it, because these wars and military operations are unnecessary, immoral, and unjust, U.S. troops have innocent blood on their hands.

Yet, I am sometimes told, even by opponents of current U.S. military actions, that it is the president, the politicians, the ruling class, the neoconservatives, the Joint Chiefs, the military brass, the defense contractors, and/or the Congress that should be blamed for these wars.

My detractors have forgotten one important group: the soldiers that do the actual fighting. They are the ones invading, occupying, torturing, killing, maiming, incarcerating, indefinite detaining, extraordinary renditioning, assassinating, destroying property, stirring up anger and hatred against the United States, and increasing the threat of terrorist retaliation—not the president, not the politicians, not the ruling class, not the neoconservatives, not the Joint Chiefs, not the military brass, not the defense contractors, and not the Congress.

That some joined the military out of a sense of patriotism after 9/11 or that some joined the military because they were deceived by a recruiter or that some joined the military out of ignorance of U.S. foreign policy or that some joined the military because they couldn't find gainful employment still doesn't change the fact that it is the soldiers who do the actual fighting.

Yes, they are pawns in the deadly game of U.S. foreign policy, but as free moral agents they are still responsible for their actions.

So, if it is true that current U.S. military actions are morally wrong, then it stands to reason that asking God to bless the troops would not only be an exercise in futility, but downright blasphemous. And if it is true that current U.S. military actions are morally wrong, then it also stands to reason that blessing the troops would be the last thing on God's mind. I get this idea from reading Proverbs 6:16–19:

> These six things doth the LORD hate: yea, seven are an abomination unto him:
> A proud look, a lying tongue, and hands that shed innocent blood,
> An heart that deviseth wicked imaginations, feet that be swift in running to mischief,
> A false witness that speaketh lies, and he that soweth discord among brethren.

We have all heard the slogan, "The Few, the Proud, the Marines." But is there anything the Marines are doing overseas that they or we should be proud of? There are the lies about defending our freedoms by fighting in Afghanistan or being stationed in Japan. There is the innocent blood being shed in Afghanistan and Pakistan. There are wicked imaginations being devised in retaliation against insurgents who killed occupying U.S. troops. There are feet swift in running to mischief that keep open the network of brothels surrounding U.S. bases overseas. There are false witnesses who kill civilians and retroactively declare them insurgents and a threat. There is discord sown among Americans over the actions of the military.

And it's not just the Marines. Soldiers, sailors, airmen, and Marines—they all take pride in their service just as Americans take pride in them. Americans greet the troops as conquering heroes in airports. They applaud them on airplanes and in sports arenas just for being in the military. They thank them for their service in the Post Office. They recognize them in church on Memorial Day, the Fourth of July, and Veterans Day, or on the Sunday before. And the troops stand up straight and stick their chest out and take it all in.

When was the last time a soldier who "served" in Iraq or Afghanistan came home and acknowledged that what was going over there was nothing short of criminal? Sure, it has happened. And I have had many current and former soldiers write me and say as much. But when was the last time one of the tens of thousands of soldiers who have returned from a tour of duty in Iraq or Afghanistan publicly stated that he was not proud of his "service"?

Perhaps they are too concerned about their career, their rank, their next assignment, or their image? In today's economy I almost can't blame members of the military for remaining in, hanging around, lying low, and staying under the radar until retirement. I suspect that many soldiers come home with serious doubts about what they were doing in Iraq or Afghanistan and are even ashamed of what they did, but come home in such horrible shape—mentally, physically, and emotionally—that they just want to forget about it.

But there is a difference between staying under the radar until retirement and just being another government employee like a clerk at the Social Security Administration and going back to Afghanistan and being put in a position where you might shed more innocent blood, devise more wicked imaginations, engage in more mischief, spout more lies, witness more falsely, and sow more discord. Yet, many willingly return.

I have never said to not pray for the troops. But praying for the troops is not the same as asking God to bless the troops.

Pray that the troops don't shed innocent blood. Pray that the troops don't commit suicide. Pray for pastors to stop recommending military service to their young people. Pray for Christian families to stop supplying cannon fodder to the military. Pray that the troops come home. Pray that young people find employment instead of join the military. Pray for the end of military recruiters preying on young, impressionable students. Pray for an end to senseless foreign wars. Pray for an end to the U.S. empire of troops and bases that encircles the globe.

Oh, there are many things regarding the troops to pray for, but God blessing the troops should not be one of them.

* * * * *

DO SOLDIERS IMITATE CHRIST?

This past Veterans Day was especially troubling to those of us who don't go to church to see and hear the military idolatry that is unfortunately all too prevalent in many churches. The reason this year was so bad is that Veterans Day actually fell on a Sunday. It is bad enough to attend church on the Sunday before Veterans Day (or Independence Day), but it is even worse when a state holiday falls on a Sunday. Thank God Memorial Day is always observed on a Monday.

So, this past Veterans Day was the perfect day for military-loving churches to give their last full measure of devotion, so to speak, when it comes to the military: veterans dressed in their military uniforms, veterans asked to stand while they are applauded, active duty military personnel recognized, the church building and grounds decorated with flags, the pledge to the flag recited, patriotic songs sung, hymns of worship to the state sung, prayers for the troops, thanks to the troops for "keeping us safe" and "defending our freedoms," the songs of the different branches of the military played on the piano before the service or during the offering, a "Support Our Troops" message on the church sign, a video tribute to the military played during the Sunday morning church service, a special message by a military chaplain from the local base, and the glorification of the military in general.

I have observed on more than one occasion that American Christians don't seem to care how many wars their great troops are involved in, how senseless the wars, or how many lies the wars are based on. They don't seem to care how many countries their beloved troops are in, how many foreign bases they are on, or how many billions the United States spends to maintain its empire of troops and bases around the globe. They don't seem to care how many foreign civilians are killed by their glorious troops, how many are maimed and injured, or how many widows and orphans they create. It doesn't seem to matter what their great troops do, where their beloved troops do it, and to whom their glorious troops do it.

This is no more apparent than in the writings of the theologically schizophrenic Michael Milton, whom I discovered and wrote about a year ago.

Milton is the Chancellor, CEO, and The James M. Baird Jr. Chair of Pastoral Theology at Reformed Theological Seminary in Charlotte, North Carolina. Milton is also a Navy veteran, an Army Reserve chaplain, an instructor at the U.S. Army Chaplain Center & School in Fort Jackson, S.C., and a member of the American Legion, the Reserve Officers Association, and the U.S Army Chaplain Corps Regimental Association. And as I also pointed out last year, he holds to every armchair warrior, red-state fascist, reich-wing nationalist, imperial Christian fallacy known to man.

"Veterans Day is a holy day, at least for me," says Milton in an article for *byFaith*, the online magazine of the Presbyterian Church in America, "And I think that Christ is glorified, at least in my heart, when I hear the Navy hymn sung by voices that have been there, in the air, in the land, and on the sea."

In his article Milton reminiscences about being a young man and seeing a neighbor named Carl leaving for Vietnam. "I felt proud to see him go. He had his uniform on, having just returned from boot camp for a final few days of family time before being flown to Vietnam, and I was impressed," says Milton, who "loved to see young men in our country's uniforms" because it reminded him of his late father, a naval officer, who died when he was five. Milton never saw Carl alive again, but he did see the men in uniform emerge from the "white government car" a month later and tell Carl's young wife that he had been killed in Vietnam.

What made my blood boil was not that Carl died unnecessarily, duped, in vain, and for a lie, just like the thousands of U.S. soldiers who have done so in Iraq and Afghanistan, but—as senseless and as tragic as Carl's death was—because of what Milton said about soldiers in recounting his Veterans Day custom:

> Each Sunday nearest Veterans Day, I would always take time in the announcements to read from Romans 13 about "showing honor unto whom honor was due." I would ask our organist or pianist to play the service songs of each of the Armed Forces branches and for veterans to stand as they were played. I would ask them to stand for those who also served but did not come home. I always reminded them to play for the Merchant Marines, too. At the conclusion, as all were standing, I asked that we go to the Lord to pray for these and give thanks for all who would imitate Christ Jesus and serve and sacrifice so that we could be free.

Taking these last statements in reverse order—

U.S. troops fighting in foreign wars are doing everything but defending our freedoms. The more they defend our freedoms—by bombing, invading, and occupying other countries—the more enemies of the United States they create and the more our real freedoms are taken away in the name of "fighting terrorism" and "national security." Since I never "served," don't take my word for it; listen (here and here) to Army veteran and now president of the Future of Freedom Foundation, Jacob Hornberger, who has been arguing this very point for years.

Something is always sacrificed for a reason and a purpose. An accidental death is not a sacrifice. An unnecessary death is not a sacrifice. A death in vain is not a sacrifice. A senseless death is not a sacrifice. A death that is not required is not a sacrifice. The thousands of U.S. soldiers who have died fighting in Iraq and Afghanistan did not sacrifice themselves for freedom or anything else. Their lives were wasted. They were wasted because their deaths were both pointless and preventable.

Do U.S. soldiers perform any service that is honorable, necessary, and worthy of thanks? Do they defend the United States by securing its borders, guarding its shores, patrolling its coasts, or watching its skies? Fighting foreign wars is not serving. Bombing and destroying Iraq and Afghanistan is not serving. Killing hundreds of thousands of Iraqis and Afghans is not serving. Occupying countries is not serving. Playing golf on a U.S. military golf course while stationed in Japan is not serving. These are just ways of earning a paycheck for being part of the president's personal attack force.

Of course, the worst thing that Milton did was to say that soldiers imitate Christ. He went on to say this once more in his article: "Christ is the captain of our salvation, and we will serve our nation, our people, in some way, as a pale but earnest imitation of His life and death on Calvary's cross." U.S. soldiers don't deserve to be mentioned in the same sentence with the Lord Jesus Christ—the Prince of Peace. Just because Christ died and soldiers die doesn't mean that the two deaths are somehow related. Jesus Christ laid down his life for us. The American soldiers killed in Iraq and Afghanistan didn't die for us, unless you mean the U.S. imperial presidency, U.S. hegemony, the U.S. empire, the U.S. military, the U.S. military-industrial complex, U.S. foreign policy, and the U.S. national security state. Do soldiers imitate Christ when they bomb and shoot, when they invade and occupy, when they plunder and pillage, or when they maim and kill?

Rather than Veterans Day being, as Milton concludes, "a holy day when mortal men and women remind us of the service and sacrifice of Jesus Christ," I think it is rather an unholy day when mortal men and women are wrongly exalted over the service and sacrifice of Jesus Christ.

* * * * *

CHAPTER 3

CHRISTIANITY AND THE WARFARE STATE

CHRISTIANITY IN ECLIPSE

The Christian's attitude toward the state, its leaders, its military, its wars, its imperialism, and its interventionism should be a no-brainer: contempt, disdain, disgust, revulsion, abhorrence, repugnance, loathing—take your pick. Yet, among Christians one continues to find some of the greatest apologists for the state, its leaders, its institutions, and its evil doings.

Biblical Christianity is becoming eclipsed by state worship. The "obey the powers that be" mantra is still recited incessantly. The state is revered by too many Protestants as a force for good or social justice instead of the criminal gang that it is. The state's latest pronouncements about this country or that country being a threat to American interests are too often accepted by evangelicals at face value. The need for the invasion of, the bombing of, the imposing of sanctions against, or the need to take some other belligerent action toward other countries is swallowed by some Catholics like a communion wafer.

Biblical Christianity is also being eclipsed by leader worship. Instead of being viewed as a war criminal, President Bush is seen as the messiah in chief by many evangelicals, with Huckabee as his heir apparent. Any president will do, however, as long as he is a Republican, claims to be a Christian, and wants to continue killing Muslims lest they kill us first because they hate our freedoms. In spite of Bush's horrendous violations of civil liberties, his doubling of the national debt, his debacle in Iraq, and his tremendous expansion of the power of the presidency, he is still revered by way too many Christians both in and out of the evangelical community.

Biblical Christianity has been partially eclipsed by war. Some of the greatest defenders of Bush's war in Iraq are Christians. This was true when the United States first invaded Iraq, and it is just as true now, five years later. It doesn't seem to matter how senseless the war, as long as it is a Republican war. It doesn't seem to matter how many times the lies that the war was based on have been exposed, it is all just dismissed as liberal propaganda. It doesn't seem to matter how long the war lasts, since if we quit fighting them "over there" we will end up fighting them "over here." It doesn't seem to matter how much the war costs, since military spending is good for the economy. It doesn't seem to matter how many thousands of American soldiers are killed, since that number is less than the number of people killed on American highways every year. It doesn't seem to matter how many thousands of American troops are injured, since they joined the military voluntarily. It certainly doesn't seem to matter how many hundreds of thousands of Iraqis are killed, since they all hate our freedoms. It doesn't seem to matter how many thousands of Iraqis are injured, since they are all terrorists anyway. It doesn't even seem to matter if the war is not in America's best interests, since we should "obey the powers that be." It is war that breeds state worship and leader worship. Christians that are otherwise sound in the faith become idolaters when it comes to war and its architects.

Biblical Christianity has been almost totally eclipsed by the military. Although some Christians may denounce some of the abuses of the FBI, the IRS, and the BATF, they usually hold the institution of the military in high esteem. In fact, many Christians, and especially those who consider themselves evangelicals, have a military fetish. Even Christians who oppose U.S. foreign policy in general and the war in Iraq in particular are some of the most vocal defenders of the military. Churches publically honor veterans and praise them for defending our freedoms, not just on Veterans Day, but on Memorial Day, the Fourth of July, and special "military appreciation" days. Although they may decry women serving in combat roles, the feminization of the military, and the pregnancy rate of women on Navy ships, churches generally have no problem with their young men joining the military to bomb, maim, and kill for the state in some foreign war that has nothing to do with defending the United States. Because Christians are in love with the military, criticism of the military is strictly verboten, regardless of the nature of the latest U.S. foreign intervention that the troops are engaged in. Christian soldiers are expected to blindly follow their leaders when it comes to the latest country to bomb or invade. Those who question the morality of their orders, and civilian Christians who do the same, are viewed as unpatriotic, American-hating traitors who don't appreciate their freedoms that the military protects.

It is the power of the state to wage war and engage in an aggressive, imperialistic foreign policy that ought to be eclipsed by Christianity. Instead, Christians have willingly supplied the state with cannon fodder for its wars and military interventions. They have bombed, maimed, and killed for the state without hesitation. They have showed no concern or compassion for the lives of foreigners for whom Christ also died. In the name of a career, they have given of themselves to be stationed or deployed where U.S. troops have no business in going. Those not in the military have become the military's greatest supporters. Christians have become apologists for the state. They have deified its leaders instead of denigrating them as criminals. They have defended its actions instead of denouncing them as immoral. They have served the state instead of the Lord Christ.

Although there have always been (and will always be) men in history who have gloried in the state and its wars, Christians should not be numbered among them. After five years of seeing the lying, stealing, killing, liberty-destroying warfare state in action, one would think that Christians, of all people, would cease their support for the state, its military, and especially its wars. Unfortunately, and to the everlasting shame of Christians, I see no end to this statolatry in sight.

* * * * *

ELIJAH VS. THE STATE

The state has always been a lying, stealing, and killing machine.

We know this is true of the Soviet Union under Stalin, Nazi Germany under Hitler, and Red China under Mao, but as I showed in "The Lying State" and "The Murdering State," and as Jeff Knaebel recently laid out in great detail here, this is just as true of the U.S. government as it is of any other.

The reason that many people don't accept this fact is because they have the mindset that lying to, stealing from, and killing foreigners in their countries doesn't really count.

Christians seeking to justify their support for, or the participation of their friends and relatives in, the U.S. government's latest military adventure often recite the mantra, "Obey the powers that be," a loose paraphrase of Romans 13:1, as if that somehow means that Christians should blindly follow whatever the government says. But because the state is, as Murray Rothbard described it, a "bandit gang writ large," Christians should always remember the reply of the apostles when they were told to stop speaking in the name of Jesus: "We ought to obey God rather than men" (Acts 5:29). The Bible alone is the word of God, not congressional legislation or resolutions, Supreme Court decisions, the Code of Federal Regulations, or presidential executive orders. God trumps the state every time.

The nature of the state can be clearly seen in a case of eminent domain gone awry found in the Old Testament story of Naboth's vineyard (1 Kings 21:1–29). Naboth of Jezreel had a vineyard by the palace of King Ahab. Ahab wanted Naboth's land for a garden of herbs. He offered to give Naboth either a better vineyard or a cash payment. Naboth refused to sell on the grounds of ancestral law. When Ahab sulked because he couldn't get Naboth to sell, his wife, Jezebel, concocted a scheme to obtain Naboth's vineyard. She sent official government letters to the elders of Jezreel instructing them to proclaim a fast and have two false witnesses testify that Naboth blasphemed both God and the king. This resulted in Naboth and his family being stoned to death. After this, Ahab, at the instigation of his wife, "rose up to go down to the vineyard of Naboth the Jezreelite, to take possession of it" (1 Kings 21:16).

Like most tyrants, Ahab did not directly involve himself with murder. The state can always find loyal subjects who, in the name of nationalism and under the guise of patriotism, are willing to kill for the state. The two false witnesses were merely to preserve the appearance of justice. The state always seeks to cloak itself with legitimacy. And just like murder, the state never lacks for those who are willing to defend its lies. To make it easier to take people's property, the state now invokes eminent domain; that is, legalized theft. Naboth was killed under the façade of religion. Add a religious element to anything and gullible American Christians will come out in droves to support it. This is easy to do in the case of the war in Iraq. Because the United States is a "Christian nation," and was attacked by terrorists who were Muslims, the war can be turned into a modern-day crusade against Islam since Iraq is a "Muslim nation." The fact that Bush himself acknowledged that Iraq was not responsible for the September 11th attacks seems to have gone unnoticed by many American Evangelicals. Although most of these Christians may not term the war a crusade, the fact that the "enemy" is a darker-skinned heathen makes them indifferent to the death and destruction meted out by U.S. troops.

There was one man in ancient Israel who certainly didn't believe in reciting the "obey the powers that be mantra":

> And the word of the LORD came to Elijah the Tishbite, saying, Arise, go down to meet Ahab king of Israel, which is in Samaria: behold, he is in the vineyard of Naboth, whither he is gone down to possess it. And thou shalt speak unto him, saying, Thus saith the LORD, Hast thou killed, and also taken possession?
> And thou shalt speak unto him, saying, Thus saith the LORD, In the place where dogs licked the blood of Naboth shall dogs lick thy blood, even thine.
> And Ahab said to Elijah, Hast thou found me, O mine enemy? And he answered, I have found thee: because thou hast sold thyself to work evil in the sight of the LORD. (1 Kings 21:17–20).

Elijah didn't make excuses for the evil deeds of the state. He considered lying, stealing, and killing to be evil—regardless of whether it was done by or for the state.

Where are all the Elijahs today? I know they are out there. Not all Christians are defenders of King Ahab. Why are most pulpits in the land silent? They are not silent about all kinds of things that are not expressly stated in Scripture.

Instead of denouncing U.S. foreign policy as evil and the latest U.S. military adventure as immoral, too many Christians defend both in the name of nationalism and patriotism.

We need Christians today who have the spiritual discernment of Elijah. We need Christians with the backbone to say that George Bush, like King Ahab of old, has sold himself to work evil in the sight of the Lord.

* * * * *

HEROD'S HENCHMEN

> "Then Herod, when he saw that he was mocked of the wise men, was exceeding wroth, and sent forth, and slew all the children that were in Bethlehem, and in all the coasts thereof, from two years old and under, according to the time which he had diligently inquired of the wise men." ~ Matthew 2:16

Christian apologists for the state, its leaders, its military, and its wars are not known for being the most consistent group of religious people. They are, in fact, some of the most inconsistent, hypocritical, duplicitous, two-faced people—religious or irreligious—that one will encounter when it comes to people who defend the state's military adventures. They may otherwise be good, godly, conservative disciples of Christ who don't drink, smoke, dance, or gamble, but when it comes to the subjects of war, the military, and U.S. foreign policy, they can turn into crazed warmongers faster than Barack Obama used the word "change" in a campaign speech.

Ignorance greatly abounds, of course. But much of this is willful ignorance. It is one thing to be ignorant, but it is stupid to make a career out of it. Who else of all people should be opposed to war, militarism, nationalism, and imperialism than Christians who claim to believe the Bible, obey its precepts, and worship the Prince of Peace? Yet, it is conservative, evangelical, and fundamentalist Christians who continue to be among the biggest defenders of Bush's war in Iraq, the U.S. military, and American foreign policy. I know this is the case, not only because they themselves write to me and call me a liberal or a pacifist (I am neither), but because many of them are pastors whose church members write to me because they are so frustrated that their pastor is so blatantly partisan, willingly ignorant, and laughably inconsistent.

We can see the inconsistency of these imperial Christians in—of all places—the Christmas story found in the Gospel of Matthew.

Most people are familiar with the details. Wise men came to King Herod after the birth of Jesus looking for "he that is born King of the Jews" (Matthew 2:2). After finding out from the leaders of the Jews that Christ was to be born in Bethlehem, Herod instructed the wise men to "go and search diligently for the young child; and when ye have found him, bring me word again, that I may come and worship him also" (Matthew 2:8). But after finding the Christ child, and after presenting him with gold, frankincense and myrrh, the wise men were "warned of God in a dream that they should not return to Herod" (Matthew 2:12). Herod, as most rulers—ancient or modern—was a despicable individual. He was guilty of many acts of brutality, including the killing of one of his many wives and some of his children. After Joseph was instructed in a dream to flee into Egypt with the young child and his mother because "Herod will seek the young child to destroy him" (Matthew 2:13), the monster Herod, "when he saw that he was mocked of the wise men, was exceeding wroth, and sent forth, and slew all the children that were in Bethlehem, and in all the coasts thereof, from two years old and under, according to the time which he had diligently inquired of the wise men" (Matthew 2:16).

Herod did nothing of the kind.

No, I am not a Bible critic who maintains that the "massacre of the innocents" never happened or dismisses it as more hagiography than history.

Herod did nothing of the kind—but his henchmen did. Not only could Herod have not possibly killed all of these children himself; the leaders of the state always rely on their nationalistic and patriotic subjects to do their dirty work.

The first martyrs for Christ were put to death before he was. They were killed by order of the state. But just like Bush and Cheney have not themselves actually killed anyone in Iraq, Herod is likewise not guilty of actually killing any of these young children. Yet, many of the same Christians who maintain that Herod has blood on his hands go out of their way to absolve Bush and Cheney of their war crimes.

Oh, the inconsistency of Christian warmongers! Oh, the inconsistency of Christian apologists for the state and its wars!

Christian, are you one of Herod's henchmen? Would you commit infanticide if the government told you to do so? Then why did you vote for a man whose motto was "Country First"? Why do you incessantly recite your "obey the powers that be" (Romans 13:1) mantra? Why do you make excuses for the genocide that the United States has unleashed in Iraq? Why do you dismiss bombed Afghan wedding parties as collateral damage? Why do you defend an imperialistic and interventionist U.S. foreign policy? Why do you encourage us to pray for the troops as they mete out death and destruction to Iraqis in a war that has nothing to do with defense of the country? Why do you continue to support the Republican Party in light of that Party's profligate spending, massive increase in government, mockery of the Constitution, destruction of civil liberties, and open-ended wars? Why do you applaud U.S. soldiers as heroes and defenders of our freedoms when they are neither?

How many Afghan and Iraqi babies and children have been killed by the U.S. military? Sadly, many Christians not only don't know, they don't even care.

* * * * *

THE WARMONGER'S BIBLE

Two tools of government propaganda used to get young men to kill, maim, and destroy for the state are nationalism and religion. Put both together and you have a deadly combination.

Imperial Christians who equate patriotism with militarism and nationalism now have a book to guide them: *The American Patriot's Bible*.

The publisher of this new Bible is Thomas Nelson Publishers. Now, this publisher has recently published some excellent books (e.g., the works of Judge Napolitano), but *The American Patriot's Bible* is certainly not one of them.

The general editor of *The American Patriot's Bible* is Richard G. Lee, founding pastor of First Redeemer Church in Atlanta and frequent speaker at conferences and on television. Dr. Lee is the author of twelve books, a trustee of Liberty University, and a board member of the National Religious Broadcasters. He was named "Father of the Year" by the Southeastern Father's Day Council and received the Ronald Reagan Leadership Award for 2007. Lee hosted a "Restoring America" conference in 2009 with assorted Republican Party apologists.

The American Patriot's Bible is not a new translation of the Bible. It uses the *New King James Version* that was published by Thomas Nelson in 1982, but "joining with the sacred text are stories of American heroes, quotations from many of America's greatest thinkers, and beautiful illustrations that present the rich heritage and tremendous future of our nation." This is done via special introductions to each book of the Bible, twelve full-color, four-page sections inserted randomly throughout the Bible, and 254 brief articles on certain virtues and various patriotic and historical themes that appear near specific Bible verses in boxes within the text, on half pages, and sometimes on full pages. None of the articles actually comment on the biblical text. Certain words in the text are merely used as a springboard to launch into the subject of the article, which usually has nationalistic, militaristic, or political overtones. Other features of *The American Patriot's Bible* include an introduction, a subject index to the articles, a concordance to the Bible, maps, a list of the U.S. presidents, and a list of the fifty states with their dates of admission to the Union.

Before I even turned to the first book in the Bible, I realized that *The American Patriot's Bible* had a militaristic and nationalistic perspective that I was going to choke on. In addition to the usual pages in the front of some Bibles that are used to record births, deaths, and other family records, *The American Patriot's Bible* has a page to record "Military and Public Service." There is also a four-page section on "The Seven Principles of the Judeo-Christian Ethic." Now, there is certainly nothing wrong with following Judeo-Christian ethics, but under principle one, "The Dignity *of* Human Life," the attempt is made to justify U.S. military interventions around the world:

> In the Declaration of Independence our nation's Founding Fathers wrote that everyone has "unalienable rights," and that among these rights are "life, liberty, and the pursuit of happiness." We Americans not only believe this for *our* land, but also we send our brave military men and women around the world to defend the rights of those who are threatened.

Principle four, "The Right to a God-Centered Education," is also problematic because it accepts the existence of a government school system as legitimate. Any parent can give a child a God-centered education, either at home or at a Christian school. The idea that we should expect the public schools to give children a God-centered education is ludicrous. Government schools don't need to be "taken back" by Christians, they need to be abandoned.

Another disturbing sign is the prominent place given in *The American Patriot's Bible* to Abraham Lincoln—a man who is neither a role model for a Christian nor an example of a president who upheld the

Constitution. In addition to the image of the Lincoln Memorial appearing on pages I-2, I-36, and on the front of the dust jacket; Lincoln's picture appears on pages vi, 488, 832, 1058, 1401, 1456, I-30, and I-32 (twice). Lincoln appears in a montage that includes his Lincoln Memorial statue on pages 236, 266, 296, 302, 339, 371, 407, 442, 475, 516, 531, and 550; Lincoln appears in a montage that includes Mount Rushmore on pages 561, 600, 704, 743, 756, and the rear flap of the dust jacket; Lincoln is quoted on pages I-2, I-32, I-36, 302, 488, 718, 823, 832, 527, 528, 1037, 1058, and 1328; Lincoln is mentioned on pages 78, 808, 1035, 1099, 1114, 1448, 1456, and I-37; Lincoln is discussed on pages I-30, 518, and 1401.

Like most study Bibles, each biblical book in *The American Patriot's Bible* is preceded by a brief one-page introduction. But there are two things that are different about these introductions.

First of all, at the top of the page of the introduction and the first page of the biblical book there is a montage that includes images of soldiers and/or naval ships, military aircraft, flags, national monuments, or national symbols. On the introduction page to each of the New Testament Gospels there is an image of soldiers raising a flag underneath the banner of the national motto "In God We Trust." All of the other books in the New Testament open with a montage containing the Statue of Liberty on the left with troops marching on the right.

The second thing that is disturbing about the book introductions is their content. Each introduction contains a paragraph that tries to relate the theme of the biblical book to some patriotic or nationalistic theme or an event in American history. For an example in the Old Testament, we can turn to the book of Nehemiah. The theme of the book is said to be "godly leadership." But who is put forth as an example of a godly leader like Nehemiah? It is the wretched Franklin Roosevelt. In the introduction to 2 Thessalonians in the New Testament, we read about how the Apostle Paul "always moved quickly to deal with heresy before it could damage the churches." We are told that he used the authority of his apostleship and did not seek anyone's permission. This is applied to George W. Bush saying that "America will never seek a permission slip to defend the security of our country." Then we are told that after the 9/11 attacks Bush "immediately announced a Global War on Terrorism, which commenced with the invasion of Afghanistan and the overthrow of the Taliban regime and Al-Quada." It is nothing short of sacrilege to mention George WMD Bush in the same paragraph with the Apostle Paul.

The subjects of the twelve four-page color sections that appear throughout *The American Patriot's Bible* are: The Bible and American Presidents, Christianity in Colonial America, Faith of the Founders, The

American Revolution, The Great Awakening, The Bible and American Education, Christianity and the American Frontier, The Civil War, Monuments to American Patriotism, World War II, Christianity and Equal Rights, The Bible and Famous Americans.

In the section titled "The Bible and American Presidents" we are given quotes about the Bible from eleven presidents. This is all well and good, but no one should think for a minute that these eleven men put into practice the precepts of the book they spoke so highly of. In "Faith and the Founders" we are told that 93 percent of the delegates to the Constitutional Convention "were members of Christian churches." If this is true then the fact that the Constitution never mentions the Lord Jesus Christ other than a reference to "the year of our Lord" is even more disturbing. The section on World War II is especially disheartening with its picture of the loathsome FDR, its claim that Japan, Italy, and Germany wanted to rule the world, and its simplistic explanation of the coming of the war. The picture of a smiling President Obama in the section titled "Christianity and Equal Rights" is also disturbing. What is a man doing pictured in a Bible who was the most liberal member of the U.S. Senate, who has spent his life in the service of racial preference, who has had the most radical of associations, who practices an aberrant Christianity, who orders and jokes about Predator drone attacks, and who is an economic corporatist that believes in the redistribution of wealth?

The third major feature of *The American Patriot's Bible* is its 254 articles on certain virtues and various patriotic and historical themes. The articles are a mixed bag of virtues, principles, patriotism, nationalism, and militarism, with a heavy emphasis on U.S. presidents.

The small articles in boxes near specific biblical verses contain quotes from famous people about God, the Bible, religion in society, or some virtue, tell us where in the Bible a particular president placed his hand when he took the presidential oath of office, and reference certain events and documents in American history. Seeing the first one, which appears on page 44, made me nauseous—it is a quote on freedom from the evil warmonger and torture master Dick Cheney. Even worse is the sight of a quote from Colin Powell on U.S. foreign military interventions that goes with John 3:16. It is implied to the reader that just as "God so loved the world that he gave" so the United States sends its "fine men and women into great peril to fight for freedom beyond our borders," asking nothing in return but enough land to bury our dead soldiers.

When these articles take up a page or half a page, it is more of the same, but with longer quotes and the addition of images. Presidential warmongers are prominently featured: FDR on page 217, George W. Bush on page 292, Woodrow Wilson on page 586, Abraham Lincoln on page

1058, and Theodore Roosevelt on page 1071. This is fitting since the focus of the articles is often times related to war. This time, however, it wasn't until the second one that I became nauseous. Appearing on page 6, it is the story behind and words of the blasphemous "patriotic" song *The Battle Hymn of the Republic*. The identification of the slave-owning George Washington as the "American Moses" (p. 64) is ludicrous as is the quote from the denier of Christ's deity and miracles, Thomas Jefferson, on the moral precepts of Jesus (p. 1096).

The last thing I want to read about in the notes of a Bible is something about a U.S. president. Although some of the historical information in *The American Patriot's Bible* is interesting and informative, it belongs in a separate book, not in the word of God. And the American history that is presented is highly selective.

Gregory Boyd, the author of the highly-recommended book *The Myth of a Christian Nation: How the Quest for Political Power Is Destroying the Church* (Zondervan, 2006), has written several times about *The American Patriot's Bible*. Because the conclusions he has reached are also my own, I will simply list some of them here:

- It unashamedly glorifies nationalistic violence
- Selective retelling of American history
- Overt celebration of America's violent victories over our national enemies
- The text of the Bible is used merely as an excuse to further the patriotic agenda of the commentators
- The glory of nationalistic violence permeates this Bible
- The commentators attempt to give their idealized version of American history divine authority by weaving it into the biblical narrative
- The biblical text has been reduced to nothing more than an artificial pretext to further a particular nationalistic and political agenda
- Saturated with this nationalistic, "fight-for-God-and-country," mindset
- A very high percentage of the commentaries sprinkled throughout this Bible exalt American wars and their heroes
- Offers no commentary on any passages related to our instruction to love and do good to our enemies
- A version of the Bible whose sole purpose is to reinforce the nationalism and celebrate the military victories of a particular country
- Virtually incarnates the nationalistic idolatry that has afflicted

the Church for centuries
- It excludes from consideration almost every aspect of American history that could blemish the image of America or its heroes
- Especially in the Old Testament, an explicit parallel is drawn between Israel and America
- This intense glorification of national violence constitutes a central theme of this ill-conceived Bible

You can read Boyd's blog posts about *The American Patriot's Bible* here and here and his review here.

"If you love America and the Scriptures, you will treasure this Bible," says the introduction to *The American Patriot's Bible.* I think it would be more accurate to say that if you love American exceptionalism, American nationalism, American imperialism, and American militarism, you will treasure this Bible. Many Christians who love America *and* the Scriptures know better than to equate patriotism with any of these things.

* * * * *

ROMANS 13 AND NATIONAL DEFENSE

> "Let every soul be subject unto the higher powers. For there is no power but of God: the powers that be are ordained of God.
> Whosoever therefore resisteth the power, resisteth the ordinance of God: and they that resist shall receive to themselves damnation.
> For rulers are not a terror to good works, but to the evil. Wilt thou then not be afraid of the power? do that which is good, and thou shalt have praise of the same:
> For he is the minister of God to thee for good. But if thou do that which is evil, be afraid; for he beareth not the sword in vain: for he is the minister of God, a revenger to execute wrath upon him that doeth evil.
> Wherefore ye must needs be subject, not only for wr ath, but also for conscience sake" (Romans 13:1–5).

Christian apologists for the state, its leaders (when they are Republicans), its military, its spy agencies, and especially its wars (and especially when they are started by Republicans) sometimes refer to the above passage from the Book of Romans as if it somehow justifies their blind nationalism, their cheerleading for the Republican Party, their childish devotion to the military, their acceptance of national-security state, and their support for perpetual war.

There is no greater abuse of this passage than when it is applied to national defense. I have come across two examples of this recently.

The first is from an exchange between a reader of my columns and his theologian friend. Earlier this year, when the United States had just begun its military adventure in Libya, a reader informed me of a conversation with a friend who happened to be a theologian and seminary professor. Said professor posted something on Facebook about Libya and how Obama the evil Democrat wouldn't hesitate to use force on Americans if they tried to institute a new government like the Libyans. My reader agreed, but then added: "So would Bush. Statism knows no party." The response of the theologian was simply: "Governments have a God-given right to defend themselves. Romans."

Pointing out the similarities between Obama the Democrat and Bush the Republican is a cardinal sin according to some Christian conservatives. Although Bush expanded federal spending on and control over education, expanded Medicare to greater heights than LBJ ever dreamed, started two unnecessary wars, doubled the national debt, had bailout and stimulus programs, increased farm subsidies and foreign aid, increased government spending and regulations, gave us the first trillion-dollar budget deficit, instituted torture, violated civil liberties, and expanded the police state—none of this matters because he was a Christian and a Republican.

As for Bush's ecumenical, inclusive, warped, and unorthodox Christianity, I have dealt with that in an article here. As for the failings (to put it mildly) of the Republican Party, I have written about them here and in many other articles.

And to say that Romans 13 has anything to do with a government defending itself is absolutely ludicrous. Being a warmonger and military apologist makes even some of the best Bible students lose their mind.

The second example of theological lunacy is from a column by Craig Parshall about the killing of Osama bin Laden (which he favored) in the magazine *Israel My Glory*. Parshall is senior vice president and general counsel for the National Religious Broadcasters.

In response to the question he raised of "Can Christians ethically support the U.S. government's deliberate targeting of individuals for death?," Parshall says:

> Christians who urge pacifism by citing Jesus' commandments about peace (i.e., Mt. 5:9) miss the point. They fail to recognize the theological distinctions between individual responsibility to seek peace with others (Rom. 12:18) and the corporate responsibility of government to use lethal force (the "sword," Rom. 13:1–7) to protect citizens from "evildoers" (1 Pet. 2:13–14).

Opposing the extra-judicial assassination of Osama bin Laden has nothing to do with pacifism. Moreover, even Christians who oppose the death penalty might change their minds if bin Laden had been lawfully tried, found guilty, and sentenced to death. And just because the "powers that be" bear the sword doesn't mean that the state should execute people without trial. More importantly, however, to say that Romans 13 has anything to do with a government defending its citizens is ludicrous.

I can't resist commenting on something Parshall says in the next paragraph of his article: "In all of the New Testament references to soldiers and Roman centurions, there is no suggestion that their work, which often involved using force and violence against others, was somehow sinful or inappropriate." So, the soldiers who scourged, smote, and crucified the Son of God didn't do anything sinful or inappropriate? I thought so.

I have been asked many times over the years to write something on Romans 13. Although this is something I have thought a great deal about and know that I must eventually do, this brief look at Romans 13 and national defense is not that article. Actually, a large monograph or small book is what is called for.

In the meantime, here is a collection of comments of mine on Romans 13 in my LRC articles.

From "Christian Killers?" (December 2, 2004):

> To justify their consent or silence, and to keep their congregations in line, Christian leaders repeat to their parishioners the mantra of "obey the powers that be," a loose paraphrase of Romans 13:1, as if that somehow means that they should blindly follow whatever the president or the government says, and even worse, that it overturns the commandment "Thou shalt not kill" (Exodus 20:13; Deuteronomy 5:17), which is repeated in the New Testament (Matthew 19:18; Romans 13:9). The way some Christians repeat the "obey the powers that be" mantra, one would think that they would slit their own mothers' throats if the state told them to do so.

From "The Warmonger's Psalm" (June 2, 2005):

> This love affair that many conservative, evangelical, and fundamentalist Christians have with the military is grounded in their blind obedience to the government, based on an unrestricted, absolute interpretation of Romans 13:1, from which they have derived the "obey the powers that be" mantra. Of course, this obedience to the state is very selective, which shows what

hypocrites these people are. None of these Christians would kill their mother if the government told them to do so, but they would see nothing wrong with killing someone else's mother if the state gave them a uniform and a gun.

From "The Hypocrisy of Christian Warmongers" (August 11, 2006):

Christian warmongers don't really believe their own mantras. When they chant "obey the powers that be," "obey magistrates," and "submit yourselves to every ordinance of man," it doesn't actually mean anything. Since the war in Iraq began, Christian warmongers have turned these portions of Scripture into their mantras in order to justify the war. None of them actually believe that a Christian should always accept the latest government pronouncement, support the latest government program, or obey the government in every respect. It was all a ruse to justify an unjust war. If the government commands one of these Christians to shoot his neighbor and destroy his property, he will choose to disobey and suffer the consequences—just like if the government commands one of these Christians to shoot an Israeli and destroy his property.

So, if a Christian warmonger doesn't really believe that Christians should always obey the state, then why does he lie and say that they should? Christian warmongers hide behind their mantras because they are trying to defend a president, a party, and a movement that are undefendable. Should a Christian have served in Hitler's army? What about Stalin's? Why not? Should a Christian have participated in the Holocaust or in one of the Russian czar's pogroms? Why not? Christian warmongers are very selective about which governments they think Christians should obey. Despite their rhetoric, they really don't think that everyone should blindly follow whatever the president or the government says. The bottom line is that the command for the New Testament Christian to "be subject unto the higher powers" (Romans 13:1) is not absolute.

From "Elijah vs. the State" (August 4, 2008):

Christians seeking to justify their support for, or the participation of their friends and relatives in, the U.S. government's latest military adventure often recite the mantra, "Obey the powers that be," a loose paraphrase of Romans 13:1, as if that somehow means that Christians should blindly follow whatever the government

> says. But because the state is, as Murray Rothbard described it, a "bandit gang writ large," Christians should always remember the reply of the apostles when they were told to stop speaking in the name of Jesus: "We ought to obey God rather than men" (Acts 5:29).

From "Herod's Henchmen" (December 25, 2008):

> Christian, are you one of Herod's henchmen? Would you commit infanticide if the government told you to do so? Then why did you vote for a man whose motto was "Country First"? Why do you incessantly recite your "obey the powers that be" (Romans 13:1) mantra?

From "Is Libertarianism Compatible With Religion?" (March 15, 2011):

> Some Christians get hung up on Romans 13 and end up making apologies for the state and its wars. It's too bad they skipped over Romans 12:
>
> Bless them which persecute you: bless, and curse not. (Romans 12:14)
>
> Recompense to no man evil for evil. (Romans 12:17)
>
> Dearly beloved, avenge not yourselves, but rather give place unto wrath: for it is written, Vengeance is mine; I will repay, saith the Lord. (Romans 12:19)
>
> Overcome evil with good. (Romans 12:21)

I have also quoted and/or discussed what three authors have written about Romans 13. "A Christian Against the State" is a review of *Christian Theology of Public Policy: Highlighting the American Experience*, by John Cobin. "The Doctrine of a Christian Warmonger" is a critique of a presentation by Pastor Tod Kennedy called "The Doctrine of God and War." "Can a Christian Kill for His Government?" is a review of a book of the same name by Bennie Lee Fudge.

There are a lot of things that could be said about Romans 13, but that it has reference to national defense is not one of them.

* * * * *

ROMANS 13 AND OBEYING THE GOVERNMENT

I said last year in my article on "Romans 13 and National Defense" that I had been asked many times over the years to write something on Romans 13, that it was something I had thought about a great deal, and that it was something I knew that I must eventually do. Unfortunately, this is still not that article. However, because of questions about Romans 13 that I recently received and answered, I thought I would expand upon my answer here.

First, the text:

> Let every soul be subject unto the higher powers. For there is no power but of God: the powers that be are ordained of God.
> Whosoever therefore resisteth the power, resisteth the ordinance of God: and they that resist shall receive to themselves damnation.
> For rulers are not a terror to good works, but to the evil. Wilt thou then not be afraid of the power? do that which is good, and thou shalt have praise of the same:
> For he is the minister of God to thee for good. But if thou do that which is evil, be afraid; for he beareth not the sword in vain: for he is the minister of God, a revenger to execute wrath upon him that doeth evil.
> Wherefore ye must needs be subject, not only for wr ath, but also for conscience sake (Romans 13:1–5).

Christian apologists for the state's military "defending our freedoms" and its wars "over there so we don't have to fight them over here" incessantly quote their "obey the powers that be" mantra derived from Romans 13 in an attempt to justify their blind nationalism, American exceptionalism, flag waving, God and country rhetoric, warmongering, prayers for the troops, illicit affection for the military, and unholy desire to legitimize killing in war—as well as justify the state's imperialism, militarism, and unjust wars.

But even worse than Christian warmongers reciting their "obey the powers that be" mantra, is the chant of "Romans 13" after some statement justifying war or the military:

> The war in Iraq was a just war. Romans 13. The troop surge was necessary. Romans 13. Dropping the atomic bombs on Japan was necessary. Romans 13. President Bush did the right thing with the intelligence he had. Romans 13. Iraq had weapons of mass destruction. Romans 13. Collateral damage happens. Romans 13.

> The Vietnam War was necessary to fight communism. Romans 13. My country, right or wrong. Romans 13. Soldiers are just following orders. Romans 13. We must fight them "over there" so we don't have to fight them "over here." Romans 13. Osama bin Laden needed to be killed. Romans 13. Governments have a God-given right to defend themselves. Romans 13. Waterboarding is not torture. Romans 13. Drone strikes are necessary to protect Americans. Romans 13. Support the troops. Romans 13.

The chant of "Romans 13" is used to put a divine stamp of approval on U.S. wars and militarism. It is never used to put a divine stamp of approval on other countries' wars and militarism, unless, of course, they are allied with the United States at the time.

Now, regarding Romans 13, I just want to briefly mention five things to provide a longer and more thought-out answer to that which I recently gave a young man who is now, thank God, out of the military.

First of all, it won't do any good to explain it away, correct it, revise it, limit it to godly governments, or limit it to the Constitution. This is because there are two other passages that are even more explicit:

> Put them in mind to be subject to principalities and powers, to obey magistrates, to be ready to every good work, (Titus 3:1)

> Submit yourselves to every ordinance of man for the Lord's sake: whether it be to the king; as supreme; Or unto governors, as unto them that are sent by him for the punishment of evildoers, and for the praise of them that do well. For so is the will of God, that with well doing ye may put to silence the ignorance of foolish men: (1 Peter 2:13–15)

Second, I continue to be puzzled that some Christians stumble over this. Only a madman would say that obeying the government in Romans 13 is absolute. Even the most diehard Christian apologist for the state, its military, and its wars would never think of saying such a thing. Although the way some Christians repeat the "obey the powers that be" mantra may make one think they would slit their own mothers' throats if the state told them to do so, they wouldn't do it no matter how they were threatened by the state. If government agents came to them and said, "Here, put on this uniform, take this gun, and go shoot your neighbor," they would likewise refuse and suffer the consequences. No Christian is going to make his wife get an abortion because the government says he has too many children. No Christian is going to accept every government pronouncement, support every government program, or blindly follow whatever the president or the government says—even when the Republicans are in control. Any admonition in Scripture to obey the government is tempered by command to "obey God rather than men" (Acts 5:29) and the sixth commandment "Thou shalt not kill" (Exodus 20:13), which is repeated in Romans 13:9.

Third, what about Christians in other countries? Shouldn't they also "obey the powers that be"? Aren't their powers that be likewise ordained of God? What if their government instructs them to conduct drone attacks in the United States, bomb the United States, commit acts of terrorism against the United States, or invade the United States? Aren't they resisting the ordinance of God if they don't do it? Should all Christian soldiers in the German army during World War II have disobeyed orders and laid down their weapons when America entered the war? Christian warmongers are such hypocrites. They are very selective about which governments they think Christians should obey. What they really mean by their mantra is that all people everywhere in the world should only obey the powers that be in the United States.

Fourth, obedience is not really the issue. Obeying the government is not absolute when the government commands something that is contrary to the word of God. The problem with the former-Marine pastor of the former soldier who wrote to me and other Christian warmongers is in what they believe to be contrary to the word of God. It is here that we are at an impasse. When someone defends unjust foreign wars (are there any other kind?), bloated military budgets, torture, drone strikes, bombing campaigns, secret prison camps, indefinite detention, CIA meddling and black ops, almost anything the military does, an empire of troops and bases around the world, and an interventionist U.S. foreign policy in general as not contrary to the word of God as long as it is Americans are doing these things to foreigners and not foreigners to Americans, I say that he is a Christian warmonger who needs to rethink his position. So the issue is not actually obedience, it is what constitutes something contrary to the word of God. The real issue is what extent of disobedience is obedience to God.

Fifth, Christians who recite their "obey the powers that be" mantra and chant "Romans 13" when they want to put a divine stamp of approval on U.S. wars and militarism are falsely leading people to believe that defending U.S. wars and military interventions has something to do with obeying the government. Obeying the government has nothing to do with believing everything the government says, accepting everything the government does, supporting the government's troops, or defending the government's wars. The U.S. government hasn't commanded any American to think or say that the war on terror is a good thing, that the wars in Iraq and Afghanistan are just wars, that U.S. foreign policy should be supported, that prayers should be made for U.S. troops, or that the U.S. Navy is "a global force for good." And the government certainly hasn't commanded any individual to go kill and maim on its behalf in Iraq and Afghanistan. There is no draft. No one was forced to join the military. And no one who bothered to study U.S. military history for five minutes would have joined before these wars began and not known that there was a chance he would have to kill and maim for the state.

In conclusion, I will just say this.

When I see a sign in a government-owned park that says "Don't Walk on the Grass," I don't walk on the grass. When I see a sign at a government-owned zoo that says "Don't Feed the Animals," I don't feed the animals. When a situation arises like when I see a sign on the Interstate that says "Speed Limit 65" while everyone is passing me doing 75, I speed up, but always mindful that some connoisseur of coffee and doughnuts might be lurking around the bend, just waiting to give me a ticket.

But when I am told to sit at a desk and kill foreigners via drone, fly over some foreign country and drop bombs, invade some foreign country that was no threat to the United States, indefinitely detain some foreigner in prison without trial, or occupy some foreign country that I would have to look up on a map to know where it was, I dissent and refuse to obey.

* * * * *

CHAPTER 4

CHRISTIANITY AND TORTURE

WATERBOARD AN A-RAB FOR JESUS

In a recent column, Eric Margolis labeled the Republicans as "America's champion of war and torture." Those are some harsh words—harsh but true.

The recent release of the Bush torture memos and the revelation that the CIA waterboarded Abu Zubaydah 83 times and Khalid Sheik Mohammed 183 times *before* Bush claimed that we don't torture has elicited a predictable response from conservative Christians who think the Republican Party is the party of God: silence.

It is also no surprise that a new survey by the Pew Research Center for the People & the Press shows that of four major religious traditions in the United States (white evangelical Protestant, white non-Hispanic Catholic, white mainline Protestant, and unaffiliated), white evangelical Protestants are more likely to believe that the use of torture against suspected terrorists can often or sometimes be justified. In fact, the more often people attended church, the more likely they were to justify torture.

A similar poll commissioned last year by Faith in Public Life and Mercer University reported that almost 60 percent of Southern evangelicals believed that torture was often or sometimes justified.

When the Spanish did it, it was torture. When the Japanese did it, it was torture. When the Germans did it, it was torture. When the Khmer Rouge did it, it was torture. But when waterboarding was done by Americans under a Republican administration, it suddenly became an "enhanced interrogation technique."

Such has not always been the case. Waterboarding-like techniques used by American soldiers during the Philippine Insurrection and the Vietnam War were condemned. But that was before the "war on terror" where anything goes in the name of "national security."

"Khalid Sheikh Mohammed was not waterboarded 183 times," says a Republican hack at Fox News. That number is "highly misleading" and a "vast inflation" because "the much-cited figure represents the number of times water was poured onto Mohammed's face—not the number of times the CIA applied the simulated-drowning technique on the terror suspect."

Okay, so how many "pours" does take to be waterboarded? If a prisoner is removed from his cell, taken to an interrogation room, forced to endure one "pour," and then taken back to his cell—can we not say he was waterboarded because he only suffered one "pour"?

And what about Abu Zubaydah? In addition to being waterboarded, he had a collar wrapped around his neck, was smashed against a wall, was forced to stay in a pitch-dark box for hours, was stripped naked, was suspended from hooks in the ceiling, and was deprived of sleep. Is it not torture if these things only happened one time?

The strict constitutionalist at Fox, Judge Andrew Napolitano, who actually read the 175 pages of torture memos, sees things differently from the defenders of the Bush regime at his network: "This is not rocket science and it is not art. Everyone knows torture when they see it; and no amount of twisted logic can detract from its illegal horror, its moral antipathy, and its attack at core American values."

Who are these CIA operatives that engage in waterboarding and other forms of torture? What kind of a man does such a thing? The FBI does profiles of serial killers. How about a profile of a CIA agent who tortures prisoners, in the interest of national security, of course?

Are these men Christians? I suppose they are. The majority of Americans claim to be a Christian of some sort. Can a Christian waterboard an A-rab for Jesus?

For the Christian, there is no other way to do it. The Bible says: "And whatsoever ye do in word or deed, do all in the name of the Lord Jesus, giving thanks to God and the Father by him" (Colossians 3:17). It also says that whatsoever we do, we should "do it heartily, as to the Lord" (Colossians 3:23). We should do everything "to the glory of God" (1 Corinthians 10:31).

Can a Christian smash someone against a wall in the name of the Lord Jesus? Can a Christian heartily lock someone in a dark box for hours at a time? Can a Christian deprive someone of sleep to the glory of God? Can a Christian give thanks to God while he hangs someone from the ceiling?

Sure he can, but not without violating the whole tenor of the New Testament.

Christians are told to put off anger, wrath, and malice (Colossians 3:8), to not render evil for evil (1 Thessalonians 5:15), to not give offense (1 Corinthians 10:30), to abstain from all appearance of evil (1 Thessalonians 5:22), to not be a brawler (Titus 3:2), and to abhor that which is evil (Romans 12:9). I think this rules out waterboarding.

Okay, but suppose the perpetrators of torture in the CIA do not claim to be Christians and don't care what the New Testament says? Well, does that mean it is okay if Christians cheer them on? If not, then what should Christians do? Should they just be indifferent?

John the Baptist told Herod: "It is not lawful for thee to have her" when he married his brother's wife (Matthew 14:4). He also told Roman soldiers to "do violence to no man" (Luke 3:14). Why aren't Christians doing likewise?

Why aren't Christians letting the CIA and the military know that waterboarding is torture and that torture is wrong? Could it be that these institutions are filled with Christians? Could it be that Christians respect these institutions? Could it be that Christians trust these institutions? I think all of the above are true.

Where is the outrage from the evangelical community over these torture memos? I'll tell you where. It is in the same place as the outrage over the invasion of Iraq, the thousands upon thousands of dead Iraqis, the over four thousand American soldiers who died for a lie, the bloodbath that Iraq has become, the Guantanamo prison camp, the CIA secret prisons, the destruction of liberty in America due to the war on terror, and America's evil foreign policy.

Christians should be leaving the Republican Party in droves. Christians should be crawling on broken glass as penance for blindly supporting the Republican Party. Christians should be repenting in sackcloth and ashes for thinking the Republican Party was the party of God.

Instead, even as more and more crimes of the Bush administration come to light, I fear that Christians who are outraged, and rightly so, at the crimes of the Obama administration and the Democrats will look in the next election to the Republicans as their savior instead of the champions of war and torture.

America needs more Christians like John the Baptist instead of John Hagee.

* * * * *

CHRISTIANS FOR TORTURE

The most ardent atheist would be rendered speechless should he hear of Christians for abortion, profanity, adultery, or drunkenness. Of all people in the world, it is certainly Christians—and especially the conservative, evangelical, and fundamentalist kind—that atheists, agnostics, and infidels expect to be opposed to these things.

So what in the world is an atheist to think when he sees the widespread Christian support for torture? Yes, torture. But don't

Christians claim to follow the ethics of Jesus and the apostles in the New Testament? Aren't Christians commanded to put off anger, wrath, and malice (Colossians 3:8), "be ready to every good work" (Titus 3:1), and "live peaceably with all men" (Romans 12:18)? Yes, Christians.

What is really tragic is that most Christians who of late have weighed in on the subject of torture are not arguing whether or not waterboarding and other "enhanced interrogation techniques" constitute torture—they readily admit that they do—but that torture is justified in the name of fighting terrorism, national security, defending our freedoms, keeping us safe, or protecting our children and grandchildren.

In my recent article "Waterboard an A-rab for Jesus," I mentioned two polls which showed that a great percentage of evangelicals supported the use of torture against suspected terrorists. Now come two additional surveys that are even more shocking. When an Allen Hunt Show poll asked for views on torture, 50 percent of the participants indicated their preference for the position: "Am A Christian—And I Support Torture." Hunt himself, thank God, is opposed to the practice. And in a story on OneNewsNow (a division of the American Family New Network) about Southern Baptist leader Richard Land saying that the use of waterboarding is unethical, a poll asked simply: "Do you agree with Dr. Land? Is waterboarding 'unethical'?" The results: less than 10 percent agreed with Land. What is interesting about Land is that he fully supports Bush's war on terror, minus the torture, of course.

These are unbelievable poll results. Christian torture advocates should be ashamed of themselves for being so ignorant of New Testament ethics. This is FrontPage Magazine Christianity. This is National Review Christianity. This is imperial Christianity at its worse. I lay a great deal of the blame on pastors for being servants of the state instead of servants of Christ. It is pastors who ought to be teaching and warning their congregations about what is wrong with the U.S. empire, the U.S. military, the CIA, U.S. wars, and U.S. foreign policy. Instead, we have pastors that lead their congregations to pledge to the flag, sing praise to the state on every national holiday, and honor the U.S. war machine on special military appreciation days.

It is one thing for Christians to think that the Republican Party is the lesser of two evils, that we should be fighting a global war on terror, that U.S. troops are defending our freedoms by fighting in Iraq and Afghanistan, that we are protecting Israel by fighting against terrorism, that it is "liberal" to be opposed to war, that we should fight them "over there" lest we have to fight them "over here," or that Iraq attacked us on 9/11 (all completely bogus ideas)—but this in no way justifies torture.

We didn't torture Nazi war criminals to reveal the names of others similarly guilty. Although we sentenced some of them to death, and some of them to prison terms, we never tortured them even though they were guilty of genocide. We don't torture serial killers to get them to reveal where all the bodies of their victims are buried. Even when we call them monsters and sentence them to death, we still don't torture them. We don't allow police to torture suspects until they confess to committing a crime, and neither do we allow confessions obtained by torture to be used in court. Heck, we didn't even torture Saddam Hussein when we captured and imprisoned him.

We associate torture with Japan (American WWII POWs), North Korea (American Korean War POWs), China (recently deceased Air Force Colonel Harold E. Fischer), and Vietnam (just ask John McCain).

We associate torture with third-world prisons, the KGB, the Stasi, and other secret police organizations, the Dark Ages, the Inquisition, the Holocaust, the Reign of Terror, mass murderers, massacres, and genocides.

We associate torture with the Soviet Union under Stalin, China under Mao, Germany under Hitler, Korea under Kim Il-sung, Cuba under Castro, Cambodia under Pol Pot, Iraq under Saddam Hussein, and Uganda under Idi Amin.

We associate torture with everything that is evil, vile, and inhuman.

What have we come to in the United States when people who name the name of Christ support torture? How dare Christians criticize Muslims for saying that Islam is a religion of peace and then advocate the torturing of suspected terrorists? By their support for torture, Christians have given "great occasion to the enemies of the LORD to blaspheme" (2 Samuel 12:14).

* * * * *

THE MORALITY OF TORTURE

Everyone follows some sort of a moral code, even atheists. Jews have the Old Testament or the Talmud. Christians have the New Testament or the Bible. Other religions have their particular holy books. Non-religious people subscribe to natural law, the Golden Rule, altruism, or some other ism.

Every moral code shares some basic similarities: it is wrong to lie, cheat, steal, rape, murder—and torture.

The current debate over the morality of the U.S. government engaging in torture has revealed many Americans who profess to adhere to a moral code to be hypocrites. Now we are being told that, because the end (saving American lives) justifies the means (torture), the use of torture is justified under certain circumstances.

Christians especially are being hypocritical since they have historically condemned situation ethics and the decline of moral absolutes. They are also cautioned in the New Testament not to do evil that good may come (Romans 3:8).

What some Americans are now advocating is the torture of suspected terrorists held in Guantánamo and other prisons. Real terrorists, like foreigners Ramzi Yousef and Zacarias Moussaoui and American José Padilla, have been charged for their crimes, convicted in federal court, and are currently incarcerated in U.S. prisons.

Let us assume for the sake of argument that terrorists are those that fight against a U.S. invasion of their country and not vice versa, that men held in places like Guantánamo are really suspected terrorists and are not there merely because they were wrongly picked up by bounty hunters paid by the U.S. government, and that torture does in fact result in valuable information being revealed that could prevent a terrorist attack and save American lives.

If it is morally permissible to torture a *suspected* terrorist in an *attempt* to gain information that *may* save American lives, then:

- Is it morally permissible to torture a suspected terrorist *who is a child* in an attempt to gain information that may save American lives? If not, then why not?
- Is it morally permissible to torture a suspected terrorist *who is a woman* in an attempt to gain information that may save American lives? If not, then why not?
- Is it morally permissible to torture *by any means* a suspected terrorist in an attempt to gain information that may save American lives? If not, then why not?
- Is it morally permissible to torture a suspected terrorist *even if it results in his permanent disability* in an attempt to gain information that may save American lives? If not, then why not?
- Is it morally permissible to torture a suspected terrorist *even if it results in his death* in an attempt to gain information that may save American lives? If not, then why not?

Is it morally permissible to do any of the above if it may save just one American life? If not, then why not?

I am afraid that many American torture advocates would not have a problem with any of the above, even if it might only save just one American life.

But if the goal is possibly saving American lives, then what about torturing American citizens who might know about American lives being in jeopardy? Is it morally permissible to torture a suspected terrorist *who is an American* in an attempt to gain information that may save American lives? If not, then why not? What about American woman and children? Are all means of torture acceptable or are there certain forms of torture that are only reserved for foreigners? What if the suspected American terrorist becomes disabled or dies as a result of the torture?

Again, if the goal is possibly saving American lives, then what about torturing American citizens who are *not* suspected terrorists but might know about American lives being in jeopardy? Is it morally permissible to torture *a suspect in police custody* in an attempt to gain information that may save American lives? If not, then why not? But what if the suspect is a woman or a child? And may any form of torture be used or are there certain forms of torture that are off limits for suspects in police custody? What if the suspect in police custody becomes disabled or dies as a result of the torture?

But why stop with suspects in police custody. I mean, if the goal is possibly saving American lives, then what about torturing Americans in their homes who might know about American lives being in jeopardy? And what about travelling overseas to torture foreigners in their homes? Is it morally permissible to torture *anyone anywhere* in an attempt to gain information that may save American lives? If not, then why not?

Just think about the potential benefits of torture for local law enforcement. Drug users could be tortured until they reveal the names of their dealers. Serial killers could be tortured until they reveal where they buried their dead bodies. Pedophiles could be tortured until they reveal the names of the children they have victimized. Burglars could be tortured until they reveal the addresses they have burglarized. Rapists could be tortured until they reveal the names of all the women they have violated. College students could be tortured until they reveal the names of those who illegally supplied them with booze. Reporters could be tortured until they reveal the names of their sources. Hey, if we torture enough people, we can get a confession for every unsolved crime in the world.

The trump card of conservative torture advocates like Thomas Sowell is always an emotionally-charged reference to one's family:

> What if it was your mother or your child who was tied up somewhere beside a ticking time bomb and you had captured a terrorist who knew where that was? Face it: What you would do to that terrorist to make him talk would make water-boarding look like a picnic.

In such a highly emotional and personal situation, it's difficult to know with certainty how someone would react. Face it: If someone thought that their loved ones were in imminent danger of death, and they thought that the only way to save them was by torturing someone, he might be willing to torture a terrorist, a terrorist's mother, a terrorist's child, or even you, your mother, or your child. But is this the right thing to do? And is this how U.S. foreign policy should be conducted?

I don't think that many Americans who say that torture is justified under certain circumstances if it may save American lives really believe what they are saying. If you really want to get a terrorist to talk, there are ways to do it without laying a finger on him. Here is one: Take his wife and son and, in front of him, rape her, crush the boy's testicles, and sodomize them both. That will get him talking more than anything you could ever do to him. If the end is gaining information that may save American lives, then why not? Now, except for some red-state conservative fascists and a few bloodthirsty Christian warmongers, I think that most Americans wouldn't go this far. But if you believe in torture in an attempt to gain information that may save American lives, where do you draw the line? Once you establish a "ticking time bomb" exception, every situation ends up becoming a ticking time bomb scenario.

And how credible is information obtained via torture? Face it: Just as someone might be willing to torture anyone and everyone if they thought the lives of their loved ones were in imminent danger, so anyone and everyone undergoing torture might be willing to admit to anything to get the torture to stop. If we took a chainsaw to Dick Cheney, he would confess to all sorts of crimes that the Bush administration didn't even commit. Even the U.S. Army's 2006 field manual on interrogation says about torture:

> Use of torture is not only illegal but also it is a poor technique that yields unreliable results, may damage subsequent collection efforts, and can induce the source to say what he thinks the HUMINT [Human Intelligence] collector wants to hear. Use of torture can also have many possible negative consequences at national and international levels.

But even if credible information could be obtained through torture, it is still immoral, barbaric, and un-American.

Seldom heard in the torture debate is why people became terrorists in the first place. A recent article by James Payne, "What Do the Terrorists Want?," shows that, contrary to neoconservative warmongers like David Frum and Richard Perle, terrorists espouse neither an ideology of conquest like the Nazi Germany and Soviets Russia nor a desire to impose on the whole world its religion and law. The majority of Osama bin Laden's venom is directed at the West for aggression, oppression, and exploitation of Muslim lands and peoples, not because he, like President Bush driveled, "hates our freedoms."

Rather than saving American lives, the torture of Muslim prisoners serves as a recruiting tool for al-Qaeda and other Islamic terrorist organizations. Yes, the crimes of terrorists are many. But why give them reasons to commit more of them? "If we forfeit our values by signaling that they are negotiable in situations of grave or imminent danger, we drive those undecideds into the arms of the enemy," says former commandant of the Marine Corps Charles C. Krulak.

It is proponents of torture that aren't concerned about American lives. If they were then they wouldn't support the senseless wars in Iraq and Afghanistan that have resulted in almost 5,000 American soldiers dying for a lie.

Who are the true patriots? Who are the real Americans? Those who defend foreign wars that send thousands of Americans to their deaths, create terrorists where there were none, and increase the hatred of foreigners toward the United States or those who want to end the U.S. foreign policy of intervening in the affairs of other countries, dismantle the Holy American Empire, and bring all U.S. troops home to stay?

* * * * *

FOR FURTHER READING

Abrams, Ray H. *Preachers Present Arms: The Role of the American Churches and Clergy in World Wars I and II, with Some Observations on the War in Vietnam*, 2nd ed. Scottdale: Herald Press, 1969.

Arner, Rob. *Consistently Pro-Life: The Ethics of Bloodshed in Ancient Christianity*. Eugene: Pickwick Publications, 2010.

Bacevich, Andrew J. *The New American Militarism: How Americans Are Seduced by War*. Oxford: Oxford University Press, 2005.

Bainton, Roland H. *Christian Attitudes Toward War and Peace: A Historical Survey and Critical Re-evaluation*. Nashville: Abingdon Press, 1960.

Bell, Daniel M. *Just War as Christian Discipleship: Recentering the Tradition in the Church Rather than the State*. Grand Rapids: Brazos Press, 2009.

Boettner, Loraine. *The Christian Attitude Toward War*, 3rd ed. Phillipsburg: Presbyterian and Reformed Publishing Co., 1985.

Boyd, Gregory A. *The Myth of a Christian Nation: How the Quest for Political Power Is Destroying the Church*. Grand Rapids: Zondervan, 2005.

Brimlow, Robert W. *What about Hitler? Wrestling with Jesus's Call to Nonviolence in an Evil World* (Grand Rapids: Brazos Press, 2006).

Brown, Dale W. *Biblical Pacifism*, 2nd ed. Nappanee: Evangel Publishing House, 2003.

Cahill, Lisa Sowle. *Love Your Enemies: Discipleship, Pacifism, and Just War Theory*. Minneapolis: Fortress Press, 1994.

Calhoun, Laurie. "Just War? Moral Soldiers?" *Independent Review*, IV, 3 (Winter 2000), 325–345.

Camp, Lee C. *Who Is My Enemy? Questions American Christians Must Face about Islam—and Themselves*. Grand Rapids: Brazos Press, 2011.

Charles, J. Daryl. *Between Pacifism and Jihad: Just War and Christian Tradition*. Downers Grove: InterVarsity Press, 2005.

_____., and Timothy J. Demy. *War, Peace, and Christianity: Questions and Answers from a Just-War Perspective*. Wheaton: Crossway, 2010.

Clough, David L., and Brian Stiltner. *Faith and Force: A Christian*

Debate about War. Washington D.C.: Georgetown University Press, 2007.

Clouse, Robert G., ed. *War: Four Christian Views*. Downers Grove: InterVarsity Press, 1981.

Eller, Vernard. *War and Peace: from Genesis to Revelation*. Scottdale: Herald Press, 1981.

Fahey, Joseph J. *War and the Christian Conscience: Where Do You Stand?* Maryknoll: Orbis Books, 2005.

Fiala, Andrew. *The Just War Myth: The Moral Illusions of War*. Lanham: Rowman & Littlefield Publishers, 2008.

Flynn, Eileen P. *How Just Is the War on Terror? A Question of Morality*. New York: Paulist Press, 2007.

Gamble, Richard M. *The War for Righteousness: Progressive Christianity, the Great War, and the Rise of the Messianic Nation*. Wilmington: ISI Books, 2003.

Griffin, David Ray, et al. *The American Empire and the Commonwealth of God: A Political, Economic, Religious Statement*. Louisville: Westminster John Knox Press, 2006.

Griffith, Lee. *The War on Terrorism and the Terror of God*. Grand Rapids: Wm. B. Eerdmans Publishing Co., 2002.

Grotius, Hugo. *The Rights of War and Peace*, edited with an introduction by Richard Tuck from the edition by Jean Barbeyrac. 3 vols. Indianapolis: Liberty Fund, 2005.

Hauerwas, Stanley. *War and the American Experience: Theological Reflections on Violence and National Identity*. Grand Rapids: Baker Academic, 2011.

Heering, G. J. *The Fall of Christianity: A Study of Christianity, the State, and War*. Fellowship Publications, 1943.

Hershberger, Guy F. *Can Christians Fight? Essays on Peace and War*. Scottdale: Mennonite Publishing House, 1940.

Hess, Richard S., and Elmer A. Martens, eds. *War in the Bible and Terrorism in the Twenty-First Century*. Winona Lake: Eisenbrauns, 2008.

Holmes, Arthur F., ed. *War and Christian Ethics: Classic and Contemporary Readings on the Morality of War*, 2nd ed. Grand Rapids: Baker Academic, 2005.

Hornus, Jean-Michel. *It Is Not Lawful for Me to Fight: Early Christian Attitudes Toward War, Violence, and the State*, rev. ed. Scottdale: Herald Press, 1980.

Isbell, Allen C. *War and Conscience*. Abilene: Biblical Research Press, 1966.

Jewett, Robert, and John Shelton Lawrence. *Captain America and the*

Crusade against Evil: The Dilemma of Zealous Nationalism. Grand Rapids: Wm. B. Eerdmans Publishing Co., 2003.

Kapusta, Philip P. *Blood Guilt: Christian Responses to America's War on Terror*. Fredericksburg: New Covenant Press, 2011.

Lipscomb, David. *Civil Government: Its Origin, Mission, and Destiny, and the Christian's Relation to It*. Nashville: McQuiddy Printing Co., 1913.

Long, Edward LeRoy. *War and Conscience in America*. Philadelphia: The Westminster Press, 1968.

Loveland, Anne C. *American Evangelicals and the U.S. Military, 1942–1993*. Baton Rouge: Louisiana State University Press, 1996.

Macgreror, G. H. C. *The New Testament Basis of Pacifism*, rev. ed. Nyack: Fellowship Publications, 1954.

Maguire, Daniel C. *The Horrors We Bless: Rethinking the Just-War Legacy*. Minneapolis: Fortress Press, 2007.

Marrin, Albert, ed. *War and the Christian Conscience: From Augustine to Martin Luther King, Jr.* Chicago: Henry Regnery Co., 1971.

Massaro, Thomas J., and Thomas A. Shannon. *Catholic Perspectives on Peace and War*. Lanham: Rowman & Littlefield Publishers, 2003.

McCarthy, Emmanuel Charles. *Christian Just War Theory: The Logic of Deceit*. Wilmington: Center for Christian Nonviolence, 2003.

McDurmon, Joel. *The Bible & War in America: A Biblical View of an American Obsession and Steps to Recover Liberty*. Powder Springs: American Vision, 2012.

McMahan, Jeff. *Killing in War*. Oxford: Clarendon Press, 2009.

Miller, Richard B., ed. *War in the Twentieth Century: Sources in Theological Ethics*. Louisville: Westminister/John Knox Press, 1992.

Morey, Robert. *When Is It Right to Fight?* Minneapolis: Bethany House Publishers, 1985.

Nelson-Pallmeyer, Jack. *Saving Christianity from Empire*. New York: Continuum, 2007.

Nuttall, Geoffrey F. *Christian Pacifism in History*. Oxford: Basil Blackwell & Mott, 1958.

O'Donovan, Oliver. *The Just War Revisited*. Cambridge: Cambridge University Press, 2003.

O'Huallachain, D. Liam, and J. Forrest Sharpe, eds. *Neo-CONNED! Just War Principles: A Condemnation of War in Iraq*. Norfolk: Light in the Darkness Publications, 2005.

Pearse, Meic. *The Gods of War: Is Religion the Primary Cause of Violent Conflict?* Downers Grove: InterVaristy Press, 2007.

Raven, Charles E. *War and the Christian*. London: Student Christian Movement Press, 1938.

Reimer, A. James. *Christians and War: A Brief History of the Church's Teachings and Practices*. Minneapolis: Fortress Press, 2010.

Roth, John D. *Choosing Against War: A Christian View*. Intercourse: Good Books, 2002.

Settje, David E. *Faith and War: How Christians Debated the Cold and Vietnam Wars*. New York: New York University Press, 2011.

Shannon, Thomas A. *What Are They Saying about Peace and War?* New York: Paulist Press, 1983.

Sider, E. Morris, and Luke Keefer, eds. *A Peace Reader*. Nappanee: Evangel Publishing House, 2002.

Sider, Ronald J., ed. *The Early Church on Killing: A Comprehensive Sourcebook on War, Abortion, and Capital Punishment*. Grand Rapids: Baker Academic, 2012).

Simpson, Gary M. *War, Peace, and God: Rethinking the Just War Tradition*. Minneapolis: Augsburg Fortress, 2007.

Swaim, J. Carter. *War, Peace, and the Bible*. Maryknoll: Orbis Books, 1982.

Swift, Louis J. *The Early Church Fathers on War and Military Service*. Wilmington: Michael Glazier, 1983.

Trzyna, Thomas. *Blessed Are the Pacifists: The Beatitudes and Just War Theory*. Scottdale: Herald Press, 2006.

Yoder, John Howard. *Christian Attitudes to War, Peace, and Revolution*. Grand Rapids: Brazos Press, 2009.

_____. *Nonviolence: A Brief History*. Waco: Baylor University Press, 2010.

_____. *The War of the Lamb: The Ethics of Nonviolence and Peacemaking*. Grand Rapids: Brazos Press, 2009.

_____. *When War Is Unjust: Being Honest in Just-War Thinking*, 2nd ed. Eugene: Wipf and Stock Publishers, 2001.

Watts, Craig M. *Disciple of Peace: Alexander Campbell on Pacifism, Violence, and the State*. Indianapolis: Doulos Christou Press, 2005.

Classic Reprints on War and Peace
Available from Vance Publications

No. 71, *Christianity and War*, Veritatis Amans, et al., 1838, 1847.
No. 102, *The Complaint of Peace*, Desiderius Erasmus, 1521.
No. 103, *Antipolemus; or, the Plea of Reason, Religion, and Humanity, Against War*, Desiderius Erasmus, 1515.
No. 108, *The Early Christian Attitude to War: A Contribution to the History of Christian Ethics*, John C. Cadoux, 1919.
No. 110, *Vicesimus Knox on War and Peace*, Vicesimus Knox, 1793–1824.
No. 121, *The Morality of War*, Jonathan Dymond, 1896.
No. 124, *The Book of Peace: A Collection of Essays on War and Peace*, The American Peace Society, 1845.
No. 125, *The Origin of the Civil War*, Robert L. Dabney, 1890.
No. 127, *A Christian View of Armed Warfare*, William Paul, 1969.
No. 129, *A Northern Defense of Secession and Rejection of the Civil War*, George W. Bassett, 1861.
No. 130, *John T. Flynn on Roosevelt and Peal Harbor*, John T. Flynn, 1944, 1945.
No. 131, *An Address on War*, Alexander Campbell, 1848.
No. 132, *Can a Christian Kill for His Government?* Bennie Lee Fudge, 1943.